CHRONICLE OF
WAR

1914 TO THE PRESENT DAY

CHRONICLE OF
WAR

1914 TO THE PRESENT DAY

EDITED BY DUNCAN HILL

Photographs by the

Daily Mail

**Trans
Atlantic
Press**

Published by Transatlantic Press in 2009

Transatlantic Press
38 Copthorne Road
Croxley Green
Hertfordshire, WD3 4AQ, UK

© Atlantic Publishing 2009
Photographs © Daily Mail Archive
(See page 318 for details)

Design by John Dunne

A catalogue record for this book is available from the British Library.

ISBN 978–0–9557949–4–0
Printed in Singapore

Contents

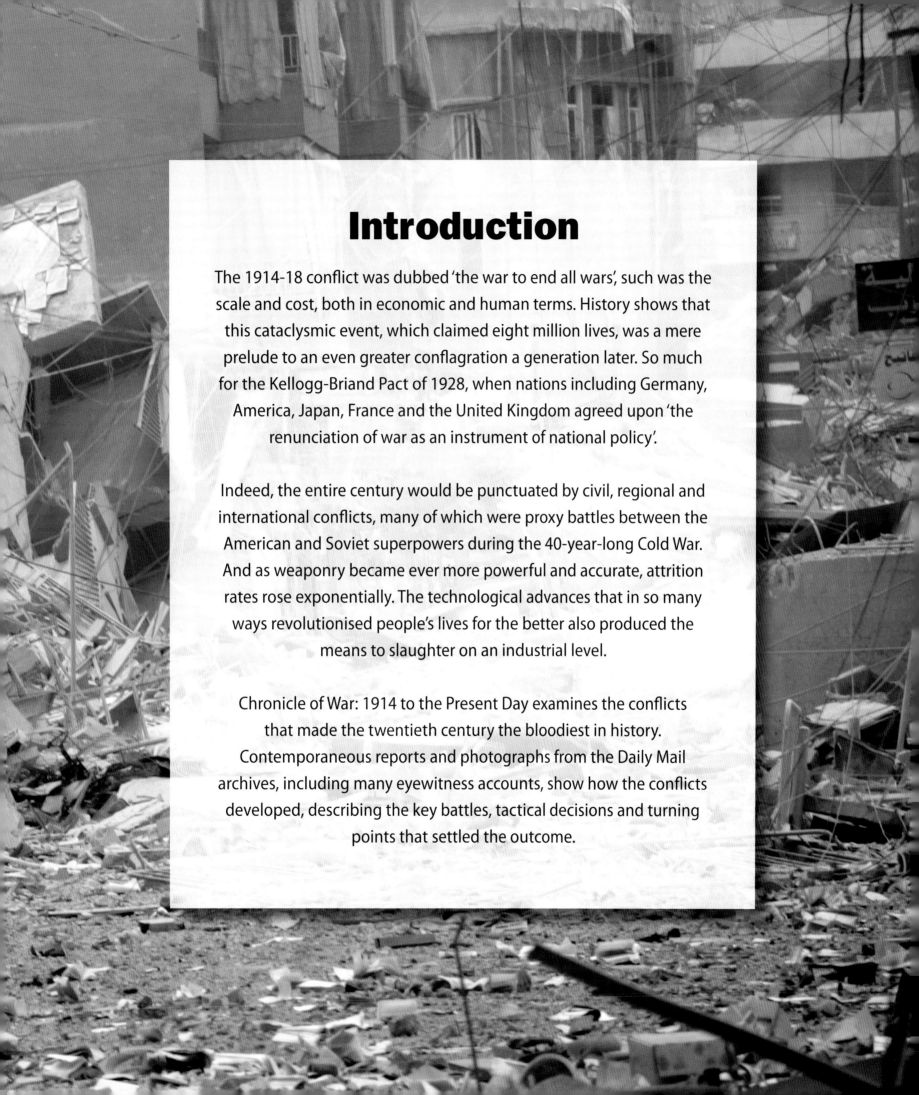

Introduction

The 1914-18 conflict was dubbed 'the war to end all wars', such was the scale and cost, both in economic and human terms. History shows that this cataclysmic event, which claimed eight million lives, was a mere prelude to an even greater conflagration a generation later. So much for the Kellogg-Briand Pact of 1928, when nations including Germany, America, Japan, France and the United Kingdom agreed upon 'the renunciation of war as an instrument of national policy'.

Indeed, the entire century would be punctuated by civil, regional and international conflicts, many of which were proxy battles between the American and Soviet superpowers during the 40-year-long Cold War. And as weaponry became ever more powerful and accurate, attrition rates rose exponentially. The technological advances that in so many ways revolutionised people's lives for the better also produced the means to slaughter on an industrial level.

Chronicle of War: 1914 to the Present Day examines the conflicts that made the twentieth century the bloodiest in history. Contemporaneous reports and photographs from the Daily Mail archives, including many eyewitness accounts, show how the conflicts developed, describing the key battles, tactical decisions and turning points that settled the outcome.

First World War
1914-1918

Setting the stage for war

By the summer of 1914, the tensions between the great powers of Europe had been mounting for some time. The continent was divided into shifting power blocs and rival ruling dynasties, and the decline of the Ottoman Empire, which had once extended across Europe from Turkey to just outside Vienna, only emphasized this.

The fact that the rulers of Great Britain, Germany and Russia were first cousins did not do anything to reduce the levels of tension. In Britain, George V, the second son of Edward VII, had acceded to the throne in 1910. Tsar Nicholas II had ruled over the vast Russian Empire since 1894, and the German Empire was headed by Kaiser Wilhelm II, who had succeeded the Iron Chancellor, Otto von Bismarck, in 1888. The Dual Monarchy of Austria–Hungary had been ruled by the Habsburg Emperor Franz Josef I since 1867 and France was a Republic, led by Raymond Poincaré.

Alliances

National security was a critical issue for all of the major states; the developing tensions meant that no single nation felt secure by itself and every one of them needed allies on whom they could depend. In 1879, Germany and Austria-Hungary had formed an alliance. They were joined by Italy because of its historic antipathy towards France. In response, Russia and France clubbed together by signing the Double Entente in 1894.

Britain had yet to decide on its position. London was suspicious of the growing might of Germany, but had clashed with France as recently as 1898 over a territorial dispute in the Sudan. In the event, Britain sided with France. King Edward VII had charmed the French public during a state visit in May 1903 and the two countries signed the 'Entente Cordiale' within the year. It was not a formal alliance, but a friendly understanding, and neither country was under any obligation to support the other in time of war. In August 1907, Britain further cemented its commitment to France by signing an agreement with Russia. Europe had become divided into two powerful blocs.

Arms race

For centuries the powers of Europe had clashed over their competing interests around the globe. During the nineteenth century, they usually reverted to diplomacy to sort through their differences, but in the early twentieth century the network of alliances emboldened both sides and diplomatic responses soon gave way to militaristic ones. To adjust to the aggressive new order of international relations each of the powers began rapidly building up their arsenals, for it had become clear that the brawniest power would get its way.

Europe was presented with four major crises between 1905 and 1913, two between France and Germany over Morocco and two between Austria-Hungary and Russia over the Balkans, but each time neither side felt sufficiently comfortable in their arsenals to risk war. However, the situation had changed by the time a fresh crisis emerged in the Balkans in 1914. On this occasion, neither side was willing to back down because both thought they could win.

OPPOSITE ABOVE: British soldiers going over the top at Arras, April 1917.

OPPOSITE BELOW: Unaware that one of the greatest wars of all time was about to start, a British family at Waterloo Station gets ready to set off on their summer holidays.

LEFT: Kaiser Wilhelm II ascended to the German throne in 1888 and quickly cast aside the shrewd 'Iron Chancellor', Otto Von Bismarck. He replaced Bismarck's conservative foreign policy, which had emphasized diplomacy and an avoidance of conflict, with a rash and belligerent quest for glory.

FAR LEFT: Kaiser Wilhelm with his cousin King George V of Great Britain. Both were grandchildren of Britain's Queen Victoria.

LEFT BELOW: Russia's Tsar Nicholas II and his family pictured shortly before the war. Russia's decision to stand with Serbia against Austria-Hungry led to the outbreak of the First World War.

BOTTOM: A young Winston Churchill, then First Lord of the Admiralty, is pictured after taking a 60-mile flight from Upavon to Portsmouth in the summer of 1914.

Assassination in Sarajevo

Archduke Franz Ferdinand, the 51-year-old nephew of Franz Josef and heir to the Habsburg throne, was on an official visit to Sarajevo in the summer of 1914. He was well aware of the potential danger as there had already been some assassination attempts by disaffected Bosnian Serbs, who were opposed to Austrian rule in Bosnia and sought to include the region in a wider Serbian state. However, he hoped to win over the locals with a well publicized trip through the streets of Sarajevo. This gave members of the Serbian nationalist Black Hand organization the perfect opportunity to strike a blow against their Austro-Hungarian oppressors.

When the visit took place on June 28, a seven-strong assassination squad was lying in wait. However, the assassination attempt failed when the bomb that was to be thrown into the Archduke's car missed its target and exploded in the street. The Archduke decided to carry on with his official visit, which gave the assassins a second chance to strike. One of them, 19-year-old Gavrilo Princip, assuming their efforts had failed had gone to eat lunch in a Sarajevo café. Luck was on his side; the Archduke's driver had taken a wrong turn and stopped to turn around close by the café. Seizing his opportunity, Princip turned his pistol on the car's occupants. Franz Ferdinand was hit in the neck and Sophie, who was expecting their fourth child, in the stomach. Both of them were quickly pronounced dead.

DAILY MAIL JUNE 29, 1914

Murder of the Austrian heir and his wife

We regret to state that the Archduke Francis Ferdinand, the heir to the throne of Austria-Hungary, and his morganatic wife, the Duchess of Hohenberg, were assassinated yesterday.

The assassination took place at Sarajevo, the capital of Bosnia, which State, together with Herzegovina, was annexed by Austria-Hungary from Turkey in 1908. Bosnia, which is bounded on the south by Montenegro and Servia, has a large Slav population that is discontented with Austrian rule.

The Archduke had paid no heed to warnings to him not to go to Bosnia on account of the disturbed state of the province. Anti-Austrian demonstrations were made before his arrival at Sarajevo on Saturday. Two attempts were made to kill the Archduke and his wife at Sarajevo yesterday. The first failed; the second was only too successful.

A 21-year-old printer of Servian nationality living in Herzegovina threw a bomb at the Archduke's motor-car in the street. The Archduke deflected the bomb with his arm. It fell to the ground and exploded. The heir to the throne and his wife escaped, but a number of other people were injured, six of them seriously.

A little while later the Archduke and his wife were driving to see the victims of the bomb explosion, when a schoolboy aged 19, apparently also of Servian nationality, threw at them a bomb which, however, did not explode, and then fired at them with a Browning automatic pistol. Both were wounded and both died shortly afterwards.

Igniting the war

The Austro–Hungarian empire was outraged by the murders, but it wanted more than mere revenge; this was an ideal opportunity to crush Serbia and also consolidate an empire that was in danger of breaking apart. Russia had strong historic ties to Serbia, but had backed down from supporting Belgrade in the two previous Balkan crises. However, Russia had since built up its military with French assistance and on this occasion was prepared to stand with Serbia against Austria-Hungary.

Austria-Hungary looked to Germany for support. Berlin had realized that it would soon be outpaced in the arms race by the Entente powers and that the window in which it could win a war was rapidly closing. As a result, the Kaiser confirmed his full support for Franz Josef's government. On July 31 Germany issued Russia with an ultimatum: to cease any mobilization immediately. No reply came, and the following day Germany declared war on its large eastern neighbour. The Great War had begun.

OPPOSITE: **A crowd forms outside the War Office in London waiting for news as to how Britain and France will respond to the outbreak of war between Russia and Germany.**

ABOVE: **Archduke Franz Ferdinand and his family. His marriage was morganatic, which** meant his children could not inherit the throne of Austria-Hungary.

LEFT ABOVE: **Archduke Ferdinand and his wife alight from their car at Sarajevo city hall after the first failed assassination attempt.**

LEFT MIDDLE: **The Archduke and his wife leave a reception at city hall. A wrong turn on the way to their next engagement results in their assassination.**

LEFT BELOW: **Crowds try to attack the assassin, Gavrilo Princip as police lead him away.**

DAILY MAIL AUGUST 3, 1914

Great war begun by Germany

The German Government declared war upon Russia at 7.30 on Saturday evening. There was still hope of peace when this action was taken. The Czar had pledged his word to the Kaiser that he would not mobilise or attack Austria while negotiations with her were in progress.

The German Army was active yesterday. It crossed the French frontier, without any declaration of war, at three distinct points. It invaded France at Longwy, 270 miles from London, close to the Luxemburg frontier; at Cirey, near Nancy; and at Delle, near Belfort.

German troops were last night in French territory.

BY THE KING.
A PROCLAMATION
REGARDING THE DEFENCE OF THE REALM.

GEORGE R.I.

WHEREAS by the law of Our Realm it is Our undoubted prerogative and the duty of all Our loyal subjects acting in Our behalf in times of imminent national danger to take all such measures as may be necessary for securing the public safety and the defence of Our Realm :

AND WHEREAS the present state of Public Affairs in Europe is such as to constitute an imminent national danger :

NOW, THEREFORE, WE strictly command and enjoin Our subjects to obey and conform to all instructions and regulations which may be issued by Us or Our Admiralty or Army Council, or any officer of Our Navy or Army, or any other person acting in Our behalf for securing the objects aforesaid, and not to hinder or obstruct, but to afford all assistance in their power to, any person acting in accordance with any such instructions or regulations or otherwise in the execution of any measures duly taken for securing those objects.

Given at Our Court at Buckingham Palace, this Fourth day of August, in the year of our Lord one thousand nine hundred and fourteen, and in the Fifth year of Our Reign.

GOD SAVE THE KING.

The Schlieffen Plan

All the pent-up tensions of the previous years ensured that events moved very fast, and Germany knew that it was only a matter of time before France entered the war on the side of its Russian ally. A two-front war posed a serious threat, but the German general staff had developed a contingency measure. Called the Schlieffen Plan, it called for a rapid strike towards Paris to effectively neutralize the threat from France, after which the German army could turn their attention back to Russia. There was one really critical factor for the Plan's success: speed. Russia's enormous size did mean that there was a small window of opportunity for Germany. It would take time for Russia to gather enough troops, giving Germany a short time to act before it faced a real threat. France, therefore, had to be effectively put out of action quickly so that the full strength of the German army could be in position on the eastern front before Russia was ready to fight. Germany knew, however, that this window would soon be slammed closed. Accordingly, even before war was formally declared between Germany and France on August 3, German forces began the march westwards. The situation in the east was largely left to Austria–Hungary.

Under the Schlieffen Plan, the German attack on France would be made through Belgium, rather than directly across the Franco–German border. This was problematic because Belgium was a neutral country, and Britain was a long-standing guarantor of its neutrality. However, the Germans were not certain that the British would intervene because they knew London was preoccupied with the question of Home Rule for Ireland and powerful members of Prime Minister Asquith's government were adamantly against Britain being drawn into any European conflict. Moreover, Britain was under no treaty obligation to take up arms in these circumstances.

Germany invades Belgium

Germany demanded unhindered passage through Belgium and, on August 3, the Belgian government rejected its ultimatum and looked to Britain for support. The Asquith government chose to honour its commitment to Belgium and did so unequivocally, to the astonishment of Theobald Bethmann-Hollweg, the German Chancellor. Britain refused to stand aside while Belgium and, eventually, France were invaded.

On August 4, London delivered an ultimatum to Germany, which expired at midnight: Britain would declare war if German forces failed to withdraw from Belgium. Midnight came and went with no response. Bethmann-Hollweg could barely believe it. 'Just for a scrap of paper Great Britain was going to make war on a kindred nation who desired nothing better than to be friends with her,' he declared. Germany had badly misjudged the situation on the far side of the North Sea. Many of the people in all the nations involved seem to have felt a kind of joy, even euphoria at this point. Sir Edward Grey was far more perceptive when he stated 'The lamps are going out all over Europe; we shall not see them lit again in our lifetime'.

OPPOSITE ABOVE LEFT: **German** soldiers in Berlin receive flowers as they march off to war.

OPPOSITE ABOVE RIGHT: **The** Palace issues a proclamation for the defence of the Realm upon the outbreak of war on August 4, 1914.

OPPOSITE BELOW: **Crowds gather** to watch Lord Gordon Lennox lead the 2nd Grenadier Guards past Buckingham Palace shortly after the outbreak of war.

OPPOSITE BELOW INSET: **Crowds** cheer outside Buckingham Palace on the evening of August 4, 1914 after hearing of the declaration of war.

TOP: **Young Britons march past** the War Office in London to show their support for the newly declared war.

ABOVE: **Onlookers watch as the** sign is taken down from the door of the German Embassy in London.

DAILY MAIL AUGUST 3, 1914
British warning to Germany

We understand that an intimation has been conveyed to the German Government to the effect that if a single German soldier is ordered to set foot on Belgian soil the British Navy will take instant action against Germany.

Germany has also seized a British liner at Kiel and a British collier at Brunsbuettel, near the canal.

The German Emperor officially ordered a mobilisation of the entire forces of Germany at 5.15 yesterday afternoon. Actually the German mobilization had been secretly begun three days ago, on July 31.

The French Government ordered the mobilisation of all its forces to begin at midnight of Saturday-Sunday. In seven or eight days the French armies, with a strength of at least 1,000,000 men, will be ready to fight on the frontier. Behind them will be other armies ready to give them all support.

Italy has intimated that she will not support Germany and Austria. Her treaty of alliance with them does not compel her to fight in a war of aggression. She was only bound to intervene if Germany and Austria were attacked without provocation. Italian neutrality will be maintained by a general mobilisation of the Italian forces.

German successes

The Central Powers – the German and Austro–Hungarian forces – received early encouragement. The German army swept through Belgium quickly and Liege, the fortress town, fell. This was a strategic victory that was essential to the success of the Schlieffen Plan. The Belgian government left Brussels for Antwerp on August 17, and only three days later the country's capital was in German hands. There were reports of atrocities committed by the German troops. Though some of these were clearly exaggeration and propaganda, it soon became clear that the German army wanted more than simple surrender from the people it conquered. It intended to obliterate any obstacles in its path, crushing the spirit of its opponents as well as succeeding in battle. The cathedral town of Louvain was sacked in the closing days of August in a manner that shocked the world; the Germans claimed that shots had been fired against their soldiers, and many civilians paid the ultimate price in revenge. Additionally, Louvain's magnificent and unique university library, with its many priceless books and manuscripts, was destroyed. A month later the magnificent Gothic cathedral at Rheims suffered a terrible bombardment, even though a Red Cross flag was flying from it.

German entry into Brussels

Brussels was unconditionally surrendered by the Burgomaster to a German advance guard. Germany has imposed a fine of £8,000,000 on the city of Brussels. A German force, 35,000 strong, with bands playing, marched into the city in the afternoon. The Germans behaved with brutal arrogance to the population and to captured Belgian officers.

The Belgians were heavily defeated, with great loss and the capture of 12 guns, by the Germans at Louvain on Wednesday. The Belgian troops offered a gallant resistance, but were overwhelmed by numbers.

The Battle of the Marne

However, Germany's success disguised several major weaknesses; the army was overstretched and undersupplied. The Russians went on the offensive in August and two corps were redeployed east, just as the British Expeditionary Force began arriving to shore up French defences. Nevertheless, the Germans were within striking distance of Paris and the Allies had to act quickly to save the French capital. The result was the Battle of the Marne, which took place in early September 1914. A great number of men were killed on both sides, but the battle resulted in a German retreat. The Germans moved to a more easily defendable position on the high ground north of the Aisne river. Neither side could make further headway and a long war of attrition set in.

DAILY MAIL AUGUST 18, 1914

The British army in France

The British Expeditionary Force is in France. This news, officially promulgated to-day, discloses the great secret. The military authorities have accomplished a thrilling feat. With perfect secrecy they have mobilised, assembled in British ports, and moved to France the largest army that ever left British shores. We may justly congratulate them on their energy and organisation. They have worked in silence with admirable efficiency.

This is not the first time that a British army has gathered on French soil. But it is the first time that British troops have entered France to aid her. The cause for which that gallant army marches today is the same as that for which its forefathers fought in 1814 and 1815. It has gone forth to defend the right, to protect the weak against lawless attack, to uphold the great cause of human freedom against the onslaught of military despotism. It stands, as the England of 1814 stood, for liberty against tyranny. And in that fight, however protracted, however terrible, it will not quail. He was a wise French soldier who said that England, when she had once taken hold, never let go. Through whatever suffering and sacrifices this army which she has sent forth with all her love and faith will carry her standard to victory.

ABOVE LEFT: The British head off to war. Less than three weeks after the outbreak of war, a 120,000 strong British Expeditionary Force stood on the continent. They engaged the Germans in their first battle at Mons, Belgium, on August 23.

OPPOSITE BELOW: Fallen soldiers strew the ground following the Battle of the Marne.

OPPOSITE ABOVE LEFT: British marines march through the Belgian coastal town, Ostend.

OPPOSITE ABOVE RIGHT: Lance-Corporal Charles Alfred Jarvis (second right) attempts to recruit men in Woodford Green, London. On August 23, 1914, Jarvis became the first British soldier of the war to be awarded the Victoria Cross for his actions at Mons.

OPPOSITE MIDDLE RIGHT: Wounded soldiers arriving at Ostend, having failed to prevent the fall of Antwerp on October 9, 1914.

ABOVE RIGHT: Lord Kitchener (left), a veteran of the Boer War and the campaign in the Sudan in 1898, was appointed Secretary of State for War by Prime Minister Asquith at the outset of the confict.

LEFT: Although conscription was not introduced in Britain until 1916, around 2,500,000 men volunteered for active service in Lord Kitchener's Army.

The Eastern Front

The Schlieffen Plan meant that Germany only allocated minimal resources to the Russian Front in 1914. The Eighth Army under the command of General Prittwitz was sent to the east to hold the line while war was waged against France in the west. The Russian army was inferior to the Germans in terms of training and leadership, but vastly superior in terms of numbers. This caused Prittwitz to panic and order a partial retreat so an angry government in Berlin replaced him with generals Hindenberg and Ludendorff.

In August 1914, the Russian generals planned to strike at the German Eighth Army, which was based to the west of the Masurian Lakes. The Russian First Army would go around the lakes to the north and the Second Army would do so from the south in order to trap the Germans in a classic pincer movement. However, things did not go according to plan because the Germans intercepted radio communication between the two armies. Knowing his troops were no match for both Russian armies, General Hindenberg marched to engage the Second Army while the First was too far away. The resulting battle near Tannenberg was a disaster for Russia; the Second Army was almost wiped out, 30,000 men were killed and 100,000 were taken prisoner.

The Battle of the Masurian Lakes

Hindenberg and Ludendorff then turned their attention to the First Army, commanded by General Rennenkampf. The Battle of the Masurian Lakes began on September 9, 1914. The battle was not quite the disaster for the Russians that Tannenberg had been, but the First Army only escaped to fight another day because of Rennenkampf's decision to retreat.

To capitalize on Germany's successes, Austria-Hungary began an offensive in Galicia in September, but the ramshackle imperial army was unable to defeat the Russians who took the strategic fortress of Lemberg. Germany's new Chief of Staff, Erich von Falkenhayn, wanted to turn its attention back to the Western Front, but he had to reinforce Austria-Hungary in the east. As a result, a major redeployment of troops from the west to the east took place.

ABOVE: The remnants of the Russian Second Army in full-scale retreat after the crushing defeat at the Battle of Tannenberg.

ABOVE LEFT: Russian soldiers march westwards. Although they were poorly trained and lacked equipment, the Russian army had strength in numbers.

LEFT: Troops on the Eastern Front face the harsh winter. Thousands would die during the conflict as a result of the cold.

OPPOSITE ABOVE LEFT: Downtime in the Russian ranks. Fighting on the Eastern Front was often gruelling; more than 30,000 men were killed in the Battle of Tannenberg alone.

OPPOSITE ABOVE RIGHT: Russian soldiers creep across no man's land to cut wires in front of German Trenches. Trench warfare was rare in the east because the front was so long.

OPPOSITE MIDDLE RIGHT: Tsar Nicholas II takes command of Russia's war effort. His failure to make any decisive improvements would become a major factor of the Russian Revolution.

OPPOSITE BELOW: Russian soldiers on training exercises.

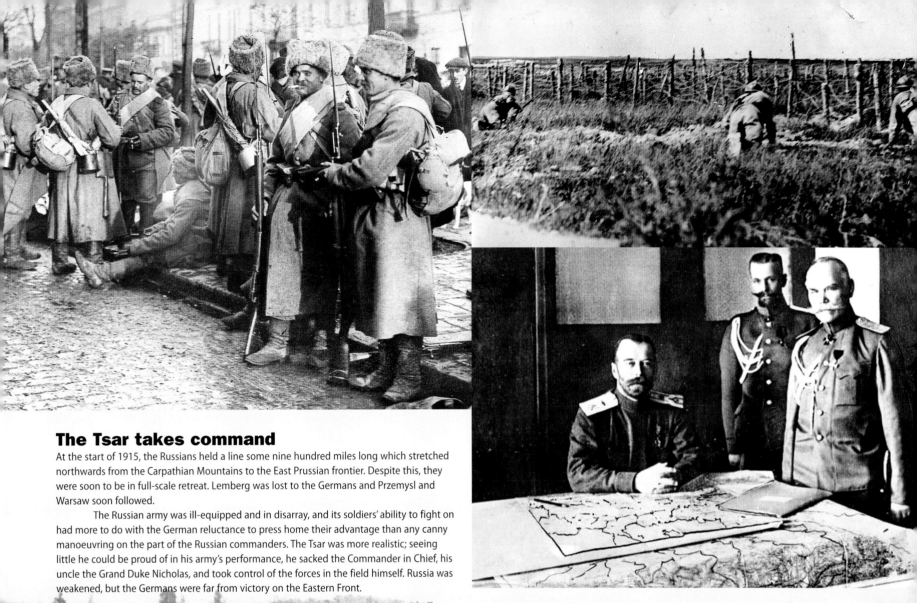

The Tsar takes command

At the start of 1915, the Russians held a line some nine hundred miles long which stretched northwards from the Carpathian Mountains to the East Prussian frontier. Despite this, they were soon to be in full-scale retreat. Lemberg was lost to the Germans and Przemysl and Warsaw soon followed.

   The Russian army was ill-equipped and in disarray, and its soldiers' ability to fight on had more to do with the German reluctance to press home their advantage than any canny manoeuvring on the part of the Russian commanders. The Tsar was more realistic; seeing little he could be proud of in his army's performance, he sacked the Commander in Chief, his uncle the Grand Duke Nicholas, and took control of the forces in the field himself. Russia was weakened, but the Germans were far from victory on the Eastern Front.

ABOVE AND OPPOSITE LEFT: **Damage in Scarborough, England, following a German raid. The German High Seas fleet shelled the British coastline on December 16, 1914, killing more than one hundred civilians.**

OPPOSITE RIGHT: **The towns of Hartlepool (above) and Whitby (below) were also struck.**

BELOW: **The historic ruins of Whitby Abbey were hit in the attack.**

DAILY MAIL DECEMBER 17, 1914

Germans bombard three English towns

The war has been brought to our shores in no uncertain manner. At the breakfast hour yesterday German warships vigorously shelled the Hartlepools, Scarborough, and Whitby, the last two being entirely unfortified towns.

Unfortunately there has been loss of life. The names of 17 dead at Scarborough are issued by the police but there are also some wounded. A considerable proportion of these are after the German's own heart – women and children. At West Hartlepool, 7 soldiers were killed and 14 wounded, and 22 civilians are among the dead and 50 wounded. The material damage is nearly all to private property. At Scarborough three churches, hotels, and many private houses were wrecked or damaged. At Whitby, sad to relate, the ruins of the famous old abbey were still further laid low. Two people were killed and two wounded.

The patrol ships engaged the Germans on the spot and a patrolling squadron went in pursuit, but the enemy escaped at full speed in the mist. But the splendid outstanding fact is that England is cool and ready for the enemy.

What was their object?

Yesterday for the first time in two centuries British towns were shelled by a foreign foe and British blood spilt on British soil. What was the German object in attacking unfortified coast resorts and a commercial harbour?

The first motive was to throw a sop to their hatred of England. Held back from Calais, checked in Poland, with Turkey staggering under redoubtable blows, and Austria dismayed, German militarism felt something must be achieved against its most detested foe.

The second motive was to take the revenge the German public has demanded for the annihilation of Admiral von Spee's squadron in the South Atlantic.

The third motive was to proclaim, especially to neutral countries, that German ships could move in the North Sea.

The fourth motive was the vain hope of creating panic so that troops might be kept here who would otherwise be sent to the Continent.

The fifth motive, and the most important, was to force the British Admiralty to keep a larger force than hitherto in the narrower part of the North Sea where that force would be liable to constant mine and submarine attacks from the Germans.

There will be no panic

Neither the British Admiralty nor the British public will fall into the snare. There will be no panic. There is rather a sense of stern content and satisfaction that the issue has at last been made clear. The war has come home to the nation and the nation is ready.

The Germans show no respect for the laws of the war. We must defend our homes against their methods. We must recognize that in this age of mines, submarines, and aircraft the conditions of war have changed. Our Scarboroughs and Hartlepools must have adequate defence. The nation is not taken aback. The German belief that a show of force on the coast or half a dozen bombs from a Zeppelin can demoralise the British people is a pitiful delusion. What the nation realizes from yesterday's events is that new and sterner efforts must be made to win, that more aid must be sent to our Allies, and that the preoccupation of every man and every woman must be to crush for ever the tyranny of German militarism.

DAILY MAIL OCTOBER 17, 1914

Life in the British trenches

Not 'over by Christmas'

Many people had believed that the war would be over by Christmas 1914, but this was hugely optimistic. German troops posed next to road signs pointing towards Paris; French troops did the same beside signs indicating the way to Berlin. But even should one of the protagonists succeed in landing a heavy pre-emptive blow against one of the others, it was never going to bring about capitulation – because this was, when it came down to it, a war of alliances.

For example, if the Schlieffen Plan succeeded and France suffered grievously from a German attack, the country was not likely to surrender as long as Britain and Russia stood by its side. As far as the Triple Alliance went, Germany and Austria–Hungary gained strength from the knowledge that they stood together, although Italy was on the sidelines and refused to take up arms with its partners. The alliances which had brought Europe into war in an almost inevitable progression also worked against there being a swift victory for anyone.

On Christmas Day the opposing forces in the advanced western trenches put their enmity to one side and met in no man's land. It was, however, only a temporary respite, for the fighting would continue for another four years.

Our men have made themselves fairly comfortable in the trenches, in the numerous quarries cut out of the hill-sides, and in the picturesque villages whose steep streets and red-tiled roofs climb the slopes and peep out amid the green and russet of the woods. In the firing line the men sleep and obtain shelter in the dug-outs they have hollowed or 'under-cut' in the sides of the trenches. These refuges are slightly raised above the bottom of the trench, so as to remain dry in wet weather. The floor of the trench is also sloped for purposes of drainage. Some trenches are provided with head cover, the latter, of course, giving protection from the weather as well as from shrapnel balls and splinters of shell.

Considerable ingenuity has been exercised in naming the shelters. Among other favourites are 'The Hotel Cecil', 'The Ritz', 'Hotel Billet-doux', 'Hotel Rue Dormir', etc. On the road barricades, also, are to be found boards bearing the notice: 'This way to the Prussians'.

Obstacles of every kind abound, and at night each side can hear the enemy driving in pickets, for entanglements, digging trous-de-loup, or working forward by sapping. In some places the obstacles constructed by both sides are so close together that some wag has suggested that each should provide working parties to perform this fatiguing duty alternately, since their work is now almost indistinguishable, and serves the same purpose.

The quarries and caves to which allusion has already been made provide ample accommodation for whole battalions, and most comfortable are the shelters which have been constructed in them. The northern slopes of the Aisne Valley are fortunately very steep, and this to a great extent protects us from the enemy's shells, many of which pass harmlessly over our heads to burst in the meadows below, along the river bank. At all points subject to shell fire access to the firing line from behind is provided by communication trenches. These are now so good that it is possible to cross in safety the fire-swept zone to the advanced trenches from the billets in villages, the bivouacs in quarries or the other places where the headquarters of units happen to be.

To those at home the life led by our men and by the inhabitants in this zone would seem strange indeed. All day, and often at night as well, the boom of the guns and the scream of the shells overhead continue. At times, especially in the middle of the day, and after dark, the bombardment slackens; at others it swells into an incessant roar, in which the reports of the different types of gun are merged into one great volume of sound.

ABOVE: **On Christmas Eve, British soldiers noticed Christmas lights appearing in the German trenches and the following morning they heard cries of 'Happy Christmas'. The British responded with similar good wishes in German, giving rise to an informal armistice. Slowly** both sides emerged from the trenches and met in no man's land to exchange pleasantries and gifts. The ceasefire also gave both sides a chance to collect and bury their fallen comrades.

OPPOSITE ABOVE: **Canadian troops being inspected by General Sam Hughes.**

OPPOSITE BELOW: **No man's land littered with German dead as pictured from the French trenches. The German trenches (the white line in the middle of the picture) are just yards away.**

DAILY MAIL OCTOBER 16, 1914

The arrival of the Canadians

Plymouth has been the scene of many memorable incidents in British history, but never of a more stirring and significant one than when yesterday the transports bearing the Canadian troops dropped anchor in its harbour. They received a west-country welcome that was local in form but absolutely national in the spirit behind it. What Plymouth was privileged to witness was something more than the arrival of so many thousands of hardy natural soldiers; it was a living picture of the Empire in action; it was the scattering of all the illusions of Imperial disintegration with which the Germans have bemused themselves; it was a spectacle, hardly to be paralleled since the Crusades, of free and self-governing communities voluntarily embracing a cause that passionately appeals to their hearts and consciences.

The Western Front, 1915

The year of 1915 was a year of dreadful casualties for very little gain on the Western Front. The Allied trenches in France and Belgium were largely manned by the French while Kitchener's British recruits were undergoing a rapid programme of military training. The National Register Bill, introduced in Britain in July 1915, required that every man and woman between the ages of 15 and 65 should their submit personal details to the authorities. However, Britain held out against conscription for another year.

With the redeployment of eight divisions to the Eastern Front, the German military used chemical warfare to make up for the shortage of manpower on the Western Front. The Germans first used gas during the Second Battle of Ypres in April 1915. It caused chaos in the Allied line, but the Germans were unable to capitalize because they could not risk exposing their own men to the deadly gas. The use of poison gas in this way was widely felt to be outrageous. Field Marshal Sir John French described its use as 'a cynical and barbarous disregard of the well-known usages of civilized war and a flagrant defiance of the Hague Convention.' But despite it, by the end of the battle on May 13, the stalemate remained.

The Battle of Neuve Chapelle

On March 10, the Allies made their first serious attempt to break through the enemy line at the village of Neuve Chapelle. The settlement itself was successfully seized from German hands, although Sir John French's report on the battle was grim (and a foretaste of worse to come): there had been a gain of some three hundred yards on a front just half a mile in length – but it had cost the Allies 12,000 men either killed, wounded or missing.

Munitions shortage

A dire situation had arisen with the production of munitions in Britain. Severe shortages had been exposed by the Battle of Neuve Chapelle and the Second Battle of Ypres, where demand had far outstripped supply. When this became public knowledge it brought about a political crisis, and the Liberal government was replaced by a coalition in May. Asquith retained the premiership, however, while Lloyd George was moved from his post as Chancellor of the Exchequer. He headed a new department, the Ministry of Munitions.

OPPOSITE ABOVE LEFT: **The First World War saw poison gas emerge as a weapon of war for the first time. These British Red Cross nurses, working on the front line, were given masks to protect themselves in case of attack.**

OPPOSITE RIGHT: **British soldiers try to relax in the cramped muddy trenches of the Western Front.**

OPPOSITE BELOW LEFT: **The Battle of Neuve Chapelle was the first planned British offensive of the war. Although, they managed to capture the village of Neuve Chapelle itself, the offensive was eventually abandoned after the British registered severe losses.**

ABOVE LEFT: **In addition to women, workers from across Britain's and France's empires were put to work manufacturing munitions.**

ABOVE: **With the shortage of shells having such an impact on the battlefield, ever more British factories were converted to munitions production. Most of the workers in this industry were women.**

LEFT: **British soldiers first started wearing bowl-shaped steel helmets after the summer of 1915. They offered greater protection when a soldier needed to look out over the top of the trench.**

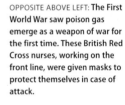

DAILY MAIL JUNE 15, 1915
Our shell shortage – a French opinion

The lack of shells and ammunition, says the Temps to-night, is the principal reason why Great Britain does not defend a larger line in France. The revelation of this shortage has caused some surprise in France.

How is it that a great industrial country like England, whose territory remains inviolate, has been unable to furnish its Army with the munitions which it needs? The fact is that the manufacture of war material, especially field artillery and shells, is a special industry demanding minute and precise attention. Representative English industries such as sheet iron, rails, and locomotives do not require the work of great precision which, on the contrary, is indispensable to most of the important French industries. It was, therefore, more difficult for England to find workmen capable of learning to turn out war material.

But England is tenacious, and every month her sword will weigh more heavily in the balance.

War in the air

The First World War witnessed the birth of aviation in warfare. Both sides had to contend with this new front and develop this new technology for use in war. German Zeppelins had bombed Paris at the start of the conflict, and the British had to face an aerial bombardment for the first time on January 19, 1915. Parts of the Norfolk coastline came under attack, and this was followed by raids on the south-east and the North Sea coast over the next few months. There were not many fatalities, but they were almost all civilians. The targeted killing of non-combatants in this way added a new dimension to the war, which was termed 'frightfulness' at the time. By employing this new tactic, the Central Powers hoped to damage morale rather than inflict huge casualties, and they soon extended it to the oceans as well.

War in the sea

Germany declared the waters around Britain and Ireland to be a war region in February 1915 and began a blockade of the seas around the British Isles using submarines and mines. However, the war at sea was, for the most part, a stalemate because neither side was keen to engage the other. The Allies feared German U-Boats and the Germans feared British naval superiority. To try to break the deadlock, the Germans announced that commercial shipping would now be attacked without any warning. This caused outrage and Winston Churchill, then First Lord of the Admiralty, condemned it as 'open piracy and murder on the high seas' when he spoke in the House of Commons.

Sinking of the *Lusitania*

The threat became reality on May 7, in a way which had profound ramifications. Over 1,000 people died when the Cunard liner *Lusitania* was sunk a few miles off the Irish coast. A week before, the German embassy in the United States had issued a statement announcing that the *Lusitania* was a potential target, but only a few among the many passengers took the threat seriously enough to cancel their voyage. The loss of 128 American lives generated a strong tide of anti-German feeling in the States and was actually the first step towards American involvement in the war. These same feelings of shock and disgust were also widespread in Britain, where anti-German sentiment rose sharply and violently. This change in the public mood led the Royal Family to change its name from the House of Saxe-Coburg to the House of Windsor.

DAILY MAIL · JANUARY 20, 1916

The deadly Fokker

The series of air fights recorded in the British official report late last night - in which two of our machines were lost and five of the enemy's were 'driven down' - shows the vital importance of combating the new German battleplane. The finest flying men in the world, the British, are being out-engined and out-powered by the deadly Fokker.

The French authorities believe that the latest type of Fokker, which is a monoplane (i.e., with a single spread of wings), is fitted with a 200-h.p. Mercedes water-cooled engine. It is probably more powerful than even the latest French Nieuport or Morane. Its immense engine power gives it an extraordinary speed in climbing. The Germans well know the position and the importance of their engine superiority; witness the constant references in their communiques from headquarters since December 16. They – and these communiques, unlike the wireless, rarely lie – record the destruction in air fights of thirteen British machines and two French.

The matter is of the greatest importance not only at the front but also here, for the Fokkers will no doubt come over to drop bombs.

OPPOSITE: The British fleet, viewed from the deck of HMS *Audacious*. This was the first major British battleship lost in the war when it hit a mine off the coast of Ireland in October 1914.

OPPOSITE LEFT: The sinking of the Kaiser's battleship, *Blücher*, at Dogger Bank in 1915. The crew scrambles along her plates in an attempt to abandon ship.

OPPOSITE ABOVE RIGHT: Bomb damage from a Zeppelin raid on Bury St Edmunds, England

ABOVE LEFT: A German Fokker. The planes were developed by the Dutch engineer Anthony Fokker.

MIDDLE LEFT: The aerodrome in Flanders used by the 'Red Baron' Manfred von Richthofen, who was one of Germany's most successful fighter pilots. He was killed in battle in April 1918.

BELOW LEFT: A German plane brought down by British gunners in Flanders.

BELOW: A member of the Royal Air Force poses with the bomb he will drop against German positions.

Gallipoli

At the outbreak of war, it had been thought that the Allies' naval strength would turn out to be a vital factor. The first six months of the conflict had shown little evidence of this, but in early 1915 an Anglo–French task force was deployed in the Mediterranean with the aim of changing the situation. The plan was to attack Turkey, which had joined the Central Powers in 1914, through the straits of the Dardanelles – the narrow waterway from the Aegean Sea which led all the way to Constantinople. If the Allies could take Constantinople, then there was every chance that they would be able to win a passage through to their Russian allies.

Accordingly, in February 1915 the forts at the entrance to the Dardanelles were bombarded by a fleet led by Vice-Admiral Sackville Carden. However, progress up the straits was slow and three battleships were lost to mines on March 18. As a result it was decided that the eventual success of the Dardanelles campaign would depend on the deployment of land forces, an obvious decision in the circumstances and one which came as no surprise whatsoever to the Turks.

The landings

On April 25 some British and French troops, together with soldiers from the Australian and New Zealand Army Corps (ANZAC), landed on the Gallipoli Peninsula. Turkish soldiers had been expecting the landings and were lying in wait in strong fortifications above the beaches. British and French troops landing at Cape Helles on the tip of the peninsula came under severe fire and barely managed to capture the beach. At the end of the first day their forces were too depleted to mount an advance beyond the beach.

To the north ANZAC troops faced an even worse situation. They landed almost a mile off course and faced an impossible terrain. Trapped between the sea and the surrounding hills, they were lambs to the slaughter.

ABOVE LEFT: **The Anglo-French fleet, consisting mostly of outdated battleships, made slow progress up the straits and fell prey to mobile batteries operated by Turkish forces. It was difficult to launch a counterattack on a moveable target without sending ground troops ashore.**

ABOVE RIGHT: **The men wait around on deck for the Gallipoli campaign to start. At the outset of battle, the Allies had relatively poor intelligence. They did not know the strength of the Turkish army, which was further strengthened during the naval** bombardment, and they were also uncertain of the terrain, having taken what they knew from old tourist guides.

ABOVE: **Australian troops in the boat on the way to Gallipoli. The boats carrying Australian and New Zealander servicemen drifted off course and the men went ashore at the wrong beach.**

LEFT: **Troops aboard SS Nile, prepare to land on the Gallipoli Peninsula.**

OPPOSITE BELOW: **British and French troops come ashore at Cape Helles on the Gallipoli Peninsula.**

OPPOSITE ABOVE RIGHT: **Marines land at Gallipoli. Capturing the Dardanelles offered the Allies a major strategic advantage: the ability to link up with their Russian allies through the Black Sea.**

OPPOSITE ABOVE LEFT: **A Turkish shell bursts out to sea as British troops take cover. The shells came from a gun nicknamed 'Asiatic Annie' by the men. When Annie ceased firing, the soldiers would dive in and collect the fish killed in the onslaught.**

DAILY MAIL DECEMBER 14, 1914

The Dardanelles

The Dardanelles (the ancient Hellespont) is a narrow channel separating Europe from Asia and connecting the Sea of Marmara and the Aegean Sea. It is about 40 miles long. The shores at the mouth are about two miles apart, but the waterway then widens considerably, gradually to contract again until it reaches 'the Narrows' eleven miles up, where it is less than a mile wide. There are two sets of defences, one at the mouth and the other at the Narrows. During the war with Italy it was stated that the Turks arranged a minefield below the Narrows.

The passage of the straits was forced by the British squadron under Sir John Duckworth in February 1807, but he repassed them with great loss in March, the castles of Seston and Abydos hurling down stone shot upon the British ships. The British Mediterranean Fleet also unceremoniously steamed through the Hellespont in 1878.

RIGHT: Allied troops navigate their way along a narrow ridge dubbed 'the valley of death' at Gallipoli.

BELOW LEFT: Members of the Australian Imperial Guards listen to music with the enemy less than 30 yards away.

BELOW MIDDLE: The locals watch with little enthusiasm as marines come ashore. Reinforcements were landed at Suvla Bay in August 1914, but they were unable to have a decisive impact on the campaign.

BELOW RIGHT: In May 1915 a truce was declared at Gallipoli for both sides to bury their dead. Many more would die from disease in the coming summer heat.

BOTTOM: Going over the top at Gallipoli. The Dardanelles campaign quickly succumbed to the deadlock and heavy losses the Allies had been experiencing on the Western Front.

DAILY MAIL DECEMBER 21, 1915
Undoing the Dardanelles blunder

The withdrawal of the British troops from two of the three points held on the Gallipoli Peninsula may be taken as a sign that the Government has at last realized the stupendous blunder it committed in venturing upon this expedition, the earlier phases of which Mr. Churchill described as a 'gamble'. A gamble it has proved in the lives of the most heroic of our race. The casualties at the Dardanelles numbered up to November 9 no fewer than 106,000 officers and men. In addition, sickness on this front accounted for 90,000 down to October. A loss of nearly 200,000 men was thus incurred without any adequate result.

Not only did the Government despatch to the Dardanelles forces which, judiciously utilized at other points, might have achieved the greatest results; not only did it divert to the Near East munitions at a time when we were perilously short of high-explosive shells. It also deceived the nation as to the position and prospects after its strokes had signally failed through initial mismanagement or the inadequacy of the army employed. The public has not forgotten the optimistic assurances of Mr. Churchill, Lord Robert Cecil, and Lord Kitchener.

Mr. Lloyd George's speech last evening really contains the gravest indictment that has as yet been drawn against the Government. Here is a confession that when the Germans were in May making 250,000 high-explosive shells a day the British production was only 2,500. Even now he implies that, despite great efforts, we have not equalled the German output. Shall we ever overtake it? Only if the nation works its hardest. The fatal words of the war, he said, were 'too late.' These words have dogged the Allies' every step.

Failure at Gallipoli

With the Allies pinned down, a fresh landing at the parched Suvla Bay was carried out in August but it came to nothing, and did so quickly. Casualties, both from enemy action and disease, were dreadful. Churchill, who had been one of the chief advocates of the Dardanelles campaign, had spoken of being just 'a few miles from victory', but by November 1915 it was clear that there were no options left: retreat was the only possibility. Sir Charles Munro replaced Hamilton, and was charged with leading the evacuation. Churchill resigned. The withdrawal from the straits, at least, was a spectacular success. It took place between December and January in almost total secrecy. The entire campaign cost the Allies more than 250,000 men.

TOP: HMS *Cornwallis* fires at Turkish positions in the mountains from Suvla Bay during the Gallipoli campaign. The *Cornwallis* was sunk in a German U-boat attack in the Mediterranean in January 1917.

MIDDLE LEFT: Marines on guard duty at Gallipoli.

ABOVE: Turkish soldiers taken prisoner during the landings at Suvla Bay.

FAR LEFT: With such great losses at Gallipoli, these Australian troops made their own crosses. They carved their names and dates of birth alongside the words 'Killed in Action', leaving only the date of death blank.

LEFT: A snapshot of the empty trenches on the Gallipoli Peninsula after the Allied soldiers pulled out. The Allies were careful to disguise the withdrawal from the Turkish army and in doing so made sure that no man was killed during the exit.

The Battle of Loos

In autumn 1915 the French commander, Field-Marshal Joseph Joffre, planned an offensive to drive the enemy off French soil. Despite the harsh experience of the spring, Joffre clung to the hope that throwing yet more men and weapons at the German lines might bring about his aim, but it failed. In the advance, in Artois and Champagne, British troops did somewhat better. The First Army, commanded by Sir Douglas Haig, took Loos. This time it was the British forces who used gas, the first time they had done so. However, a lack of available reserves prevented the attack from being completely successful and the German forces were able to rally. The British reserves had been too far from the action, and Sir John French was blamed for this error of judgement. In December he was replaced by Field-Marshal Sir Douglas Haig as Commander in Chief of the British Expeditionary Force.

TOP: Britain launched a major offensive to capture the Belgian town of Loos on September 25, 1915. The offensive marked the first occasion that the British used poison gas, but the gas was blown back towards the British lines in places injuring at least 2,500 men. Haig abandoned the offensive after taking 50,000 casualties.

ABOVE MIDDLE: British soldiers returning from front-line duty at the Battle of Loos.

ABOVE: British soldiers fixing their bayonets in preparation for a fresh offensive in 1915.

RIGHT: Sappers, responsible for engineering work, made a crucial contribution to the war effort.

OPPOSITE ABOVE LEFT: Members of the cycling corps mend their bikes under shellfire. Bikes proved to be an important line of communication, especially in conditions where motor vehicles were liable to struggle.

OPPOSITE ABOVE RIGHT: Rollcall in an Allied labour camp. The names of these Chinese men are inscribed on streamers attached to a rotating drum.

OPPOSITE MIDDLE RIGHT: The Turkish Army marches through Damascus in the Middle East.

OPPOSITE BELOW: British infantryman enjoy the modest spoils of war. One is wearing a German greatcoat while another has attached an eagle emblem to his helmet.

Fighting in the Middle East

As the year drew to a close, the Central Powers had the upper hand. Britain experienced a major blow in Mesopotamia, where the nation's interests had become vulnerable when Turkey entered the war. In September a force led by General Charles Townshend took Kut-el-Amara but an attempt to push on to Baghdad proved to be futile and, as at Gallipoli, a bold offensive turned into retreat. Townshend's exhausted troops struggled back to Kut, where they held out for 143 days. The rations were poor – they only had a little flour and horsemeat by the end – and the outcome was inevitable. They finally surrendered in April 1916, and some 13,000 men were taken prisoner by the Turks, but Turkey's success in preventing the Allies from gaining access to the Black Sea via the Dardanelles (and linking up with the Russian army) was its most significant contribution to the Central Powers' war effort.

DAILY MAIL   MARCH 18, 1915

War work for women

Any woman who by working helps to release a man or to equip a man for fighting does national war service. Every woman should register who is able and willing to take employment.

The object is twofold. In the first place it is an effort to overcome the shortage of labour in many trades. In the second, it is thought that employers engaged in other than government work will be prepared to release from civil service much male labour if women can be found competent to do the work now performed by men of military age and fitness.

Every woman employed will be paid at the ordinary industrial rates. The pay ranges from 32s. a week including overtime in some of the munition factories to 8s. and 10s. a week in agriculture. There is immediate need for women workers in munition and other factories, in offices and shops, as drivers of commercial motor vehicles, as conductors of cars, and above all in agricultural employment. The shortage of workers on the land and in the businesses associated with it runs into many thousands.

The appeal is made to every section of the community. It is recognized that in many instances it will be desirable that women of the same class shall be employed together, and efforts will be made to organize 'pals' battalions' of labour. Endeavour will be made to billet those who elect to assist in agriculture in hostels in suitable centres, and already county people have been approached with a view to making adequate arrangements.

What women can do

'The scheme,' said an official of the Board of Trade, 'has been under consideration for some time, and it is felt that with Lord Kitchener's appeal for "speeding up" in commerce the time is opportune for launching it. If the full fighting power of the nation is to be put forth on the battlefield, the full working power of the nation must be made available to carry on its essential trades at home.

And this is where women who cannot fight in the trenches can do their country's work, for every woman who takes up war service is as surely helping to the final victory as the man who handles a gun in Flanders. With a fortnight's training women can fill thousands of existing vacancies, and also take the places of thousands of men anxious to join the fighting forces but at the moment compelled to keep in civil employment.

Every woman so employed will receive ordinary industrial treatment in the matter of pay from the start, and parents can rest assured that every precaution will be taken to safeguard the welfare of young women employed in factories and elsewhere. Every woman's society, suffrage and otherwise, has been approached, and many have promised their help and the assistance to lay down a hard-and-fast rule as to the trades and employment women can follow, but there are many occupations in which they can be substituted for men.

It is hoped that the first registration of women will be made on Monday. As to the age of those suitable, it is hardly likely that anyone younger than 17 will be needed at the moment, but in the other direction there is hardly a limit. Those who are ready to help the nation should go to the local Labour Exchange and register there.'

Changing roles for women

The First World War brought about a major change in the roles of women in society. Before the outbreak of war few women were in paid employment and most of these worked in domestic service. As men signed up for service, women were required to make up for labour shortages in all sectors of the economy. The shortage of labour became especially acute when conscription was introduced in 1916.

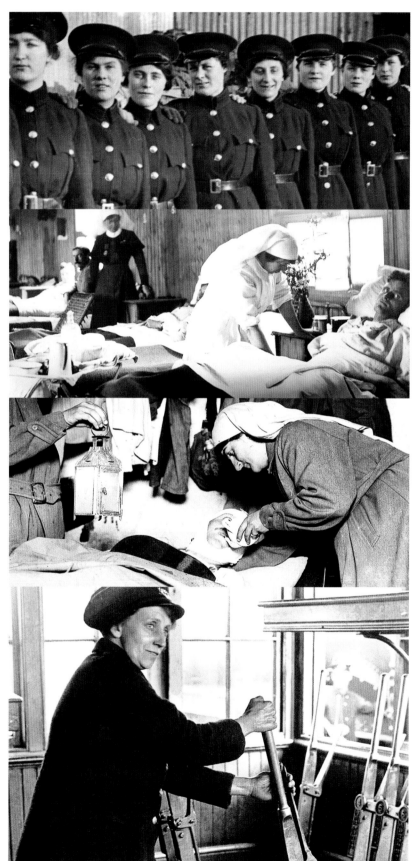

Bulgaria joins Germany and Italy switches sides

The great German advance in the east had provided some astonishing territorial gains: Ukraine, Lithuania, the territory covered by modern-day Poland and parts of Belarus. There was more to come, this time in the Balkans. In the autumn Austro–Hungarian forces mounted another assault on Serbia, with German support. This was bad enough for the Serbs, yet another attack from the north-west, but now they also faced another difficulty – a threat from the east. Bulgaria joined the Central Powers in October. Ferdinand, the Bulgarian ruler, had been offered of parts of Serbia, a bribe which went down well in a country that had been forced to cede territory to Serbia during the earlier Balkan wars. The addition of Bulgaria was crucial. Anglo–French forces tried to help their Balkan ally by entering Serbia through Greece, but Bulgarian troops blocked their way and Serbia was alone. The Serbian capital of Belgrade was quickly overrun and many Serbs were forced into a full-scale evacuation, travelling through the difficult mountain regions of Montenegro and Albania. Thousands of people died on their flight westwards, towards the Adriatic coast, and the survivors were taken to the island of Corfu in Allied ships.

But despite the considerable successes the Central Powers had enjoyed in 1915 they had not achieved their major aim, which was to force one of the Allied nations to the negotiating table. The Allies had also been bolstered by the addition of Italy, as the former Triple Alliance member switched sides in May 1915. The new year would bring fresh attempts to break the deadlock, and a long-anticipated sea battle between the naval superpowers, Britain and Germany.

OPPOSITE ABOVE: 'Land Girls' freed up British agricultural workers for armed service. They helped maintain domestic food production to sustain the war effort.

OPPOSITE MIDDLE: Women pulp paper in Purfleet on the Thames.

OPPOSITE BELOW: Women take over from men in the newspaper printing industry.

LEFT TOP: Women form a 24-person-strong fire brigade at a munitions factory in Middlesex, England. Eight of them were on duty at any one time and the day was divided into three eight-hour shifts.

LEFT MIDDLE ABOVE: A Voluntary Aid Detachment Nurse of the Red Cross and the Order of St John tends to a wounded soldier. VADs, as they were known, performed a variety of duties from assisting in hospitals to driving ambulances.

LEFT MIDDLE BELOW: In a scene reminiscent of the Crimean War sixty years earlier, a nurse holds a lamp over a wounded soldier while another feeds the patient from an invalid cup.

LEFT BOTTOM: A woman takes charge of railway signalling in Birmingham, England.

ABOVE: A woman chops down trees for firewood.

Verdun

Germany's plan for the new year involved a major fresh assault in the west. Falkenhayn, the German commander, believed that France could be defeated if his men launched an attack at the historic fort city of Verdun on the River Meuse. The general contended the city was so important to France's self-esteem and patriotism that the Allies would invest all their resources in defending it.

The offensive, 'Operation Gericht' (Judgement), was launched on February 21, 1916. 1,200 guns – including the huge and notorious 42-centimetre Big Bertha – launched what was to be one of the fiercest bombardments of the entire war.

Within four days the Germans had taken Fort Douaumont which was the largest of the city's famous defensive strongholds.

Pétain takes Command

Falkenhayn's trap was sprung and, as predicted, the French refused to cede a city that was a symbol of national pride, regardless of the fact that it was of no great strategic value. However, the French were not content merely to become cannon fodder for a hopeless cause. Under General Pétain, who assumed command of the city's defences, they determined to fight fire with fire. Pétain, the man who would be later be reviled as a Nazi collaborator in World War II, became a national hero for the part he played in helping to save Verdun. Contrary to his later reputation, Pétain was a general of the modern school. He saw that the tradition of noble sacrifice – the usual French military response – had now to become subservient to modern technology, and his own artillery began inflicting heavy casualties on the German ranks.

Lines of communication were inevitably badly damaged, but Pétain ensured that one vital road to the south of the city remained open. This became known as the 'Voie Sacrée' or 'Sacred Way' and would be remembered for the ceaseless lines of trucks carrying fresh troops and supplies to the front. They also, of course, brought exhausted and shell-shocked men in the opposite direction for treatment, rest and recuperation. And the losses were heavy; the battle raged fiercely until June.

German redeployment east

As time dragged on there was some wavering among the German hierarchy. This was not surprising; the victory which had been confidently expected to happen within days had failed to materialize after four whole months. Then, with a decision on Verdun in the balance, the news came of a major Russian offensive in the east where General Alexei Brusilov had routed the Austro–Hungarian army. This forced Falkenhayn into a large-scale redeployment of troops eastwards. No sooner had this happened than the British forces began their own offensive on the River Somme. The Germans had lost their opportunity and Falkenhayn scaled down the action at Verdun. The net effect was that during the remainder of the year the French regained all the territory they had lost. The combined death toll was about 700,000, with French losses marginally greater. Once more there had been carnage on an unbelievable scale for no discernible benefit. Verdun was proudly declared to be an 'inviolate citadel' defended by men who had 'sowed and watered with their blood the crop which rises today' by the French President, Poincaré. Verdun cost Falkenhayn his job as commander of the German forces, with Hindenburg replacing him as Chief of Staff in August.

The greatest battle

'The greatest battle of the greatest war' – for so the Germans already describe it – sways to and fro on the hills north of Verdun and seems steadily to extend. The Germans are attacking in enormous force and with the utmost fury. The incomparable French are maintaining the defence with that tenacious coolness and readiness to riposte which distinguish their modern army. There is as yet no sign of any decision and there is a good deal to suggest that the conflict is only in its first stage.

It has been suggested that the Germans are mad in attacking at one of the strongest points of the French line. The German staff, however, has every reason to be anxious to impress neutrals whose decision is believed to hang in the balance by dealing a terrific blow at the French. It has always held that any fortress and any position can be taken provided the necessary sacrifices are made.

The preliminary methods have been the same at Verdun as against the Russians on the Dunajetz – but with this immense difference, that at Verdun the French are well prepared, have numerous lines of defence behind their advanced positions, and are abundantly munitioned. Their most dangerous difficulties are that some new form of attack may be attempted by the enemy, whether by aircraft or by gas. The German bombardment is described as being of a fury which has never been approached before. That gives some measure of its violence. In the culminating point of Mackensen's assault on the Dunajetz 700,000 shells were discharged by the enemy in four hours, while, in addition, many new and devilish devices were employed in the shape of liquid fire, asphyxiating gas, and aircraft dropping asphyxiating bombs. The artillery fire in the present battle, we are told, is changing the very appearance of the country. But the monster guns are not this time all on Germany's side; the French are well equipped with rivals of the monster 17in. Kruppe.

OPPOSITE LEFT: French poilus manning the trenches.

OPPOSITE RIGHT ABOVE: French troops pictured outside Fort Douaumont on October 26th 1916 after it had just been retaken from the Germans.

OPPOSITE RIGHT MIDDLE: French soldiers capture a German dug-out at Verdun. A German infantryman from the 242nd regiment lies dead in the foreground.

OPPOSITE RIGHT BELOW: Women make munitions at a factory in France.

LEFT: Casualties of Verdun. Around 700,000 men lost their lives in the capaign.

RIGHT: Kaiser Wilhelm and his son meet German troops at the start of the Verdun offensive.

Jutland

Despite the passage of nearly two years of war, the British and German fleets had managed to avoid any full-scale confrontation. The British navy had more ships and greater firepower, even though Germany had made determined attempts to overtake them in the run-up to war. The mighty Dreadnoughts, with their turbine engines taking them up to a speed of 21 knots, and with their 12-inch guns having a ten-mile range, were formidable fighting machines. However, the first Dreadnought had appeared in 1906 and Germany had used the intervening decade to create a response. In addition, Britain's Royal Navy had not been used in battle since the days of Nelson a century earlier, and it was led by the cautious Admiral Sir John Jellicoe.

DAILY MAIL JUNE 3, 1916

Great battle off Danish coast

On the afternoon of Wednesday, May 31, a naval engagement took place off the coast of Jutland (Denmark.) The British ships on which the brunt of the fighting fell were the battle-cruiser fleet, and some cruisers and light cruisers, supported by four fast battleships. Among these the losses were heavy.

The German battle fleet, aided by low visibility, avoided prolonged action with our main forces, and soon after these appeared on the scene the enemy returned to port, though not before receiving severe damage from our battleships.

6 British cruisers sunk

The battle-cruisers Queen Mary, Indefatigable, Invincible, and the cruisers Defence and Black Prince were sunk. The Warrior was disabled, and after being towed for some time had to be abandoned by her crew. It is also known that the destroyers Tipperary, Turbulent, Fortune, Sparrowhawk, and Ardent were lost and six others are not yet accounted for. No British battle-ships or light cruisers were sunk.

German battleship and battle cruiser blown up

The enemy's losses were serious. At least one battle-cruiser was destroyed, and one severely damaged; one battleship reported sunk by our destroyers during a night attack; two light cruisers were disabled and probably sunk.

The exact number of enemy destroyers disposed of during the action cannot be ascertained with any certainty, but it must have been large.

Scapa Flow

Jellicoe's fleet was based at Scapa Flow in the Orkney Islands, north of the Scottish mainland. Scapa Flow's position gave Britain a natural stranglehold on the North Sea and the German fleet had been confined to harbour for long periods, meaning the Central Powers were being slowly starved of resources. In January 1916 the new commander of Germany's High Seas Fleet, Admiral Reinhard Scheer, came up with a plan to neutralize Britain's naval superiority. He recognized that he had to attack, and formulated a plan to split up the enemy fleet and so increase his chance of victory. The Germans began to carry out raids on Britain's east coast, which forced Jellicoe to deploy a battle-cruiser squadron south from the Orkneys to Rosyth. This was exactly in accord with phase one of Scheer's scheme. His plan's second phase was to lure the battle-cruisers into the open sea by sailing a few German ships off the Norwegian coast. The British battle-cruiser squadron, led by Sir David Beatty, took the bait – and lying in wait for them, not far from the German outriders, was the entire High Seas Fleet. Everything seemed to be proceeding smoothly, but there was one serious flaw in their plans which was completely unknown to the Germans. British intelligence had cracked their naval code. Scheer had hoped to overpower Beatty's squadron of battle-cruisers and escape before the main British fleet could reach the scene but, thanks to the code-breakers, Jellicoe was already steaming into action.

BELOW: **The British Fleet pictured shortly before war was declared.**

ABOVE: **The two greatest naval forces in the world in battle in the North Sea off the Danish coast. Although German ships inflicted heavier losses, they suffered severely and did not risk a second engagement for the duration of the war.**

OPPOSITE: **Men gather on Fleet Street, the heart of London's newspaper industry, to read news of the latest sea battle.**

Battle commences

Beatty's squadron engaged the German fleet at around 4.00 p.m. on May 31, 1916, and both HMS *Indefatigable* and *Queen Mary* exploded and sank within twenty minutes of each other. Out of *Indefatigable's* crew of 1,019 only two men survived, and 1,286 died on the *Queen Mary*. A bewildered Beatty said 'There seems to be something wrong with our bloody ships today.' He was right: later investigation suggested that the way in which the cordite was stored had been at fault.

By now, German gunnery was having the better of the exchange and Scheer was closing in fast, but he was still unaware of the approaching Grand Fleet. When Beatty sighted the main body of the German navy he turned his cruisers northwards towards Jellicoe and the main British fleet. It was now his turn to try and lure the enemy into a trap, and they duly followed. When the battle lines were finally drawn up it was Jellicoe who had a huge tactical advantage. By the time the two fleets engaged each other, his ships were arranged broadside across the German line, a manoeuvre known as 'crossing the T'. The Germans were coming under heavy bombardment and, despite the loss of HMS *Invincible* in yet another spectacular explosion, Jellicoe seemed certain of success.

Uncertain victory

In response, Scheer executed a brilliant 180-degree turn, his ships disappearing into the smoke and confusion. Jellicoe was reluctant to follow them, as always aware of the threat posed by torpedo fire, but he soon discovered that he didn't need to. For some reason, Scheer's forces performed another about-face manoeuvre and headed straight towards the British line. Jellicoe was in a dilemma. The Germans now had torpedoes within range – which could cause enormous losses – but engaging the enemy directly could bring an outright victory. He chose discretion and retreated, and by dawn the next morning the German fleet had slipped away. The battle was over.

Germany declared the Battle of Skaggerak, as they called Jutland, to be a great victory. There was some justification in this since Britain's losses were substantially higher. Fourteen British ships had been sunk, while Scheer had lost 11, and over 6,000 British sailors lost their lives while Germany's casualties were less than half that. There was certainly some disappointment in Britain, both among the ordinary people and in the government, but Germany never threatened Britain's mastery of the seas again. In fact, Scheer advised the Kaiser that their strategy should now focus on the deployment of U-boats, rather than on using surface ships.

The Somme

The British now launched their own offensive on the Somme, with France playing a supporting role. An enormous week-long artillery bombardment began; it was a prelude to an attack by front-line soldiers which happened on July 1. Optimism was great among the British troops (as it had been among the Germans in February), and they sang: 'We beat 'em on the Marne, we beat 'em on the Aisne, we gave them hell at Neuve Chapelle and here we are again'. However, the artillery attack had not done its job properly. The Germans were heavily entrenched, and the bombardment proved to be ineffectual. Even worse, it also acted as a warning of the imminent assault. The Allied infantry left their trenches and moved across no man's land, attacking the German positions in close ranks. They were easy prey for the Germans' Maxim machine guns and by nightfall the casualty figure stood at about 57,000 – the worst losses on any one day in British military history. The French had been more tactically astute and made some gains, but overall it was a thoroughly bad day for the Allies.

Haig miscalculates

Haig, however, was undeterred by the losses. Although the casualty figures were never so bad again, the overall verdict on the Somme offensive was grim. The positions that Haig had hoped to secure on the very first day were still in German hands over four months later, in mid-November. The casualties on the Allied side exceeded 600,000, with German losses almost as bad at up to half a million. British tanks had been deployed for the first time during the Somme campaign but they did not make the impact on the overall outcome that had been hoped for, and by the end of the year a decisive breakthrough on the Western Front remained as elusive as it ever had.

DAILY MAIL JULY 3, 1916

The first day's gains

A great battle had been fought. Another is being fought, and many more have yet to be fought. It will probably be called in England the Battle of Montauban and in France the Battle of the Somme. But, whatever we call it, or however we judge it, we must think of it as a battle of many battles, not to be likened in duration or extent, or perhaps intention, to such affairs as Neuve Chapelle or Loos.

It is and for many days will continue to be siege warfare, in which a small territorial gain may be a great strategical gain; and the price we must pay is to be judged by another measure than miles or furlongs or booty.

We are laying siege not to a place but to the German army – that great engine which had at last mounted to its final perfection and utter lust of dominion.

In the first battle, which I saw open with incredible artillery fury at 6 o'clock this morning, we have beaten the Germans by greater dash in the infantry and vastly superior weight in munitions. I may, perhaps, claim to be in some position to estimate methods and results. I watched the night bombardments, both German and British. I saw at close quarters the hurricane of the morning bombardment, which heralded that first gay, impetuous, and irresistible leap from the trenches, many of which I had visited earlier, knowing what was to come.

OPPOSITE ABOVE LEFT: **Men of the Black Watch eat breakfast on the morning of July 19 ahead of a successful attack on German positions at the Somme.**

OPPOSITE ABOVE RIGHT: **German casualties in a trench taken by the Allies, July 11, 1916.**

OPPOSITE BELOW: **The 'Black Watch' pipers play in celebration of the capture of Longueval on July 14, 1916. The village was taken in just twenty-five minutes. The pipers began playing just as soon as they realized there would be no immediate German counterattack.**

ABOVE: **Men wait for the orders to advance from their reservist trench at the Somme.**

RIGHT ABOVE: **Soldiers pack tightly into a trench in preparation for an assault during the Somme offensive.**

RIGHT MIDDLE: **South African soldiers distinguished themselves in the battle for Delville Wood, renamed 'Devils Wood' by the Allies. At the height of the battle, German shells had rained down at a rate of 400 per minute, stripping the landscape bare.**

RIGHT: **The Battle of the Somme saw the first use of tanks by the British Army. Although this new technology did not prove decisive at the Somme, it would help the Allies overcome the deadlock of trench warfare in future battles.**

BELOW: **Members of the Wiltshire Regiment rush on the Leipzig Salient, just south of Thiepval.**

Conscription in Britain

The year of 1916 saw the death of Lord Kitchener, whose recruitment campaign had seen more than two million British men enlist since the outbreak of war. He was aboard HMS *Hampshire* bound for Russia when the ship was sunk off the Orkney Islands. Despite Kitchener's efforts, the rate at which men were volunteering to serve had slowed considerably by the start of 1916 and the British Government responded by introducing the Military Service Bill on January 5. This meant that single men aged between 18 and 41 could now be conscripted into the armed forces. Asquith, the Prime Minister, had originally wanted the sons of widows to be exempted from conscription, but this did not last. The nature of the war – and the extraordinary and appalling losses on the Western Front in particular – meant that married men up to the age of 41 were also being called up before the year was over.

Romania joins the Allies

In addition to Britain's new conscripts, the ranks were swelled by the addition of a new ally, Romania, in August. It was originally hoped that Romania's decision to join the Entente Powers might tip the balance in their favour in the Balkans – but that hope quickly proved to be groundless. 'The moment has come to liberate our brothers in Transylvania from the Hungarian yoke,' said the Romanian King, but Bucharest fell almost without a struggle on December 5. It looked as though recruiting either new allies or new soldiers had made no real difference.

ABOVE RIGHT: **While en route to Russia for talks, Lord Kitchener (left) was killed when his ship was sunk off the Orkney Islands on June 5, 1916.**

MIDDLE: **8-inch Howitzers deployed in the Fricourt-Mametz Valley, August 1916. The Allies used over 400 heavy guns at the Somme, one for every 60 yards of the front on which the attack took place.**

BELOW: **A smokescreen masks an Allied attack at the Somme.**

OPPOSITE BELOW: **The barren landscape of the Somme battlefield.**

OPPOSITE ABOVE LEFT: **Reserves move up to support the advance on Morval.**

OPPOSITE MIDDLE LEFT: **Wounded men are lifted out of an ambulance wagon at a makeshift hospital station set up in an old farmhouse.**

OPPOSITE BELOW RIGHT: **King George V visited the trenches five times during the course of the war. He visited during the Somme offensive in August 1916.**

DAILY MAIL AUGUST 16, 1916

The King on the Somme battlefield

The King returned yesterday from another visit to the front. The following is the General Order to the Army in France which his Majesty sent to General Sir Douglas Haig:-

Officers, N.C.O.s, and men.

It has been a great pleasure and satisfaction to me to be with my Armies during the past week. I have been able to judge for myself of their splendid condition for war and of the spirit of cheerful confidence which animates all ranks, united in loyal co-operation to their Chiefs and to one another.

Since my last visit to the front there has been almost uninterrupted fighting on parts of our line. The offensive recently begun has since been resolutely maintained by day and by night. I have had opportunities of visiting some of the scenes of the later desperate struggles, and of appreciating to a slight extent the demands made upon your courage and physical endurance in order to assail and capture positions prepared during the past two years and stoutly defended to the last.

I have realized not only the splendid work which has been done in immediate touch with the enemy – in the air, under ground, as well as on the ground – but also the vast organizations behind the fighting line, honourable alike to the genius of the initiators and to the heart and hand of the workers. Everywhere there is proof that all, men and women, are playing their part, and I rejoice to think their noble efforts are being heartily seconded by all classes at home.

The happy relations maintained by my Armies and those of our French Allies were equally noticeable between my troops and the inhabitants of the districts in which they are quartered, and from whom they have received a cordial welcome ever since their first arrival in France.

Do not think that I and your fellow countrymen forget the heavy sacrifices which the Armies have made and the bravery and endurance they have displayed during the past two years of bitter conflict. These sacrifices have not been in vain; the arms of the Allies will never be laid down until our cause has triumphed.

I return home more than ever proud of you.

May God guide you to Victory.

George R.I.

Unrest on the Home Front

Despite Verdun, the Somme and Jutland, 1916 was to be as indecisive as its predecessor. In addition, war weariness began to set in. By the end of the year each of the main protagonists faced a new and unexpected threat: internal destabilization. The privations of a long-drawn-out conflict meant that the enthusiasm of August 1914 was nothing more than a distant memory. Each country sought to actively encourage unrest within its enemies' borders, while simultaneously stamping on it at home. During 1916 the seeds of revolution were sown; the following year would witness a dramatic harvest which would affect the course of the war.

Britain's greatest crisis came early, at Easter, when members of Sinn Fein took over Dublin's Post Office. Their uprising was brutally put down and its leaders were executed. Meanwhile Britain was actively trying to encourage revolution in the Ottoman-controlled Middle East. The Arabs of the Hijaz were moved to rise up against the Ottoman Empire and recieved British promises of independence afterwards. T. E. Lawrence, later known as Lawrence of Arabia, who played a prominent part in the guerrilla war that the Arabs began to wage, knew from the start that Britain had no intention of honouring its pledge.

Half-hearted peace proposal

As general disaffection grew, and the strain of the conflict became more and more apparent, the desire for an end to the war naturally gathered momentum. Germany actually sued for peace on December 12, 1916, but the note that was passed to the Allies was somewhat unusually worded, given its aim. It spoke of the 'indestructible strength' of the Central Powers and stated that 'a continuation of the war cannot break their resisting power'. Perhaps not surprisingly, such language did not have the intended effect; not even the most generous of the Entente Powers could see this as being in any way conciliatory. Lloyd George, who had replaced Asquith as Britain's Prime Minister in December 1916, responded accordingly.

It was a 'sham proposal', he said, and entering into discussions on the basis of its contents 'would be putting our heads in the noose with the rope end in the hands of the Germans'. Though all sides may have been eager to end hostilities, they were hardly willing to do so at any price.

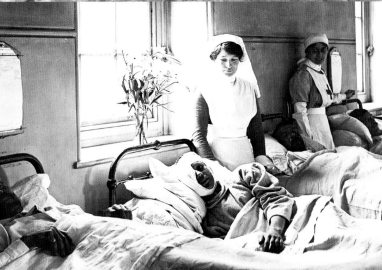

OPPOSITE ABOVE RIGHT: A panoramic view of the devastation wreaked upon Dompierre-sur-Authie during the Somme offensive.

OPPOSITE LEFT: British soldiers carrying stove pipes during the harsh winter of 1916–17.

OPPOSITE BELOW INSET: The makeshift grave of an unknown British casualty of the Somme offensive at Ginchy. His cap is at the head of the grave and his rifle is fixed to the ground at its foot.

OPPOSITE BELOW: A snapshot of death and destruction on the Western Front at Christmas, 1916.

LEFT: British soldiers protect themselves by wearing German body armour picked up off the battlefield. Plans to devise body armour for British troops were still underway at this stage.

LEFT: Injured veterans of the campaign arrive home in England for treatment in late 1916.

ABOVE: Soldiers eat their Christmas dinner in a shell hole at Beaumont Hamel, December 25, 1916. Beaumont Hamel was taken on November 13, one of the final successes before Haig ended the Somme offensive.

BELOW: Men of the Royal Warwickshire Regiment take a well-earned rest out in the open during the Somme Campaign.

German retreat

Withdrawals on the Western Front were central to Germany's new plan. As early as September 1916, work had begun on a new defensive line. It would shorten the front by about 30 miles and, as a consequence, provide a welcome reduction in the demand for resources. The German forces withdrew to the Siegfried Line (or the Hindenburg Line as the Allies called it) in the early months of 1917. A thousand square miles of land, which had been fought over so bitterly and which had cost so many casualties, was conceded almost at a stroke. But the withdrawal was not an unmitigated benefit for the Allies. As they retreated, the Germans adopted a comprehensive scorched-earth policy. The ground which they gave up would have no useful resources left – not even a drop of water, as all available supplies had been poisoned.

LEFT: The German army left a trail of devastation in their wake. The Allies discover Bapaume ablaze as they enter the town on March 21, 1917.

ABOVE: German soldiers left a note in reference to the destruction on Peronne's town hall. It read: 'Don't be angry, just be amazed'.

BELOW: Troops from Australia and New Zealand patrol in Bapaume on March 29, 1917.

TOP LEFT: The French town of Peronne was razed to the ground during the German withdrawal.

ABOVE LEFT: French civilians liberated by the German withdrawal welcome the Allies. .

TOP RIGHT: Back on the Home Front, women taxi drivers first appeared on the streets of Birmingham in 1917. While women made inroads into many professions dominated by men, they were still not allowed to drive taxis in London.

ABOVE RIGHT: The devastation in Bapaume as pictured from the town hall on March 30, 1917.

BELOW: German trenches lie abandoned following the tactical withdrawal to the Hindenburg Line.

Nivelle's spring offensive

The Allies met to plan their own strategy for 1917 long before they became aware of the German withdrawal. This was essentially more of the same: concerted offensives on every front, with the aim of stretching the enemy forces to the limit. However, such a plan carried with it the prospect of another Somme – and that possibility haunted Lloyd George, who had become Prime Minister late in 1916. As it happened, a change in France's command structure dramatically changed the Allies' thinking, much to his relief. Joffre was replaced by General Robert Nivelle, in December. The new Commander in Chief of the French Army had distinguished himself at both the Battle of the Marne and Verdun. As a result his reputation was so good that he had little difficulty in bringing the political leaders with him – not least because he told them just what they wanted to hear. His scheme was for a joint Anglo–French spring offensive, on the Aisne. First would come saturation bombardment of the enemy positions, followed by a 'creeping barrage', behind which the infantry would advance. Nivelle predicted that a decisive breakthrough would come in only a few days. Haig did not agree – and nor did others – but Lloyd George's approval of the plan meant that his hands were effectively tied.

DAILY MAIL FEBRUARY 15, 1917

Sir D. Haig on his plans

'This year will be decisive in this sense: that we shall see the decision of the war on the fields of battle – that is to say, an event from which Germany will emerge beaten by force of arms.'

Speaking in French the purity and fluency of which surprised his visitors, the field-marshal, in answer to questions, said:

As to the next great offensive, it does not matter who makes the first move. If the enemy begins, whether it be in the north or the south, in salients which tempt him or on former battlefields, we are ready to receive him. His temerity will cost him dear. Our armies are well trained and in working order, so that the enemy's defeats will become a rout, depriving him at any moment of the possibility, even far behind his lines, of re-entrenching.

Shall we break through? Without the slightest doubt, with irresistible impulse and in many places. The German defence includes behind the lines a powerful system of railway lines. The first attacks in the great offensive may, therefore, at the beginning be limited. It has taken months and months to hold back this people of more than 50,000,000. It will take several more months yet to annihilate them. But we shall strike terribly and ceaselessly until we have accomplished the total destruction of their armies.

Mutiny in the French ranks

The offensive finally got underway on April 9, by which time it had already been undermined by Germany's withdrawal to the Hindenburg Line. Nivelle, though, pressed on. The Allies received early encouragement, as the Canadian Corps took Vimy Ridge and the British attacked Arras. But when the main thrust came it proved to be yet another false hope, and the French army sustained over 100,000 casualties in the attack on Champagne. And, not surprisingly, the strict time limit that had been imposed fell by the wayside too. On May 15 Nivelle paid the price for his mistake: he was replaced by General Pétain. Popular though Pétain was, his appointment was not enough to assuage the emotions of the French infantry. After more failed promises and yet more mass slaughter they had had enough. There was mutiny on a massive scale.

Fortunately, the German Army was unaware of the situation, or they might have seized their chance. Pétain responded to the mutineers with a mixture of carrot and stick: the offensive was cancelled and attempts were made to improve the dire conditions on the front line. Anarchy could not go unpunished, however, and 23 mutineers faced a firing squad 'pour encourager les autres'.

OPPOSITE ABOVE LEFT: **A corner of the battlefield at Arras. The British launched the attack on April 9, 1917 as a diversionary operation in advance of Nivelle's main offensive on the Aisne.**

OPPOSITE ABOVE RIGHT: **Canadian troops prepare to go over the top at Vimy Ridge as the Battle of Arras begins.**

OPPOSITE MIDDLE LEFT: **A battery of 60-pounders in action at Arras.**

OPPOSITE BELOW: **British troops in Arras, June 7, 1917. The offensive cost the British 160,000 lives.**

ABOVE: **Canadian troops cheer their victory at Vimy Ridge. In a single assault they took the ridge, where so many French soldiers had perished in 1915.**

LEFT: **The battle-scarred slopes of Vimy Ridge after the offensive.**

BELOW: **Soldiers pass through the ruins of Athies during the Battle of Arras.**

The United States enters the war

At the start of 1917, Woodrow Wilson, recently elected as US president for a second term, was fighting to keep his country out of the war. He invited the opposing sides to state the terms on which hostilities could end. The Central Powers did not reply, but the Allies' response, issued on January 10, 1917, stated that the aggressors, whose conduct had been 'a constant challenge to humanity and civilization', had to evacuate all the territories that they had invaded and also pay substantial reparations. They reaffirmed their commitment to 'peace on those principles of liberty, justice and inviolable fidelity to international obligations', but Wilson's decision was far from straightforward. Although the Central Powers had violated other nations' sovereign territory, Britain and France were also great imperialist powers. Altruism played no part in Wilson's decision-making, though; he wanted whatever was in America's interests. He also recognized that it might be necessary to commit to war in order to shape the peace in the most favourable way.

LEFT: The inauguration of President Wilson, March 1913. Wilson, a Democrat, was able to defeat the incumbent President Taft because ex-President Roosevelt ran as an independent and split the Republican vote.

ABOVE: Woodrow Wilson, the 28th President of the United States, had tried to keep his country out of the war, but Germany's attempts to incite a war between Mexico and the United States proved a step too far.

OPPOSITE ABOVE RIGHT: A meeting of Allies, France's General Balfourier talks to English and Russian officers whilst being flanked by Serbian and Japanese officers.

OPPOSITE LEFT: Winston Churchill addresses munitions workers in Glasgow after becoming Minister of Munitions in July 1917.

OPPOSITE BELOW: Kaiser Wilhelm with the 26th President of the United States, Theodore Roosevelt. Roosevelt supported intervention on the side of the Allies in the First World War.

The Zimmerman Telegram

Germany launched its tactic of unrestricted submarine warfare on February 1, 1917, but Wilson would still not be drawn in. America severed all diplomatic relations with Germany, but pursued a policy of 'armed neutrality' for the next two months. Three US cargo ships were sunk in March, increasing the pressure. However, the final straw soon came for many people – Germany attempted to exploit Mexico's long-standing grievances against the United States. Arthur Zimmerman, Germany's Foreign Secretary, sent a telegram to Mexico offering support for any action undertaken to reclaim territory lost to the US in the previous century, which included Arizona and Texas. The telegram was intercepted by the Allies and its contents revealed. It had an immediate impact in the States, and the large numbers of people who had previously been strongly committed to isolationism now became equally in favour of war.

Congress approves military action

On April 2, the President went to Congress to seek approval for a declaration of war; the decision was ratified four days later. The US had thrown in her lot with the Entente but would not sign the Pact of London, the agreement which bound the Allies to act together and not conclude separate peace deals. Wilson even studiously avoided using the term 'ally'. In these circumstances, the formal declaration of war on April 6 was more of a psychological turning point than a military one, and it would be some time before the US would be able to make a significant contribution to the armies in the field, something which Germany's high command relied on. Hindenburg and Ludendorff, who were both doubtful about the possibility of victory on the battlefields of the Western Front, put their faith in the war at sea – or rather, in the war beneath the sea. The German U-boats, which were now unrestricted in their choice of targets, could crush Britain while America was still preparing for war. On land all they had to do was play a defensive game.

DAILY MAIL FEBRUARY 2, 1917

Germany defies US

Germany has sent a Note to the United States which in effect declares a hunger war on that country and on the world. A Washington report says that President Wilson may, in reply, warn Germany against unrestricted submarine warfare and threaten a breach in relations if Berlin is unheeding.

The Note announces that German submarines will observe no restraints, and forbids neutral shipping to enter the waters round Great Britain, France and Italy, and the Eastern Mediterranean. It imposes on United States trade these conditions:

1. Only one steamer a week between the United States and Britain.

2. That vessel must run to and from Falmouth.

3. It must be painted in a particular way and lighted at night.

4. The United States Government must guarantee that it carries no contraband, and must warn other ships not to enter the 'barred zone'

All previous promises given by Germany to President Wilson are repudiated. The German demand is a violation of the sovereignty of all neutrals, as the above regulations are not permitted by international law and interfere with neutral rights at sea.

The Note says that the German Government is actuated by 'the highest sense to serve humanity,' and hopes that the people and Government of the United States will 'appreciate the new state of affairs from the right standpoint of impartiality.'

Passchendaele

Following Nivelle's disastrous spring offensive, the French were in no position to instigate another attack on the Western Front. Haig, however, was determined to do so; his authority had been restored by the failure of Nivelle's offensive, which he had opposed. His idea was to break through the German line at Ypres and then push through to the Belgian coast, severing the enemy's right flank. Such a plan also meant that the Allies would be within striking distance of the German U-boat bases at Ostend and Zeebrugge. All the Entente Powers were still deeply concerned by Germany's U-boat policy and any action which might harm their submarines was therefore a tempting one. Pétain was sceptical, favouring a defensive operation until the US could mobilize in significant numbers, and Lloyd George was still concerned about the possibility of another Somme. But the United States was a long way from being ready, and there were still weaknesses in the French army. Haig saw the chance of Britain gaining a glorious victory. He got his wish and his plans for the third Battle of Ypres – or Passchendaele, as it would come to be known – got under way.

The battle for Messines Ridge

Haig's first target was the Messines Ridge south of Ypres which was a key vantage point; the Germans had held it for two years. On June 7 General Sir Herbert Plumer led a successful attack on the ridge. From then on preparations for the main assault could continue unobserved and unhindered by targeted enemy action. However, these preparations took six weeks – time which the Germans put to good use.

OPPOSITE ABOVE RIGHT: The terrible weather meant that the trenches at Passchendaele often flooded. There were many cases of trench foot, a form of frost-bite, that resulted from prolonged exposure to the cold and damp.

OPPOSITE LEFT: British soldiers watch as wounded German prisoners of war are marched to the rear.

OPPOSITE BELOW: A Belgian woman sells oranges to British troops as they head to the front in Flanders.

ABOVE LEFT: Canadians medics carry a wounded comrade by stretcher across the muddy fields during the Battle of Passchendaele.

LEFT: An 18-pound field gun gets stuck in the mud. The summer and autumn of 1917 would be the wettest Flanders had seen in living memory.

BELOW LEFT: Lancers making their way through the ruins of a French village, September 22, 1917.

RIGHT: The scene at a field dressing station on the afternoon of June 7, 1916, the first day of the battle for the Messines Ridge.

BOTTOM: The war causes congestion in Fricourt, France, August 8, 1917.

DAILY MAIL   JUNE 8, 1917

Haig strikes

We attacked at 3.10 a.m. the German positions on the Messines-Wytschaete Ridge [south of Ypres] on a front of over 9 miles. We have everywhere captured our first objectives, and further progress is reported to be satisfactory along the whole front of attack.

The Battle of Messines Ridge, as the sequel to the Battle of Vimy Ridge, will be almost the greatest battle in our history, if we keep what we have won. At the moment that I write our skied observers see German divisions in mass gathering for attack, but whatever may happen in the future it remains that we took what we meant to take exactly as we meant to take it and at the precise minute we meant to take it.

Rain and mud at Passchendaele

The rain came earlier than usual and was especially heavy. Haig had planned massive bombardment to signal the start of the main assault on Passchendaele, but the shells broke up muddy ground whose drainage system had collapsed in the deluge. The advancing British soldiers had to contend with thick sticky mud and water-filled craters as well as enemy fire, but the Germans were not in the same position. They had abandoned the idea of trying to keep to entrenched positions in such appalling conditions, and defended their lines with machine guns housed in pillboxes instead.

It took another month before the weather improved and the Allies finally gained a glimpse of Passchendaele Ridge, which had been one of the first-day objectives. The rain returned in October but Haig remained unwavering in his aim. He was convinced that the German army was about to crack and was consumed by the need to capture Passchendaele itself. Passchendaele was eventually taken on November 2, though at enormous cost. The line had only advanced five miles, but more than 250,000 casualties had been sustained for that short distance. Haig's plans were a complete failure. The ports of Zeebrugge and Ostend continued to maintain the U-boats that had been inflicting terrible losses on Allied shipping, and the German army was far from surrendering.

OPPOSITE ABOVE LEFT: The corpses of German soldiers killed in an attack on October 12, 1917. On this day Anzac troops suffered heavy losses as they made the first attempt to take Passchendaele.

OPPOSITE MIDDLE LEFT: A soldier takes cover in the flooded trenches of Passchendaele.

OPPOSITE BELOW: One regiment marches to the front as another one rests at the roadside on October 14, 1917.

OPPOSITE MIDDLE RIGHT: Soldiers shelter in the flooded shell holes of the Passchendaele battlefield.

ABOVE: Wounded men are wheeled through the mud to makeshift hospitals behind the lines.

ABOVE LEFT: Donkeys cart supplies through the muddy fields around Passchendaele on October 31, 1917. The day before, the Germans had repelled an Allied attack with mustard gas.

LEFT: Canadian sappers mark the ground for road construction. All the roads and buildings in Passchendale were destroyed during the battle.

BELOW: British casualties mounted to almost 250,000 during the battle for Passchendaele. Here the wounded lie in open fields awaiting treatment.

DAILY MAIL   OCTOBER 15, 1917

Swamp of death and pain

Every inch we gained in Friday's battle is worth a mile as common distance is reckoned. Some troops went forward 1,700 yards or even more, fighting all the way; and when their relic came back some part of that heroic journey no enemy dared follow them, so foul and cruel was their track.

They left behind them a Golgotha, a no man's land, a dead man's land. Five or six miles separate our troops from any place where you can step firm, where you can find any break in the swamp. It is a nightmare journey to traverse it, in spite of the ceaseless labour of pioneers.

Our soldiers coming out of this swamp of death and pain maintain incredible serenity. If we could advance so far in such conditions we could go anywhere in fine weather. We were nowhere beaten by the enemy, though more defensive wire was left round shell-holes and pill-boxes and fewer machine gunners knocked out than in any recent attack. We were beaten by the rain that began to fall in torrents at midnight before the attack, so they all say and feel, and so it was.

One of them, still full of humour, said he considered Friday an unlucky day for him. 'You see,' he argued, 'I was first hit in the shoulder by a machine-gun bullet, and as I stumbled was hit in the foot, and as I lay another hit me in the foot and another hit me in the side. Decidedly Friday is an unlucky day.' It was a terrible day for wounded men, and alternate advance and retreat now always leave a wide, indeterminable no man's land from which escape to the mercy of either side is hard. But the best is being done, and the immortal heroism of the stretcher-bearers was backed by both the daring and skilful work of doctors at advance dressing stations and ambulance drivers a little farther back.

The trouble was how to find people or places. Wounded men, runners, contact officers, and even whole platoons had amazing journeys among shells and bullets searching for dressing-station headquarters, objective or what not, and, as we know, even Germans on the pure defensive had similar trouble and their units were inextricably confused. It was all due, as one of them said, to the sump, or morass.

All that can be said of the battle is that we are a little higher up the slope than we were and a little further along the crest road to Passchendaele. How we succeeded in capturing over 700 prisoners is one of the marvels of the day. A marvel, too, is the pile of German machine guns. They are some small concrete proof of the superhuman efforts of our infantry. If the world has supermen they were the men who waded forward up to their hips astride the Ravelbeck and stormed concrete and iron with flesh and blood. They were at least the peers of the men who fought 'upon their stumps' at Chevy Chase.

To-day the artillery fire has died down, the sun is bright, though the cold west wind threatens showers.

The Russian Revolution

The French were not alone in having discontented, dissatisfied and angry troops. There was dissent in the ranks of all the major combatants, provoked largely by hardship and the privations they suffered – and by the impact of mass slaughter for no discernible gain whatsoever. It seemed as though the consensus between government and people which was required to continue the war was in danger of breaking down, in every nation. All the leaders recognized that the morale of both troops and civilians needed careful monitoring.

In Russia, however, dissent spilled over into full-blown revolution. By the winter of 1916–17 both Russia's army and people were at breaking point. The poorly fed, poorly equipped and badly led troops refused to fight, and the civilian population was faced with soaring prices in the face of dwindling food supplies. Workers in Petrograd – St Petersburg – went on strike on March 8 and took to the streets. In 1905 a similar protest had been quashed with great force, but this time the troops' sympathies lay with the protestors, and the Duma announced that it no longer recognized the Tsar. On March 15, Nicholas II abdicated and a moderate provisional government under Alexander Kerensky was established. This government believed that the war still had to be won and the fighting continued. However, an offensive in Galicia in June 1917 failed badly, leaving the ordinary Russian soldiers believing they were no better off than they had been under the Tsar.

DAILY MAIL NOVEMBER 9, 1917

Lenin overthrows Kerensky

The Petrograd Extremists, with Lenin, the pro-German, in the forefront, announce that they have overthrown Kerensky, that he is in flight, that some half dozen Ministers have been arrested, including Terestchenko, the Foreign Minister, and that their policy is an immediate peace and the land for the people.

They have seized the Winter Palace, after firing several shells at it from a cruiser, and several railway stations, and have issued orders undoing what has been done to try to restore Army discipline.

Petrograd Manifesto

The following, transmitted from Russian wireless stations, is the document announcing Kerensky's overthrow:-

To the army committee of the active army, and to all the workmen's and Soldiers' councils: The garrison and proletariat of Petrograd have deposed the Government of Kerensky, which rose against the revolution and the people. The change was accomplished without bloodshed. The Petrograd Workmen's Council solemnly welcomes the change, and proclaims the authority of the Military Revolutionary Committee until the creation of a Government from the Workmen's Councils. In announcing this to the Army at the front the Revolutionary Committee calls upon the revolutionary soldiers to watch closely the conduct of the men in command. Officers who do not join the accomplished Revolution immediately and openly must be arrested at once as enemies.

The Petrograd Workmen's Council considers as the programme of the new authority:

The offer of an immediate democratic peace.

An immediate handing over of the large proprietorial lands to the peasants.

The handing over of all authority to the Workmen's Councils.

An honest convocation of the Constitutional Assembly.

The Revolutionary Army must not permit uncertain military detachments to leave the front for Petrograd. Use persuasion, but where this fails oppose any such action without mercy. This order must be read immediately to detachments of all arms. To withhold it from the rank and file is equivalent to a great crime against the Revolution and will be punished by all the strength of the Revolutionary law.

Soldiers! For peace, for bread, for land, for the power of the people.
The Military Revolutionary Committee

The Bolsheviks seize power

The overthrow of the Tsar presented exiled revolutionaries with the opportunity to return to Russia and take advantage of the situation. One such revolutionary was Vladimir Ilich Lenin, leader of the Bolshevik faction of Russia's Marxist Party. He returned to Russia from exile in Switzerland in April 1917 with the assistance of the Central Powers and called for an immediate end to the war. His message proved popular among soldiers and workers who were deserting in droves and facing severe food shortages. On November 7 – October 25 in Russia, which was still using the old Julian calendar – the Revolution began. In an almost bloodless coup, the Bolsheviks stormed and captured the Winter Palace in Petrograd (St Petersburg), which was being used as the headquarters of the provisional government. With the seat of government in their hands, the Bolsheviks began consolidating their power in what would become a bloody civil war.

In March 1918 the Bolsheviks ended the war with Germany by signing the punitive Treaty of Brest Litovsk. Desperate to end the war and keep soldiers and workers loyal to their new regime, the Bolsheviks were forced to negotiate from a position of great weakness. They were forced to give away vast swathes of territory of in the west, including some of Russia's best industry and agriculture. For Germany, the Treaty of Brest Litovsk was one of the greatest successes of the war. They gained vast swathes of territory and could now concentrate on the Western Front.

OPPOSITE BELOW: **Soldiers of the Keksgolm Regiment stage a protest on the streets of Petrograd.**

OPPOSITE MIDDLE: **Russian officers are taken prisoner by their own men.**

OPPOSITE ABOVE RIGHT: **Bolshevik militias fire in the Nevsky Prospect during the October Revolution.**

ABOVE LEFT: **Paralysed by disorganization, Russian soldiers hold a meeting at the Front in August 1917 to collectively decide their next move.**

FAR LEFT: **Lenin speaks to huge crowds in Petrograd (St Petersburg) upon his return from exile in April 1917.**

LEFT: **One of the first issues of the Bolshevik newspaper to be published after the revolution. The Bolsheviks used newspapers to convey propaganda to the Russian public.**

BELOW: **Provisional Government forces open fire on Bolshevik protestors in the Nevsky Prospect during a failed uprising in July 1917. Lenin fled into exile once again in order to avoid arrest. He did not return until just before the revolution in October.**

The Battle of Cambrai

To maintain momentum after Passchendaele, the Allies launched a last offensive for the year on the Western Front. At the Battle of Cambrai, which opened on November 20, over 400 tanks were deployed, spearheading the attack. This was the first time tanks had been seen on a battlefield in such numbers. There were some encouraging early gains, but a combination of direct hits and mechanical breakdowns meant that tank numbers were severely reduced after the initial breakthrough. In the end, the German Army counterattacked and the usual stalemate was restored.

Mixed review for the Allies

1917 had been a year fraught with difficulties for the Allies, but it ended on a rather brighter note as news came through that Field Marshal Allenby's Egyptian Expeditionary Force had marched into Jerusalem on December 9, capturing Beersheba and Gaza on the way. There was little reason for celebration on the other main fronts on land. There was a complete collapse in the east following the Russian Revolution; there had been the fiasco of Nivelle's spring offensive and Passchendaele in the west, and defeat at Caporetto in Italy. However, the German U-boat war, which had been devastating to the Allies in the early months of the year, had moderated somewhat. The Allies had been using a convoy system, with merchant ships travelling together under the protection of warships, and this had helped to improve survival rates. Even so, rationing had to be introduced in Britain at the end of the year, and even the royal family succumbed to it. Germany's attempt to bring Britain to her knees had, ultimately, failed. And 1918 might be much better – there was the prospect of the American Expeditionary Force led by General John Pershing becoming a key part of the effort on the Western Front. Their recruits and conscripts were completing their training and becoming ready for frontline duty.

ABOVE: Highland Territorials jump across a German communication trench during an attack on Flesquieres during the Battle of Cambrai.

LEFT: British Infantry dodge machine gun fire near Cambrai. The Allies soon became victims of their own success; the tanks, which had been vital to the spectacular gains on the first day, pushed on too far ahead of the troops, allowing for an easy German counterattack.

BELOW LEFT: The East Anglian division occupies a German trench on the first day of the Battle of Cambrai.

Time running out for Germany

The German high command had little room for any manoeuvring by the end of 1917. It was clear, even to them, that the threat from the U-boats had declined; they could no longer regard their submarines as being an instrument of victory. It was also obvious that the condition of both the German army and the ordinary people – and those of the other Central Powers – meant that the war could not continue for much longer. The Allied blockade was continuing to bite. It was causing suffering, although it was failing to starve Germany into submission. The troops and people could only really be expected to bear such hardships while a great military victory over their enemies remained a distinct possibility. However, 1918 would bring American forces across the Atlantic in much greater numbers. The German generals knew they would have to play their final cards in France and Belgium, and do so before most of the US forces arrived.

TOP: **A long ammunition column moves up to the front on November 24, 1917 during the Battle of Cambrai.**

ABOVE: **Medics rush to pull a wounded man off the battlefield. Thousands of medics lost their lives during the war as they tried to rescue the wounded.**

RIGHT: **In December 1917 the troops spend a fourth Christmas at the Front.**

BELOW AND INSERT: **The ruins of Cambrai in the aftermath of the battle.**

Operation Michael

The year started with the German high command having to initiate a redeployment of troops from east to west. A spring offensive around Arras was planned, which would shatter the Allied line and see the German army move relentlessly northeastwards to the Channel coast. This was Operation Michael, and it relied on a new tactic. Ludendorff decided to put his faith in a rapid infiltration of the enemy line by specially trained 'Sturmtruppen' or storm troops. The Allies were to be given no time to recover, and sheer momentum was the key to its success. This was a huge risk, and some senior German officers thought that Operation Michael was far too ambitious, especially given that up to a million men remained on the Eastern Front while Treaty negotiations were still ongoing. But Ludendorff was virtually forced into this action; if he could succeed in driving a wedge between the British and French forces, then victory might yet be possible.

On the other side there was complete contrast; the Allies were in a more defensive frame of mind. There were several reasons for this, and they were partly due to the reverses of 1917. The legacy of Passchendaele meant that Lloyd George felt Haig was too ready to embark on futile offensives, and far too willing to play with the lives of his troops. Accordingly, he was wary of committing significant numbers of men into Haig's care. The Entente Powers also realized that time was now on their side.

German successes

By the time the Germans launched Operation Michael on March 21, only about 300,000 US troops had reached Europe. In stark contrast, trains had been transporting German troops westwards day and night for weeks. This huge logistical undertaking gave some of them an opportunity to desert but, even so, Germany still had a numerical advantage on the Western Front for the first time since the very beginning of the war. The Allies did suspect that an attack was imminent but had no idea exactly where or when it would begin.

The start of the offensive was finally announced by a heavy artillery bombardment, including the use of gas shells, during the early hours of March 21. The main point of attack turned out to be between Arras and St Quentin, and the British Third and Fifth Armies bore the brunt of it. The heavy shelling then switched to a creeping barrage as the German infantry began to move forwards. Their initial gains were indeed spectacular. Succeeding waves of fresh troops joined the attack in a rolling spearhead, a tactic which maintained the forward momentum which was essential to success. The German forces swept across the old Somme battlefield and quickly took Peronne, Bapaume and Albert. The assault threatened to separate the French and British, which could have had catastrophic consequences, and growing disagreement between Haig and Pétain about the Allies' response was an added bonus for the Germans.

DAILY MAIL MARCH 23, 1918

The greatest battle of all time

This morning the enemy renewed his attacks in great strength along practically the whole battle front. Fierce fighting has taken place in our battle positions and is still continuing.

The enemy has made some progress at certain points. At others his troops have been thrown back by our counter-attacks.

Our losses have inevitably been considerable, but not out of proportion to the magnitude of the battle.

From reports received from all parts of the battle front the enemy's losses continue to be very heavy, and his advance has everywhere been made at a great sacrifice.

Our troops are fighting with the greatest gallantry. When all ranks and all units of every arm have behaved so well it is difficult at this stage of the battle to distinguish instances.

Identifications obtained in the course of the battle show that the enemy's opening attack was delivered by some 40 German divisions [possibly 600,000 men], supported by great numbers of German artillery, reinforced by Austrian batteries. Many other German divisions have since taken part in the fighting, and others are arriving in the battle area.

Further fighting of the most severe nature is anticipated.

OPPOSITE LEFT: **A runner waits for a response to the message he has just delivered. The use of runners was vital for maintaining good communications at the front.**

OPPOSITE MIDDLE RIGHT: **Kaiser Wilhelm meets with his top generals Hindenburg and Ludendorff.**

OPPOSITE BELOW: **A soldier shields himself as a shell bursts close by during the German offensive.**

OPPOSITE ABOVE RIGHT: **Conscientious objectors in Dartmoor, England. The caption published with this picture in the Daily Mail read:** 'Working for the Camera – The Dartmoor, "conscientious" objectors are here seen professedly cultivating the soil, but they spend much of their time "on leave" or in "strolling on the moors, smoking, reading and talking." Devon people are meeting next Wednesday under the chairmanship of the Mayor of Plymouth to protest'.

LEFT: **Soldiers of the Worcester Regiment doff their caps for a photograph as they head to the frontline.**

BOTTOM: **A Red Cross advanced operating station comes under German artillery fire.**

BELOW: **Back on the Home Front, two women arrive for their shift on the London underground.**

President Wilson's Fourteen Points

On January 8, 1918 Woodrow Wilson, the US President, delivered an address to Congress. He outlined his ideas for a post-conflict Europe in his 'Fourteen Points' speech, in which he envisioned a Europe made up of nations based on democracy and self-determination, which were armed only as much as was necessary for internal security. A 'League of Nations' would provide collective security and oversee international relations. Wilson did not confer with the Allies before delivering his speech, and not all of it would have been well received had he done so. Complete freedom of navigation on the seas at all times (whether at peace or war), for instance, was a stipulation which would not have pleased Britain, a great naval power. In addition, Wilson's call for transparent pacts between governments was far removed from the secret deals by which many of the minor combatants had been persuaded to support one side or the other. But President Wilson knew that he held a strong hand in January 1918, and he was determined to be the prime mover in shaping the new world order.

Britain grows weary

In Britain the situation had become delicate. Over six million working days were lost to strikes in 1918, an indication that the government's exhortations to show restraint and support for the war were finally wearing thin. And as insurance against future manpower needs, the 1918 Military Service Bill raised the age at which men were liable to be conscripted from 41 to 50. The Defence of the Realm Act was amended in March to make it an offence for women to pass on sexually transmitted diseases to servicemen, the incidence of which was reaching epidemic proportions, and offenders were threatened with a heavy fine or imprisonment. This was not especially connected to public morality; it had much more to do with the need to have men fit for active duty.

It wasn't just the American soldiers who were eagerly awaited. The war had left Britain close to bankruptcy. By 1918, 75 per cent of the country's national income was directed at the war effort; the nation's resources had never been so overwhelmingly devoted to a single aim. In the end, the final bill would be £10 billion, of which some £7 billion was borrowed. It meant that the financial backing of the US would be every bit as welcome as its manpower and machinery.

OPPOSITE: **President Wilson delivers his Fourteen Points to Congress.**

OPPOSITE ABOVE LEFT: **Artist Lucille Patterson takes on the job of painting billboards on 42nd Street in New York in order to release men to join the army.**

BELOW: **The USS *Michigan* transports American troops to Europe. It spent the remainder of the war being used for training exercises in American waters.**

ABOVE: **American sailors watch the Changing of the Guard ceremony at Buckingham Palace soon after arriving in London.**

RIGHT: **The first female naval recruit in the United States, Loretta Walsh, is sworn in as 'chief yeoman' to do clerical work for the navy.**

Ludendorff's offensives

Marshal Ferdinand Foch became the de facto Supreme Allied Commander of the Western Front on March 26. He had the immediate problem of pulling together the Allied defences and stopping the potentially disastrous German advance. The town of Amiens, Foch quickly realized, would be an immediate target for the enemy and he decided that it must be defended at all costs. In this he was helped, paradoxically, by the Germans and specifically by Ludendorff, who decided to advance on a wide front instead of concentrating his efforts on taking Amiens itself. As the days passed, the Allied line became much stronger and better reinforced, while the German line was getting overstretched and weaker. The German advance finally petered out on April 8. It had lost its vital momentum.

Ludendorff decided to change the point of attack in the hope of revitalizing the attack. A fresh offensive was launched around the River Lys to the north, which had originally been considered as an alternative to Operation Michael. It now became the focus of a secondary onslaught, and once again there was an immediate breakthrough which offered encouragement to the Germans. Haig issued a Special Order of the Day on April 11. This was, in effect, a rallying call to all the ranks: 'There is no other course open to us but to fight it out. Every position must be held to the last man; there must be no retirement.'

Romania surrenders

By the end of April the latest German offensive had fizzled out as well. Ludendorff was now caught between the need to make a decisive breakthrough and the necessity of trying to conserve his resources, which were rapidly diminishing. Romania signed the Treaty of Bucharest on May 7, and now posed no threat to Germany; a glimmer of hope. Romania had felt dangerously isolated after Russia's withdrawal from the war and saw the need for an early armistice. Germany exacted a heavy price from the defeated country but it made little difference; the war was now in its final phase.

Germans within striking distance of Paris

The final stages had to be played out on the Western Front. Ludendorff tried yet another initiative on May 27, this time against the French Sixth Army along the Chemin des Dames. The German army swept across the Aisne and reached the Marne. This suddenly threatened Paris, which was only some 50 miles away, and there was a partial evacuation of the city. Paris did come under fire from the German guns, but the attack was halted. The German army had made great territorial gains and inflicted considerable losses on the Allies in three short months of concerted effort. However, more and more American divisions were arriving, and the Allied losses were not as critical as those sustained by Ludendorff. In a single month

DAILY MAIL   APRIL 14, 1918

The line holds but the crisis is not past

The British Army has made its valiant answer to Sir Douglas Haig's general order calling upon it to stand and fight – to the last man - for 'the safety of our homes and the freedom of mankind.'

For the past 48 hours, in the face of repeated attacks by masses of Germans and of a terrific bombardment, our devoted lads have held their ground firmly and unflinchingly. The line is still unbroken, and though the crisis is not yet by any means over, there is at least good hope that the men of 1918 will hold fast and win through like the heroes of 1914. There must still be considerable danger so long as there are signs of a powerful German

concentration in another quarter, between Arras and Albert. But each hour gained in the north is of priceless importance.

During the last two days our troops have beaten off an attack at Festubert. They have held Bailleul, a point of supreme importance, as it threatens the communications of Ypres. They have recovered Neuve Eglise, on the flank of the Ypres defences, and they have kept it against repeated attacks. They have maintained their positions on the high ground. They still have the enemy below them in the intricate marsh and meadow land, where movement is not facilitated by the nature of the ground.

– June – his army suffered over 200,000 casualties. June also saw the arrival of the flu epidemic in the German ranks, diminishing their strength even further.

On July 15, Ludendorff made a final effort to achieve a breakthrough. There was an offensive around Rheims. Three days later the French, who were supported by fresh American troops, counter-attacked. This became known as the Second Battle of the Marne, and proved to be the turning point. From this time on, right until the end of hostilities in November, Germany would be on the retreat.

OPPOSITE BELOW: The British army retreats from General Ludendorff's latest offensive on April 3, 1918.

OPPOSITE LEFT: A soldier watches an explosion at a munitions dump during a tactical withdrawal on the Western Front.

OPPOSITE ABOVE RIGHT: Soldiers barricade themselves amongst the rubble during street fighting in Bailleul.

BELOW: Wounded British troops at an advanced dressing station following a German attack. Injured soldiers are put on stretchers in preparation for transport to regular hospitals further behind the lines. German prisoners are put to use as stretcher bearers.

ABOVE: A labour battalion builds a road through captured British territory on the Western Front. Many of the members of these battalions were veterans who went to France to help with the war effort in any way they could.

The Amiens offensive

The Allies were now forcing Ludendorff's army backwards relentlessly. The morale of the rival forces changed accordingly – and the poor situation of the German forces did not improve. The Battle of Amiens took place on August 8, with General Rawlinson leading a combined Allied force. They caught the Germans completely off guard and quickly shattered any remaining hopes of victory which they might have had. Over 2,000 guns bombarded the German line and about 400 tanks were deployed to support the infantry as they advanced.

Allied air supremacy

The Allies now had massive air supremacy, partly due to the RAF, which had recently been formed. Reconnaissance aircraft had improved, and information about enemy positions and batteries could now be relayed much more efficiently. The backroom staff had also finally come up with a solution to the problem of synchronizing machine-gun fire with the rotation of the propellers, some three years after Anthony Fokker had achieved the same thing for the Germans. The rate of attrition among the flyers was high, however: on the first day of the Amiens offensive the RAF lost 45 planes to anti-aircraft fire. Despite this, their contribution to the Allies' ultimate success was significant.

The Amiens offensive was undoubtedly disastrous for the Central Powers, and Ludendorff declared it to be 'the black day of the German army'. The final blow would be for the Allies to breach the Germans' Siegfried Line, and this finally happened on September 29. Even before that, both Ludendorff and the Kaiser knew that the outcome was now set. The only thing left was to bring the war to an end.

OPPOSITE ABOVE RIGHT: British soldiers in the trenches on the outskirts of Thiepval, September 5, 1918.

OPPOSITE LEFT: General Pershing decorates Captain Douglas MacArthur, who would go on to lead the United States to victory in the Pacific during the Second World War.

OPPOSITE BELOW: Animal carcasses litter the battlefield following fighting around Pilkem, August 1918.

RIGHT: A British soldier checks the papers of a local civilian while searching for German deserters in June 1918. Morale among the German army was beginning to collapse as an influenza epidemic set in.

FAR RIGHT ABOVE: German dead lie abandoned in a field as the Germans withdraw from their positions on the Western Front.

FAR RIGHT MIDDLE: A lone Allied soldier enters Peronne Square, shortly after the German army's withdrawal.

FAR RIGHT BELOW: Allied soldiers fight the Germans in Albert in August 1918.

BOTTOM: Cavalry passing the ruins of Albert Cathedral. Albert was captured by the Allies on August 23, 1918. Atop the Cathedral stood a statue of the Virgin Mary which became legendary for the troops who fought in the region. Constant bombardment caused the statue to lean at right angles. A popular myth for both sides held that when the statue finally fell, the war would end. The 'hanging Virgin' was finally knocked down during a British artillery bombardment in April 1918.

The final stages

The Allies' grip on the Central Powers was tightening everywhere. Bulgaria began negotiating for peace on September 27. It was the first of Germany's allies to fall. There had been widespread resentment among the Bulgarians that they had been treated as second-class citizens by the German state, not as trusted allies. The German army had even commandeered scarce food supplies, leaving Bulgarian soldiers and civilians hungry. The Allies launched a large-scale offensive from Salonika in mid-September, and Bulgaria's desire to resist was effectively non-existent.

This was soon followed by the defeat of the once-great Ottoman Empire. General Allenby had taken Jerusalem in December 1917, but had been hampered by the redeployment of resources to the Western Front since then. He was finally ready to mount an attack once again in September 1918. Allenby tricked his opposite number, Liman von Sanders, into thinking that the point of attack would be inland – and then struck along the coast, near Megiddo. The Turkish army, which had suffered heavily from guerrilla raids organized by the Arabs assisted by T. E. Lawrence, was particularly weak there and there was a swift breakthrough. The cities of Damascus, Beirut and Aleppo fell in quick succession and, on October 30, Turkey finally surrendered.

ABOVE AND BELOW: **French towns fell to the Allies in quick succession as the Germans were beaten back or withdrew during the autumn of 1918.**

OPPOSITE LEFT: **Canadian troops in Cambrai, which fell on October 8, 1918.**

OPPOSITE MIDDLE: **Allied troops climbing the banks of the St Quentin canal in early October 1918.**

OPPOSITE RIGHT: **An Allied column marches unopposed towards the town of Cambrai. Thousands of men had lost their lives fighting for the town less than a year earlier.**

DAILY MAIL NOVEMBER 1, 1918
Turkey surrenders

Turkey has surrendered. An Allied fleet is to proceed to Constantinople and the Black Sea.

On the day that the armistice was signed, Wednesday, our Army captured the last 7,000 Turks in Mesopotamia and are marching to Mosul.

Austria has sent a white flag party to General Diaz to negotiate an armistice. The Italians, meanwhile, are advancing at a great pace, and have scooped up 50,000 prisoners and 300 guns. The whole line is now bending. Revolutions have begun in Vienna and Budapest. The soldiers have seized control and are shouting, 'Down with the Hapsburgs.'

The Czecho-Slovaks have occupied railways on the enemy's line of retreat, and have cut the lines from Berlin to Vienna and Budapest.

British, French, and Americans attacked yesterday on the Scheldt front and gained their objectives. Our men took 1,000 prisoners.

Austria-Hungary falls

Austria–Hungary surrendered four days later. For months the Dual Monarchy had seemed to have been on the point of collapse, both militarily and politically. A major problem was that it contained so many disparate peoples, different ethnic groups who felt little or no allegiance to the empire. They were becoming increasingly unwilling to suffer any more hardship on its behalf.

In June 1918 came the Battle of the Piave. The Austro–Hungarian army was defeated by the Italians, and this wore away the commitment of the Hungarians, Croats, Czechs and Slavs even more. Franz Josef had died in November 1916, and his successor Emperor Karl had already gone behind Germany's back in an attempt to secure a peace deal and save his country from whatever fate awaited it. He offered autonomy to the main ethnic states in the empire, but it was a futile attempt to hold the various countries together, and the prospect of some form of federal status actually split the empire further apart instead of binding the army more closely together. The immediate effect was one of mass desertion as the soldiers from previously subject ethnic groups sought to reach their homelands, which now had a new political identity. On October 24, the Italians launched an offensive. Austrian resistance evaporated and, on November 3, the Dual Monarchy accepted the Allies' terms.

DAILY MAIL OCTOBER 18, 1918

Capture of Ostend

Yesterday was the Allies' greatest day

The British landed at and took Ostend, captured Lille, entered Douai, and reached the outskirts of Tourcoing. The Belgians are on the edge of Bruges and the French are at Thielt, 16 miles only from Ghent.

British, Americans, and French between Le Cateau and the Oise advanced 2 miles towards the Hun line of retreat from the south and took 3,000 prisoners.

Lille's ecstasy

The Germans left Lille at 4 o'clock this morning. Our airmen saw people in the streets waving flags, and an hour after it was reported that our patrols were in the streets. The first people to enter were received with such ecstasy that it was impossible to move and escape without the help of the civic authorities. Cars were laden with flowers and gigantic bouquets; women and children crushed forward to embrace the English who entered, and cheers for England resounded down all the streets.

The German retreat is apparently general along the coast, but the enemy is holding hard for the moment in Courtrai and north of it, where our troops are fighting hard.

Germany looks for peace

The German leadership recognized that it had now reached the end, that it was time to give in and stop fighting a war it could no longer hope to win. They did so even before the country lost its chief ally. The new chancellor Prince Max of Baden sent a note to Washington on October 4 hoping to secure an armistice based on Wilson's Fourteen Points, which was considered to be the least worst option. But if Germany expected more favourable terms from America than from Britain or France, it was to be disappointed. The Germans had nothing to bargain with and had to accept whatever terms the Allies would impose, a fact not lost on President Wilson. He didn't tell the British or French of the exchanges between Washington and Berlin which the US had entered into, and Germany accepted US terms on October 27.

Marshal Foch continued to put pressure on the retreating German forces. General Pershing's American troops, supported by the French, were at the forefront of a huge offensive in the Meuse–Argonne region. This began on September 26 with the aim of capturing vital rail links, Germany's main line of communication. The American army sustained over 100,000 casualties in the next five weeks, but the final breakthrough of the First World War came on November 1.

DAILY MAIL NOVEMBER 12, 1918

Germany surrenders

The armistice was signed at 5 a.m. yesterday. The 'Cease fire' sounded at 11 a.m. The terms are such that Germany cannot fight again. She surrenders most of her arms for land, sea, and air: and she must repair and repay.

London gave itself up to joy yesterday. The scenes were beyond credence. The King toured the capital and addressed the crowds. Throughout the country and the world rejoicing is unexampled. Parliament, after acclaiming the Premier, went to St Margaret's to give thanks to God. The King attends a thanksgiving at St. Paul's to-day.

The news was announced in London at 10.20 a.m. by the Prime Minister in the following terms :-

The armistice was signed at 5 a.m. this morning, and hostilities are to cease on all fronts at 11 a.m. to-day. This was followed in half an hour by the text of Foch's 'Cease fire.'

Marshal Foch to Commander-in-Chief:

Hostilities will cease on the whole front as from November 11 at 11 o'clock (French time). The Allied troops will not, until a further order, go beyond the line reached on that date and at that hour.

Armistice

Ludendorff had already fallen and it was only a matter of time before his entire country followed. There was revolt on the streets of Berlin and the German navy mutinied at Kiel on November 3. On November 8 Marshal Foch received an armistice delegation from Germany in a railway carriage in the forest of Compiegne. The Germans were given seventy-two hours to agree to the terms laid down, which included the introduction of democracy to the country, but the delegates didn't need that much time. The following day Kaiser Wilhelm abdicated, leaving for neutral Holland. The armistice was signed at 5.00 in the morning on November 11, and was to come into force six hours later, at 11 a.m. There was some fighting until the very last minute.

OPPOSITE ABOVE LEFT AND RIGHT: The war exacted a heavy toll on both sides; some 4.5 million of Allies had fallen and the death toll for the Central Powers was in the region of 4 million, although the exact figure is not known.

OPPOSITE BELOW: Allied soldiers cheer their victory after more than four years of fighting.

ABOVE: The Allied delegation disembarks the train after signing the Armistice with the Germany.

RIGHT: The first military bridge is opened across the Scheldt at Tournai on November 23, 1918.

LEFT: Nurses bring flowers to the grave of a fallen soldier in France.

Revolution in Germany

Von Hindenburg led his defeated troops home to a country in chaos. All the years of deprivation and hardship had failed to produce a glorious victory and the mobs began appearing on the streets demainding political change. The sailors' mutiny in Kiel had rapidly spread across the country and Kaiser Wilhelm was forced to abdicate on November 9. A new democratic government was formed, but some leftwing radicals, wanted to capitalize on the public mood and engineer a Russian style revolution in Germany.

In January 1919 the communist Spartakist movement, led by Rosa Luxemburg, Leo Jogiches, Clara Zetkin, and Karl Liebknecht, staged an uprising against the new government in Berlin. Despite his left-wing leanings, the new Chancellor of Germany, Friedrich Ebert, wanted to avoid the kind of full-scale social revolution that had happened in Russia, so he called in the German army and the Freikorps (paramilitaries) to crush the rebellion. By January 13 the Spartakist leaders had been captured and executed.

Meanwhile revolution had also broken out in Bavaria, where Communists had declared independence from German and had begun to rounding-up enemy suspects and expropriating private property. Chancellor Ebert ordered the army and the Freikorps into Bavaria where they soon took control, capturing and executing an estimated 700 men and women.

TOP LEFT: **British soldiers shop at a market in Bonn during their short occupation after the war.**

TOP MIDDLE: **The Belgian Rhine Army mans a machine-gun post on the Homburg Bridge at Duisburg as a precaution against 'Red' troops invading the occupied area.**

TOP RIGHT: **A German officer, decorated with the Iron Cross, reading the proclamation of a state of siege in Danzig in April 1919. The city's predominantly German population bitterly opposed being included in a Polish state. The Treaty of Versailles made Danzig a 'Free City' under League of Nations administration.**

ABOVE: **Freikorps pose for photographers in the Wilhelmsplatz in Berlin.**

BELOW INSET: **Trying to regain a sense of normality, these children celebrate Christmas in Berlin in 1919.**

BELOW: **French troops march into Frankfurt for a brief period of occupation.**

DAILY MAIL NOVEMBER 11, 1918

Kaiser in flight

The Kaiser has abdicated and fled to Holland with the Crown Prince, and apparently also Hindenburg and the General Staff. If they went in uniform they must be interned.

He signed the abdication following a revolution in Berlin, where the Social Democrats under Ebert have hoisted the red flag on the palace and are forming a Government. Most of the army seems to have gone over to the 'Red' workers.

The courier with the armistice terms from Foch arrived at Spa, the German headquarters, only yesterday morning. Further emissaries have arrived there from Berlin and have wirelessed to the envoys at French headquarters that 'a delay of some hours' is probable. It is not clear who will sign.

Our cavalry are racing along the Brussels road. The infantry are outside Mons. Maubeuge they took on Saturday, and east of it they have captured many trains, as, farther south, have the French, who are well beyond Hirson and Mezières. France is nearly freed.

1,561st day of the war

Three weeks ago the Kaiser, aged 59 and a monarch for 30 years, called on his people to rally round him. Shortly after, he left German soil for his headquarters at Spa, in Belgium, 20 miles south of the Dutch frontier. He has not since set foot on German territory so far as is known.

Following the revolt in the Fleet and Army at home and the Republic in Bavaria, soldiers' and workmen's councils were formed in the chief cities and in many of the smaller German States.

Finally, revolution broke out in Berlin on Friday. By Saturday authority there was in the hands of the Socialists. Most of the garrison, including Guardsmen and a number of Guards and other officers, joined the revolutionaries. There was little fighting except at the cockchafers (or cadets') barracks, where some firing took place.

A large crowd proceeded to the Reichstag, where Friedrich Ebert announced that he had been charged by Prince Max of Baden to take over the Chancellorship. He is a harness maker of Heidelberg, one of the group of Socialists who supported the war so long as it was successful.

He is introducing general suffrage for men and women, who are to elect a Constituent Assembly. This will decide the form of the future Government and the position in it of the former German States. He has appealed for unity and the preservation of the food machinery. Associated with him is Scheidemann, another German Socialist leader, hitherto generally subservient to the Government. The banks have closed temporarily, to prevent a run.

It must be remembered that most of the information now available comes from the Socialists, who control the wires and the wireless.

Armistice envoys

Meantime, on Friday morning the German envoys reached Marshal Foch's headquarters and sent back a courier with the Allies' terms to German Army, which was exploding its dumps near the road he had to follow. He got to Spa only at 10.15 a.m. yesterday. More emissaries were sent thither from Berlin, and new delays seem likely.

Whose signature is valid if the armistice terms are accepted is not clear. Herr Ebert has announced that, so far as the Army is concerned, all orders must be countersigned by himself or a representative. The enemy is given till 11 this morning to say 'yes' or 'no.'

The Kaiser clung to his position almost to the last and clearly refused to abdicate till news of the revolution in Berlin arrived. Then, 'shivering and trembling,' he gave way. The Crown Prince renounced the succession, and together the two fled, accompanied, it is reported from Holland, by Hindenburg and all the staff. They did not wait to learn Foch's terms. They passed over the very ground in Belgium first violated by German troops late on August 3, 1914.

The Kaiser was in uniform and the staff was armed. Under international law they should be interned by the Dutch Government.

TOP: French troops mount a machine gun on a café table in central Frankfurt as a precaution against disorder in the town.

ABOVE: Germans surrender their planes to the Allies after the war.

RIGHT: The exiled son of Kaiser Wilhelm, ex-Crown Prince Wilhelm (holding stick) is pictured amongst a group of supporters.

Paris Peace Conference

It was now down to the victors to shape some sort of workable peace, but it was to be one in which principles and ideals would inevitably clash with self-interest. The Allies had given little thought to the actual peace terms they would demand, largely because leading a war in which some 10 million people had lost their lives had been such an enormous task. The only coherent document that was already in existence was Woodrow Wilson's Fourteen Points.

The Paris Peace Conference opened on 18 January 1919, and President Wilson laid out his vision for a new organization to oversee conflict resolution. This League of Nations was a good idea in theory, but it was emasculated from the start when the US Senate, anxious about possible involvement in distant disputes, obstructed American membership. Nevertheless, by the end of 1919 the Covenant of the League of Nations had been incorporated into the various peace treaties and the organization set to work promoting collective security.

Treaty of Versailles

There were five separate peace treaties which were signed between the Allies and each of the defeated powers. The first, and the most important, was the settlement with Germany. On June 28, 1919, the Treaty of Versailles was signed in the palace's Hall of Mirrors. The terms were severe. Alsace-Lorraine was returned to France and most of East Prussia was lost to the reunited Poland, which was also given access to the sea via the port of Danzig. Belgium and Denmark also gained territory at Germany's expense. The Saar region was to be administered by the League of Nations, and there would be a 15-year occupation of the Rhineland by the Allies. All of Germany's colonies were also forfeit. The country was not allowed to maintain either a U-boat fleet or an air force, while her army was not to exceed 100,000 men. The German High Seas Fleet was interned at Scapa Flow.

OPPOSITE ABOVE: **Delegates trawl through paperwork as they hash out the terms of the Treaty.**

OPPOSITE MIDDLE: **The delegations from Canada and New Zealand arrive in Paris for the peace conference. Both countries sustained heavy losses in the war.**

OPPOSITE BELOW: **Soldiers stand guard outside the Palace of Versailles as the Treaty is signed within.**

ABOVE LEFT: **General Pershing, commander of the US forces in Europe, arrives in Versilles.**

LEFT: **President Wilson doffs his cap to the crowd outside the Trianon Palace Hotel in Versailles.**

TOP: **The Big Four at Versailles. From left to right: Prime Minister Vittorio Orlando of Italy, Prime Minister David Lloyd George of Great Britain, Prime Minister Georges Clemenceau of France and President Woodrow Wilson of the United States.**

ABOVE MIDDLE: **Germany's representatives listen to Clemenceau's speech during a meeting at the Trianon Palace Hotel in Versailles where the Peace Treaty was officially handed over to them.**

ABOVE: **Australian Prime Minister Billy Hughes gives instructions to his driver in Paris. Australia sustained more than 200,000 casualties in the war.**

Treaty of Versailles: reparations and war guilt

LEFT: The Peace Treaty is signed in the Hall of Mirrors at Louis XIV's monumental Palace of Versailles.

ABOVE: **Large crowds gather outside the Palace of Versailles waiting for news that the peace treaty has been signed.**

There were two further stipulations to the Treaty of Versailles which were even more controversial and would have severe ramifications in the future. The first was the question of reparations. France had been made to pay heavily following the Franco-Prussian War of 1870–71, and Clemenceau demanded that Germany should now be subject to similarly heavy financial penalty. France and Britain were left to settle this issue because the US did not ratify the treaty and waived all claims to reparations itself. At this point, Lloyd George and Clemenceau imposed an interim order for Germany to pay $5 billion in cash and goods, with the issue set to be reviewed at a future date. These punitive reparations, at such a high level, were impossible for the defeated country, and within four years Germany had defaulted. By the end of the 1920s it was clear that the reparations payments were completely unsustainable and they were allowed to lapse. However, the inevitable economic hardship, and the levels of resentment that it brought about, would provide an exceptionally fertile breeding ground for Adolf Hitler's National Socialist Party, established in 1921.

Secondly, the Allies insisted on adding a moral dimension to the peace settlement and a clause was included stating Germany's sole moral responsibility for the conflict. This Germany could not agree with, and the country even gathered some support among its former enemies on this point. Many high-ranking Germans, including the Kaiser, were supposed to face trial for war crimes, though in the event these never happened. Many people viewed this as overly vindictive and supported the appeasement of Nazi Germany when it went about reversing the treaty in the period before the Second World War.

Treaty of Saint Germain

A new Republic of Austria was created in the Treaty of Saint-Germain, signed on 10 September 1919, and Italy regained some of her former territory. The disparate Austro–Hungarian empire was broken up, and the independence of Czechoslovakia, Poland and Hungary was also recognized. Serbia's pre-war wish for a Slav state could also be granted. The Kingdom of Serbs, Croats and Slovenes – later renamed Yugoslavia – was created, with Alexander I as its first head of state. However, this new country also included Macedonians, Bosnians and Albanians, an volatile ethnic mix that would create tensions and, 70 years later, lead to war and break up the country.

The settlement with Bulgaria came with the Treaty of Neuilly which was signed on November 27, 1919; Bulgaria ceded land to Greece, Romania and Yugoslavia, including its outlet to the Aegean Sea. The Treaty of Trianon, signed on June 4, 1920, reduced Hungary to a fraction of its former size. Romania got Transylvania, for which it had gone to war, while Czechoslovakia and Yugoslavia also benefited.

Treaty of Sèvres

The final document in all these peace agreements, the Treaty of Sèvres, was signed with Turkey on August 10, 1920. Mesopotamia and Palestine both became British mandates while Syria became a French one, and Turkey also lost territory to Greece and Italy. This particular treaty fell apart very soon. A nationalist movement led by Mustafa Kemal (Ataturk) resented the conciliatory approach adopted by the Ottoman Sultan Mehmed VI, and Kemal swept to power on a promise of recovering some of the country's lost territory. On July 24, 1923, following a bitter struggle against Greece, the Treaty of Lausanne was signed. Turkey regained Thrace and Smyrna, which had been allocated to Greece under the Treaty of Sèvres three years earlier.

Resentments grow

The peace treaties caused much more ill feeling, and not just in those countries which had experienced financial and territorial losses. Italy thought it should have been given a greater share of the spoils and Benito Mussolini formed a new political party, Fasci di Combattimento, in 1919, with the chief aim of restoring the country's national pride. One method of achieving this was by the acquisition of new territory, and Italy looked to Africa to provide this.

Internally, post-conflict Europe was far from being settled and peaceful; it was bedevilled by border disputes and economic hardship. The redrawn map of the continent left all of the newly formed states with disaffected minorities, though Germany remained the greatest problem. The country had not been dismembered in the way the Austro–Hungarian and Ottoman empires had, though it had been badly injured. The terms of the peace agreements were harsh enough to provoke an acrimonious response but Germany was not permanently shackled in the way that France had wanted – as, indeed, future events would show. Germany was admitted to the League of Nations in 1926. Adolf Hitler assumed power seven years later and one of his earliest acts was to withdraw from it; he then repudiated the military constraints of the Treaty of Versailles and the country embarked on a massive rearmament programme. The apparent vindictiveness of the 1919 Versailles treaty was instrumental in Hitler's rise to power, and in the events which followed. Some prescient individuals were already warning – as early as 1919 – that war had not been concluded, only suspended for the moment. The so-called 'war to end all wars' would eventually be widely regarded as being a prelude to the Second World War.

OPPOSITE ABOVE RIGHT: **A spoil of war; a German U-Boat lies in the Thames off the Houses of Parliament in December 1918.**

OPPOSITE ABOVE LEFT: **Members of the Women's Legion ASC leave London bound for France on the same day the peace treaty was signed. They will take the places of men awaiting their demobilization.**

OPPOSITE BELOW LEFT: **General Pershing gets a hero's welcome when he visits London after the war.**

OPPOSITE BELOW: **The 21st Canadian Infantry Battalion crosses a bridge over the River Rhine at Bonn.**

ABOVE RIGHT: **The graves of unknown British dead pictured in France in 1920. On Armistice Day of that year, the body of one unknown soldier was buried at Westminster Abbey with full military honours in tribute to them all.**

BELOW RIGHT: **Repatriated British prisoners of war arrive home to tea and biscuits in London.**

ABOVE LEFT: **General Pershing visits the men busy building 'Pershing Stadium' at Joinville, France in June 1919.**

BELOW LEFT: **The emergence of the 'special relationship': President Wilson with King George V after the war.**

BELOW: **Veterans of the Ypres campaigns march past the town's famous Cloth Hall, May 21, 1920.**

War and Partition in Ireland 1916-1923

Easter Rising

The 1800 Act of Union had united Britain and Ireland, but was opposed by many Irish politicians who campaigned for home rule. However, Protestant Ulster Unionists were opposed to home rule and campaigned just as vigorously against it. As arguments raged the population of Ireland dropped by 2.5 million as people either perished during the Great Famine (1845–51) or emigrated. By the early 1900s housing conditions in Dublin were the worst in Europe with many thousands of families living in only one room.

In 1914 the British government passed the Home Rule Act, which offered a degree of devolved government to all of Ireland, excluding an undefined area of Ulster in the north where Protestants were in the majority. However, the First World War intervened and the implementation of the Act was postponed.

Soon after the war broke out, a militant nationalist group named the Irish Republican Brotherhood (IRB) began to call for an independent Irish Republic, believing that home rule would continue to give London too much influence over Irish affairs. They began planning an uprising and on Easter Monday in 1916 around 1,500 men gathered in Dublin. Many were not armed, but they managed to take and hold key points in the city, including the Magazine Fort in Phoenix Park and the Four Courts. They also briefly entered Dublin Castle, the seat of Britain's government in Ireland. One of the focal points of the uprising was the General Post Office, where the rebels held out for almost a week until food and ammunition ran out.

DAILY MAIL APRIL 26, 1916

Rebels capture Dublin Post Office

At noon yesterday serious disturbances broke out in Dublin.

A large body of men identified with the Sinn Feiners (meaning 'ourselves alone,' the extreme Nationalist body), mostly armed, occupied St. Stephen's Green and took possession forcibly of the Post Office, where they cut the telegraphic and telephonic wires.

Houses were also occupied in St. Stephen's Green, Sackville-street, Abbey-street, and along the quays.

In the course of the day soldiers arrived from the Curragh, and the situation is now well in hand.

So far as is known here, three military officers, four or five soldiers, two loyal volunteers, and two policemen have been killed, and four or five military officers, seven or eight soldiers, and six loyal volunteers wounded. No exact information has been received of casualties on the side of the Sinn Feiners.

War of independence

After the uprising, sixteen of the leaders and their associates were given quick military trials and then executed. The British imposed martial law and hundreds of captured rebels were imprisoned on the British mainland. Until the executions many ordinary Irish people had been apathetic about independence from Britain and wary of the Easter Rising, but the deaths ignited a fire of patriotism that led to widespread rebellion against British rule. Support for the republican Sinn Fein political party skyrocketed and it won 73 of Ireland's 105 parliamentary seats in the 1918 General Election. Its candidates stood on a policy of abstentionism, which meant that, if elected, they would refuse to take their seats in the UK parliament. Irish republicans saw Sinn Fein's election victory as a mandate for independence and established an Irish Parliament in 1919. The Irish Volunteers were reorganized into the Irish Republican Army (IRA) and began waging a ruthless guerrilla campaign to oust the British and secure independence. The British responded with similar levels of brutality, and a cycle of reprisals and counter-reprisals developed. Public opinion in Britain became alarmed at the conduct of British forces in Ireland and the government was under pressure to come up with a political solution.

OPPOSITE ABOVE: **Dubliners pass food through the barbed wire during visiting hours at the Richmond Barracks where participants of the Easter Rising were being detained. Many Irish people were apathetic about the uprising, but the heavy-handed British response inspired people across the country to back the republican cause.**

OPPOSITE ABOVE RIGHT: **The scene at the intersection of Sackville Street and Earl Street in Dublin on Easter Monday 1916. The shops in the right of the picture have been looted and rebels and locals are crowding around a hijacked streetcar.**

OPPOSITE BELOW RIGHT: **The aftermath of the uprising; Sackville Street (now O'Connell Street) lies in ruins.**

RIGHT ABOVE: **Soldiers guard the entrance to Seaforde Street in the Short Strand aea of Belfast following severe fighting in the city in September 1921.**

RIGHT: **Soldiers conduct a search on premises suspected of housing IRA weapons in Cork.**

Partition and civil war

The British government had been seeking a political settlement in Ireland since the end of the First World War, and in November 1920 the Government of Ireland Act was passed. This Act effectively partitioned Ireland by establishing two home rule parliaments, one covering 26 majority Catholic counties in the south and the other covering the remaining six counties in the north where Protestants were in the overall majority. This did not stop the war because the IRA rejected partition and home rule. To stop the bloodshed, the British proposed a treaty whereby southern Ireland would become the Irish Free State, an essentially independent entity with Dominion status within the British Empire. The treaty was signed in December 1921, but republicans were bitterly divided on whether to accept a treaty that excluded the six northern counties.

As the war with the British ended, it gave way to a civil war between supporters and opponents of the Anglo-Irish Treaty. The outgoing British troops assisted the pro-treaty forces and their anti-treaty opponents were steadily beaten in the major towns and cities. Anti-treaty forces continued to wage a guerrilla campaign, but finally ceased firing in May 1923 with the realization that they lacked public support; a 1922 election had shown that the majority of the public were in favour of the treaty. The fighting in southern Ireland had ended, but the troubles in northern Ireland were far from over.

ABOVE: **Sandbags and barbed wire are added to shore up the defences of a British Army post in Belfast as the Irish War of Independence begins.**

LEFT: **British soldiers man a barricade in Belfast after reports that IRA snipers are in the vicinity.**

BELOW: **Mourners recite the Rosary outside Cork Gaol following the death of eleven IRA prisoners who had been on hunger-strike, October 1920.**

Russian Civil War 1917-1922

Treaty of Brest-Litovsk

One of the immediate consequences of the Russian Revolution, especially as far as the outside world was concerned, was the end of Russia's war with Germany. The failed Galicia initiative of June 1917 had demoralized the Russian army, leading to mass desertion. The Bolsheviks took over four months later, and pulling out was an easy decision for the new leadership to make. Not only were they firmly against the war, they also needed peace to consolidate their position within Russia, and the treaty of Brest-Litovsk was signed in March 1918.

Under its terms Russia relinquished control of many of its western territories, which angered many people and fuelled internal opposition to the Bolshevik government. The Allies were outraged at what they saw as treachery and defection, but were also worried about the effect the Revolution might have on their domestic populations; the Bolsheviks were open in their desire to see an international workers' revolution and began propaganda campaigns. The Allies also had valuable investment interests in Russia. It was not altogether surprising, then, that they would intervene, supporting the 'Whites' or the anti-Bolsheviks.

ABOVE: Soldiers loyal to the Bolsheviks demonstrate on the streets of Petrograd in the weeks following the Russian Revolution.

FAR RIGHT: Tsar Nicholas II and his family were killed by the Bosheviks at Ekaterinburg during the Civil War to prevent the Whites from liberating them.

RIGHT: Vladimir Ilych Lenin led the Bolsheviks during the Civil War. He imposed a ruthless economic policy called 'War Communism', which involved requisitioning food from peasants to keep the towns and armies fed. The policy resulted in a reduction in food supplies as it failed to incentivize production. It was eventually scrapped by Lenin himself in favour of a more moderate 'New Economic Policy'.

The Whites

The White forces drew their support from a variety of areas, from priests of the Orthodox Church to monarchists, landowners, army generals, nationalists and local warlords. There were also some left-wing groups who were equally opposed to the Bolsheviks and who sided with the Whites. Their foreign supporters provided financial backing, but also – eventually – troops, and the most intense fighting was to take place between 1918 and 1920. Initially, foreign backing for the Whites came from the Germans and the troops of the Austro-Hungarian Empire, but the Allies – Britain, France and the United States – were also to contribute, preparing their intervention even before the war had actually ended on the Western Front. Other nations also became involved, notably Japan in the east.

BELOW: Lenin addresses Red Army troops in Red Square in Moscow in May 1919.

RIGHT: Leon Trotsky became head of the Red Army in 1918. He turned it into an effective fighting force, helping secure the ultimate victory of the Revolution. This picture was taken in France in 1932 after he had been exiled by Stalin.

LEFT: Trotsky delivers a speech from his motorcar during a visit to the Northern front in September 1919.

The Reds

Leon Trotsky, one of the Bolshevik leaders and a civilian rather than a military man, formed the Red Army to defend the Bolshevik Revolution and resist the Whites and their foreign supporters. Initially, the Red Army was pushed back, suffering a serious defeat in the east against White forces led by Admiral Kolchak, but it actually had several major advantages. It quickly developed military superiority over the White armies, which were bedevilled by ignorance, muddle and incompetent officers. The Bolsheviks were also able to keep most of their industrial plants, including armaments factories, working. In contrast production effectively ceased in areas controlled by the Whites. And the White forces were disunited, inclined to operate independently, with leaders who quarrelled viciously among themselves.

Red Victory

In the east, the Whites under Kolchak had managed to advance from Siberia to beyond the Volga, but he was unable to hold his forces together and defeats followed. Many of his troops deserted, any local support dried up and Siberia was reduced to chaos as the Red Army advanced; they took control of most of the territory in February 1920. In the north, General Nikolai Yudenich got as far as the suburbs of Petrograd (St. Petersburg), but he was forced back after Trotsky led the defence of the city in person in November 1919. Further south and west, the Whites were led by General Anton Denikin, and later by General Peter Wrangel. The Red Army checked Denikin's attempts to advance and forced Wrangel to play a defensive game. He was able to hold parts of the Crimea for several months until November 1920 when his troops were forced to leave or surrender. Red Army forces were also able to regain control of Central Asia, the Caucasus and the Ukraine. The Civil War was effectively over in the west and south, though Vladivostok on the Pacific coast held out until October 1922. By this time Russia was in an appalling state. The country was devastated, there had been epidemics and famines, and immense loss of life. It is estimated that 15 million people died during the Civil War.

ABOVE: Members of the Moscow Soviet address Muscovites from the roof of an armoured car in February 1920.

BELOW: Thousands of Bolshevik soldiers languish in a German prisoner of war camp. These men were arrested when they crossed the frontier into the German province of East Prussia.

LEFT: Lenin's embalmed body is carried to his mausoleum in Moscow following his death in January 1924. His untimely death led to a power struggle, which was ultimately won by Joseph Stalin.

Polish-Soviet War
1919-1921

Border disputes

The map of Eastern Europe was almost completely redrawn by the treaties drawn up at the end of the First World War. One of the main results was the creation of an independent state of Poland, which had been partitioned since 1792.

However, the new frontiers were undefined and in the chaos many states began fighting over borders. The Poles tried to gain as much Lithuanian, Belarussian and Ukrainian territory as they could – these had been part of the original, unpartitioned Polish state and had substantial Polish populations – and by 1919 they controlled most of western Ukraine.

The war between Poland and Soviet Russia initially appeared to be yet another border dispute; the first serious conflict between them took place in February 1919. Russia was embroiled in the Civil War, and though the anti-Bolshevik Whites could have been useful allies, the Poles distrusted them as they were not committed to Polish independence. Nonetheless, Polish forces advanced eastwards, taking Minsk in August and enjoying a series of successes. They reached further into Ukraine, to the city of Kiev.

By now – spring 1920 – the Russian Red Army was less distracted by the Civil War and also experienced several victories. They counter-attacked and pushed the Poles back to Warsaw, but then the Poles counter-attacked in their turn and forced a Russian retreat. Lenin decided to sue for peace. Both sides claimed to be victorious; the Poles had successfully defended their state and the Russians had stemmed the Poles' eastward advance.

ABOVE: Minsk lies in ruins following the Polish-Soviet War. The Poles captured and occupied the city in August 1919.

LEFT: Josef Pilsudski, Poland's leader and highest ranking army officer, sought to expand his country's territory in the east at the expense of Soviet Russia.

Spanish-Moroccan Rif War 1919-1925

Spain in North Africa

There has been a Spanish presence in North Africa for centuries, but by the start of the twentieth century, France had a more significant colonial position. By 1912, anarchy had increased in Morocco, and Sultan Abdelhafid gave sovereignty to the French under the Treaty of Fez. The treaty also granted Spain some land around Tangiers and in the Rif, the mountainous area of northern Morocco.

General local hostility to the Spanish presence soon grew into more open resistance following the emergence of a inspirational leader, Abd el-Krim. Spain established small forts along the main road through the territory in an attempt to shore up its control. The Spanish commander, Fernandez Silvestre, spread his men thinly among these forts, leaving them isolated and vulnerable.

Riffian attack

Krim and the local Riffians began striking Spanish positions, quickly establishing a pattern of attack: isolated posts were surrounded and cut off, the men inside the posts were left to starve or die of thirst, and anyone who attempted to escape was killed. Any troops sent to relieve the fort would be ambushed and killed. To prevent further attacks, Silvestre ordered a retreat to the coastal town of Melilla. On July 22, 1921, thousands of Spanish soldiers were killed as they tried to evacuate from the largest Spanish fort at Anual, and Silvestre committed suicide amid the bloodshed. By mid-August the Riffians had trapped the remaining Spanish in Melilla which they could have taken, but they retreated to the hills.

Republic of the Rif

Krim's victory inspired other tribes to join him and the short-lived Republic of the Rif was created. However, the tribes were difficult to unite, which gave the Spanish an opportunity. They reached agreement with those tribes closest to Tangier, enabling them to concentrate their forces on Krim further to the east. The Spanish force was raised from 25,000 to 150,000 men. This was a different army, led by tough, professional officers including Franco, the future Spanish dictator. They started bombing villages in 1924, but progress was slow and the Riffians began advancing again in November.

ABOVE: Spanish troops hurriedly evacuate a fort before it is attacked by the Riffians.

ABOVE RIGHT: Spanish irregulars launch an attack on an enemy position.

BELOW RIGHT: Spanish soldiers bolster their defences in Melilla following their great defeat at Anual.

French intervention

The French, alarmed by Krim's independence movement, moved their troops to attack the Riffians. Krim attacked them on April 13, 1925, meeting initial success, but his position was ultimately untenable. By June the French and Spanish developed a joint approach, and there were now 360,000 French and Spanish troops opposing the tribesmen. In September the French advanced, regaining the territory captured by Krim, and Spanish troops made a successful amphibious attack. Krim was forced into retreat; the French continued advancing, and he surrendered on May 27, 1926. He was able to escape and sought asylum in Egypt where he died in 1963.

ABOVE LEFT: Hundreds of volunteers line up outside the Spanish Consulate in London, anxious to join the Spanish Foreign Legion and fight in Morocco.

ABOVE MIDDLE: Wounded Spanish troops receive medical attention in the field.

ABOVE: Moroccan servants carry wounded Spanish soldiers from the trenches in September 1924. The number of Spanish troops had just been raised by a factor of six.

Italian invasion of Ethiopia 1935-1936

In the 1930s Benito Mussolini the fascist ruler of Italy began seeking new colonies in Africa. Ethiopia, then called Abyssinia, was the obvious choice; it was one of only two remaining independent states on the continent and bordered Eritrea and Somalia, which had been Italian colonies since the nineteenth century. In January 1935 Mussolini signed an agreement with France essentially giving him a free hand in Africa in exchange for a tougher stance against Nazi Germany. One month later he expanded conscription and poured troops into Eritrea. The invasion of Abyssinia began in October 1935 and was over within seven months following a campaign that saw the use of airstrikes and chemical weapons by the Italians. The Italian invasion underscored the ineffectiveness of the League of Nations, which was unable to impose meaningful sanctions or prevent the invasion of one member state by another.

ABOVE: Mussolini inspects Bersaglieri units in Littoria after their return from Abyssinia in December 1936.

RIGHT: Ethiopian soldiers gather to listen to a speech given by their Emperor, Haile Selassie, ahead of an attack on Italian positions.

Sino-Japanese War
1931-1945

The Japanese invasion of Manchuria

At the end of the nineteenth century, Japan began to create an overseas empire. China, weak and increasingly divided, was an obvious target. Expansionist Japan undertook a series of invasions and occupations of its neighbour from the First Sino-Japanese War in 1894 to the end of the Second World War. Until 1941, when the Japanese attacked Pearl Harbor, the Chinese fought alone.

Under a treaty made in the 1890s, Japan administered the 'South Manchuria Railway Zone' in China. Guards were stationed in the area to protect the railway system, but these were not ordinary railway personnel; they were Japanese army regulars, and they often exercised outside the immediate area of the Zone. Then, on September 18, 1931, a section of railway track outside the Chinese garrison town of Mukden was blown up. The damage was comparatively minor, but the consequences were not. The Japanese accused the Chinese of having sabotaged their railway.

The Mukden Incident

The actual events are still rather confused, but it is generally believed that the explosion was staged by Japanese militarists – with or without Tokyo's knowledge – to provide a pretext for annexing the whole of Manchuria. Local Japanese troops attacked the Mukden garrison, and had overwhelmed the inexperienced 7,000-strong Chinese army by the evening. About 500 Chinese had died, but there were only two Japanese fatalities. The 'Mukden Incident' was a perfect excuse for action, and Japanese forces soon occupied major Manchurian cities. There was some resistance, but it was not long before the Japanese army was in complete control of Manchuria, with its valuable natural resources, and both the army and navy were pressing for further expansion.

The Shanghai War

The Mukden Incident and the subsequent invasion of Manchuria led to a wave of protests, both abroad and within China. Many were in Shanghai, a city where many foreign powers (including Japan) had concessions. On January 27, 1932 Japan issued an ultimatum to the Shanghai administration, demanding suppression of the protests. They agreed on the afternoon of the following day, but at about midnight on January 28 the city was attacked by Japanese aircraft in the first major action supported by aircraft carriers in the Far East. Ground troops also moved in, but the Chinese put up fierce resistance and the Japanese were forced to retreat.

The other major powers tried to open negotiations, but the Japanese army moved additional troops to the area and attacked again. By mid-February, however, they were still not able to conquer the city and even more soldiers were drafted in, taking the strength of the attacking army to about 90,000. This turned the situation around, and on March 2 Chinese forces began leaving Shanghai. There was still some sporadic fighting, but an agreement was finally signed two months later and Shanghai became a demilitarized zone. The Chinese saw this as a further humiliation, which was augmented by the Japanese declaration of a 'protectorate', a puppet state known as Manchukuo, in Manchuria. Japan now dominated a large area of China.

OPPOSITE ABOVE: **Crowds of civilians cheer as infantry of the Japanese First Division leave their barracks en route to Manchuria.**

OPPOSITE MIDDLE RIGHT: **Chinese soldiers man barricades, as one prepares to throw a hand grenade during the Shanghai War in February 1932.**

OPPOSITE BOTTOM RIGHT: **Chinese soldiers set up gun batteries in the ruined Chapel district of Shanghai during the Japanese attack in 1932.**

BELOW: **Japanese troops move into Jehol province in early 1933. Japan pushed into the province in order to extend its Manchurian colony to the Great Wall of China.**

ABOVE RIGHT: **A Chinese defence line straddles a frozen river bed along the Jehol Front as they try to stop the Japanese advance on the Great Wall.**

RIGHT: **The Chinese retreat through a snowy mountain pass as Japanese troops move into Jehol province.**

Outbreak of war

There was sporadic fighting during the next few years, but the conflict flared into all-out war in 1937 following another incident, this time at the Marco Polo Bridge outside Beijing. It developed into what was to become the largest Asian war of the twentieth century.

Following the 'Marco Polo Bridge Incident' near Beijing and successful Japanese attacks on two Chinese towns, the Chinese Nationalist Kuomintang army mobilized. They attacked Japanese marines in Shanghai on August 13, 1937 in an action which began one of the largest battles of the war. The Japanese launched an amphibious counter-attack ten days later, which was followed by fierce house-to-house fighting in the city. By the end of October the defeated and collapsing Chinese army was forced into a retreat, and by the end of November the Japanese controlled Shanghai. The fighting did not stop, however; it merely continued along the road to the Nationalist stronghold of Nanking.

Rape of Nanking

In Nanking, there was chaos – low morale among both soldiers and civilians, people attempting to flee, troops deserting – as the Japanese approached. By December 9, Japanese troops had surrounded the city, occupying the countryside around it, and were demanding immediate surrender. This was refused and they attacked the city, entering it on December 13. The Chinese army had retreated.

In the following six weeks, one of the greatest war crimes of the twentieth century took place. This was the Nanking Massacre, otherwise called the 'Rape of Nanking'. Rape was varied and almost commonplace, but so were random murders, executions – of both civilians and prisoners of war – and widespread looting. A third of the city was also destroyed by arson. Casualty figures cannot be exact in such circumstances, but physical evidence supports a figure of more than 200,000 deaths in this six-week period. Many more died in the area around Nanking before the occupation. There was widespread outcry. Many Westerners had been in the city before it fell, and though most had managed to get away, some remained and were witnesses to the horrors for the outside world. There were even journalists, both Western and Japanese, and a film was made at the time, attesting to the terrible events.

Scorched earth

Other cities fell shortly afterwards, and soon Japan controlled the six largest cities in China. There was often bombing of civilian targets – one example is Canton, where wave after wave of bombers inflicted enormous damage. When the Japanese finally took over the city in October 1938, they found that the retreating Chinese had destroyed any remaining industrial or military establishments. The Chinese were not alone in applying a scorched-earth policy, however; such action was to become something of the norm on both sides. For sheer destruction, however, the ultimate was probably the deliberate flooding of the Yellow River in June 1938, with which the Chinese hoped to slow the Japanese advance and protect the city of Wuhan. It did that, but only to a degree; it also caused a vast number of deaths, maybe almost a million.

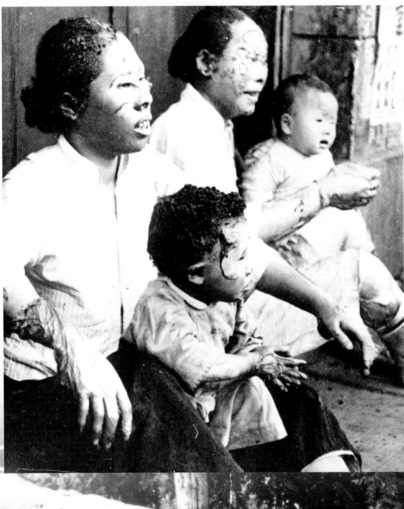

OPPOSITE BELOW: **Japanese soldiers 'mopping up' in the villages around Shanghai. One soldier knocks down the door with an axe, while the others wait to shoot any soldiers who try to escape.**

OPPOSITE ABOVE RIGHT: **Japanese soldiers attack Woosung near Shanghai.**

OPPOSITE LEFT: **Prince and Princess Chichibu of Japan on a goodwill tour of Europe at the outbreak of the Sino-Japanese war.**

ABOVE: **A soldier hurls an incendiary bomb at the enemy camped in a row of houses in Shanghai. The photographer was shot shortly after this picture was taken.**

BELOW: **Japanese infantry defend the town of Tungchow on the outskirts of Beijing in July 1937. The town's entire Japanese civilian population was massacred during the attack.**

LEFT: **Victims of incendiary bombing in Shanghai are photographed to attest to the horrors of the Sino-Japanese War. These mothers received terrible burns trying to protect their children; despite their brave efforts the children were also badly burnt.**

Resistance

China had a comparatively low industrial base, was mired in a civil war between the Nationalists and the Communists, and had little experience of modern warfare. However, the Japanese still met fierce resistance, which they failed to anticipate, and there was guerrilla fighting in many areas. They finally suffered a defeat at Taierzhuang, partly because they failed to consider the impact that local resistance could have – railway lines were sabotaged and communication links severed – and partly because they also underestimated the Chinese generals. The main Chinese objective since the fall of Shanghai had been to slow Japanese progress and resistance was a crucial part of this. 'Trading space for time', as it was known, was also intended to give the Nationalists time to retreat, moving Chinese industry as well, to a provisional capital, the more easily defended city of Chongqing.

The Japanese went on to capture the city of Wuhan in October 1938, and in the process almost eliminated the Chinese air and naval forces, though ground troops did survive. The war dragged on, now in effective stalemate, and the scale of horror rose as the Japanese began massive air attacks on almost every Chinese city. These caused huge loss of life, appalling injuries and a massive increase in the number of displaced people.

The Three Alls

In the meanwhile, guerrilla resistance continued; the countryside was becoming almost impossible for Japanese troops as the Chinese refused to give up despite heavy losses. The Japanese only really controlled the major cities and the lines of communication running between them. In yet another attempt to break the stalemate and force a conclusion to the war, the Japanese introduced the Three Alls policy – kill all, loot all, burn all. During the time this policy was in operation, it has been estimated that about ten million Chinese civilians were forced into labour companies. Most of the atrocities for which the Japanese in China are now notorious also happened at this time, in an attempt to break the deadlock. When it came to administering their Chinese 'empire', the Japanese installed more puppet governments, similar to that which had been introduced in Manchuria. However, they had little or no support because committing atrocities and 'winning hearts and minds' do not go together, and opposition continued. They did succeed, however, in raising collaborationist forces in the areas they controlled. These men, who were often forcibly 'recruited' en masse, maintained local security. The local population saw them as traitors to China.

War in the Pacific

The Chinese Nationalist government was also now receiving international aid, which the Japanese blamed for their refusal to surrender. The Japanese, on the other hand, now urgently needed a reliable source of supplies such as oil in order to continue the war, and this meant having freedom of movement in the South China Sea and the Pacific. On December 7 1941, the Japanese attacked Pearl Harbor and the war became part of the Second World War. This gave China new allies, and gave the struggle against the Japanese in the country a new international importance.

There were millions of deaths during the course of the Second Sino-Japanese War, as well as appalling hardship for the survivors. Many Western historians put the number of Chinese dead at about 20 million, most of whom were civilians, and the Japanese lost about 1.75 million in their futile attempt to rule China. Many Chinese died from starvation and many were displaced; their homes, livelihoods and, in many cases, their families destroyed. The scars of the conflict influence the relationship of the two countries to the present day.

OPPOSITE ABOVE RIGHT: **Japanese soldiers patrol the streets wearing their new bullet-proof armour.**

OPPOSITE LEFT: **A Chinese anti-tank unit gets into position ahead of a Japanese advance.**

OPPOSITE BELOW: **High in the mountains, Chinese soldiers set up resistance to the Japanese Army.**

ABOVE: **A Japanese soldier sets up a machine gun post to help maintain order in an occupied Chinese city.**

ABOVE RIGHT: **Japanese naval officers marching during the Sino-Japanese war. The Imperial Navy was jealous of the glory being won by the army in China and pushed for an invasion of the French and Dutch colonies in the South China Sea. This decision put Japan on the path to Pearl Harbor.**

RIGHT: **Japanese marines defend against stiff Chinese resistance.**

Spanish Civil War 1936–1939

The Second Republic

In 1930 the dictatorship of General Miguel Primo de Rivera collapsed, ushering in a brief and tumultuous period of democratic government in Spain. With Primo de Rivera in exile, the legitimacy of the Spanish King, Alfonso XIII, hung by a thread. He had strong links to the dictatorship and the local elections of April 1931 were widely regarded as a referendum on the future of the monarchy. When the republican left scored a decisive victory, Alfonso went into exile, and Spain became a republic for the second time.

Radical reform

Two months later, Spain held parliamentary elections, which were won by a coalition of leftwing parties. The new government quickly embarked upon a programme of radical reform; the Catholic Church was disestablished, the Jesuit order was dissolved, universal suffrage was introduced, the army was democratized and limited autonomy was granted to Catalonia. These radical changes alarmed the right and forced landowners, army officers, monarchists, big businesses and the Catholic Church to recover from the collapse of the dictatorship and to work together to defeat the left.

Reversing the reform

While the right was galvanizing itself, the left was being weakened by incumbency. Unable to hold together its broad support base, the government began fracturing and the right regained control through the ballot box in 1933. The new government devoted its time to reversing the changes made under the previous administration. However, this government was crippled by instability; workers went on strike, Catalonia declared its independence and miners revolted in Oviedo in the Asturias. With a weak, rightwing government in power it was the left's turn to coalesce with the help of the Communist International (Comintern). A Popular Front was established to paper over the cracks and secure electoral victory in 1936.

Military conspiracy

The democratic experiment had severely polarized the country and the new Popular Front government offered no solution to the crisis. Instead it had further antagonized the right by replacing the rightwing President Niceto Alcala-Zamora with the leftwing Manuel Azana. With Spain on the verge of collapse, a group of military leaders began plotting a coup to restore order, stop the march of Communism and halt separatism in the regions. Among the conspirators was a forty-three-year-old general named Francisco Franco who had been relocated to a remote command post in the Canary Islands to reduce his chances of subverting the Popular Front government.

Midnight Battle Near Gibraltar
CIVIL WAR RAGING IN SPAIN
Anti-Reds From Morocco Marching On Madrid | La Argentina Dies
BOMBING & SHELLFIRE IN MANY CITIES
British Warships and Troops Stand By:
Malaga "Burning": 200 Britons in Town
CABINET ARMS WORKERS

DAILY MAIL FEBRUARY 18, 1936

Spain in grip of red riots

Martial law was spreading throughout Spain last night following a day of Communist rioting arising out of the surprise Left-Wing victories in Sunday's general election. Here are the chief incidents of the past few hours:

*Martial law proclaimed in the provinces of Valencia, Alicante (where rioters released lepers), and Saragossa (where there is a general strike). 'State of Siege' in Huesca.

*Shooting in the streets of Madrid, where police joined Communist rioters, led to one person being killed and 14 injured.

*Gaols fired by prisoners in the cities of Cartagena, Saragossa, and Valencia, where mutineers held troops at bay with rifles last night.

*Government of Barcelona seized by 'rebel' City Council.

Disorders follow left-wing triumph at polls

Although the election returns are not yet complete – latest estimates give the Socialist Coalition 250 and Conservatives 178 out of a total of 473 seats – the Premier, Señor Valladares, indicated last night that a Left-Wing Government will be formed on Friday. There is considerable speculation as to the future of Señor Azana, the nominal leader of the Left-Wing coalition. In some quarters it is expected that when the new Government is installed Señor Largo Caballero, the Socialist Party chief, whose programme is frankly revolutionary, will take steps to assume supreme power.

OPPOSITE ABOVE: **Streetfighting during the Spanish Civil War. These Republican forces have barricaded themselves into a doorway as Nationalist forces enter their village.**

OPPOSITE BELOW: **Huge crowds cheer General Francisco Franco and General Emilio Mola, the leaders of the Nationalists, as they walk to the cathedral in Burgos, the seat of the Nationalist government during the war.**

ABOVE: **Volunteers for Franco's army walk through the streets of Pamplona in the Navarre region.**

OPPOSITE BELOW: **Republican Government forces prepare for an attack on the Balearic island of Majorca which was being held by the insurgent Nationalists during the Spanish Civil War.**

DAILY MAIL APRIL 15, 1931

Alfonso abdicates

King Alfonso of Spain signed a provisional decree of abdication at 5.30 yesterday afternoon, and left Madrid by car last night for Cartagena, south-eastern Spain, where he went on board a Spanish warship. This morning his Queen, a beloved English princess, and their family of two daughters and four sons, will also set out from their palace into exile. It is stated in Madrid that the King and the Royal Family propose to come to England.

For 36 hours, ever since the results became known of the overwhelming victory of the Republicans over the Royalists at the municipal elections, the King had been urged to abdicate but Alfonso, like the brave man he has always been, fought grimly for his throne until he was deserted by his friends and by the army. A Republic has been proclaimed throughout Spain and a Cabinet has been formed in Madrid of men who were recently in gaol for political offences.

I am informed that before leaving the Palace the King issued a manifesto to the Spanish nation. In this document, after explaining the reasons for his departure, he says that he does not believe that the Spanish nation is really Republican at heart and that he feels sure he will be the means of recalling once more the old dynasty which has reigned for so long over the destinies of the Spanish people. The King concludes by saying that he remains at the disposal of the Spanish people.

The streets of Madrid are full of shouting, demonstrating crowds. Some of them are waving the new purple, yellow and red republican flag, but many of them have the red Socialist flag, which is largely cheered. One such procession, composed of motor-cars decorated with scarlet flags, has just passed down the Prado, accompanied by about 2,000 men and women on foot. On the roof of the foremost car was a girl dressed in red waving a Communist flag. It was strange to see the police and Civil Guards, who up to late last night were engaged in charging such crowds, standing aside and stopping the traffic for the passage of these demonstrators.

The Civil War begins

On July 13, 1936, the conspirators were given a pretext to launch their coup when the Popular Front government became embroiled in the assassination of a rightwing politician named Calvo Sotelo. Within days the military had risen up in rebellion across Spain. However, the coup did not succeed in overthrowing the government as planned. Military uprisings in urban areas and the industrial heartlands were suppressed as workers rallied around the government. An uprising at the Montana Barracks in Madrid was brutally put down and it was to be almost three years before the capital fell to Franco's men. The failure of the coup sparked the very disorder the generals had sought to prevent and it set Spain on course for a long civil war between supporters of the government (Republicans) and supporters of the military insurrection (Nationalists).

LEFT: The bloody aftermath of the failed uprising at the Montana Barracks in Madrid. Franco did not have enough supporters in most of the major urban areas for his coup to succeed instantly. His men in the capital, outnumbered by government loyalists, were penned into the Montana Barracks and slaughtered.

ABOVE: Crowds cheer General Franco in the town of Burgos, Northern Spain.

BELOW: Militiamen loyal to the Republican government walk triumphantly down a Madrid street having secured control of the capital following the fall of the Montana Barracks, July 30, 1936.

DAILY MAIL   JULY 20, 1936

Midnight battle near Gibraltar

Despite a vigorous censorship and severance of telegraphic communication, special Daily Mail despatches report that anti-red insurgents who on Friday seized Spanish Morocco are in control of the Canary and Balearic Islands, have landed in large numbers at Algeciras and Cadiz, and are marching northward against Madrid. At midnight heavy fighting was in progress at La Linea, the Spanish frontier town on the outskirts of Gibraltar. Following artillery and machine-gun fire the streets were reported 'littered with dead.' Two British warships are standing by at Gibraltar to evacuate British subjects from Spanish territory if necessary.

Civil war was raging in Spain early this morning.

Spain changed her Cabinet three times yesterday, though for the moment, with Señor Jose Giral at the head, it remains Red. Here are other incidents of the revolt:

*Malaga, where there is a British colony of 200, reported 'in flames.'

*Telephone communication between London and Gibraltar and London and Portugal cut off. The services pass through Madrid.

*Rebels bombed by warplanes at Cadiz, Ceuta, Melilla, Tetuan – where children were killed – and other places. Barcelona reported 'either bombed or shelled.'

In an effort to check the insurrection, the Spanish Government has ordered all cities to organize 'combat squads' of citizens who are to be given arms.

Franco takes Toledo

After the uprising began, Franco flew from the Canary Islands to take command of the rebels in Spanish Morocco, where the bulk of Spain's army was based. With German and Italian assistance his troops were transported onto the mainland to bolster the rebels in cities where they were on the defensive. In the city of Toledo, supporters of the rebellion had fled with their families to the town's Alcazar fortress after the uprising failed. They fought off attacks from supporters of the Republic for more than two months until Franco's men took the city on September 27, 1936. The following month Nationalist forces relieved their besieged comrades in the city of Oviedo, which had been the location of the miners' uprising just two years earlier.

DAILY MAIL SEPTEMBER 28, 1936
Fall of Toledo

Toledo, the Spanish Red stronghold and key to Madrid, fell before the onslaught of General Franco's columns last evening and the heroic garrison of the Alcazar was relieved on the seventieth day of one of the most terrible sieges in history. This historic event which marks the beginning of the end in the Spanish civil war was officially announced by General Franco in a laconic communiqué issued from anti-Red headquarters at Burgos shortly before 2 o'clock this morning. It said:

'Toledo was captured by our troops at 9.30 this evening, and the besieged cadets in the Alcazar were liberated by General Varela (commander of the column which stormed Toledo) himself.'

Almost at the same moment came messages from Madrid admitting that Toledo had fallen.

Reds' last bid to destroy garrison fails

Shortly before they were relieved the defenders beat off a last desperate attempt by the Reds to storm the ruins, while their 400 wives and children sheltered in the dungeons from dynamite and petrol flame attacks. Throughout yesterday a great battle raged in the suburbs of the city, and when late last night it was reported that the anti-Reds had seized the main Toledo-Madrid road the fate of the city was sealed.

BELOW: To stop the advance of Franco's men on the capital, the Republicans destroyed key bridges around the city, including this one at Getafe to the south.

ABOVE: Nationalist forces search for Republican snipers in the ruins of Toledo.

LEFT: A survivor of the siege of the Alcazar in Toledo clasps a food parcel as she stumbles amid the wreckage of the ruined citadel.

DAILY MAIL   APRIL 29, 1937

Mystery surrounds the fate of Guernica, the ancient capital of the Basque country

Reports were received yesterday in news agency messages stating that it had been reduced to a blazing mass of ruins after one of the most appalling air raids in modern warfare. More than 800 civilians were said to have been killed in three and a half hours' bombing by German aeroplanes.

Early this morning messages from Marquina denied the reports that Guernica had been set on fire by air bombs. No anti-Red aeroplanes have bombed Guernica, it was declared, and if houses had been set on fire, it was the work of anarchists or Red extremists.

Relays of bombers

According to the earlier reports bombers, starting at 4.30 p.m. on Monday, came over in relays, seven at a time, accompanied by the same number of fighters. It was market day, and the town was crowded. From the first 'planes the crews, it was stated, leaned out, dropping hand grenades, while the frightened populace rushed to a few bomb shelters. Hundreds raced desperately for the fields, where they were systematically followed and machine-gunned from the air by swooping fighters. Then relays of bombers dropped high explosive bombs, more than 1,000, it is estimated, hitting the town. Incendiary bombs followed.

At 10 p.m., when the raids were said to have ceased, the whole town was ablaze, including architecturally precious churches. Fire fighters and salvage crews were helpless. In one blazing street, which nobody was able to enter, was a bomb shelter in which 50 women and children were reported to have been trapped and incinerated. Guernica was the ancient seat of the Diet of Viscaya, the oldest and original of the three Basque provinces.

Guernica

After failing to capture Madrid in March 1937, the Nationalists opened a new front in the north. It was during this campaign, on the evening of April 26, that a volunteer legion of Nazi Germany's Luftwaffe razed the Basque city of Guernica to the ground. The destruction revealed the devastating potential of modern aerial warfare and instilled terror across Europe. Britain's inability to defend against a Guernica-style attack became a crucial factor in Neville Chamberlain's appeasement of Hitler in the late 1930s. The ruined city fell to the Nationalists within days of the air raid, paving the way for the capture of Bilbao less than two months later. By the end of the year, the Nationalists had conquered the whole of northern Spain.

International intervention

The Popular Front government in France initially sent support to the Spanish Republicans, but were quickly discouraged in this venture by the British who called for a Non-Intervention Agreement to prevent the conflict from spreading. The Great Powers of Europe all signed this Agreement, but only Britain and France adhered to it. Nazi Germany and Fascist Italy began providing financial and military aid to Franco from the outset of the war and were undeterred by the Non-Intervention Agreement. In addition to the obvious ideological reasons for supporting the Nationalists and the military training the war offered their troops, Hitler and Mussolini were enticed by substantial mining concessions as well as military bases in Spain in the event of a war with France.

Communist Russia did not initially intervene in the Civil War. However, by the end of 1936, Stalin started sending men and materiel to shore up the Republic. Soviet assistance often proved counterproductive because it was unpalatable to the moderate, democratic left and served to split the Republican movement. Soviet aid did not come cheap and the entire Spanish gold reserve, estimated at $520 million, was shipped to Moscow at the end of the war.

The Republic was also helped by the 'International Brigades', individuals from around the world who volunteered to fight against the Nationalists. Although the International Brigades were organized by the Communist International, most were motivated by an anti-fascism rather than an active support of Communism. These international recruits played a crucial role in the defence of Madrid.

OPPOSITE TOP AND OPPOSITE MIDDLE: **The ruins of the Spanish city of Guernica after it was attacked by Germany's Condor Legion. The Spanish Civil War offered pilots in Germany's Luftwaffe an opportunity to train. The exact death toll is not known because the Nationalist forces did not investigate when they took control of the city. Estimation is difficult because the raid took place on market day. Normally this would have caused a large influx to the town, but many may have stayed away on account of the nearby fighting.**

OPPOSITE BELOW AND LEFT: **Images of the ruined city struck horror around the world and played a key role in Britain's decision to appease Nazi Germany. The destruction of the city was later immortalized in the painting 'Guernica' by Pablo Picasso.**

ABOVE LEFT: *Deutschland*, **a German pocket battleship helping the Nationalists, was attacked off the Spanish coast by two Republican bombers on May 29, 1937.**

ABOVE: **Basque children arrive as refugees in Southampton, England in May 1937. The British government intially opposed taking in the children for fear that it would abrogate the Non-Intervention Agreement. However, the Archbishop of Canterbury took up their cause and the government was soon forced to allow the children into the country. They were cared for by individuals and private organizations across Britain and most were repatriated at the end of the war.**

The Nationalists take Barcelona

In early 1938 Aragon became the main theatre of the war. The Republicans launched an attack at Teruel to relieve pressure on Madrid during the winter of 1937-8. After scoring initial successes, the Nationalists counterattacked with German aerial assistance and retook Teruel in February 1938. The Republicans tried to maintain the offensive in the Ebro Valley between July and November, but the Nationalists had the upper hand and used the battle as a launching pad for their attack on Barcelona. The city had been a staunch Republican stronghold since the right had opposed any form of Catalan autonomy. So when Barcelona fell to the Nationalists in January 1939, it became clear that the war was almost over.

Madrid falls

The Nationalists attempted to take Madrid on numerous occasions during the war. Franco's forces had made a triumphant entrance into the city limits in November 1936, but the capital's defences held out. They tried once again in vain with Italian volunteers in March 1937 during the Battle of Guadalajara, a town just to the northeast of the capital. The Nationalists then put their resources into conquering the rest of Spain and Madrid was largely spared until the end of the war. By the time the city fell, together with Valencia, on March 28, 1939, the Republican government had already fled into exile and Britain and France had recognized Franco's regime. With the capital and much of the country under his command, Franco declared ultimate victory on April 1, 1939.

Franco went on to rule Spain until his death in 1975. After that time, Juan Carlos, the grandson of King Alfonso XIII, assumed control. He presided over a steady return to parliamentary democracy, which has lasted to this day.

Battle for Madrid

SPAIN CALLS UP ALL MEN UNDER 30

Government Claim Revolt Has Been Quelled

WHILE MOB VIOLENCE AND TERROR CONTINUED THROUGHOUT SPAIN LAST NIGHT, A SPECIAL CORRESPONDENT OF "THE DAILY MAIL" WAS TOU...

DAILY MAIL FEBRUARY 27, 1939

Recognition for Franco today
Volunteers to leave Spain

Today's moves in Britain, France and Spain may mark the virtual end of two and a half years of civil war. Those moves are:

1.- President Azana, who last night left Paris, arrives at Collonges-sous-Saleve, near Geneva, to-day. He will live in retirement. This means the legal end of the present Republican regime.

2.- The Prime Minister, in Parliament this afternoon, will announce Britain's recognition of Franco. Sir Robert Hodgson will become Charge d'Affaires at Burgos. In his announcement Mr. Chamberlain will state that General Franco has informed the British and French Governments that he does not intend to pursue a policy of reprisals. This is assuming that hostilities are not continued much longer.

There were further indications in London last night that the Republican leaders will shortly scatter and the war will be terminated by surrender.

General Franco has also told the British Government that he will maintain the integrity of Spain. He will require, as soon as the war is over, the withdrawal of all foreign troops.

There are rumours in well-informed quarters in London that before very long General Franco will restore the Spanish Monarchy with limited prerogatives.King Alfonso's son, Prince Juan, is likely to be invited to ascend the throne.

OPPOSITE ABOVE: **Italian officers captured during the Battle of Guadalajara are pictured under guard in a Madrid cell.**

OPPOSITE BELOW: **Nationalist forces search for survivors amongst the rubble of a monastery having just pushed the Republicans out of Teruel in February 1938.**

ABOVE: **A soldier bids farewell to his wife and child before leaving to fight on the Aragon front during the Spanish Civil War.**

TOP: **Locals survey the damage done to Barcelona following the latest Nationalist bombing raid.**

BELOW: **Expecting heavy fighting, Republican forces construct stone barricades in the streets of Barcelona.**

RIGHT: **General Francisco Franco watches Spanish tanks rumble past during the 12th anniversary parade to commemorate the end of the Spanish Civil War.**

Second World War 1939-1945

The rise of Hitler

The end of the First World War had not really brought about any improvement in the level of tension between nations; it had simply changed the nature of the grievances and added some new ones. After the war, hopes for future peace in the world had been enshrined in the League of Nations, created to provide for a policy of 'Collective Security', but there were some doubts about how effective it would be, doubts which were to be fully vindicated.

Adolf Hitler had first come to public attention in 1923 when he made an unconstitutional attempt to seize power in Bavaria, known as the 'Munich Putsch'. It failed and he was sent to prison for nine months as a consequence. While imprisoned, he used the time to write *Mein Kampf* (My Struggle), which became his political programme. He claimed that Germany had not really been defeated as such in 1918, and that both the apparent defeat and the post-war settlement had been a betrayal, for which he blamed the Jews. One of the consequences of the Munich Putsch was that Hitler was now determined to seek power by legitimate means, as far as that was possible. Following his release in 1924, he reorganized his political party, creating what was in effect a private army. This paramilitary organization was known as the SA (Sturmabteilung), and by 1927 there were over 30,000 people in it. They were the 'Brownshirts', who intimidated their opponents and instigated violent conflicts with both Communists and Jews. In the meanwhile, the economic situation went from bad to worse.

ABOVE: **American soldiers approach the Normandy beaches on D-Day, June 6, 1944.**

RIGHT ABOVE: **Nazi supporters line the streets of Weimar during Hitler's visit to the town in July 1936.**

RIGHT: **Crowds fawn upon Hitler as he attends Labour Day celebrations in Berlin's Lustgarten in May 1934.**

OPPOSITE LEFT: **Upon becoming Chancellor, Hitler set about consolidating his power. He had his closest rivals murdered on the 'Night of the Long Knives' in July 1934.**

OPPOSITE RIGHT ABOVE: **Hitler poses for a photograph with a Polish delegation led by Poland's Foreign Minister, Colonel Joseph Beck. One of Hitler's first foreign policy achievements as Chancellor was to conclude a Non-Aggression Pact with neighbouring Poland.**

OPPOSITE BELOW LEFT: **German soldiers marching at a military parade in Berlin in 1935.**

OPPOSITE BELOW MIDDLE: **Hitler addresses a crowd of Hitler Youth at the annual Nazi Party Congress in Nuremberg.**

OPPOSITE BELOW RIGHT: **German troops in Berlin swear an oath of allegiance to Adolf Hitler in 1934.**

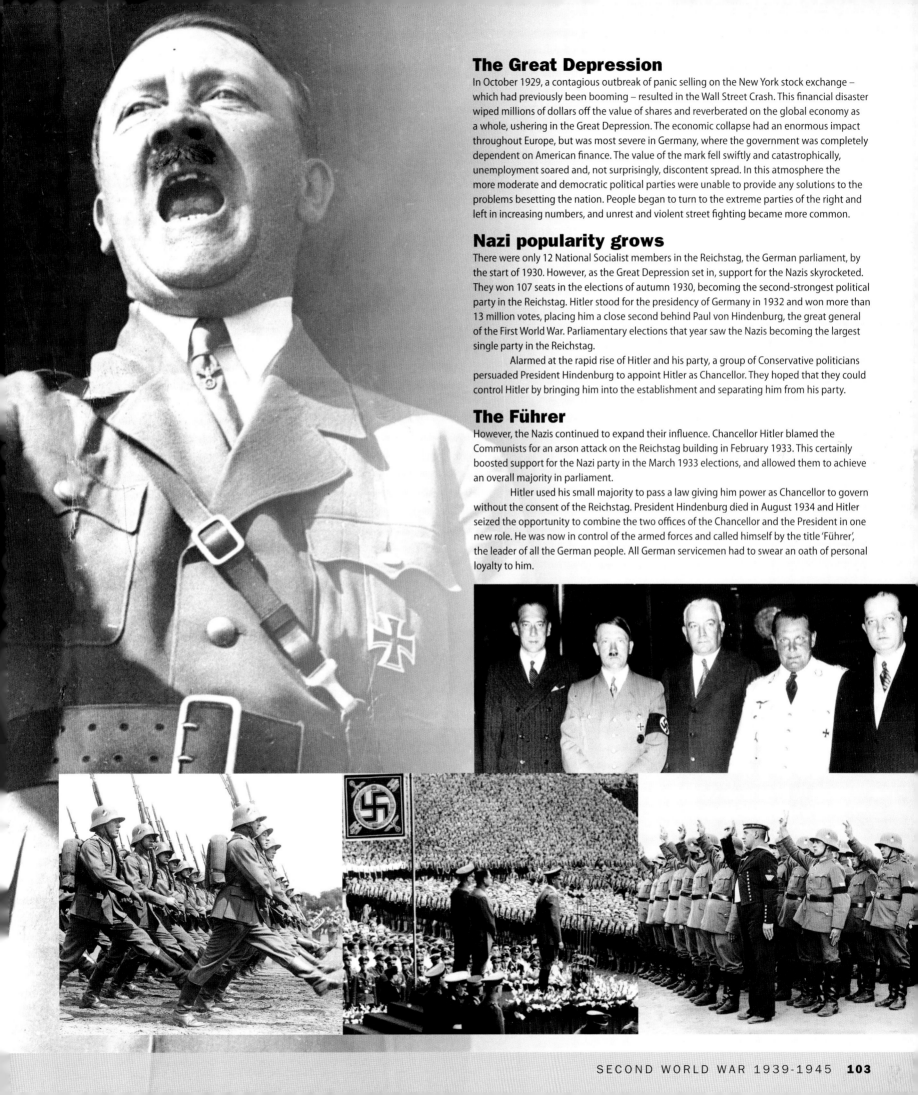

The Great Depression

In October 1929, a contagious outbreak of panic selling on the New York stock exchange – which had previously been booming – resulted in the Wall Street Crash. This financial disaster wiped millions of dollars off the value of shares and reverberated on the global economy as a whole, ushering in the Great Depression. The economic collapse had an enormous impact throughout Europe, but was most severe in Germany, where the government was completely dependent on American finance. The value of the mark fell swiftly and catastrophically, unemployment soared and, not surprisingly, discontent spread. In this atmosphere the more moderate and democratic political parties were unable to provide any solutions to the problems besetting the nation. People began to turn to the extreme parties of the right and left in increasing numbers, and unrest and violent street fighting became more common.

Nazi popularity grows

There were only 12 National Socialist members in the Reichstag, the German parliament, by the start of 1930. However, as the Great Depression set in, support for the Nazis skyrocketed. They won 107 seats in the elections of autumn 1930, becoming the second-strongest political party in the Reichstag. Hitler stood for the presidency of Germany in 1932 and won more than 13 million votes, placing him a close second behind Paul von Hindenburg, the great general of the First World War. Parliamentary elections that year saw the Nazis becoming the largest single party in the Reichstag.

Alarmed at the rapid rise of Hitler and his party, a group of Conservative politicians persuaded President Hindenburg to appoint Hitler as Chancellor. They hoped that they could control Hitler by bringing him into the establishment and separating him from his party.

The Führer

However, the Nazis continued to expand their influence. Chancellor Hitler blamed the Communists for an arson attack on the Reichstag building in February 1933. This certainly boosted support for the Nazi party in the March 1933 elections, and allowed them to achieve an overall majority in parliament.

Hitler used his small majority to pass a law giving him power as Chancellor to govern without the consent of the Reichstag. President Hindenburg died in August 1934 and Hitler seized the opportunity to combine the two offices of the Chancellor and the President in one new role. He was now in control of the armed forces and called himself by the title 'Führer', the leader of all the German people. All German servicemen had to swear an oath of personal loyalty to him.

Appeasement

While he consolidated his power inside Germany, Hitler moved cautiously in his foreign policy. He signed a non-aggression pact with Poland and agreed to negotiate with European powers over disarmament. However, from 1934 he secretly began rearming Germany so that it would become strong enough to achieve his main foreign policy goal: the reversal of the Treaty of Versailles.

As the 1930s progressed, the German military grew stronger and the international situation became ever more favourable. The failure of the League of Nations to tackle both Japanese aggression in Manchuria in 1931 and Italian aggression in Abyssinia in 1935 made it obvious that the organization would not seriously challenge Hitler's attempts to reverse the Treaty of Versailles. The ineffectiveness of the League revealed that the Great Powers were distracted and indifferent. The United States, Britain and France were still grappling with the Great Depression and Stalin was busy purging and collectivizing in the Soviet Union.

Reoccupying the Rhine

In 1936, Hitler decided to test the waters and send troops into the Rhineland, which had been established as a demilitarized zone under the terms of the treaty. His officers had been instructed to withdraw should they encounter any resistance. However, there was no response from the Great Powers, and an emboldened Hitler began building a line of fortifications along the French and Belgian borders.

Austria was the next country to attract his attention. The Treaty of Versailles had decreed that Austria and Germany should never be united. Austria was, however, in chaos – much of it caused by Austrian Nazis – and Hitler used this as a pretext for sending the German army into the country. On March 13, 1938, his troops marched into Vienna and Austria was integrated into the Reich. Hitler, himself an Austrian, returned in triumph to the capital where he had lived in poverty before the First World War.

Next on Hitler's agenda was Czechoslovakia, a democratic country that had been created by the Versailles Treaty. Some three million Germans lived in Czechoslovakia, mainly in a region along the German border called the Sudetenland. Hitler insisted that this region should be absorbed into the Reich.

ABOVE RIGHT: **Hitler follows his army into Linz, Austria to oversee the 'Anschluss', the Union of Austria and Germany, in March 1938.**

ABOVE RIGHT INSERT: **Neville Chamberlain returns home waving a 'piece of paper' signed by Hitler promising a peaceful resolution to European disputes in future. Chamberlain declared that he had returned bringing 'peace with honour, peace in our time.'**

ABOVE: **American President Franklin Delano Roosevelt pictured in his home in Hyde Park, New York in 1938. The United States stayed out of European disputes while it tried to rebuild its battered economy in the 1930s.**

BELOW: **Hitler's position was further strengthened in May 1939 when he signed an alliance, 'The Pact of Steel' with Mussolini.**

The Munich Agreement

These demands caused concern in London, but Britain was in no position to challenge Germany in Central Europe. The British military was greatly overstretched across the vast Empire and the public had no appetite for a new European conflict. Instead, the British Prime Minister, Neville Chamberlain went to Germany to negotiate with Hitler. At their meeting in Munich on September 29, 1938, Hitler and Chamberlain agreed that the Sudetenland should join Germany, but that this would be Hitler's last territorial demand in Europe. Chamberlain returned, claiming he had secured 'peace for our time', but his critics labelled this as 'appeasement'.

In March 1939, under the pretext of unrest in Slovakia, Germany occupied the rest of Czechoslovakia. The Munich Agreement was in tatters and the British public were outraged. Hitherto, many people had believed that Hitler's demands had been reasonable, but overt aggression in Czechoslovakia was a step too far, and the public called for firm action. In response, the British government issued guarantees to protect Poland, Romania and Greece against German aggression.

The Nazi Soviet pact

The British government began preparing for a war during 1939 by speeding up programmes of rearmament and civil defence. However, the government's inherent anti-Communism meant that it was slow to develop ties with the Soviet Union, which was vital if Germany was to be threatened with a two-front war. Given the violent ideological differences between the Soviet Union and the Nazis, the British believed that Stalin would inevitably support a war against Hitler and did very little to strengthen relations. The announcement on August 23 that Germany and the Soviet Union had signed a non-aggression pact came as a complete surprise to London. The pact was expedient; Hitler avoided a two-front war and Stalin avoided a war he was not yet ready to fight. A secret clause of the pact also promised Stalin a free hand in the Baltic states and in eastern Poland. On September 1, 1939, with his Eastern Front secure, Hitler risked war in the West by invading Poland.

ABOVE: **Hitler and Chamberlain meet at Bad Godesberg in Germany on September 23, 1938, where Hitler detailed his demands for the Sudetenland. Chamberlain spent the week convincing the Czechoslovak government to agree the terms before signing the Agreement with Hitler in Munich a week later.**

ABOVE RIGHT: **Hitler congratulates his Foreign Minister, Joachim von Ribbentrop, upon his return from signing the Nazi-Soviet Pact in Moscow.**

BELOW: **Hitler salutes as he walks through a sea of flowers in the Sudetenland, October 3, 1938.**

TOP RIGHT: **Joseph Stalin, leader of the Soviet Union, pictured at a conference in January 1938. In the late 1930s, Stalin was preoccupied with industrial development, agricultural collectivization and purging Russian society of 'saboteurs'.**

DAILY MAIL   APRIL 1, 1939

British pledge to Poland is without reserve

The pledge: ... In the event of any action which clearly threatened Polish independence, and which the Polish Government accordingly considered it vital to resist with their national forces, His Majesty's Government would feel themselves bound at once to lend the Polish Government all support in their power. - The Premier in the House yesterday.

Britain has offered Poland a mutual anti-aggression pact to which other Powers will be invited to subscribe. It is hoped that Col. Beck, Polish Foreign Minister, will sign it when he comes to London next week. The pledge given by the Prime Minister in the House of Commons yesterday to support Poland if she is attacked was purely to cover an interim period following rumours - which have not been confirmed - of German troop movements.

Apparently the Cabinet thought that the situation in Eastern Europe was sufficiently urgent to justify a unilateral declaration by the British Government. Ministers were also becoming acutely aware of the necessity to give the country some idea of their intentions.

The pledge given by the Prime Minister goes far beyond any commitment entered into by Britain since the end of the Great War. It is meant to form the basis of a strong anti-aggression front, by which it is hoped to preserve peace.

The Prime Minister's pledge to Poland is without reservation. Contrary to assertions made in London yesterday, there are no British conditions regarding Danzig or the Polish Corridor.

German invasion of Poland

In the early hours of September 1, 1939, German troops crossed the border into Polish territory triggering the largest war the world has ever seen. The Polish army, consisting mainly of cavalry divisions, was no match for the modern, mechanized German army. The Luftwaffe quickly won air superiority over the smaller Polish air force and began pummelling Polish cities. As Poland met its fate, frantic debates ensued in London and Paris over how to respond. By evening, the decision was made to issue an ultimatum demanding that Hitler withdraw promptly from Poland or face war.

The British and French Ambassadors handed the text of their ultimatums to the German foreign minister, Ribbentrop, who agreed to pass them on to Hitler. The British and French ultimatums expired at 11 a.m. and 5 p.m. on Sunday September 3 respectively. Neither country heard back from Hitler and consequently a state of war ensued.

BELOW: **Hitler addresses the Reichstag in the Kroll Opera House on the day of the invasion of Poland. In the speech he blamed Poland for starting the war by firing upon German territory that morning. He** warned that 'whoever departs from the rules of humane warfare can only expect that we shall do the same'.

ABOVE: **Poles march through Warsaw on their way to dig trenches for the defence of the city.**

ABOVE RIGHT: **Polish refugees stream out of Warsaw to escape the relentless bombardment.**

DAILY MAIL SEPTEMBER 4, 1939

War 11 A.M., September 3, 1939

Great Britain and France are at war with Germany. We now fight against the blackest tyranny that has ever held men in bondage. We fight to defend, and to restore, freedom and justice on earth.

Let us face the truth. This was inevitable whether it began with Austria, Sudetenland, Bohemia, or Danzig. If it had not come over Danzig it would have come later upon some other issue. It became inevitable from the day Hitler seized power in Germany and began his criminal career by enslaving his own people. For his one aim since then has been gradually to enslave all others by the methods of brute force.

Once more Britain, her Empire and her friends are engaged in a conflict to uphold Right against Might.

If the democracies had flinched now, they would have been compelled to abdicate for ever their title to be called the champions of liberty. The fate of these small nations who have already lost their rights would have been theirs in turn.

This was the dominant thought in the inspiring message broadcast by the King to his people last night. We go to war because we must. In His Majesty's words: 'For the sake of all that we ourselves hold dear, and of the world's order and peace, it is unthinkable that we should refuse to meet the challenge.'

Stalin invades Poland

The Polish commander, Marshal Smigly-Rydz, hoped in vain that Polish defences could hold out until Britain and France attacked in the west. However, his men were sitting ducks for Germany's 'Stuka' dive-bombers, and Polish cavalrymen were gunned down with ease as they futilely tried to take on German tank units.

On September 17, Stalin moved his troops into eastern Poland to fulfil the secret clause of the Nazi-Soviet Pact. He disguised his land grab as a mission to liberate Ukrainians and White Russians from Polish domination. The Red Army encountered little resistance from the Poles who were completely tied up on the Western Front. On September 28, Ribbentrop met with his Soviet counterpart Vyacheslav Molotov to sign the German-Soviet Boundary and Friendship Treaty, which officially carved the spoils of Poland between them. There was some resentment among Germans that the Soviets were to be handed territory that had been won by the Wehrmacht, especially as Stalin waited more than two weeks before declaring war.

The fall of Warsaw

The Polish capital, Warsaw, held out for several weeks against the Wehrmacht, which feared that street fighting would be too costly. Instead, the German army besieged the city and then bombed it into submission. The devastating attacks resulted in thousands of civilian deaths and the destruction of the town. The troops defending the town surrendered on September 27 in order to relieve the suffering of the town's civilian population, but the German occupation that followed was to make their lives much worse. Politicians, academics, soldiers and ordinary civilians were massacred as the Nazis immediately set about destroying any potential opposition. The Germans began to ethnically cleanse Poland by expelling the 'subhuman' Poles from their homes and sending German families to replace them, unless they were deemed sufficiently Aryan and agreed to be 'Germanized'.

Polish Jews were singled out for the harshest treatment; they were subjected to barbaric attacks and forced to move to ghettos, cut off from the outside world. However, this was only to be a temporary arrangement, and Poland's Jewish population was to suffer even worse when the Nazis decided upon their 'Final Solution'.

ABOVE LEFT: **Polish POWs line up for food in German prison camps.**

ABOVE RIGHT: **Hitler observes the destruction of Warsaw from a hill overlooking the city.**

LEFT: **German troops train in preparation for air raids after the Allied declaration of war.**

BELOW: **Polish troops wait for the Germans to arrive in Warsaw after the city's capitulation.**

Britain prepares for war

For the first few months, there seemed to be little change. In Britain, rationing began. A night-time blackout was introduced and children were evacuated from cities to the country – both measures designed to protect the country from German air raids, which were not to happen for another nine months. There were, however, some raids on shipping by German submarines. A large French army and a much smaller British Expeditionary force maintained defensive positions in Northern France, preparing for the possibility of invasion. However, as the months passed, it seemed increasingly unlikely that Hitler would strike in western Europe, and talk of a 'phoney war' spread. Further to the east, though, the situation was different. During the period of the phoney war in the west, bitter fighting continued in Poland, Lithuania, Latvia and Estonia.

ABOVE: Troops marching into Piccadilly Circus, London, in 1939. Little funds had been made available for the military during the 1920s and 1930s and rearmament and civil defence programmes had to be rapidly stepped up after the Sudetenland crisis in 1938.

LEFT: Shop signs supporting the government's declaration of war against the Nazi regime became commonplace.

BELOW: A group of British children wave goodbye to their families as they wait to board a train.

BOTTOM: The statue of Eros at Picadilly Circus, London, is boarded up to protect it from the impending air raids.

DAILY MAIL SEPTEMBER 2, 1939

"The children have all behaved marvellously"

The greatest organised movement of a human population in the world's history started yesterday. As if by some quiet smooth-working machine, nearly 1,000,000 children, mothers, blind and maimed people were taken from danger to safety. In three days - perhaps less - 3,000,000 will have made the journey across the invisible frontier. Thousands of households all over Britain yesterday welcomed small strangers who were to be for a time members of the family.

Most homes in the evacuated areas were adapting themselves bravely to a sadder change which had robbed them of their children. London has lost much of its laughter. Nearly half of the 3,000,000 are being evacuated from the Greater London area. The rest are from the naval and shipping areas and the industrial districts of the Midlands, North, and Scotland.

Everywhere the task of moving this enormous number of children was carried out with great ease, owing to the thorough preparation and the co-operation of officials, parents, and children. And officials everywhere said 'the children behaved simply marvellously.'

War in Scandinavia

At the end of 1939 the Red Army invaded neutral Finland because the Finnish government had refused to accept Stalin's territorial demands. Helsinki was badly damaged by Soviet bombing raids, but the winter snow came to the aid of the Finns. Finnish soldiers used guerrilla tactics to slow and reverse the Soviet advance during December and January. The Soviets struck back with a major offensive in February, forcing the Finnish government to accept a punitive peace agreement.

On April 9, 1940, Hitler launched simultaneous attacks against major ports in Denmark and Norway. There were some contingents from Britain and its Allies already in Norway, and these were rapidly deployed in defence. But the German command of the air – and a general lack of reinforcements, despite strong naval support – meant that the defenders were quickly forced to withdraw. There was one possible bright spot, though: the Allies had managed to inflict significant losses on the German fleet in the Norwegian campaign.

TOP: **Iron railings were removed** from many public places such as parks, gardens and squares in order to be resmelted for use in munitions. Private owners were encouraged to do the same.

ABOVE: **Signposts and street** names were removed across Britain in case they assisted invading German troops.

RIGHT: **Children are taught how** to use gas masks. The British government feared the Germans would mount a gas attack and implored people to 'always carry your gas mask'. In the event the Germans never used of poison gas during their raids on Britain.

BELOW RIGHT: **British Boy Scouts** collect waste paper as the country embarked on a recycling drive.

BELOW: **Sandbags being filled** in Hampstead. They were used to protect buildings across the country.

The fall of France

Just before dawn on May 10, the German assault on Western Europe finally began. In a swift and comprehensive move, soon to be widely known as blitzkrieg, German paratroopers and bombers successfully struck at positions in Holland, Belgium and Luxembourg, facilitating rapid infantry assaults deep into these countries. In response, the Allies committed a large part of their forces to Belgium.

The Germans advanced at speed through the Low Countries, aiming to cut the Allied forces in two and push many of their troops towards the coast. At the same time armoured Panzer divisions broke through the French lines at Sedan. They stormed across northern France, heading towards the Channel coast within a matter of days. There was comparative chaos in the Allied forces; the speed and scope of the assault had stunned everyone. Their troops in the north, now successfully caught in the German pincer movement, began to retreat towards the Channel ports, notably to a perimeter around Dunkirk. A huge evacuation from France was authorized on May 26. This evacuation would be the first test for Winston Churchill, who had replaced Neville Chamberlain as Britain's Prime Minister sixteen days earlier; Chamberlain had finally resigned following severe criticism over the government's response to the German advances in Norway and Denmark.

TOP: French soldiers march towards the front line. Germany unexpectedly invaded France through the dense forest of the Ardennes region of Belgium, and in doing so, circumvented France's heavily defended 'Maginot Line' fortifications along the German border.

ABOVE: French troops take aim at German positions from the first-floor windows of a ruined house in a village near the Belgian border. The French military censor forbade the publication of the name of the village.

LEFT: More troops rush up a rickety stairway to man the first-floor windows, while their commanding officer issues orders from a niche in the wall in the right of the picture.

BELOW: With fierce fighting occurring on the other side of the building, French troops run from house to house to take up more positions in a desperate attempt to stem the German advance until reinforcements arrived.

Dunkirk

In the event, the evacuation, codenamed Operation Dynamo, was an enormous success. It had been thought that some 45,000 Allied troops could be rescued from Dunkirk – but 338,226 men were rescued from the beaches between May 26 and June 4, in often appalling conditions. There were many naval ships, but the evacuation was marked by the use of hundreds of small ships – whatever vessels were available on the south coast of Britain. The weather, by and large, was favourable and the RAF were also able to help, but the evacuation beaches were under almost constant attack. Dynamo was a success in terms of the sheer number of lives saved, but thousands of vehicles, weapons and tons of supplies were left behind.

The Vichy government

Hitler had now succeeded in gaining control of the Channel coast, and the rest of France was soon to fall. The German army entered Paris some ten days later, on June 14 – just a month after the initial attacks on the country. Italy entered the war in support of Hitler, and by June 22, with all of northern France occupied by German troops and columns advancing southwards towards the border with Spain, the French Premier, Marshal Pétain, agreed to an armistice with Hitler. Under its conditions, France had to disarm and was to be divided into two basic sections. The northern zone and the northern and western coasts were under direct German control, but the southern part of the country would be governed by a collaborationist government led by Pétain and based at the spa town of Vichy. By the end of June the British-owned Channel Islands, so close to France, had also fallen to Germany.

TOP RIGHT: French tanks on manoeuvres in January 1940. This period was known as the 'Phoney War' because both sides had declared a state of war existed, but neither side had launched an attack.

MIDDLE RIGHT: French soldiers return from manning border posts during the 'Phoney War' period.

RIGHT: Reservists dig air-raid shelters in Paris in September 1939.

ABOVE: Paris experiences its first air raid, September 1939. There was relatively little aerial bombardment of the city in comparison with other European capitals.

BELOW: Columns of Allied soldiers await evacuation from the beach at Dunkirk.

The Battle of Britain

Most of Western Europe was now under Hitler's control, but Britain remained a serious obstacle to his ambitions. He set his sights on invading the country, and developed a plan called Operation Sea Lion. In order for this to be successful, however, the Germans had to effectively control the Channel and subdue Britain's south coast. As a result attacks were initiated, both on the sea and from the air. Shipping convoys were the first victims, and then, by August 1940, attacks began on the vital airfields of southern England. This was the start of the Battle of Britain.

The RAF was heavily outnumbered by the German Luftwaffe. Initially, there were heavy losses, but the RAF had some advantages, notably ground radar, and began to regain control of the skies over Britain in late August. The Germans, who had been incurring increasing losses themselves, changed their strategy – moving from fighter attacks on airfields to bomber raids on the factories and docks of London, marking the beginning of the Blitz. One unintentional result of this was that it allowed time for repairs to the airfields, which had been almost destroyed, and there was some opportunity for the RAF to regroup.

The Luftwaffe began to lose many more aircraft – and pilots – than the RAF, and it was becoming obvious to the Germans that their estimates of British losses were inaccurate, not to say wildly over-optimistic. They had underestimated Fighter Command in every way, and the invasion of Britain was called off in September.

OPPOSITE: An aerial view of the Luftwaffe flying over Britain.

OPPOSITE ABOVE RIGHT: Squadron Leader Douglas Bader had a distinguished career as an RAF pilot, despite having lost both of his legs in a crash in 1931.

OPPOSITE MIDDLE RIGHT: A German plane plummets to the ground over Sussex in August 1940.

OPPOSITE BELOW RIGHT: Britain's new Prime Minister, Winston Churchill, visits Ramsgate, one of the most heavily affected areas of Britain during the Battle of Britain in 1940.

ABOVE LEFT: Much of the Battle of Britain was confined to the southeast of England. However, German fighters menaced the skies all over the country. This reconnaissance plane was brought down in Scotland.

MIDDLE LEFT: Vapour trails mark the scene of a dogfight between the RAF and the Luftwaffe. Curious civilians often came onto the streets to watch and cheer on the RAF.

BELOW LEFT: Bren gunners kept a watchful eye on the skies over Britain.

BELOW: A squadron of Hurricane fighters fly in close formation. Along with the Spitfire this aircraft was the best defence Britain had against the Luftwaffe.

BELOW RIGHT: Members of the Women's Auxiliary Air Force (WAAF) at a lookout post.

DAILY MAIL JUNE 19, 1940
The Battle of Britain

The Prime Minister gave the House of Commons last night 'some indication of the solid, practical grounds upon which we are basing our invincible resolve to continue the war.'

The professional advisers of the three Services, he said, unitedly advised that we should do it and that there were good and reasonable hopes of final victory.

In this island there were now over 1,250,000 men under arms, backed by 500,000 Local Defence Volunteers. We might expect very large additions to our weapons in the near future. And, 'after all we have a Navy, which some people seem to forget.' Our fighter air strength is stronger at present in relation to Germany's than it had ever been.

'The Battle of Britain' said Mr. Churchill, 'is about to begin. On this battle depends the survival of Christian civilisation. I look forward confidently to the exploits of our fighter pilots, who will have the glory of saving their native land and our island home from the most deadly of all attacks.

'There remains the danger of the bombing attacks, which will certainly be made very soon upon us by the bomber forces of the enemy. It is quite true that these forces are superior in number to ours, but we have a very large bombing force also, which we shall use to strike at the military targets in Germany without intermission.

'What General Weygand called the Battle of France is over. The Battle of Britain is about to begin. On this battle depends the survival of Christian civilisation. Upon it depends our own British life and the long continuity of our institutions and our Empire. The whole fury and might of the enemy must very soon be turned upon us. Hitler knows he will have to break us in this island or lose the war. If we can stand up to him all Europe may be freed and the life of the world may move forward into broad, sunlit uplands. But if we fail, the whole world, including the United States and all that we have known and cared for, will sink into the abyss of a new dark age made more sinister and perhaps more prolonged by the lights of a perverted science.

'Let us therefore brace ourselves to our duty and so bear ourselves that if the British Commonwealth and Empire last for a thousand years, men will still say, 'This was their finest hour'.'

Blitz on Britain's cities

Even though the invasion of Britain was called off, Germany continued to bomb Britain's cities in the hope of breaking civilian morale. The Blitz began in September 1940 with attacks on London. Civilian targets were struck across the city from the docklands in the east to Buckingham Palace in the west. Londoners were especially vulnerable because few people had space for air-raid shelters. Consequently many people crammed into underground Tube stations. These undoubtedly saved many lives, but were not without risk. On October 14, 1940, sixty-four people were killed at Balham Tube station when a bomb hit a water main, flooding the station.

Britain had been prepared for such an aerial bombardment since the beginning of the war, and many targets had been anticipated. The country had made provision for air raids: blackout conditions were imposed at night, air-raid shelters had been built, and there had even been a mass issue of gas masks, on the assumption that Hitler might make use of chemical weapons. Although poison gas was never used in the Blitz, casualties were high as densely populated areas were subjected to sustained bombardment. Though a lot of children had been evacuated to the countryside from the cities at the start of the war, most of them had returned during the period of the 'phoney war', and many of them died.

ABOVE RIGHT: **Civilians shelter during an overnight air raid in the relative safety of Holborn Tube station.** Few people in London had space at their homes for an air-raid shelter so many crowded into Underground stations. The government assisted them by putting bunkbeds and latrines in the shelters.

ABOVE: **An anti-aircraft battery at work during a raid on the north of England.**

BELOW: **St Paul's Cathedral stands shrouded in smoke after a major air raid on London on Sunday December 29.**

BELOW RIGHT: **The King, Queen and Prime Minister Winston Churchill inspect the wreckage of Buckingham Palace following a raid on September 13, 1940.**

Bombing of Coventry

The Blitz was widened beyond London and the industrial city of Coventry was targeted on the night of November 14. The city's weak defences offered little opposition to the Luftwaffe, allowing them to utterly devastate the city centre, causing great loss of life. The German tactic was to drop incendiary devices to start fires that would continue to wreck the city long after the bombers' departure. A long list of other cities followed suit. Britain's seaports and shipyards at Southampton, Liverpool, Bristol, Portsmouth, Plymouth and Glasgow were subjected to particularly severe raids. The raids petered out after the Germans invaded the Soviet Union in June 1941 and the Luftwaffe was redeployed east. By this time, tens of thousands of civilians had been killed and hundreds of thousands had been made homeless. Although Germany would continue to bomb Britain intermittently, the worst of the raids were over for British civilians. However, for the German civilians, the Blitz had barely begun.

TOP: Liverpool suffers a pre-Christmas raid on December 21, 1940.

ABOVE: A row of taxis destroyed by bombing in London's Leicester Square.

RIGHT: The ruined city centre of Coventry still smoulders after the air raid on November 14, 1940.

LEFT: Firemen tackle a blaze at a factory in Birmingham after a raid in November 1940.

DAILY MAIL   NOVEMBER 16, 1940

Homes for all in smitten city

Coventry, hard-smitten by as heavy a night of bombing as even London has suffered, has shown itself to-night as a city of good Samaritans. Throughout the suburbs and the city the well-to-do and the poor alike have thrown open their houses to the homeless. Hundreds of men, women, and children whose homes were wrecked 24 hours ago have been welcomed to-night in those of people they had never seen before.

In working-class districts particularly I saw hastily scrawled notices in the windows of house after house: 'Room for two,' 'Room for three,' 'Will take four children.' No one who knocked at these doors was refused admission. People who had lost everything were told by complete strangers, 'You're welcome to share everything we've got.'

The aftermath of death and suffering has been a wave of warm humanity. In schoolrooms, empty mansions, and church halls, the homeless have gone to sleep to-night. 'No one is without a bed, and no one has gone to sleep hungry,' a city council official told me. 'It's marvellous the way people have rallied round.'

As the people were preparing their makeshift accommodation gunfire was heard again to-night. But Coventry went on with the work of restoration. I saw men and women still living in the wrecks of their homes. On houses whose roofs had been blasted away the people had rigged makeshift covers. 'Hitler?' said one

housewife to me. 'No fear! We stay put. And we're going to go on sleeping here.'

A pall of smoke hung over many areas of Coventry to-day. Two thousand high-explosive and thousands of incendiary bombs were rained indiscriminately on the city last night in a dusk-till-dawn air raid. Main streets were reduced to acres of rubble, and famous public buildings, cinemas, shops, houses, were obliterated. A thousand people were killed and injured and thousands more found themselves without homes. Yet the spirit of the people is unconquerable.

Only a shell of walls remains of Coventry's famous cathedral. Churches, public baths, clubs, cinemas, hotels, and hundreds of shops and business premises have been damaged.   In the suburbs hundreds of houses have been demolished and thousands of people made homeless. The attack lasted eleven hours. It is estimated here that at least 100 'planes, arriving in waves, took part. The first raiders to arrive dropped incendiary bombs, and many fires were started. As the intensity of the attack grew, the din became terrific.

There are no greater heroes in the city now than the staff of a hospital which suffered a direct hit. The operating theatre was wrecked, but to-night doctors and nurses who have been working throughout last night and to-day are still on duty tending the wounded people being rescued from the debris.

Lend-Lease

At sea, the Battle of the Atlantic was underway. It was vital that Britain could continue to be supplied by sea; the country's survival depended upon it. The essential convoys of supplies were under constant attack from both the Luftwaffe and U-boats, which were now able to operate from bases along the coastline of France, much extending their range. Most of the supplies came from the United States, but their cost was beginning to prove prohibitive to Britain's straitened wartime economy. President Roosevelt was willing to give any support short of actual military involvement, despite the USA's reluctance to become involved in what it saw as an essentially European affair. Churchill appealed to him for help in March 1941, and Roosevelt persuaded Congress to pass the Lend-Lease Act. This allowed the United States to lend war materials to a country whose defence was seen as necessary for the ultimate safety of the States. The relationship between Britain and the United States was strengthened further when Churchill and Roosevelt met in August 1941. They issued the 'Atlantic Charter', in which they stated their mutual reasons for resisting aggression.

ABOVE: President Roosevelt signs the Lend-Lease Act into law.

BELOW: A great merchant flotilla of British and Allied ships assembles near New York as they prepare to take war materiel to Britain under the Lend-Lease Act.

LEFT: An Allied merchant ship is guided through a minefield by means of semaphore.

Italian defeats

Italian forces had invaded British Somaliland in August 1940. This had initially forced a retreat, but the British had begun to gather a large force of tanks in the area. This meant that when the Italian army staged an invasion of Egypt from Libya in September, the British and Commonwealth forces were able to push them back to Benghazi with comparative speed. Abyssinia, which had been invaded and occupied by Italy in 1935, was also liberated. Mussolini faced a similar disaster in Greece; after invading in October 1940, the Italians met with stiff resistance and were pushed back to Albania by November 1940. To make matters worse, the British attacked the Italian navy at Taranto, its main base, on November 11. Torpedoes were dropped by aircraft and were, for the first time, effective in shallow water – the British lost two planes, but the Italians lost half their fleet.

To reverse Italy's losses, Hitler intervened. His troops had been steadily moving across the Balkans, bringing Romania, Bulgaria and Yugoslavia under his domination. In April 1941 he ordered his Panzers southward to complete the invasion of Greece. He also strengthened the Axis powers in North Africa. By the end of April his Afrika Korps, under the command of General Erwin Rommel, had driven the British out of Libya, back across Egypt and to within range of the Suez Canal.

Sinking of the Bismarck

In May 1941 the German battleship *Bismarck* sailed from the Baltic to the Atlantic on a mission to attack the vital Atlantic convoys, where she could have done great damage. She was undoubtedly the greatest surface threat to their safety. As she passed through the Denmark Strait on May 24 she was intercepted by Britain's great battleship HMS *Hood*. The ships opened fire. The *Hood* received a series of direct hits and sank within minutes with the loss of 1415 men; only three survived. This served to further demonstrate the danger the *Bismarck* represented, and efforts to sink it were redoubled. Once the *Bismarck* was out in the Atlantic she was pursued by British warships and rather elderly torpedo-carrying Swordfish planes. Skirmishing by the Swordfishes disabled the *Bismarck's* steering mechanism leaving her vulnerable. The warships moved in and finished the ship off on May 27.

TOP: German paratroopers board transport planes in Greece bound for Crete, to where the remainder of the Greek and British armies had retreated.

ABOVE: German paratroopers deploy in Crete with minimal equipment, as most of their supplies were dropped separately. This provided a twofold advantage to the Allies, for the Germans were outgunned, and much of their kit was captured.

ABOVE LEFT: The Germans had taken control of Crete by the end of May 1941. Many of the Allied troops were evacuated, but about 18,000 were captured.

BELOW: South Africans charge through an Italian smokescreen in Libya.

LEFT: The Indian army faces the Italians in Eritrea in April 1941.

PANEL: Survivors of the *Bismarck* are picked up by the Royal Navy.

Germany invades Russia

On Sunday June 22, 1941, Hitler launched Operation Barbarossa, his invasion of Russia. He had reneged on the Nazi–Soviet Pact of 1939, and Stalin is thought to have been caught completely by surprise, despite the fact that the invasion force had been amassing for some time. He had originally intended the attack for about a month earlier, but it had been delayed by a combination of weather and heavy fighting elsewhere. This would prove to be important as it gave the Germans less time to advance east and northwards before the winter began. Churchill immediately pledged support for Russia, and during the summer the Americans agreed to extend their policy of Lend-Lease to Russia as well.

Scorched-earth policy

At first the Russians retreated from the advancing Germans. They took anything that could be useful to the invaders with them and simply destroyed everything else – not just supplies but fields of ripening crops, bridges and railways: a complete scorched-earth policy. German troops were besieging Russia's second city of Leningrad by September, the Ukrainian city of Kiev fell in October and Hitler's troops had reached the outskirts of Moscow by the end of November. This was not as good for the Germans as it might have appeared. Not only was the bitter Russian winter now setting in, but the Russians were also well equipped to defend both Leningrad and Moscow. Towards the end of the year, on 6 December, they launched a counter-attack against the Germans, who were now faced with the problem of surviving the savage weather as well as beating off the determined Russians.

OPPOSITE ABOVE RIGHT: **Women help to construct defences around Leningrad as the German forces advance.**

OPPOSITE MIDDLE RIGHT: **A woman and her two sons are among the last to leave their town. Following Stalin's orders, the inhabitants laid waste to it themselves.**

OPPOSITE BELOW RIGHT: **A residential district burns in Kiev, in the Ukraine.**

OPPOSITE LEFT: **Civilians are hanged by the Nazis near Smolensk. The Soviets intercepted this image of Nazi brutality and sent it to newspapers around the world.**

OPPOSITE BOTTOM: **The Soviets destroy anything that might be of use to the German armies as they retreat. It was the same tactic used by Russian troops to defeat Napoleon more than a century earlier.**

TOP: **German troops wait by the roadside while a burning village is searched.**

ABOVE: **German troops advance through a burning farm. The crops, farmhouse and farm vehicles were all destroyed.**

ABOVE RIGHT: **German troops pass the burned-out shell of the Electrical Industry building in Kharkov.**

BELOW: **The last inhabitants flee Kerch as German and Romanian divisions enter the city.**

DAILY MAIL JUNE 23, 1941

Germans thrusting at Leningrad

German armies were last night reported to be making three main attacks in their great offensive against Russia along a front of 1,500 miles; from Finland towards Leningrad; from East Prussia towards Moscow; and from Rumania towards the Ukraine.

These distances are great. A hundred miles of difficult country lie between the Finnish frontier and Leningrad. Moscow is 600 miles from East Prussia. The Ukraine is almost immediately menaced, but the territory stretches 600 miles into Russia.

A fourth thrust is being made in Poland. Berlin radio claimed last night that German troops had crossed the Bug River, which flows in an arc around Warsaw. Long columns were said to have penetrated deep into Russian territory.

Berlin correspondents of Swiss newspapers said the Germans were using several thousand tanks to drive an opening in the Russian front and were expecting 'tremendous results.' The attack towards Leningrad is being made by German and Finnish divisions across the Karelian Isthmus - the battleground between the Soviet and Finland only 18 months ago.

Reports reaching Stockholm said a revolt which had broken out in Estonia was being successfully dealt with by Red troops. Some of the rebels seized ships in Tallinn harbour and opened fire on Russian troops in the capital.

Large formations of the Soviet Air Force have already attacked East Prussia, according to the Swiss radio. They were met by German fighters, and there were fierce and prolonged battles. German radio boasted of the superiority of the Luftwaffe over the Soviet air force. 'The German pilots,' said one of their war correspondents, 'found the Russian airmen completely inexperienced and they behaved like children.'

Three hundred divisions, or over 4,000,000 men will be locked in battle along this vast new front. Germany is estimated to have massed 125 divisions, including those she used against Greece - now policed by Mussolini. She has as allies 25 Rumanian and probably five or six Finnish divisions. Russia's western army is believed to consist of 150 divisions. Many others are available, but the state of their equipment is doubtful.

Pearl Harbor

On Sunday December 7, 1941, the war became a truly global one. Just before eight in the morning, Pearl Harbor, the US naval base in Hawaii, was attacked by almost 200 Japanese fighter planes. The strike came without a declaration of war and caught the navy completely unaware. An hour after the planes had returned to the six aircraft carriers which had escorted them, a second wave of a similar size struck. In total, 19 warships were damaged or destroyed and more than 2,400 people were killed. The scale of the destruction might have been even worse had the US Navy's aircraft carriers not been out on manoeuvres.

Tension between the United States and Japan had been mounting for some years. Japan desired to be the dominant power in East Asia, and the decline of Britain, France and the Netherlands had made this possible. However, the United States, with its presence in the Philippines and interests in the resources of the East Indies, continued to pose a major hurdle. Japan felt squeezed by the United States since Washington had imposed an oil embargo and aided China in the Sino-Japanese War in response to Japan's aggressive expansionism. Attempts to reach a diplomatic solution to their dispute failed as Roosevelt was anxious not to be seen as appeasing Japan in the manner that Hitler had been appeased before the war.

By November 1941, Japan's fuel supplies were running dangerously low and the navy resolved to capture the oilfields of the Dutch East Indies. Fearing that the United States might declare war as a result, and convinced that a war was one day inevitable, Japanese pilots launched a pre-emptive strike on the US fleet.

DAILY MAIL DECEMBER 8, 1941

Japan declares War on Britain and America

Japan to-night declared war on Britain and the United States after launching full-scale naval and air attacks on two of America's main bases in the Pacific - Pearl Harbour, in Hawaii, and Guam, between Hawaii and the Philippine Islands.

Already the Dutch East Indies have announced themselves at war with Japan, and the formal British and American declarations are expected in a matter of hours.

Quickly recovering from the first attacks, American warships steamed out of Pearl Harbour, and it was later reported that a Japanese aircraft-carrier had been sunk. Four Japanese submarines and six aircraft are also said to have been destroyed.

The Columbia Broadcasting System claims to have picked up a message saying that two British cruisers were sunk by Japanese planes attacking Singapore. This report is completely without confirmation. Another message, equally without support but well within the bounds of possibility, is that

Japanese warships have been engaged by British and American naval units in the Western Pacific. This report emanates from the Tokio correspondent of a Japanese newspaper in Shanghai quoting an announcement by Imperial Headquarters.

Early reports that Manila, the American base in the Philippine Islands, had been raided were followed by messages that all is quiet there, apart from aircraft taking off either on reconnaissance or to engage Japanese shipping.

Mr. Stimson, Secretary of War, has ordered the entire United States Army into uniform. This applies to 1,600,000, including thousands of officers and men who are on duty in administrative posts and hitherto have been allowed to wear civilian clothes.

To-night Mr. Roosevelt ordered the Army and Navy to carry out undisclosed orders, already prepared for 'the defence of the United States.'

OPPOSITE ABOVE RIGHT: **Smoke and debris fill the air as the Japanese attack Pearl Harbor.**

OPPOSITE MIDDLE RIGHT: **The USS** *Arizona* **sinks, engulfed in smoke and flames.**

OPPOSITE BELOW: **Smoke billows from the USS** *Shaw* **turning the blue Hawaiian sky black.**

TOP: **The Japanese attack on Pearl Harbor disabled the US Pacific allowing Japan to push into southeast Asia with little opposition.**

ABOVE: **Stunned Americans rushed to enlist in the armed services. Here men enrol for the US Army Air Force (USAAF) under the shadow of Lady Liberty in New York.**

RIGHT: **A line of Japanese battleships with the** *Mitsu* **nearest the camera.**

BELOW: **The huge propeller and part of the hull of the** *Arizona* **protrude from the water after the attack.**

America declares war

The day after Pearl Harbor, President Roosevelt delivered a speech to a joint session of Congress saying that December 7, 1941 was a 'date that will live in infamy' and requesting that Congress declare a state of war against Japan. Within hours both houses had voted overwhelmingly in favour of the war. Only one vote was cast against in either chamber, Congresswoman Jeanette Rankin from Montana opposed the war on account of her pacifist beliefs. Britain declared war against Japan on the same day. Three days later, on December 11, Japan's allies, Germany and Italy, declared war on the United States.

RIGHT: The President signs the declaration of war against Japan, just hours after delivering his speech to Congress.

BELOW RIGHT: Roosevelt is flanked by Vice President Henry Wallace, Speaker Samuel Rayburn, and his son, Captain James Roosevelt as he delivers his 'Infamy speech' in the House of Representatives.

BELOW LEFT: Factories engaged in war work were asked to put up this poster to inspire their employees.

BELOW: President Roosevelt addresses a joint session of the US Congress requesting a declaration of war against Japan.

TO ALL DEFENSE WORKERS . . .

The President of the United States said:

"I APPEAL . . .

"to the owners of plants
"to the managers
"to the workers
"to our own Government employees
"to put every ounce of effort into producing these munitions swiftly and without stint. And with this appeal I give you the pledge that all of us who are officers of your Government will devote ourselves to the same whole-hearted extent to the great task which lies ahead.

"We must be the great arsenal of democracy. For us this is an emergency as serious as war itself. We must apply ourselves to our task with the same resolution, the same sense of urgency, the same spirit of patriotism and sacrifice as we would show were we at war."

★ ★ ★

Let's get squarely behind our President's appeal.

★ ★

Let's work together building that "GREAT ARSENAL OF DEMOCRACY" in record time.

★

Increase PRODUCTION! - That's our No. 1 job!

Let's go!

ABOVE LEFT: **Police in Paducah, Kentucky, exchange their patrol cars for pedal bikes in order to conserve rubber, an import from the East Indies, which would inevitably grow scarce.**

LEFT: **Americans register for sugar ration books, May 1942. Sugar was America's first rationed commodity of the war.**

TOP: **Japanese men leave a California hotel after being picked up by the FBI.**

ABOVE: **The camp at Manzanar, California, that housed more than 60,000 Japanese citizens and Japanese Americans during the war.**

BELOW: **Hundreds of residents of Tillamook, Oregon, meet to discuss civil defence in the event of a Japanese invasion of the West Coast.**

DAILY MAIL DECEMBER 9, 1941

Congress declares war on Japan

Marines with fixed bayonets guarded the Capitol to-day as the United States Congress formally declared war on Japan. They voted 25 minutes after President Roosevelt, in a message denouncing Japan's aggression, had called for this action.

Mr. Roosevelt was frequently and loudly cheered during his address. He described yesterday as 'a date that will live in infamy.' The United States, he said, was at peace with Japan, and at her solicitation was still in consultation with her Government's representatives. 'Indeed, one hour after Japanese air squadrons had commenced bombing the American island of Hawaii, the Japanese Ambassador and his colleague delivered to our Secretary of State a formal reply to a recent American message. It contained no threat or hint of war,' he said.

'It will be recorded that the distance of Hawaii from Japan makes it obvious that the attack was deliberately planned many days or even weeks ago. During the intervening time the Japanese Government has deliberately set out to deceive the United States by false statements and expressions of hope for continued peace.

'The attack yesterday on the Hawaiian Islands has caused severe damage to American naval and military forces. I regret to tell you that very many American lives have been lost. In addition, American ships have been reported torpedoed on the high seas between San Francisco and Honolulu. Yesterday the Japanese Government also launched an attack against Malaya.

'Last night, Japanese forces attacked Hongkong. Last night Japanese forces attacked Guam. Last night Japanese forces attacked the Philippine Islands. Last night the Japanese attacked Wake Island. And this morning the Japanese attacked Midway Island.

'As Commander-in-Chief of the Army and Navy, I have directed that all measures be taken for our defence, but always will our whole nation remember the character of the onslaught against us. No matter how long it may take us to overcome this premeditated invasion, the American people in their righteous might will win through to absolute victory.'

Southeast Asia falls to Japan

The conflict in the Pacific escalated rapidly. On December 10, the British navy suffered an appalling blow when two of its largest battleships, the *Repulse* and the *Prince of Wales*, were sunk by Japanese bombers. Japan made several lightning-fast strikes throughout the area, and by the end of the year the US bases at Guam and Wake Island had been captured. Hong Kong fell on Christmas Day. Japanese forces moved swiftly in an attempt to seize control of southeast Asia following the attack on Pearl Harbor and their run of victories in Malaya, Hong Kong, Thailand and the Philippines. They now launched attacks throughout the Pacific; in January 1942, Manila, the Dutch East Indies, Kuala Lumpur and Burma were invaded.

Burma

This put the Allies under immense pressure. British troops in Malaya were forced to retreat to Singapore by February. The city fell on February 15, and about 80,000 British and Australians were captured. Later in February, Japan attacked Australia itself, bombing the northern city of Darwin. Then the Japanese landed on the island of Java on February 26, defeating British and Dutch naval forces in the Battle of the Java Sea. By early spring, it seemed that the Japanese were almost invincible. British troops had been forced to withdraw across the mainland of Burma towards the Indian border, and the Japanese were continuing to capture islands throughout the western Pacific.

DAILY MAIL DECEMBER 27, 1941
Hong Kong's last stand

The full story of the Battle of Hongkong was issued by the War Office last night.

It starts with December 8, when the Japanese attacked our troops on the mainland and we withdrew into 'Gindrinkers' Line,' and ends with Christmas Day when the last of the island garrison was forced to capitulate.

The Hongkong garrison consisted of two British, two Canadian, and two Indian battalions and the Hongkong Volunteer Defence Force. These were: the 2nd Bn. Royal Scots, 1st Bn. Middlesex Regt., a battalion of Winnipeg Grenadiers, a battalion of Royal Rifles of Canada, 2/14th Bn. Punjabis, and 5/7th Bri. Rajputs, with the normal complement of R.A., R.E., R. Sigs. units, and auxiliary services. Units of the Royal Navy and the Hongkong Naval Volunteer Reserve and detachments of Royal Marines co-operated with the military forces.

The geographical features of the colony, states the War Office, its isolation, and the fact that its only aerodrome was on the mainland precluded the possibility of air support.

On the morning of December 8, a Japanese division, with a second division in immediate reserve, crossed the frontier on the mainland. Demolitions were made, and our troops withdrew. There was patrol activity, and a men-carrier patrol ambushed and annihilated a Japanese platoon on Castle Peak road.

On the morning of December 11, strong enemy pressure developed on our left flank, held by the Royal Scots. Two companies were driven off by heavy mortar fire, but the situation was stabilised by using all available reserves. The Royal Scots suffered severe casualties. By midday it was decided to evacuate all the mainland except the Devil's Peak position.

Stonecutters Island was heavily bombarded all day. The island was evacuated during the night of the 11th after demolitions had been made.

The island was sporadically bombarded by artillery and from the air. The civil population was reported to be calm, but their morale considerably shaken. Monetary problems and rice distribution gave cause for serious anxiety.

December 13 was a difficult day.

The enemy sent a delegation to negotiate surrender. The proposal was summarily rejected by the Governor (Sir Mark Young).

On December 16 serial bombing and artillery shelling were increased. One enemy aircraft was brought down into the sea.

On the 17th aerial bombardment was directed against the Peak wireless station and other places. No military damage resulted.

On December 22 the enemy landed further troops on the north-east coast. A counter-attack on the 21st from Stanley towards Ty Tan Tak had failed, although a certain number of the enemy were killed at the cost of about 100 Canadian casualties.

On December 23 some ground on Mount Cameron lost during the night was recaptured by the Royal Marines, but counter-attacks by the force at Stanley towards Stanley Mound failed. However, the Middlesex Regiment successfully repulsed a determined attack at Leighton Hill.

It was impossible to conceal the fact that the situation had become exceedingly grave. The troops, who had been fighting unceasingly for many days, were tired out. The water and food supply was desperate. The reservoirs and depots were in enemy hands.

On December 24 the enemy continued to subject the garrison to heavy fire from dive-bombers and mortars, and by means of incendiary bombs set the countryside all round Mount Cameron on fire.

On December 25 the military and naval commanders informed the Governor that no further effective resistance could be made.

America's first victories in the Pacific

The Battle of the Coral Sea took place from May 4-7, 1942. American aircraft carriers off New Guinea intercepted a Japanese invasion force heading towards Papua and the southern Solomon Islands. This was the first naval battle in which all the fighting was done by the pilots of planes launched from aircraft carriers; it was also the first defeat for the Japanese. There were losses on both sides, but the Japanese fleet was turned back with the loss of an aircraft carrier, making the Coral Sea America's first victory in the war with Japan.

Midway and Guadalcanal

One month later, four more Japanese aircraft carriers were destroyed at the Battle of Midway, severely reducing their capabilities. This heralded a clear change in the Allies' fortunes; they were beginning to gain the advantage in the Pacific in terms of the balance of both air and sea power. Allied attacks were launched in the Solomon Islands, and the first landings took place at Guadalcanal on August 7. At first there was little resistance, but the Japanese troops were very swiftly reinforced and fierce fighting was to rage for the rest of 1942. Naval battles also continued, and the Americans inflicted further heavy damage to the Japanese navy and to a supply convoy off Guadalcanal in November. The island was finally won in February 1943 at a cost of thousands of lives. Within days the Americans moved to assist the Australians in pushing the Japanese out of New Guinea. The Australians had already dealt the Japanese their first defeat of the war at Milne Bay in September 1942, and the addition of the Americans was sufficient to win back control of the island by the end of 1943.

OPPOSITE ABOVE: A Japanese soldier skirmishes with British troops in Burma.

OPPOSITE MIDDLE: A scout group of British, American, Chinese and native Kachin troops wade through a river in the Burmese jungle.

OPPOSITE BELOW: One of the US Navy's amphibious trucks brings supplies ashore at New Caledonia in the South Pacific. American troops landed on the Free French island-colony in April 1942.

ABOVE: A US bomber attacks a Japanese plane in New Guinea.

MIDDLE LEFT: American soldiers manning a howitzer launch an attack in Burma.

MIDDLE RIGHT: Men of Britain's 14th Army patrol through swamps in Burma.

LEFT: Marines board an LCM landing craft in the Aleutian Islands before setting off to push the Japanese off Kiska Island.

BELOW: US troops fire on Japanese positions on the Aleutian island of Attu. The Japanese navy attacked the Aleutians to try to divert the Americans from Midway.

The Americans arrive in Britain

Meeting in Washington in December 1941, Churchill and Roosevelt agreed that the Allies should concentrate on winning the war in Europe before turning their attentions fully towards the Pacific theatre. This 'Germany First' policy had its critics, but it was agreed that the US and Britain would be stronger fighting together, and that logistically Britain had to confront the Nazi threat first. Nevertheless, the US would keep piling the pressure on Japan and won some key battles at Coral Sea and Midway during 1942.

American troops had begun landing in Britain within weeks of the attack on Pearl Harbor and Hitler's subsequent declaration of war on the US; throughout 1942 they were to arrive in vast numbers. These were the GIs (their equipment was stamped 'General Issue'; hence the name) and they were widely welcomed in Britain.

The GIs proved especially popular with children – they were widely seen as purveyors of treats that had become impossible to find, such as chocolate and sweets. They were also very popular with some British women, some 20,000 of whom would become 'GI brides' by the end of the war. As a result of this, many British men would complain that the Americans were 'oversexed, overpaid and over here'.

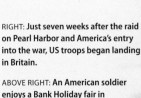

RIGHT: Just seven weeks after the raid on Pearl Harbor and America's entry into the war, US troops began landing in Britain.

ABOVE RIGHT: An American soldier enjoys a Bank Holiday fair in Hampstead.

MIDDLE RIGHT: American marines land in Iceland on their way to Britain.

ABOVE: A US Jeep makes for an unusual sight amongst the London traffic.

FAR LEFT: General Eisenhower watches Charlton Athletic take on Chelsea in the Southern Cup Final at Wembley Stadium.

FAR LEFT MIDDLE: Britain was awash with Allied troops. Here Winston Churchill visits Czechoslovak troops with the Czechoslovak President Eduard Benes.

FAR LEFT BELOW: American tank crews on manoeuvres in England.

LEFT: Eleanor Roosevelt tours through buildings destroyed in the Blitz in London in October 1942.

BELOW LEFT: Many women were thrilled that the arrival of the GIs meant that luxury items such as stockings became easier to obtain. Until then many women had painted their legs to give the impression of a seam.

BOTTOM: British and American troops arrive in port in advance of the Allied invasion of North Africa, November 1942.

Stalingrad

Russia's Red Army had managed to hold out over the winter of 1941 and even had some success in pushing the Germans back from Moscow in January. By late spring, however, the German Army had regrouped and a new campaign was planned. This time the intention was to strike towards the Crimea in the south, which would ultimately enable the Germans to take control of the Caucasus where there were significant oil reserves.

In June and July the Germans captured Rostov and Sevastopol, but this initial success was not to last. The German army turned north in August, heading for the important city of Stalingrad, and their advance was slowed by Russian resistance. It finally ground to a halt in the suburbs of Stalingrad itself, and the Germans had to settle in for a long siege instead of a swift advance. Stalingrad was desperately defended, with every patch of ground contested bitterly, and then the Russians launched a counter-offensive as the winter of 1942 began. They inflicted heavy casualties on their enemies and eventually surrounded the Germans to both the north and south of the city. Trapped between the relieving troops and the city's desperate defenders, the German Sixth Army and the Fourth Panzer Division awaited help from a relieving army, as well as urgent supplies of all kinds.

ABOVE: **Russian marines engage the Germans on the Black Sea coast, July 1942.**

TOP RIGHT: **New Red Navy torpedo boats set out on a mission in the Black Sea.**

MIDDLE RIGHT: **A family crouch over the body of their father, murdered during a massacre in the town of Kerch. The bandaged man on the left of the picture was wounded in the head during the massacre and lay still covered with earth and corpses until the Nazis departed.**

BELOW RIGHT: **The scene of Nazi terror against the civilian population of Russia in Rostov-on-Don.**

BELOW: **The ruins of Stalingrad's Factory District, where much of the fighting took place.**

Russian victory

It was astonishingly cold – the temperature reached 24 degrees below freezing – and the Germans lacked winter uniforms, food and medicine. Ammunition was also running low, but Hitler refused to allow their surrender – nor could he manage to supply them, effectively condemning the army to a form of mass suicide. By December there was no longer much doubt about the ultimate result, and January 31 saw a massive defeat for the Germans southwest of Stalingrad. On February 2, 1943 the German commander, Von Paulus, finally surrendered, disobeying Hitler. The Russians took over 90,000 prisoners, amongst whom were twenty-four generals; many more, on both sides, had died. This was the German army's greatest-ever defeat and a major turning point on the Eastern Front. The Russians now began to push the Germans back to the west.

TOP: Soldiers raise the Red Flag above a building in a recaptured part of Stalingrad.

ABOVE: Stalingrad residents welcome reinforcements from the Red Army.

BELOW: Many Soviet civilians were trapped in the city and had to make their homes amongst the rubble, in basements, or even in shell holes.

LEFT: Once the Germans had been defeated, these women were free to emerge from the basement which had been their home for the duration of the battle.

DAILY MAIL FEBRUARY 1, 1943
Stalingrad army wiped out

Field-Marshal Paulus, Commander-in-Chief of the German Sixth Army and Fourth Tank Army at Stalingrad, was captured by the Russians yesterday a few hours after he had been promoted to the highest rank by special proclamation from Hitler's headquarters.

He was seized with his staff when Soviet troops stormed the Ogpu headquarters in the heart of the city and completed the greatest disaster that has befallen Germany in this war.

It is now revealed as a disaster of unsuspected proportions. Instead of 220,000 men, the trapped army consisted of 330,000 troops, it was announced by Moscow in a special communique last night.

In addition to the Sixth Army, the Fourth Panzer Army has been trapped and destroyed. Thirteen German and two Rumanian generals and 46,000 troops have been captured. Five thousand were taken prisoner with Marshal Paulus yesterday.

Booty taken between January 10 and 30 includes 744 aircraft, 1,517 tanks, and 6,523 guns.

Resistance and collaboration

During the Second World War the Nazis controlled a vast swath of Europe from France to the Soviet Union. Throughout their occupied territories and vassal states the Germans found people prepared to work with them and people intent upon working against them. Those who collaborated usually did so because they were sympathetic to Nazi ideology or were pragmatists willing to work with whoever was in charge. They assisted the Germans by forming puppet governments, deporting Jews and arresting members of the resistance; some even joined voluntary units of the dreaded Waffen SS. Those opposed to German occupation or to Nazi ideology joined organized resistance movements or engaged in individual acts of defiance. Their activities ranged from hiding Jews and sabotaging communications to killing collaborators and providing intelligence to the Allies. Many others did not actively participate in resistance or collaboration and simply tried to survive the occupation – these people have sometimes been criticized as passive collaborators.

The reaction to the German occupation was not uniform across Europe; there was inevitably more resistance activity wherever the German presence was stronger and German rule more direct. Different national groups also responded to the German presence in different ways and some nations even welcomed the Germans as liberators from other oppressors – such was the case in Croatia and Estonia where the Germans were regarded as liberators from Serb and Russian domination respectively.

Français ! souvenez-vous

ici habite un

COLLABORATEUR

Ce papillon ne peut être apposé sur la porte d'un COLLABORATEUR qu'après enquête et autorisation des Services du Contre Espionnage.

Uprisings in Warsaw

From November 1939 Warsaw's Jewish population was forced to move into a ghetto, which was sealed-off from the rest of the city the following year. Jews from all over Poland and Europe were sent to live in the Warsaw Ghetto where thousands died from starvation and disease. From July 1942 the Nazis began a major purge of the Ghetto and hundreds of thousands of people were sent to their deaths at Treblinka. In early 1943, after news of the exterminations had reached the Ghetto, the remaining population rose up in rebellion. Using weapons that had been smuggled in or improvised, the rebels held out against the German army for almost a month. Thousands were killed during the uprising and the survivors were deported to death camps or executed on the spot.

The following year the Polish Home Army, the main Polish resistance movement, rose up in rebellion hoping to liberate Warsaw before the fast-approaching Soviet troops arrived. The uprising began on August 1, 1944 and the 50,000 strong Polish Home Army met with some early successes. However, the Germans soon sent in reinforcements and the Luftwaffe began a relentless bombardment of the city. The rebels were slowly worn down and no relief came from Soviet forces, which had stopped just short of the city – ostensibly on the orders of Stalin who did not want the Polish Home Army to take over. With more than 200,000 dead and much of the city destroyed, the rebels surrendered on October 2, 1944. The Russians seized the city three months later.

OPPOSITE MIDDLE LEFT: **Marshal Pétain inspects French troops at Châteauroux, in unoccupied France. Pétain ruled Vichy France in collaboration with the Nazis in order to spare southern France from direct German rule. The Vichy government actively supported Nazi racial policies against the Jews, and thousands were rounded up, placed in concentration camps, and later transported to death camps in the east.**

OPPOSITE TOP LEFT: **Vidkun Quisling awaits his trial in Oslo at the end of the war. The name of the wartime Premier of Norway, who was appointed upon the orders of Hitler, has become synonymous with collaboration.**

OPPOSITE TOP RIGHT: **Quisling gives the Nazi salute as he inspects German troops in Norway.**

OPPOSITE MIDDLE RIGHT: **The Allies drop supplies to the Resistance in Nazi occupied Belgium.**

OPPOSITE MIDDLE: **'Here lives a collaborator'. Anyone suspected by the Resistance of collaborating with the Germans might have woken to find this sign posted on their front door during the night.**

OPPOSITE BELOW: **French Resistance fighters are drilled on the edge of a field close to the treeline so they can duck for cover.**

ABOVE: **In hunger and dispair, members of the Polish resistance await the arrival of the Nazis following their surrender.**

FAR LEFT: **This still from a film smuggled out of France reveals daily life in the French resistance. When possible, the day began with the raising of the Tricolour.**

LEFT ABOVE: **Resistance fighters practise shooting in the foothills of the French Alps.**

LEFT: **Italian Resistance fighters launch an attack against Fascists in a Milan street.**

BELOW: **The ruins of Warsaw following the failed uprising in August 1944.**

El Alamein

The start of 1942 saw something of a stand-off in North Africa; both sides were regrouping on either side of the Gazala Line. Rommel launched his next attack on the British in May, as the Germans were attacking in Russia. His army outflanked the British and forced them to make a rapid withdrawal to Tobruk – which was lost by June. Following that, the British Eighth Army retreated eastwards to El Alamein. Here it was possible for them to be reinforced, both swiftly and to a considerable extent, from the Suez Canal. There were sustained German attacks during July and August, but the British were able to hold the defensive Alamein Line. They were ready to strike back by October, under the inspirational command of General Montgomery, who was sent to lead the Eighth Army in August. During the night of October 23 an enormous artillery bombardment began, followed by a frontal assault against Rommel's forces. Progress was steady though slow initially, but the advance picked up speed and Rommel began to retreat on November 3. The Germans were then quickly pushed back into Libya.

ABOVE RIGHT: **An American-built Maryland bomber of the South African Air Force strikes a German supply convoy in the Libyan desert.**

ABOVE: **Part of the vast Allied armada heading to the North African coast during Operation Torch.**

MIDDLE RIGHT: **Troops bring stores ashore on the North African coast during the Torch landings.**

RIGHT: **Wading through the Mediterranean Sea, American troops come ashore in Algeria.**

BELOW: **Headed by a standard bearer, US troops march towards an airfield near Algiers on the first day of Operation Torch.**

Operation Torch

Five days later, on November 8, a large-scale invasion of French North Africa was launched under the command of US General Dwight Eisenhower. It was known as Operation Torch, and had the honour of being the largest seaborne expedition in history until it was dwarfed by the Normandy landings.

Stalin had been demanding that the Allies open a second front in Europe to relieve some of the pressure on the Red Army, which was defending an enormous front. Roosevelt agreed with the strategy in principle, but was advised against it by his generals. Churchill was also sceptical; he had authorized 'a reconnaissance in force to test the enemy defences' at the French port at Dieppe in August 1942. It was a disaster. The force was withdrawn after only nine hours, by which time thousands of troops — mostly Canadians — had been either killed or captured. Instead, Churchill advocated opening a new front in North Africa. By capturing Tunisia, the Allies would severely disrupt the enemy's supply lines and could engage them on two fronts.

Pushing Germany out of Africa

There was little resistance to the Allied landings, and Admiral Darlan, the commander of Vichy France, whose forces were occupying the area, ordered a ceasefire just two days later. He also appealed to the French navy to leave Toulon, where they were based, and join the Allies. Hitler immediately scrapped Marshal Pétain's collaborationist Vichy government and ordered the full occupation of France, which took place on November 11. The French immediately scuttled their fleet to deny the Germans additional naval power.

By the end of January 1943 Montgomery's army had pushed the Germans back westward from Egypt through Libya and General Eisenhower was pushing east. Trapped between the two, the position of the Axis armies was hopeless. Rommel himself left for Europe, handing over to General von Arnim. The Axis army – about 250,000 men – surrendered to the Allies in May.

LEFT: **Old Glory, the American Flag, flies above the ruins of a North African town.**

TOP LEFT: **The liberated French population of Algiers give the V-for-Victory sign as American troops march through the town.**

ABOVE: **Italian soldiers are driven through the streets of Algiers on their way to internment camps. American troops were charged with maintaining order as locals poured onto the streets to jeer at them.**

ABOVE LEFT: **America's General Eisenhower (left) with Britain's General Montgomery (right). After pushing the Germans out of Africa, the two men would lead the Allies to victory in Western Europe.**

LEFT: **General Eisenhower and General Giraud inspect a Guard of Honour of French troops during a victory parade in Tunis, Tunisia in May 1943.**

The home front in Britain

In Britain, women had begun to be conscripted into war work or the forces in December 1941. By 1943, 90 per cent of single women were either serving in the forces themselves or working in war industries – such as munitions and armaments factories and shipyards – replacing the men who were now in the armed forces. They also worked in agriculture, where there were eventually some 80,000 'land girls' in the Women's Land Army.

Life in Britain during the war was often difficult as bombing raids continued and most things were in short supply. Everything from clothes to food and from soap to petrol was rationed and people were encouraged to 'make do and mend', by repairing and reusing everyday items.

With everybody devoting their lives to fighting for their country in some way, there was widespread agreement that post-war British society would have to change to benefit the majority of the population. The way forward was set out in the Beveridge Report, which became an unlikely bestseller. In it, Sir William Beveridge proposed that a system of social security for everyone should be set up after the war, with a National Health Service and a system of family allowances.

The Baedeker Raids

Following a devastating British air raid on the historic city of Lubeck, Hitler vowed to terrorize Britain's cities with renewed vigour. The result was the Baedeker raids on picturesque and historic cities such as Bath, Canterbury, Exeter, Norwich and York. The name Baedeker comes from the German company who produced the travel guide used to select the targets. These cities had far fewer air defences than Britain's industrial centres meaning the destruction was extensive. The raids lasted from April to June 1942, killing 1,600 people and destroying 50,000 homes. They were mainly vindictive and offered little in the way of strategic value. A number of German planes and pilots were lost, while the only effect on civilian morale was to strengthen the public's resolve against Germany.

Easing of restrictions

By 1943, the Allies had superiority in the air, but smaller-scale bombing raids did still occur, particularly over London, and usually in response to attacks on German cities. Perhaps the most tragic incident happened on the night of March 3 during a minor raid in the East End of London; it was not directly attributable to the enemy, however. People were hurrying to enter Bethnal Green Underground station and take shelter, when somebody lost their footing at the top of the stairs and fell. Pressure from behind meant that those in front could not stop, and the resulting crush caused the deaths of 178 people.

The end of the Blitz had brought some small relaxation in regulations, though rationing still continued. Early in 1943 it was ruled that lights in railway carriages could be left on when trains were standing at stations (they had previously been extinguished so that the trains – and thus stations – could not be easily detected from the air), and it was later agreed that traffic lights could be used; pedestrians were allowed to carry undimmed torches.

OPPOSITE ABOVE RIGHT: A female bricklayer repairs part of a wall damaged by bombing.

OPPOSITE MIDDLE RIGHT: Land girls reap the corn harvest on a Buckinghamshire farm.

OPPOSITE BELOW RIGHT: German bombing resulted in temporary evacuations and diversions, further disrupting daily life in Britain.

OPPOSITE ABOVE LEFT: German attacks on merchant shipping would bring Britain dangerously close to running out of essential supplies. Bacon, butter and sugar were the first products to be rationed, quickly followed by other foodstuffs and household goods.

OPPOSITE BELOW LEFT: York's five-century-old Guildhall burns following a Baedeker raid on April 28, 1942.

TOP LEFT: Making a phone call between protective sandbags in London.

LEFT: British people were encouraged to 'Dig for Victory' by growing vegetables wherever there was space. Even bombsites were converted into allotments.

TOP: Schoolboys take tea in the garden of their damaged home following a raid.

ABOVE LEFT: Clothes rationing began in Britain on June 1, 1941. Owing to a shortage of material, people were encouraged to 'make do and mend' by repairing older garments.

ABOVE RIGHT: Despite being bombed out of their office building, work continues in the street.

Bombing Germany

For the first two years of the war, Britain did not launch a comprehensive air offensive against Germany's cities. There was strategic bombing of military and industrial targets within Germany, but it was not until 1942 that Britain began indiscriminately raiding Germany with the intention of breaking civilian morale. Arthur 'Bomber' Harris took charge of Bomber Command in February 1942 and began planning for the aerial bombing of German cities. The test case for the new tactic was the historic city of Lubeck in northern Germany, which was struck on the night of March 28, 1942. The town's old buildings were easily set alight by the incendiary bombs dropped by the RAF, causing widespread destruction and loss of life.

1,000-Bomber Raids

Two months after Lubeck, Harris assembled his bombers for a strike against Cologne, an industrial city on the Rhine. Operation Millennium, as it was codenamed, employed 1,047 aircraft, making it the largest fleet yet seen in aerial warfare. The raid was originally intended for Hamburg, Germany's second-largest city and a major site of U-boat production, but it was switched to Cologne because of poor weather. On the night of May 30, the aircraft flew in a tight stream, maintaining height and speed, both to avoid collisions and to limit German radar detection. The mission was achieved more quickly than had ever been attempted, even for a much smaller force. Although some of the crews missed their intended target, almost 900 planes bombed Cologne, releasing 1,455 tons of bombs, two thirds of which were incendiary devices.

ABOVE RIGHT: **Members of the German Safety Service tackle a blaze caused by incendiary bombs.**

FAR RIGHT: **An American Liberator bomber plunges towards the ground after being damaged by anti-aircraft fire.**

RIGHT: **Low-flying RAF bombers strike a power station in Cologne.**

BELOW: **Berliners clear away debris following an air raid.**

Hamburg and Dresden

The RAF proceeded to relentlessly bomb Germany by night, and from 1943, they were joined by the American Air Force (USAAF) which bombed by day. This relentless round the clock bombardment never directly achieved its aim of forcing Germany into submission by breaking civilian morale, but it did play a vital role in wearing Germany down in preparation for the overland invasion.

In late July 1943, the RAF and the USAAF launched Operation Gomorrah, a series of devastating raids on Hamburg. Almost 3,000 sorties were flown over the city leading to the deaths of an estimated 40,000 people, most of whom perished in a great firestorm that engulfed the city on the night of July 27. A firestorm caused by a heavy raid on Dresden killed a similar number of people in February 1945. Dresden was singled out for the raid because it was an important transport hub and was being used to send troops and supplies to the Eastern Front. The death toll was higher than might have been expected because Dresden's population had swelled in number as a result of the thousands of refugees who had poured into the city in the empty trains returning from the front.

LEFT: US airmen report back to an officer following a successful raid on industrial sites near Berlin. The markings on the back of this navigator's jacket indicate the number of missions he has completed.

BELOW LEFT: A Swastika is draped over a bombed-out building to commemorate Hitler's 55th birthday in April 1944. Despite the relentless bombing campaign, there was no revolution against the Nazi regime. Some continued to support Hitler, others feared his terror network or Soviet reprisals; the rest became stoically resigned to their fate.

BELOW: Factories and an airfield in Berlin burn after heavy bombing. Initially, Berlin was spared the worst of the aerial onslaught because it was too far away for the RAF to mount a sustained campaign. However, improved technology and the arrival of the Americans changed that and Berlin was bombed severely from November 1943 until the last months of the war.

TOP: The Mohne Dam is successfully breached by a bouncing bomb during the 'Dambuster' raids of May 1943.

ABOVE LEFT: A B17 Flying Fortress crew study their new remote-controlled chin-turret which provided better protection against frontal fighter assaults.

ABOVE RIGHT: Despite massive damage to the tail of this B17, the pilot managed to return from his bombing mission over Germany and land safely back in Britain.

The liberation of Italy

The Allied victory in North Africa in May 1943 altered the state of play in the Mediterranean, making an attack on Italy possible. Italy was in bad shape: the country had lost an estimated 200,000 soldiers in North Africa, more than 200,000 were fighting on the Eastern Front, and about 500,000 were deployed in the Balkans. So when American, British and Canadian troops invaded Sicily in July 1943, the island fell within just six weeks. This rapid defeat in Sicily, combined with the devastating bombing of the mainland, led to the overthrow of Mussolini by the Fascist Grand Council; he was arrested and sent to prison.

In September, the Allies had crossed to the mainland and the new Italian government surrendered. However, this did not bring peace as the Germans in the country continued to resist the Allied advance. Italy was now treated as another of Germany's vassals: Jews were rounded up and deported to Auschwitz, partisans were executed and the country was plundered of its historic artworks. German glider pilots even rescued Mussolini from his remote mountain prison and made him leader of their new puppet state, the 'Italian Social Republic'.

ABOVE LEFT: Italian soldiers in Sicily surrender.

LEFT: Anzio lies in ruins in the aftermath of Allied raids in preparation for the landings in February 1944.

BELOW LEFT: First news of Italy's surrender reaches London. However, the fighting would get much worse once the Germans took over.

MIDDLE LEFT: Roman women gives a rapturous welcome to Allied troops.

FAR LEFT: The people of Naples greet the Allies after having seen off the Germans themselves.

BOTTOM LEFT: A church in Turin damaged during Allied air raids on the major industrial centres in northern Italy on August 8, 1943.

BOTTOM RIGHT: As food grows scarce, the grounds of Milan Cathedral are turned into a cornfield.

The fall of Rome

After encountering some initial difficulties at Salerno, the Allies raced through southern Italy in September 1943. They reached Naples at the end of the month to discover the population of the city had already risen up and pushed the Germans out. The lightning advance ground to a halt in November after the Germans retreated to the 'Gustav Line', a highly defendable position running across the country from the Tyrrhenian to the Adriatic Seas.

Attempts to break the Line during the winter proved costly to the Allies, so a surprise landing was made north of the Gustav Line, at Anzio, on January 22, 1944. In February the Germans counter-attacked in this area and the Allied advance came to a halt. To relieve the pressure on their men at Anzio, the Allies launched an invasion across the Gustav Line at Monte Cassino, the site of an ancient Benedictine abbey. The town did not fall until three months later, and only after the town and abbey had been completely reduced to rubble with great loss of life. With the Gustav Line breached, the Allies linked up with their comrades at Anzio and marched on Rome, liberating the city on June 4, 1944.

Mussolini executed

The Germans continued to resist in Italy for almost a year, and it was not until April 29, 1945 that they finally surrendered. The day before, Mussolini and his mistress had been captured and executed by Italian partisans. Their bodies, along with fifteen others, were hung upside-down from the girders of a petrol station in Milan.

ABOVE LEFT: Monghidoro, just south of Bologna, is liberated by the Allies in October 1944.

MIDDLE LEFT: British troops kick down the door of SS Headquarters in Florence.

BELOW LEFT: Italian partisans search for German stragglers in the town of Cesena following its liberation.

BOTTOM: Seventeen merchant ships in the liberated Italian port of Bari are bombed in a surprise German raid in December 1943.

DAILY MAIL FEBRUARY 16 1944

Cassino Abbey bombed to a ruin

Front-Line troops of the Fifth Army watched in awed silence to-day the destruction by bomb and shell of Cassino Abbey. They looked on at the terrible bombardment with memories of comrades who had fallen under the guns of the Germans entrenched behind the abbey walls.

It had to be done - this razing of one of the great monuments of the Western World. And it has been done thoroughly after repeated warnings and with all due consideration for civilian life.

Seven waves of Fortresses, Mitchells, and Marauders have reduced the monastery to ruins. When I turned away from the scene an hour ago, the great, grey oblong monastery was nothing but a jagged silhouette against the pale blue sky. The German guns mounted in the abbey have been silenced. No longer is it the strong fortress dominating Cassino and denying us access along 'Highway Six' to Rome.

Doubtless there will be argument for many years to come about the deed that was done between 9 a.m. and 2 p.m., but I don't believe there was one man on our side of the Rapido Valley to-day who felt any regret or remorse, or, indeed, any other emotion save acute interest.

The attack was directed not only against the monastery but against the system of pillboxes and strong-points on the slopes below it.

TOP: American artillery pounds Monte Cassino in February 1944. The abbey was initially spared, but the Allies began shelling it to deny the Germans a key observation post on the Gustav Line.

ABOVE: Monte Cassino Abbey lies in ruins after the battle.

LEFT: Not a building is left undamaged during the Allied offensive on Monte Cassino.

D-Day

Preparations for the invasion of Occupied France had proceeded apace in Britain throughout the winter of 1943 and the spring of 1944. The Dieppe raid in 1942 had cost many lives, but it had also shown that it was going to be virtually impossible to capture and hold a major French port. 'Operation Overlord' was therefore planned to land on the less well-defended Normandy beaches to the east of the Cherbourg peninsula. This meant that a vast invading army would have to be both deployed and supplied without the advantages of a proper harbour, so artificial 'Mulberry' harbours were built to be towed across the English Channel to the landing beaches. In preparation for the invasion, special landing craft and amphibious vehicles were built, and large numbers of troops started assembling in southern Britain. In addition, a pipeline named 'PLUTO' was laid across the seabed from the Isle of Wight to Normandy to ensure this enormous army had enough oil supplies once the invasion was underway.

TOP: **American soldiers train for the Normandy landings. Barrage balloons were floated across the Channel to offer some protection against enemy aircraft.**

ABOVE MIDDLE: **General Eisenhower, Supreme Commander of the Allied invasion, plans 'Operation Overlord' from his headquarters in Britain.**

ABOVE: **A 'duck' is loaded onto its transport. These vehicles were ideal for seaborne invasions as they functioned both on land and water.**

ABOVE LEFT: **The American army trains for D-Day at Slapton Sands in Devon. The beach was selected for its similarity to Utah beach.**

MIDDLE LEFT: **General Eisenhower addresses camouflaged paratroopers just before they fly off on their mission to drop behind enemy lines in Normandy in the early hours of D-Day.**

LEFT: **The last items of equipment are loaded onto the transports ahead of D-Day.**

The landings

The overall commander, General Eisenhower, gave the order for the long-awaited attack on the Normandy beaches to begin on June 6, 1944: D-Day. Soon after midnight a vast invasion fleet of nearly 7,000 vessels closed in on the designated beaches, and parachutists and glider-borne troops landed behind German lines in Normandy. At first light, after an initial assault from thousands of aircraft, the invasion proper began.

Five beaches were designated for the landings; the Americans landed at the westernmost beaches, codenamed 'Utah' and 'Omaha', while the British, supported by the Free French, came ashore further east at 'Gold' and 'Sword' beaches. The landing at 'Juno', in the middle of the two British beaches, was undertaken by the Canadian military, under the command of the British.

By the end of the first day some 130,000 men had landed in Occupied France and were able to establish a bridgehead in Normandy. This had come at a cost of many lives, especially at Omaha beach, where the preliminary aerial bombardment had missed the German defences along the sea wall. As the Americans came ashore, the Germans fired relentlessly from their pillboxes, gunning down hundreds of men before the beach was finally taken.

ABOVE: **An aerial view of Omaha beach on the morning of D-Day. Military vehicles attempt to exit the beach while small dots of men and beach obstacles can be seen in the water.**

LEFT AND FAR LEFT: **American troops come ashore in Normandy.**

ABOVE LEFT: **American soldiers await their fate in a 'Higgins Boat' as it approaches Omaha Beach.**

TOP: **Red Cross personnel and British infantry wade onto the beaches on 'D-Day+1', June 7, 1944.**

BELOW: **The Allied armada sets sail for Normandy in the early morning light of June 6, 1944.**

DAILY MAIL, JUNE 7, 1944

The last act

June 6, 1944, will stand as one of the memorable days of all time. Upon this day was launched the greatest act of war in history - the invasion of Europe. This day saw well begun the campaign which will end the war in an Allied victory.

The Germans are beaten, and they begin to know it. Rome was one portentous symbol in their darkening sky. The Allies have the advantage in men, material, morale - everything. On the Eastern Front Russia awaits her moment. No secret weapon or tactical trick can save the Third Reich now.

This is the thought that must be uppermost in our minds as we watch unfolding the gigantic combined operation of the Allied land, sea, and air forces.

'The battle,' says Mr. Churchill, 'will grow constantly in scope and intensity for many weeks to come.' It will go well at one moment and not so well at the next. The fortunes of war will not always favour us.

After nearly five years of mingled triumph and disaster the British people are not likely to be led astray by excessive hope or unreasoning despair. Rather will they respond to the words of the King, who last night asked for a revival of the crusading spirit which sustained us in the dark days.

A great team

There have been warnings from high places. 'A long period of greater effort and fierce fighting lies ahead,' says President Roosevelt. General Eisenhower gives an inspiring Order of the Day to his troops, but, he says: 'Your task will not be an easy one.'

These warnings spring not from apprehension but from a just appraisal of the situation. They are based on the confidence so well expressed by General Montgomery: 'We are a great allied team.'

The mighty forces sweeping across the Channel are equipped with all the best that modern science and ingenuity can provide, and are trained to the last ounce. Supporting them is the terrifying punch of 11,000 war-planes, and transporting them are 4,000 large vessels, besides many thousands of smaller ones, backed by the power of six battleships and numerous other naval craft.

We can but marvel at the extent and intricacy of the operation. Beside these hosts of craft and myriad of aeroplanes, the record armadas of North Africa and Sicily become small.

According to plan

Of the actual fighting we know little, but things are going well. 'The operation is proceeding in a thoroughly satisfactory manner,' says Mr. Churchill, and nothing could be more emphatic. It may be that these landings are among the feints which the Prime Minister mentioned some weeks ago. The Germans appear to expect landings elsewhere. Let them speculate. We are content to wait on events.

Events are inspiring enough. The largest massed airborne landing yet attempted anywhere has been successfully made. Other troops have pushed several miles inland from the beaches.

There will be many conflicting reports in the next few days. Those which do not come from official sources or accredited correspondents should be treated with reserve.

The first three days will be the most critical. If our fine men, who carry with them all our thoughts and hopes, can establish themselves firmly during that time, the first big obstacle will have been victoriously overcome.

LEFT: A snapshot of Omaha beach after the initial landings hints at the vast scale of Operation Overlord. During D-Day, over 130,000 men were brought ashore in nearly 7,000 vessels.

TOP: German prisoners carry an injured comrade as they load onto boats destined for detention camps in Britain.

ABOVE MIDDLE: After facing down German guns, Allied soldiers had to contend with other parts of Germany's coastal defences. Mines and barbed wire were two such impediments which the advancing armies had to contend with.

BELOW MIDDLE: Troops start to move inland after securing a beachhead.

ABOVE: Wooden slat and wire runners are offloaded on the beaches. They were vital for getting the thousands of vehicles off the beaches.

Liberation of France

The Germans were not prepared for the invasion force to come ashore at Normandy. They had been fooled into believing that the attack would come along the coast near Calais by considerable decoy activity. Nevertheless the fighting was bitter and the men encountered stiff resistance across Normandy. Within a few days the Allies began linking up their five beachheads as ever more troops poured ashore. All the plans for increasing and supplying the invasion force worked and, on June 27, American forces captured the port of Cherbourg. On July 8 Caen was taken after fierce fighting and the Allies began to push out of Normandy towards Paris.

A second invasion force landed in the south of France near Toulon on August 15 and drove the Germans northwards along the Rhone valley. In all their advances the Allies were given invaluable assistance by the French Resistance, who harried the retreating Germans. The village of Oradour-sur-Glane in central France was to pay the price for increased resistance activity: members of the 2nd SS Reich Panzer division massacred the entire village on June 10 as they made their way to the front in Normandy.

Liberating troops finally reached Paris on August 24, where serious street fighting had erupted some days earlier. French troops under the command of General Leclerc were given the honour of being the first to enter the city. They were followed a day later by the leader of the Free French, General Charles de Gaulle, who was treated to a rapturous welcome, despite the residual threat of snipers.

ABOVE RIGHT: **Refugees hurry past an upturned German military vehicle and its dead driver in a Brittany village.**

MIDDLE RIGHT: **A French civilian takes her frustrations out on a German prisoner as he is marched through the streets of St-Mihiel at gunpoint.**

BELOW RIGHT: **French villagers watch as German prisoners are marched through the village of Ouistreham, on the Normandy Coast at 'Sword' Beach.**

RIGHT: **Eight days after D-Day, the leader of the Free French, General Charles de Gaulle, lands on the Normandy beaches.**

BELOW INSET: **A German soldier surrenders to the Allies days after the invasion.**

BOTTOM: **German POWs marched through Cherbourg by American troops.**

DAILY MAIL   AUGUST 26, 1944

Germans in Paris surrender

THE battle for Paris is over. General Leclerc's tank columns broke into the capital early yesterday and in less than 12 hours' fighting smashed German resistance. The end came suddenly last evening when Leclerc, according to the Patriot radio, delivered an ultimatum to the general commanding the German garrison. The two, with the Maquis chief of Paris, then went to Montparnasse Station, where the terms of the capitulation were signed.

Under these, the German general at once ordered the cease fire. His men, unarmed, were to assemble at selected points to await orders. Their arms were to be piled and handed over intact.

At about the time Leclerc dictated his terms to the German, and while fighting was still in progress, General de Gaulle entered the city. Huge crowds greeted him with the 'Marseillaise' and cries of 'Vive de Gaulle!' to which he replied: 'I wish simply and from the bottom of my heart to say to you, Vive Paris!'

Later, in a broadcast to the people of Paris, General de Gaulle declared: 'France will take her place among the great nations which will organise the peace. We will not rest until we march, as we must, into enemy territory as conquerors.' De Gaulle said that France has the 'right to insist' that she shall never again be invaded by Germany.

TOP: De Gaulle makes his way through the crowds on the Champs Elysees in Paris.

ABOVE: French armoured divisions pass through the Arc de Triomphe in Paris.

RIGHT: German troops surrender to the Americans at Metz.

BELOW: The spire of Rouen Cathederal towers above a city in ruins.

The Liberation of the Low Countries

From France, the Allies raced into Belgium and liberated Antwerp and Brussels in the first week of September 1944. From Belgium, the Allies could have concentrated their forces on the industrial Ruhr region of Germany, but General Montgomery feared that an attack on the well-defended Siegfried Line would be too costly. Instead, he devised 'Operation Market Garden,' a plan to outflank the Siegfried Line through the Netherlands. His audacious operation involved dropping troops behind enemy lines to capture vital crossing points over a series of Dutch rivers and then following through with a swift ground invasion. The early stages were successful, but the British 1st Airborne Division met with strong German resistance at Arnhem on the Lower Rhine. The overland troops sent to relieve them were held up and then withdrawn, having sustained heavy casualties. Operation Market Garden was called off and the northern Netherlands remained under German control until the last months of the war. The Germans finally surrendered the country on May 5, 1945, just days before the end of the war.

ABOVE RIGHT: **Paratroopers get ready to jump from their plane behind enemy lines in Occupied Holland.**

MIDDLE RIGHT: **The Belgian Brigade, an independent infantry group formed in Britain, enter Brussels.**

BELOW RIGHT: **A soldier miraculously survives as a shell explodes right next to him at Arnhem.**

LEFT: **Allied paratroops deploy during Operation Market Garden.**

TOP LEFT: British troops advance on Venray, a transport hub in the Netherlands.

MIDDLE LEFT: American troops help salvage possessions from homes set alight by the retreating Germans.

TOP RIGHT: The British Second Army patrol through the Dutch town of Susteren.

MIDDLE RIGHT: A smiling Belgian woman accompanies a British soldier as he marches a group of captured Germans through Antwerp.

ABOVE: German prisoners watch as British tanks pour into Belgium.

BELOW: British troops crawl from house to house through a Dutch village.

DAILY MAIL   SEPTEMBER 26, 1944

Arnhem front

Alexander Clifford, in a delayed cable, tells below the story of the first corridor battle.

The Germans have tried the obvious thing. They cut through our corridor behind us, and - if you like to put it that way - technically surrounded us.

The moment came at noon on Friday. It was a long time before anyone worked out exactly what happened. But the effective news was that German tanks and infantry were across our lines about 17 miles north of Eindhoven. All convoys must halt. The attack came from Germany itself. It may have been combined with an attempt to rescue some of the estimated 70,000 Germans who are partly cut off in Western Holland. Its main purpose was certainly to cut the axis.

From that moment the campaign abandoned all the rules again and became a series of personal adventures of each individual. For many truck drivers it meant sitting patiently by the roadside and listening to the firing ahead. For the men on the Arnhem front it meant the queer feeling that they were no longer fighting at the end of lines of supply but were temporarily in a military vacuum. For me it meant that I was cut off from my kit, which I had left in a little inn in the village where the Germans had attacked. It had been a gay, clean little inn, with an innkeeper who still managed to provide comfort and good Dutch food. And now the German mortars were falling on it.

Good humour

For the men on that section of the road it meant a sudden inferno of battle at a spot technically 30 miles behind our front lines. British and German trucks were blazing along the road and out into the fields. The possibility had been clearly enough foreseen. We always knew we could deal with anything of the sort if it occurred, and around Nijmegen there was a great deal of good-humoured banter as people who had been cut off began to go round trying to find billets for the night.

In the desert one would have joined some unit and slept in its laager. Here in civilised Europe one hardly knew what to do. In the end I and those with me decided to sleep on the billiards tables of a wayside pub. We ate sumptuously off German rations which we found in a train at Nijmegen railway station.

The night was a succession of wild alarms. Dutchmen, either honestly misinformed or deliberate Fifth Columnists, kept streaming in to tell us that the Germans were a mile away, that the British were evacuating Nijmegen, and so forth. None of it was remotely true. But the whole position was so unorthodox that it was understandable.

There was plenty of shooting during the night. But as often happens near the front, when morning came no one knew what it had been about. The only certain news was that the Germans were still across our path. Tanks had been sent to deal with them.

I followed down behind the leading patrol. It was necessary to reach that little inn quickly if any of my kit was to be saved. The Germans were reported to have been in the village itself for quite a few hours.

The ruptured stretch of axis was a trail of wrecked vehicles. It was almost like Normandy again, for the fields were strewn with dead cows. The tarmac was churned to dust where swerving tanks had ground it up. Half a dozen cottages along the way were still burning.

Methodical

While our patrol was still passing through all this we looked up and saw a new mighty phase of this three dimensional campaign. The sky filled fuller than I have ever seen it with planes and gliders. They came low, flying in steady and majestic patterns. They were simply reinforcements for the front. The Germans began to shoot at them. It was alarming to hear how near the Germans still were to the centre-line of our axis. They were firing from the nearest woods two fields away and their bullets were spangling the cloudy sky all round the great air fleet.

They got some hits. Extraordinarily few in the circumstances, but they could hardly help getting some. A towing plane began to burn and circled from the rest. Two or three gliders slipped loose and swung round towards what they knew were our lines.

But the Germans had given their positions away and firing broke out savagely once more from our land forces. A battle started chaotically among the fields and copses and farmhouses round about. It looked chaotic. But there was plenty of method in the way the Germans were being elbowed aside. You could piece it all together by watching the positions of the tanks along the roads and the places where the anti-tank guns were being dug in and the columns of smoke where our shells were falling.

And then we came to the gay, neat little village in whose inn we had left all our kit. Now it was empty and splintered and broken. It was grey with a pall of dust. Its streets were a tapestry of fallen branches and loose tiles and scattered bricks.

The inn itself was windowless and derelict. The innkeeper and his family were alive - they were down in the cellar steadfastly singing hymns. Almost everything they possessed was broken. Their yard was full of dead chickens. We dug what remained of our things out of the wreckage of our bedrooms. An American paratrooper came and told us to be quick about it, the village still wasn't very healthy.

Soviet advances in the east

The Soviet victory at Stalingrad in January 1943 marked a reversal of fortunes in the East. Within weeks the Red Army had liberated Kharkov and Kursk, but the Wehrmacht was not yet entirely on the defensive, and managed to recapture Kharkov one month later. In July 1943, Hitler launched an enormous offensive to retake Kursk and deal a resounding blow to the Red Army. 'Operation Citadel' as the attack was codenamed, was the largest tank battle in history, with more than 6,000 taking part in total. Despite suffering heavy losses, the Red Army won the battle and began an unrelenting march westward towards Berlin.

After Kursk, Soviet cities were liberated one after another; Kharkov was taken for the second time in August, followed by Smolensk in September and Kiev in November. The Soviet advance continued throughout early 1944, and by June, the Red Army had reached Belarus. Although the key to the Red Army's success was sheer manpower, it also benefited from a superior number of tanks and aircraft. Minsk fell on July 3 — along with 100,000 German prisoners— and by the end of the month they had advanced into eastern Poland. On October 1, with the Red Army just miles away, the residents of Warsaw rose up in rebellion against German rule. However, Stalin halted the Russian advance and left the fighters, who were largely anti-Communist, to their fate. German revenge was terrible and some 200,000 Poles died. When the Soviet Union did finally enter Warsaw in January 1945, it was far from the liberation that most Poles had hoped for.

Conspiracy against Hitler

With the Allies closing in on both fronts, it seemed that Germany's defeat might be within sight. This undoubtedly encouraged conspirators within the German army to go ahead with plans to assassinate the Fuehrer. With Germany standing on the edge of an abyss, some German generals, who had always been lukewarm about Nazism, believed peace should be made with the Western Allies so the army could concentrate on keeping the Soviets from advancing on the Reich. One of the officers, Count von Stauffenberg, who was attached to Hitler's general staff, placed a bomb under a table at his headquarters in East Prussia on July 20, 1944. However, the bomb failed to kill Hitler and the conspirators were 'strung up like cattle' upon his orders.

OPPOSITE LEFT: Residents of Kursk return to their homes in March 1943 after the city had been liberated by the Red Army. The city would once again see heavy fighting when Hitler launched Operation Citadel in July 1943.

OPPOSITE ABOVE RIGHT: Soviet troops install an anti-aircraft gun in Kharkov after its first liberation in February 1944. The Germans recaptured the city the following month.

OPPOSITE BELOW RIGHT: Anti-aircraft gunners take up a position in Kharkov after liberating the city for a second time in August 1944.

OPPOSITE BELOW: The Red Army on the offensive in northern Russia.

LEFT: The people of Rostov pours onto the streets to celebrate the liberation of their city.

BELOW LEFT: A Russian soldier takes cover amongst the rubble as the Red Army attempt to lift the siege of Leningrad.

BELOW: Soviet troops continue westward after lifting the siege of Leningrad.

The Siege of Leningrad

During the war Leningrad (St. Petersburg) was subjected to one of the longest sieges in modern history. The city was blocked-off by the German army from September 1941 until January 1943, during which time more than a million people died of starvation. The Soviets were able to get some supplies in and civilians out across Lake Ladoga, but convoys ran the gauntlet of German guns and millions remained trapped and starving inside the city. In January 1943, the Red Army launched Operation Iskra, a major offensive which punched a hole through the German siege lines within days. Fighting around the city continued for another year until the German army was forced to retreat in January 1944.

DAILY MAIL JANUARY 19, 1943

Leningrad free

The siege of Leningrad, second city of Russia, which has been blockaded by the German armies for more than 16 months, has been raised. Russian troops storming across the Neva River have smashed through the enemy's mighty defence zone and advanced 45 miles.

This tremendous news was given to the world in a special Moscow communiqué last night. A second special communiqué announced equally momentous successes on the southern front. Here Russian troops have crossed both the Donetz and Manych rivers - last great natural barriers protecting Rostov. Today the road to Rostov lies open. Thousands more prisoners have been taken on both these fronts; more towns captured in the North Caucasus, and the encircled German army at Stalingrad split in two.

South of Voronezh the enemy are falling back, abandoning their equipment and large quantities of supplies. Over 1,000 motor vehicles were captured intact on one stretch of road.

Here are the texts from the communiqués: A few days ago our troops concentrated south of Lake Ladoga launched an offensive against the German Fascist troops besieging Leningrad. They were given the task of destroying the enemy defences and thereby lifting the siege of Leningrad. It must be borne in mind that during the many months of the siege of Leningrad the Germans converted their positions on the approaches to the city into a strongly fortified area consisting of concrete emplacements and other fortifications.

The offensive of our troops was launched from two directions - from the western bank of River Neva, south-west and south-east of Schluesselburg, and from the east from the area south of Lake Ladoga. Having breached the enemy's defences, which extended to a depth of about nine miles, and having crossed the Neva, our troops in the course of seven days of severe fighting occupies the town of Schluesselburg. They also seized the large fortified points of Maryino Moskovskaya-Dubrobskaya, and Lipka; eight workers settlements and the railway stations of Sinyavino and Podgornaya.

Thus, after the first battles, the troops of the Volkhov and Leningrad fronts joined up on January 18, and broke through the investment of Leningrad. According to incomplete data our troops took prisoner 1,261 officers and men. In the course of the battle our artillery and mortars destroyed 470 fortified centres and block-houses, 25 strongly equipped observation posts, and 172 artillery and mortar batteries were silenced.

The break-through was carried out partly by the forces of the Leningrad front commanded by General Govorov and partly by the forces of the Volkhov front commanded by Army General Meretskov. Co-ordination of action of troops on both fronts was achieved by the representatives of Supreme Headquarters. Marshals of the Soviet Union Zhukov and Voroshilov.

Island-hopping

After securing Guadalcanal and New Guinea in 1943 the Americans continued with their offensives in the Pacific, jumping from island to island moving ever closer to Japan in a strategy known as 'island-hopping'. In the summer of 1944 the US liberated Saipan, Guam and Tinian in the Marianas Island chain, and the invasion of Peleliu and Angaur in the Palau island group followed shortly after. The capture of these islands helped put America's B-29 bombers within range of Japan's main island, and from June 1944 the US Army Air Force began a bombing campaign against Japanese cities with the intention of forcing the country into submission. In 1945 the bombing became relentless, especially in Tokyo, where thousands of people were killed in firebombing raids, but the Japanese government still refused to surrender.

TOP: In September 1944, US troops wade ashore almost unopposed on Morotai, one of the Moluccas Islands in the Dutch East Indies.

ABOVE: An American tank rolls through Garapan, the main city on Saipan island after the Japanese had been pushed out in July 1944.

ABOVE LEFT: Marines take cover as they meet with Japanese mortar fire on the beaches of Peleliu in the Palau island group.

LEFT: A long line of amphibious tanks come ashore at Tinian Island in the Marianas chain, August 1944.

BELOW: With the help of a jeep, US troops push an anti-tank gun ashore on the island of Angaur in the Palau group.

Battle for the Philippines

The United States had shared a close relationship with the Philippines ever since the islands were ceded to Washington at the end of the Spanish-American War of 1898. Thousands of American troops were in the Philippines when the Japanese invaded within hours of the attack on Pearl Harbor. Many were captured and, together with Filipino POWs, they were forced to endure an infamous death march to their internment camp in Bataan. The battle to liberate the Philippines from Japanese rule began on October 20, 1944 when US troops under the command of General Douglas MacArthur landed on the island of Leyte. The Japanese attempted to obstruct the landings in what became the largest naval battle of the entire war. The US scored a decisive victory, neutralizing the Japanese navy and allowing US and Australian forces to steadily recapture the Philippines. The Battle for Manila began in February 1945 and ended up being the only major urban battle fought in the Pacific campaign. Fighting was fierce and it took American soldiers more than one month to secure the city. By the time it fell on March 3, thousands of civilians had been killed and the city was almost utterly destroyed.

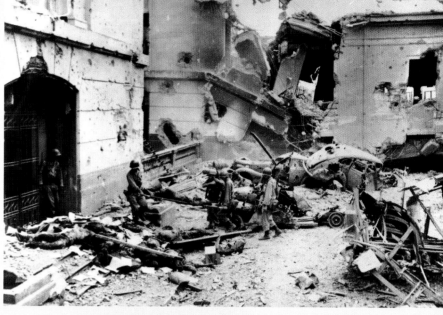

ABOVE: **An American soldier is carried by stretcher past the bodies of dead Japanese soldiers to a dressing station set up amid the debris of Manila city hall.**

LEFT: **An aerial view of the devastation caused during the fight for Manila. It was to be the only major urban battle of the Pacific campaign.**

BELOW: **Plumes of smoke rise above Manila during fierce fighting between US and Japanese forces in February 1945.**

Hitler's last stand

Although the Allies had made great strides through France and Belgium, Hitler would not accept the inevitability of defeat. A fresh offensive was planned in the Ardennes where the Allied line was weakest and his new 'wonder' weapons were ready to rain down a new terror upon London.

Battle of the Bulge

The German army launched its attack in the Ardennes in mid-December 1944. The plan was to split the Allied forces in two and create a corridor to the sea at Antwerp. The Allies managed to halt the advance on Antwerp, but not before it created a large bulge in the Allied line. The Wehrmacht found itself up against the might of the United States army and air force and by January the attack had waned. The attack only served to delay the Allied invasion of Germany temporarily and came at a cost of thousands of German lives.

TOP: **Refugees flee from the Germans' December 1944 offensive in the Ardennes.**

ABOVE MIDDLE: **A small infantry group of the US 82nd Airborne ambush a German patrol near Bra in Belgium.**

ABOVE: **Allied troops cycle past damage done to the town of Bastogne during the German offensive.**

ABOVE LEFT: **German soldiers lie dead in the snow after attempting to storm Allied positions at Bastogne in Belgium during the 'Battle of the Bulge'.**

LEFT: **Members of the US Third Army, under the command of General Patton, advance on Houffalize in Belgium.**

BELOW: **The frozen body of a German soldier lies in the snow near Nefte. Many Germans questioned the wisdom of the Ardennes offensive, which cost many lives and diverted resources from the Eastern front.**

'Wonder weapons'

In addition to his offensive in the Ardennes, Hitler had placed his faith in a new generation of secret weapons that would, he believed, inflict devastating damage on Britain. The first of these was the V1, a pilotless flying bomb, which began falling on London and South East England from June 1944. They caused casualties and heavy damage, as well as a dip in morale since most people had thought that the dangers of the Blitz had passed. They also somewhat helped Hitler reverse his rapidly declining popularity at home. Many Germans wanted retribution for the relentless Allied bombing campaign and Hitler's new weapon offered just that; the letter V was short for 'Vergeltung' the German word for revenge. The threat from the V1 decreased as the Allied troops overran the launch sites in northern France. Between June and early September, it is thought that almost 7,000 were launched; over half were destroyed before reaching their intended targets.

London came under attack from another German 'wonder' weapon, the V2, from September onwards. These, in contrast to the V1s, were long-range rockets and were fired from sites in places still controlled by the Nazis. The renewed threat from the skies revived the need to evacuate children from the threatened areas, and some 200,000 mothers and their children were forced to leave London. Nevertheless, Hitler's 'wonder weapons' were too little too late. Hitler had promised the German public great things from his 'wonder weapons', and when it became obvious that they would not alter the outcome of the war, the Nazis lost whatever public support they still had.

DAILY MAIL NOVEMBER 9, 1944

V2 Terror in London

Hour by hour last night Germany put out claims that V2 is causing widespread damage in London. Here, said radio spokesmen, was a long-range weapon more dangerous than V1. They said it had destroyed Euston Station, smashed a railway bridge, and devastated five named areas.

Goebbels seized on V2 as a morale builder to replace the anniversary celebrations of the Munich beer cellar putsch, abandoned this year for the first time.

The weapon - neutral sources have described it as a rocket-shell 'like a flying telegraph pole with a trail of flame behind it' - was said to have been in use for some weeks. But Berlin made no mention of it until yesterday.

First came a brief reference in the High Command's communiqué and then a spate of boosting radio reports and commentaries. Among all the claims there was one significant admission - that the launching of the 'deadly weapon' caused sacrifices 'among the crews.'

The Germans claimed to be in possession of full information of the damage caused by V2. 'The British Government,' said one radio spokesman, 'has so far concealed from its people that a more effective, more telling, and therefore more dangerous long-range weapon has been in action in addition to the so-called flying bomb, which everyone knows about now.

'The German Command possess exact reports on the success and the effect of V2. If they required further proof of its accuracy, official British reports have supplied it by announcing, after nights in which London was exclusively attacked with V2, that flying bombs had again been over the capital.

'For the time being nothing further can be made known about the technical details of this missile. According to reports from England, the characteristic feature of the new weapon is that it cannot be heard or seen before its extraordinarily heavy detonation.'

Reports from Sweden and other neutral countries have credited V2 with a range of between 200 and 300 miles and a warhead of something under a ton of high explosive. Bases in Germany, Holland, Denmark, and Norway have been claimed as feasible for attacks on Britain. A rocket, it is said, would have to rise some 50 miles into the sky to achieve any considerable range, and it would travel at well over 700 miles per hour.

ABOVE LEFT: **A tragic image reveals the aftermath of a V-2 attack on the Belgian coast.**

ABOVE: **Rescue workers pull casualties from the wreckage caused by a V-2 bombing of Smithfield Market in London in April 1945.**

LEFT: **An anti-aircraft gun shoots down Hitler's 'wonder weapons' over Belgium.**

Iwo Jima

On February 19, 1945 the 3rd, 4th and 5th divisions of the United States Marine Corps staged an amphibious invasion of Iwo Jima, an island some 700 miles south of Tokyo. The fighting was among the fiercest in the Pacific theatre, costing almost 7,000 American lives, making it the deadliest battle in the history of the US Marine Corps. Countless more Japanese died as they defended the island to the death, first engaging the marines in the open and later resisting from hiding place in caves. The battle ended on March 26, by which time 27 American servicemen had performed acts of bravery that would later win them the Medal of Honor.

TOP: **The marines move up the beach under the shadow of the extinct volcano, Mount Suribachi.**

ABOVE: **Marines of the 4th Division storm the shores of Iwo Jima..**

LEFT: **An aerial view of the American invasion force approaching the shore of Iwo Jima, February 19, 1945.**

BELOW: **The American flag is raised on Mount Suribachi on February 23, 1945.**

OPPOSITE ABOVE RIGHT: **US marines attempt to flush Japanese soldiers out of a cave on Okinawa.**

OPPOSITE MIDDLE RIGHT: **Marines brace themselves as they detonate a satchel charge in a cave used by the Japanese to attack their positions on Okinawa.**

OPPOSITE BELOW RIGHT: **After capturing the Marianas islands in 1944, the US established several large military bases from where B-29 Superfortress bombers could attack the Japanese home islands.**

OPPOSITE LEFT: **Three marines kneel to pray in their fox holes in a rare quiet moment during the Iwo Jima campaign.**

OPPOSITE BELOW: **The cemetery of the Fifth Marine Division on Iwo Jima. Almost 7,000 American servicemen lost their lives in the battle for the island.**

Okinawa

In mid-March as the Battle for Iwo Jima was drawing to a close, the US began the next offensive against the island of Okinawa. At just over 300 miles from Kyushu, the southernmost of Japan's four main islands, Okinawa was to be a springboard for the invasion of Japan proper. After a week long 'softening up' bombardment from the air, US troops of the Tenth Army came ashore largely unopposed. However, the Japanese were lying in wait at better-defended locations and the battle soon became a bloodbath. It took the US almost three months to wrestle control of the island and defeat the Japanese, who once again fought to the death. Unlike Iwo Jima, Okinawa had a large civilian population, which had been warned by Japanese propaganda not to expect any mercy from the Americans. Such scaremongering had terrible consequences; thousands of civilians committed suicide and thousands more died in the fighting. By the end of the battle an estimated 100,000 Japanese and 12,000 American servicemen had lost their lives.

Advancing through Germany

The early months of 1945 saw events moving fast, as the German will to fight on began to diminish. Throughout January the Russian armies advanced remorselessly upon the country from the east, liberating the Nazi concentration camp at Auschwitz on January 27. By now it was obvious to almost everyone involved that the final defeat of Germany was inevitable and imminent and Roosevelt, Churchill and Stalin met at Yalta in the Crimea to discuss the post-war division of Germany between February 4–11.

On April 14, the Red Army took Vienna and then turned its attention towards Berlin. The Russians crossed the Oder and two armies encircled Berlin on April 25. They joined to the west and then turned back towards the semi-ruined city, now devastated by artillery bombardment as well as by heavy bombing. Meanwhile the Allies were pushing on to the Rhineland and American troops captured the bridge at Remagen intact on March 7, at last establishing a much-needed bridgehead across the Rhine. Other Allied crossings were made and their forces now moved much further into Germany. American troops were just sixty miles from Berlin by 12 April.

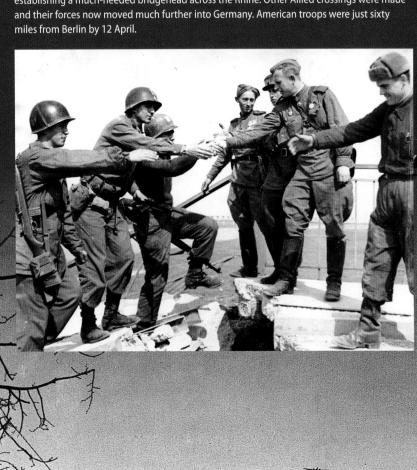

DAILY MAIL MARCH 9, 1945

The Rhine crossed

We've done it. Early this morning strong infantry forces of General Hodge's American First Army are streaming across the Rhine into our newly won bridgehead on the east bank of the river. The final drive to meet the Russian armies in the heart of Germany - the last heave to end the war - has begun.

You can throw your hats in the air to-day. The success of our lightning stroke undoubtedly shortens the war by months. We are massing substantial forces in our rapidly expanding bridgehead 290 miles from Berlin.

This historic moment in the war came at 4.30 p.m. on Wednesday, when a spearhead task force of the First Army crossed the river in a sudden thrust which took the Germans completely by surprise. The crossing was made between Bonn and Coblenz. Opposition was light. Once on the other side the Americans spread out to get elbow-room. Then our main forces poured over. Before their tremendous onslaught the German defences cracked - then collapsed like a pack of cards.

More and more men swarmed across the river, and swiftly, efficiently, the bridgehead was built up.

OPPOSITE TOP RIGHT: **Stalin and Roosevelt discuss the post-war settlement in Europe at the Yalta Conference in February 1945.**

OPPOSITE ABOVE MIDDLE RIGHT: **Russian POWs show their gratitude to one of the American GIs who liberated their prison camp.**

OPPOSITE BELOW RIGHT: **Civilians in the German city of Rheydt, birthplace of Joseph Goebbels, cautiously emerge with white flags as the Americans approach.**

OPPOSITE LEFT: **American and Soviet troops link up for the first time at Torgau on the River Elbe on April 25, 1945.**

OPPOSITE BELOW: **While bridges were being constructed across the Rhine, thousands of paratroops were dropped into Germany by the largest airborne fleet ever assembled for a single mission. German civilians watch in amazement as the fleet, stretching some 500 miles, passes overhead.**

TOP: **Russian soldiers advance across open fields in Germany.**

ABOVE LEFT: **British troops pass the bodies of dead Germans as they move along the eastern bank of the Rhine.**

ABOVE FAR LEFT: **A fourteen-year-old boy is taken prisoner by the Allies. As the Allies closed in, Hitler futilely ordered that children help defend the Reich.**

ABOVE: **Winston Churchill crosses the Rhine with American troops and General Montgomery.**

BELOW: **As the German army retreated from the advancing Allies, they destroyed most of the bridges across the Rhine. Engineers had to build makeshift bridges so the Allies could cross into Germany.**

YOU ARE NOW CROSSING THE RHINE RIVER THROUGH COURTESY OF 'E' CO. 17 ARMD. ENGR. BN. AND 'C' CO. 202 ENGR. C. BN.

The Holocaust

The Nazi regime subscribed to the belief that the German people sat atop of a global racial hierarchy and that other races – particularly Jews but also Gypsies and Slavs – were inferior and a threat to German racial purity. After they came to power in 1933, the Nazis began an incremental process of government-sponsored persecution against the country's Jewish population. They passed laws to deny Jews of their citizenship, to forbid them from marrying Aryans and to force them out of their jobs and businesses. The night of November 9, 1938, 'Kristallnacht', witnessed the first coordinated nationwide attack against Jews; many of Germany's synagogues were damaged and people were rounded up and sent to concentration camps. The following year, the war intervened and Germany's treatment of the Jews took an even deadlier turn.

ABOVE RIGHT: **Polish Jews are rounded up in Warsaw and marched to a concentration camp in March 1940.**

MIDDLE RIGHT: **German soldiers massacre Jews in newly-occupied Poland in retaliation for the death of a German soldier.**

BELOW RIGHT: **The Warsaw Ghetto burns as the Nazis try to suppress the uprising in April 1943.**

BELOW: **British soldiers liberated Belsen concentration camp on April 15. Thousands of people were found still alive but threatened by typhus, typhoid and dysentery, which were running rampant in the camp.**

Final Solution

From October 1939, as the Nazis consolidated their control of Poland, the country's large Jewish population was forced to live in walled-off ghettoes where thousands of people died of starvation and disease. After the invasion of the Soviet Union in June 1941, the Nazis began directly killing Jews using mobile killing units called 'Einsatzgruppen', which murdered more than one million men, women and children behind the German lines. In late 1941 the Nazis began constructing death camps and by early 1942 they had decided upon a 'Final Solution': the extermination of all the Jews of Europe. Millions of people were sent to death camps such as Auschwitz, Treblinka, Sobibor and Belzec, where they were murdered in specially designed gas chambers. The 'lucky ones' were sent to work camps, where they faced gruelling labour and death from disease, hunger and maltreatment. By 1945, as Allied soldiers closed in on the camps, thousands of inmates were moved by train or on forced 'death marches' to prevent them from being liberated and to prolong their suffering. By the time the war was over, more than six million Jews had lost their lives, which is an estimated two thirds of Europe's pre-war Jewish population.

In addition, the Nazis dehumanized, detained and murdered hundreds of thousands of other people deemed to be racially undesirable or politically unsound. These groups included gypsies, homosexuals and Communists, as well as people with physical or mental illnesses who were also subjected to forcible sterilizations as part of a campaign of so-called 'racial hygiene'.

ABOVE RIGHT: A mountain of shoes belonging to the deceased inmates of Belsen are used for fuel.

FAR RIGHT: A snapshot of life around a water pump in a Nazi concentration camp after its liberation.

RIGHT: Josef Kramer, the 'Beast of Belsen', was the only senior officer remaining at the camp when it was liberated by the British. He was put on trial and hanged in December 1945.

BELOW: During 1945 the full extent of Nazi atrocities was slowly realized. Here shallow graves have been discovered in woods ouside Luneburg, Germany. A train on its way to Belsen stopped near the city and some prisoners were instructed to get out and bury those who had died in the overcrowded wagons during the journey. Those who dug the graves were shot dead by the guards and buried with the rest.

DAILY MAIL MAY 9, 1945
VE Day - it's all over

London, dead from six until nine, suddenly broke into victory life last night. Suddenly, spontaneously, deliriously. The people of London, denied VE-Day officially, held their own jubilation. 'VE-Day may be tomorrow,' they said, 'but the war is over to-night.' Bonfires blazed from Piccadilly to Wapping.

The sky once lit by the glare of the blitz shone red with the Victory glow. The last trains departed from the West End unregarded. The pent-up spirits of the throng, the polyglot throng that is London in war-time, burst out, and by 11 o'clock the capital was ablaze with enthusiasm.

Processions formed up out of nowhere, disintegrating for no reason, to re-form somewhere else. Waving flags, marching in step, with linked arms or half-embraced, the people strode down the great thoroughfares - Piccadilly, Regent-street, the Mall, to the portals of Buckingham Palace.

They marched and counter-marched so as not to get too far from the centre. And from them, in harmony and discord, rose song. The songs of the last war, the songs of a century ago. The songs of the beginning of this war - 'Roll out the Barrel' and 'Tipperary'; 'Ilkla Moor' and 'Loch Lomond'; 'Bless 'em All' and 'Pack Up Your Troubles.'

ABOVE RIGHT: **VE Day in London.** Thousands gather for celebrations in Trafalgar Square.

RIGHT: **VE Day in Moscow.** Aircraft searchlights are used to light up the night sky.

BELOW: **VE Day in New York.** Thousands of people pour into Times Square in celebration of Germany's unconditional surrender.

Victory in Europe

By mid-April 1945, Russian troops were fighting their way through Berlin street by street, heading towards the Reichstag. Hitler had ordered 'fanatic determination' from all Germans in the defence of Berlin. However, he retreated to his underground bunker on April 16 and began to lose his grip on reality. On April 30, after nominating Admiral Karl Doenitz as his successor and blaming the Jews for the war, Hitler and his new wife Eva Braun committed suicide. On the same day, above ground, the battle for Berlin was won and the Soviet flag fluttered atop the ruins of the Reichstag building. The following day Hitler's propaganda minister Joseph Goebbels and his wife supervised the deaths of their six children before killing themselves. The remains of the German armies now began to surrender and, on May 7, General Eisenhower formally accepted the unconditional surrender of Germany. VE Day was celebrated across the world the following day, but the world was not yet at peace.

ABOVE RIGHT: **Street parties were held in towns and villages across Britain. Five and a half years of war had taken its its toll on the British public, and shortages and rationing would continue for several years.**

ABOVE FAR RIGHT: **Revellers pile onto a van as it drives through the crowds in Parliament Square, London, on VE Day.**

RIGHT: **With Britain and America pounding the city from above, and the Soviets attacking on the ground, Berlin is left as a shell of its former self.**

ABOVE: **The Soviet Union holds its official victory parade in Red Square, Moscow, on June 24.**

BELOW: **The Reichstag, the symbolic heart of Berlin, lies in ruins after the war.**

Victory in Japan

While victory was being celebrated in Europe, the war against Japan was still raging, but here too the Allies were pushing steadily forward. British forces finally liberated Burma from Japanese control on August 2, 1945, and the American push through the Pacific was bringing US troops gradually closer to Japan.

Roosevelt had died suddenly on April 12 and the new President, Harry Truman, was confronted with the challenging task of winning the war in the Far East. In July 1946, America successfully tested the first nuclear device and it was up to Truman to decide whether this potentially devastating piece of military technology should be used in the Pacific Theatre. Truman realized how costly an invasion of the Japanese mainland would be; he had been given a foretaste when an estimated 12,000 Americans died taking Okinawa Island in March. He was also aware that the Allies were exhausted and that many people had lost focus on the Pacific campaign amid the jubilation of the victory in Europe. In addition, the Soviet Union was preparing to declare war on Japan and Truman was keen to stem Stalin's influence in the region. All these considerations encouraged Truman to take the momentous decision to use the bomb.

Dropping the atom bombs

On August 6, 1945 an American B29 Superfortress, the Enola Gay, flew high above the Japanese city of Hiroshima. It dropped an atomic bomb that exploded above the city with devastating effects. Most of Hiroshima was utterly destroyed and over 78,000 people were killed instantly, but there was still no surrender. Three days later a second bomb was dropped over the city of Nagasaki, killing 24,000. The previous day, August 8, Russia finally declared war on Japan and invaded Manchuria, which meant the Japanese were faced with a brand-new front. The Japanese government became locked in a dispute over whether or not to capitulate.

Finally on August 15, Emperor Hirohito announced Japan's unconditional surrender.

DAILY MAIL AUGUST 8, 1945
City of 300,000 vanishes

Hiroshima, Japanese city of 300,000 people, ceased to exist at 9.15 on Monday morning. While going about its business in the sunshine of a hot summer day, it vanished in a huge ball of fire and a cloud of boiling smoke - obliterated by the first atom bomb to be used in the history of world warfare.

Such is the electrifying report of the American crew of the Super-Fortress which dropped the bomb as a cataclysmic warning to the Japs to get out of the war or be destroyed. Hiroshima, the whole crew agreed, was blotted out by a lash more brilliant than the sun.

They told their astonishing story here at Guam to-day. The explosion, they said, was tremendous and awe-inspiring. The words 'Oh my God' burst from every man as they watched a whole city blasted into rubble. Although they were ten miles away from the catastrophe, they felt the concussion like a close explosion of A.A. fire.

The men had been told to expect a blinding flash. They wore special black goggles. Only three of them knew what type of bomb was being dropped. 'It was hard to believe what we saw.' That was how Col. Paul W. Tibbits, pilot of the Super-Fort, described the explosion.

He said: 'We dropped the bomb at exactly 9.15 a.m. and got out of the target area as quickly as possible to avoid the full effect of the explosion. We stayed in the target area two minutes. The smoke rose to a height of 40,000ft.

'Only Captain Parsons, the observer; Major Ferebee, the bombardier; and myself knew what was dropped. All the others knew was that it was a special weapon. We knew at once we had got to get the hell out of there. I made a sharp turn in less than half a minute to get broadside to the target.

'All of us in the plane felt the heat from the brilliant flash and the concussion from the blast. 'Nothing was visible where only minutes before there was the outline of a city, with its streets and buildings and piers clearly to be seen. 'Soon fires sprang up on the edge of the city, but the city itself was entirely obscured.'

OPPOSITE ABOVE: Nagasaki, after the bomb.

OPPOSITE LEFT: A survivor walks amid the scorched wreckage of Hiroshima.

OPPOSITE RIGHT: A huge mushroom cloud rises 20,000 feet above Nagasaki, August 9, 1945.

ABOVE: The city of Hiroshima pictured after its obliteration.

FAR LEFT ABOVE: Troops from America and New Zealand hold a British policeman aloft on VJ Day. It was the middle of the night in Britain when Japan surrendered and the celebrations started. They continue well into the daylight hours.

FAR LEFT BELOW: Japan signs its official surrender to the British in Burma on September 12, 1945.

LEFT: Three months after VE Day, people once again pour onto the streets of Allied cities in celebration of VJ day.

Peace

On July 17, 1945 the Allied leaders met at Potsdam near Berlin. Churchill and Stalin met with the new US President, Harry Truman, and during the conference, Churchill was replaced with Clement Attlee, the new British Prime Minister. He had defeated Churchill in a General Election on July 5 with the promise of nationalizing major industries and introducing a welfare state. At Potsdam, the Allied leaders agreed that Germany would be disarmed, 'de-nazified' and divided into four zones of occupation, controlled by Britain, the United States, the Soviet Union and France.

'Iron Curtain'

A final peace agreement was never signed and the Second World War soon gave way to the Cold War. The erstwhile Allies could not agree on the post-war make-up of Europe because of the ideological gulf between them. In southern and western Europe, Britain and America promoted democracy, free trade and anti-Communism, while in Eastern Europe, the Soviet Union imposed centrally planned economies and Communist governments. According to Winston Churchill an 'iron curtain' had descended across Europe. A final resolution to the Second World War in Europe would elude the world until after the fall of the Berlin Wall and the collapse of Communism at the end of the 1980s.

In the Pacific Theatre a peace treaty was more forthcoming. Japan was placed under American military occupation from 1945 until 1952. In the early 1950s, the United States had to turn its attention to the war in Korea and sought a peace treaty with Japan. The Treaty of San Francisco was signed in September 1951, officially ending the War in the Pacific when it came into effect the following April.

ABOVE RIGHT: **Prime Minister Winston Churchill meets the new American President, Harry Truman for the first time at Potsdam on the outskirts of Berlin.**

RIGHT: **Eisenhower returns to a hero's welcome as crowds throng Broadway in New Yorks in the hope of seeing the general.**

FAR RIGHT: **The devastated city of Tokyo is pictured from the heavily-defended US embassy in September 1945.**

BELOW: **On a trip to Berlin, Churchill sits on a chair that was said to have been in Hitler's bunker.**

OPPOSITE ABOVE LEFT: **Stalin acknowledges a British Guard of Honour as he makes his way to the British residences at Potsdam for a dinner party hosted by Churchill.**

OPPOSITE MIDDLE LEFT: **In a sign of things to come, a large portrait of Stalin hangs outside the Adlon Hotel in Berlin in July 1945.**

OPPOSITE BELOW LEFT: **Two women walk past a Russian roadsign on the Kurfürstendamm in Berlin as life returns to something near normal.**

OPPOSITE RIGHT: **The defendants listen as the verdicts are read out at Nuremburg on October 1, 1946.**

OPPOSITE BOTTOM: **During a memorial service in Cardiff, the remains of fallen American heroes are loaded aboard the USS *Lawrence Victory* bound for home.**

The Nuremberg trials

Once the war was over, there was widespread agreement that the Nazi leaders should be brought to trial as war criminals. Some of them had escaped in the confusion of the final days of the war, and others like Goebbels and Hitler himself had avoided retribution for their actions by committing suicide. Those who had been captured were brought before an International War Crimes Court. This met at Nuremberg in November 1945 and sat for several months, during which time it considered enormous amounts of evidence and heard very many witnesses. Of the twenty-one defendants, three were acquitted, seven received prison sentences ranging from ten years to life and the remainder were sentenced to death. The most notable among those to be executed were Field Marshal Goering and Joachim von Ribbentrop, the German Foreign Minister. Hours before he was due to be hung, Goering committed suicide by swallowing a cyanide capsule which he had managed to keep hidden, but on October 16, 1946 the executions of the others took place. Their bodies, together with that of Goering, were taken to Munich to be cremated and, according to the official announcement, their ashes were 'scattered in a river somewhere in Germany'.

Chinese Civil War 1945-1949

Unifying China

There was near anarchy in China in the early years of the twentieth century. The establishment and the imperial court were widely believed to be corrupt and had lost of control of large parts of the country. A republican revolution, which overthrew the Manchu emperor in 1911, did not solve the country's problems. China fragmented into fiefdoms as local warlords took power and opposed efforts to reunify the country. In 1931, the Japanese seized Manchuria in northeastern China, further complicating the situation.

The leader of the republican movement, Sun Yat-sen, formed several governments in an attempt to unite China. To that end he also established a political party named the Kuomintang (KMT). Sun encouraged links with the emerging Communist Party of China (CPC) as they shared the nationalist goal of the KMT. He died in 1925 and was succeeded by Chiang Kai-shek, a military man who had been appointed head of the Whampoa Military Academy by Sun. In 1925 he became commander-in-chief of the National Revolutionary Army.

The Shanghai massacre

In April 1927, Chiang Kai-shek, who was on the political right of the KMT, broke with the Communist Party and massacred its members in Shanghai. Fighting broke out in several places, and there was an unsuccessful CPC uprising in Hunan, which was led by a young revolutionary named Mao Zedong. By late 1927, the split between the KMT and the CPC caused China to have three capitals: Beijing, which was internationally recognized; Nanking, the KMT base; and Wuhan, the Communist capital. However, by June 1928, the KMT had driven the Communists out of Wuhan and captured Beijing. Most of eastern China was now under their control, and Chiang had largely destroyed the CPC in the cities.

The Long March

It took Chiang time to control his rivals in the KMT before he could return his attention to the Communists, and during this period they became armed and better organised. The KMT launched five campaigns to encircle the Communists in their strongholds in the rural areas of Jiangxi, finally overwhelming them in late 1934. From then until 1936, the Communists began a series of retreats, undertaking lengthy journeys northwards through the mountainous territory of western China. The most famous of these was the Long March involving the First Front Army, led by Mao Zedong. The casualty rate was high on all the marches and many people also dropped out en route; it's been estimated that 300,000 set out but only 30,000 made it to their target, the area around the city of Yan-an in Shaanxi. There were only about 8,000 survivors of the Long March itself. Mao was now the almost undisputed leader of the Communists, but internal divisions were present: the Fourth Army, which was led by one of Mao's rivals, was barred from Yan-an and diverted towards remote Gaotai, where they were later largely destroyed by KMT forces.

War with Japan

The Second Sino-Japanese War now flared up, and the Communists began fighting the Japanese invaders; the CPC was becoming effective politically, and Communist armies were developing into an increasingly efficient force. The Communists stressed nationalism, the desire to rid China of foreign influence, which further increased their popularity. Chiang, meanwhile, was still trying to suppress his domestic rivals and refused to make peace with the Communists despite the threat from Japan. In December 1936 two of his generals mutinied to draw his attention to the greater threat from Japan and to force him into a United Front with the Communists. This, known as the Xi'an Incident, was the first example of cooperation between a part of the KMT and the CPC since the death of Sun Yat-sen. The war against the Japanese proved to be an excellent training ground for the Communists, as well as helping them with recruitment. Their invaluable military experience against the Japanese gave them the upper hand when fighting between them and the KMT began again after the Japanese surrendered to the Allies at the end of the Second World War.

OPPOSITE ABOVE: **Mao Zedong proclaims the establishment of the People's Republic of China, October 1, 1949.**

OPPOSITE BELOW: **Chiang Kai-Shek's men round up Communists for execution during the Shanghai massacre in 1927.**

OPPOSITE RIGHT: **Nationalist troops pass the bodies of dead Japanese soldiers as they move in to reoccupy the country.**

RIGHT: **Soldiers defend foreign interests in Shanghai during the KMT purge in April 1927.**

ABOVE: **Mao on horseback near Yan-an in 1947.**

BELOW: **Aided by Soviet volunteers, Chinese Communists capture the headquarters of an anti-Communist warlord.**

Japanese surrender

The atomic bombs dropped on Hiroshima and Nagasaki in August 1945, meant that the Japanese surrender came much sooner than either the Communists or Nationalists had expected. A temporary truce was put in operation with the encouragement of the United States, who wished to avoid instability in post-war Asia. However, it quickly fell apart, as the two sides raced against one another to capture territory from the retreating Japanese. The trigger was to be the province of Manchuria, in northeastern China, which had been seized by Japan in 1931. It was a formidable prize because it had undergone significant development during fourteen years of Japanese rule.

The battle for Manchuria

It was to be the Soviet Union who had first pick at this prize. Under the terms of the Yalta Agreement in February, 1945, the Soviets agreed to declare war on Japan, and moved into Manchuria just days before the Japanese surrender. Officially, the Soviets remained neutral, but they allowed the Communists to seize much of the arms and ammunition confiscated from the Japanese. Japanese troops usually tried to surrender to the KMT – and indeed were supposed to do so under the terms of the surrender agreement. However, this was not always possible because the Communists usually reached the occupied areas first.

The Soviet Union withdrew from Manchuria in April 1946 and the United States airlifted KMT troops in to fill the power vacuum and prevent the Communists from taking over the region. However, the Communists were now stronger militarily and had greater support among the public. Mao pushed moderate policies, which contrasted favourably with Chiang Kai-shek, whose regime appeared corrupt, too much linked to the pre-war warlord past and to massive inflation. As a result, the KMT experienced an enormous loss of popular support and the CPC were eventually victorious in Manchuria.

The fall of Nanking

Despite setbacks in Manchuria, the KMT managed to take the Communist base of Yan-an in March 1947. However, the Communist command retreated to new bases further north and continued the fight. In April 1948 they captured Loyang, cutting the KMT off from the major city of Xi'an. More and more provinces fell in late 1948 and early 1949 because the Communist ranks were swelled by the addition of captured KMT troops, and because public support for the CPC surged as a result of the popular land reform they had initiated behind the lines. On April 21, 1949, the Communist Party forces crossed the Yangtze River and captured the Nationalists' stronghold of Nanking.

Communist victory

The US, which had been supporting the Nationalists, had began to cut back both financial and military aid in 1948, and the KMT had gone even further downhill as a result. Soon there was no significant Nationalist military force still intact on the mainland of China, and approximately 2 million supporters withdrew to the island of Taiwan. The US withdrew their aid while this operation was underway, citing the inadequacies of the KMT regime as justification. On October 1 Mao Zedong was able to proclaim the establishment of the People's Republic of China, with its capital in Beijing; only a few pockets of resistance remained. On December 10 the final Nationalist base, the city of Chengdu, fell to the CPC's army, and the last members of the Nationalist government fled to Taiwan.

The Communist Party formed the first strong government that a united China had experienced in many decades. Hostilities finally ended in 1950 after over 20 years of fighting, most of it vicious. The end of the Civil War was unofficial, however, and no peace treaty has ever been signed. The People's Republic of China controls the mainland, and the Republic of China is restricted to the island of Taiwan.

OPPOSITE BELOW: **A Communist soldier with a fixed bayonet keeps watch on positions held by the Nationalist forces.**

OPPOSITE LEFT: **Communist soldiers are held in camps after being captured by the Nationalists at Suchow.**

OPPOSITE ABOVE RIGHT: **Police in Hong Kong's New Territories train in preparation for a possible Communist attack on the British colony.**

OPPOSITE BELOW RIGHT: **Chinese Nationalists gunners eject a shellcase from a 105mm gun on the Suchow front after it had been fired at the Communists.**

LEFT: **Mao Zedong announces the establishment of the People's Republic of China from the rostrum of Tiananmen Gate in Beijing, October 1, 1949.**

DAILY MAIL JANUARY 20, 1949

The fall of China

One of the great events of human history is taking shape in China. Sooner or later it will affect the destinies of everyone in the world.

The Chinese Nationalist Government are suing for peace. This can only mean that they are finished and that Chiang Kai-Shek is on his way out.

Before he goes we should pause to pay him tribute. He was a good soldier and a sincere idealist - a disciple of Sun Yat-Sen. He brought order to China. He was one of the Big Four in the last war. What really finished him was the corruption and inefficiency which have been the curse of China for generations. And now another takes his place upon the stage - Mao Tse-Tung, boss of the Chinese Communists.

These in themselves are big events. They mean the end of the civil war which began long before the recent world conflict and outlasted it by nearly four years.

The map

But more, much more, lies behind them. The fall of China is not only a triumph for the local Communists. It is the biggest victory Russia has won since the Allied defeat of Germany gave her the key to Eastern Europe.

Look at the map. The enormous land mass under Stalin's rule is now rounded off by the vast expanse of China.

Let us not delude ourselves into believing that Chinese Communism is different from any other Communism. Mao Tse-tung is Moscow-trained and indoctrinated. He is Marxist, Leninist, Stalinist.

Let us not imagine, either, that because the Communists have proposed a Coalition Government for China that they have gone democratic. We have seen that bubble burst in half a dozen European countries.

The east

No - China has fallen and will be submerged by Communism. She is becoming detached from Western influences and will merge into the Eastern sphere. It is as though a dam had broken and a mighty torrent had come rushing through the gap, to find fresh strength in new waters.

In China live 450,000,000 patient, diligent, malleable people who could provide millions of excellent fighting men to carry the banner of the Hammer and Sickle.

Here is a land of primitive agricultural and industrial processes which could be collectivised and socialised, mechanised and organised, making the Chinese the most formidable of the races of the earth.

Look, too, at the political possibilities. China borders on India, Burma, and Indo-China. All, in varying degrees, have caught the germ of Communism. Now the risk of infection has reached epidemic proportions.

The west

Finally, there is the strategic aspect. A month ago General Macarthur said that the Communist victories in China were a grave menace to American security, and he demanded reinforcements. His view was that with China in Communist hands Russia would be in a position to seize Japan and to drive the United States from the Western Pacific. He did not say this would happen, but that it could happen - and certainly the Chinese Communists' victory has shifted the balance of strategical advantage against the Western Powers.

It is, of course, too late for them to take any action in China now. But they should concentrate on their strength and on the recovery of Europe while neglecting no opportunity of seeking lasting peace with the East.

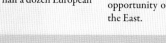

Greek Civil War 1946-1949

Nazi occupation

The tensions that caused the outbreak of a civil war in Greece had been building for some time before the conflict began in 1946. The war was part of a longer struggle between the political right and left that had begun while Greece was under Nazi German occupation. It was a bitter conflict which still has repercussions, and was the first post-war conflict in which anti-Communist forces received Western aid.

When the Nazis invaded in 1941, King George II and the Greek government escaped to Egypt, where a government in exile was established. It had little impact back in Greece and resistance was largely directed by the Greek Communists. The Communist militias of the Greek National Liberation Army (ELAS) waged a successful war of liberation against the Nazis, and by the time the Western Allies entered Athens on October 13, 1944, ELAS was already in control of much of the country.

Arrival of the British

During the war, Stalin had agreed that Greece fell within the British sphere of influence and he did not help the Communists finalize their takeover. British forces moved into the country and staged elections in March 1946. However, the Communists boycotted the vote, allowing a rightwing party to secure victory, and fighting quickly flared up again. Members of ELAS formed the Democratic Army of Greece (DSE) and began attacking government targets. In response the British began providing funding and training to the army of Greece. Stalin did not directly send aid to the DSE, but support was offered by neighbouring Yugoslavia and Albania.

The Truman Doctrine

By 1947 Britain was feeling the effects of the Second World War and could no longer afford to support the Greek government. After much debate, the United States government agreed that it could not let Greece fall to Communism and took over Britain's assisting role. This decision laid the foundations of the Truman Doctrine and gave rise to the Marshall Plan, a major aid programme to help war-torn European countries revitalize their economies.

Fighting increased throughout 1947, with the DSE operating as guerrillas, melting away into the mountains when attacked. By September, after being officially banned by the government the Communist Party formed a provisional government and set about trying to capture a town as an appropriate base. They were unsuccessful, but the size of the Greek Army had to be increased to respond to the new challenge. The DSE remained a major threat through 1948 and at one stage managed to close in on Athens.

End of the Civil War

By 1949, the Communists were facing defeat. The international situation was changing as Stalin no longer supported Tito, the ruler of Yugoslavia. The Greek Communist Party was forced to choose, and chose Stalin. In response Tito barred Yugoslavia to them in July 1949 seriously diminishing their operational capabilities. Meanwhile, the Western contribution to the Greek Army was taking effect and a string of offensives resulted in significant defeats for the DSE. By September, most DSE fighters had either surrendered or fled to Albania. Then the Albanian government announced that it no longer supported the DSE. On October 16 the Communist radio station announced a 'temporary ceasefire' – the end of hostilities.

Greece was in a terrible state. There were deep political divisions and economic chaos. Casualty figures have been estimated at between 50,000 to 100,000, and more than half a million people were displaced; about 10% of the population were homeless. Greece now fell firmly in the Western sphere of influence, and became a founding member of NATO.

OPPOSITE ABOVE: **Greek troops set off from Athens as reinforcements for the forces fighting the rebels, July 1947.**

OPPOSITE ABOVE LEFT: **Greek Army regulars consolidate their position along the Albanian frontier in the mountainous region around Konitsa.**

OPPOSITE BELOW RIGHT: **Paratroopers patrol past a gasworks near Athens.**

OPPOSITE MIDDLE RIGHT: **Greece's King George II departs from London Airport on his journey back home. The results of a September 1946 referendum on the restoration of the Monarchy found in favour of reinstating the King. The Communists disputed the election, further fuelling the civil war.**

TOP RIGHT: **British troops train the Greek Army in Konitsa.**

ABOVE MIDDLE RIGHT: **The villagers of Drosopigi turn out to welcome home Communist militias after a raid near Florina.**

RIGHT: **A military convoy patrols through Amyndeon in northern Greece in an attempt to prevent Communists from crossing the Yugoslavian border.**

BELOW LEFT: **Newly trained government troops set out on their first mission, July 1947.**

BELOW RIGHT: **Greek government soldiers and US military observers watch an assault on guerrilla positions in the Mount Grammos Sector near the Albanian frontier in September 1949.**

Arab-Israeli War 1948

Decolonization in the Middle East

Many countries in the Middle East had been calling for complete independence from colonial powers. Syria and Lebanon were under French mandates and they achieved their aim in 1946; as did Jordan, which was under a British mandate. Palestine, also controlled by the British, was increasingly problematic and the question of a potential Jewish state – which had been raised before the Second World War – was intensified in the aftermath of the Holocaust.

Many Jewish refugees headed for Palestine and the United Nations suggested that the territory be divided into two states, one Jewish and one Arab, with the city of Jerusalem as an international zone. The already high levels of tension between the two communities rose, and by November 1947 there was a civil war under way as each side attempted to control strategically significant positions.

ABOVE: **Arab fighters attack a Jewish settlement in March 1948 as the two communities clash in the run-up to Britain's departure.**

MIDDLE: **David Ben Gurion declares the founding of the state of Israel on May 14, 1948, just hours before the expiration of Britain's mandate.**

RIGHT: **Jewish immigrants arrive at Tel Aviv Harbour in May 1948. Many immigrants who arrived in the newly-created state of Israel had suffered during the Holocaust.**

Birth of Israel

This in turn developed into an international conflict following the declaration of the state of Israel on 14 May 1948 and the withdrawal of the British. On the night following the declaration, armies from Iraq, Egypt, Lebanon, Syria and Jordan, together with some volunteers from other Arab nations, invaded the Arab areas with the aim of establishing a Palestinian state. Their action was condemned by both the United States and the Soviet Union.

Initially the numbers involved were relatively small, but both sides quickly increased the size of their forces. The Israeli Defence Forces were officially established on May 26, and they consistently managed to field more troops than their opponents. Their ground troops were supported by the Israeli air force which was initially outnumbered, though the balance began to swing in its favour by the end of May, when the first bombing raid on an Arab capital, Amman, was made.

The heaviest fighting took place around Jerusalem and between there and Tel Aviv. There was heavy fighting in Jerusalem itself at the end of May, and by May 28 it was controlled by the Arabs and all the Jewish inhabitants of the old city had to leave. Elsewhere, Arab advances were halted, and a UN-negotiated truce was developed which held for almost a month. The Egyptians attacked and fighting resumed in July.

Israeli Victory

A large Israeli offensive was aimed at securing the road between Jerusalem and Tel Aviv, and the towns which lay between them were quickly taken. This prompted the first large-scale movement of Palestinian refugees, as about 50,000 people fled. Intense diplomatic efforts led to a second truce, and this held until October 15 despite the assassination of the UN envoy, Count Bernadotte. From then until the eventual end of the conflict in July 1949, the Israelis launched a series of military operations to pursue and drive out the Arab armies and secure their borders, both of which aims they were able to achieve. A variety of armistice agreements were reached, and the last one was signed with Syria on 20 July 1949.

Israel had withdrawn from the Gaza strip following international pressure, and it was now occupied by Egypt; Jordan occupied the West Bank. Though thousands of troops – and some civilians – had lost their lives, by far the biggest overall impact came in the sheer number of refugees who had fled their homes. There were thought to be at least 700,000 Palestinian refugees in either Gaza, the West Bank or in other Arab countries – and probably as many as a million. Nor were they the only ones affected; it is estimated that about 600,000 Jews were also forced to leave their homes. The situation could only lead to further conflict and suffering for the people of the area.

TOP: **Arab soldiers rest in Jerusalem after capturing the city in late May 1948. The United Nations wanted to place the city under international control, but this did not happen and sovereignty over Jerusalem remains in dispute today.**

ABOVE: **An Israeli guard hands food to Arab prisoners at a camp near Ramle.**

BELOW: **Arabs surrender to the Israel Defence Forces in Ramle on the road between Jerusalem and Tel Aviv in July 1948.**

Korea
1950-1953

Division of Korea

After the defeat of Japan at the end of the Second World War, its colony on the Korean Peninsula was divided up between the United States and the Soviet Union along the 38th Parallel. With the Americans in charge of the southern portion and the Soviets dominating the north, Korea rapidly found itself on the frontline of a new Cold War.

The original plan was to reunify the two zones before granting their independence, but this became impossible as the United States and the Soviet Union began creating two irreconcilable states in their own images. In the South, the Americans fostered a democracy, albeit with some hostility towards the left. Elections were held in May 1948 and Syngman Rhee became President. In the North, the Soviets supported the Communists and the Democratic People's Republic of Korea was established under the rule of Kim Il Sung. Both governments believed that they were the single legitimate government for the whole peninsula, which was to lead to one of the largest and most destructive conflicts of the Cold War.

Withdrawal of the Superpowers

Soviet troops withdrew in December 1948, and by June the following year most US troops had also gone, except for the US Korea Military Advisory Group, which had 480 members. However, they did not leave behind an entirely peaceful peninsula. Both North and South experienced uprisings and sporadic guerrilla fighting, most of which was connected to problems with landlords. There were also reports of incursions by the North across the 38th Parallel, but the US thought that the Republic of Korea (ROK) army would be able to deal with them.

DAILY MAIL   JUNE 28, 1950
Americans in action

America last night joined the war in Korea. Naval and air forces were ordered into battle against the Communists, and warships, bombers, and fighters began the attack immediately. General MacArthur is in supreme command.

At the same time America sent a plain-spoken Note asking Russia to use her influence with North Korea to stop the war or take responsibility for what happens. It promised the US will not fight north of the 38th Parallel.

President Truman, in a 'thus far and no farther' statement, ordered the US Seventh Fleet to protect Formosa (Taiwan), and announced help to French Indo-China and reinforcements for the Philippines.

Britain and other nations were asked to take similar action to help Korea. Mr. Attlee and the British delegate to the Security Council promised full support. So did several other nations.

Seoul, capital of South Korea, was saved by a fierce counter-attack yesterday. Communists retreated nearly 20 miles, then advanced again.

With their eyes open

The world faced its gravest post-war crisis tonight as American bombers and fighters strafed Communist tanks in South Korea.

President Truman's decision to order American planes and warships into defence against the Communist invasion was followed by a frank admission in high official quarters here that the situation held the gravest possibilities. But it is being followed by intense diplomatic activity designed to align other Western Powers solidly behind the dramatic American initiative.

President Truman's announcement said:

In Korea the Government forces, which were armed to prevent border raids and to preserve internal security, were attacked by invading forces from North Korea. The Security Council of the United Nations called upon the invading troops to cease hostilities and to withdraw to the 38th Parallel.

I order ...

This they have not done, but, on the contrary, have pressed the attack. The Security Council called upon all members of the United Nations to render every assistance to the United Nations in the execution of this resolution.

In these circumstances, I have ordered United States air and sea forces to give the Korean Government troops cover and support.

International peace and security

The attack upon Korea makes it plain beyond all doubt that Communism has passed beyond the use of subversion to conquer independent nations and will now use armed invasion and war. It has defied the orders of the Security Council, issued to preserve international peace and security.

In these circumstances the occupation of Formosa by Communist forces would be a direct threat to the security of the Pacific area and to US forces performing their lawful and necessary functions in that area.

Accordingly I have ordered the 7th Fleet to prevent any attack on Formosa. As a corollary of this action, I am calling upon the Chinese Government on Formosa to cease all air and sea operations against the mainland.

The 7th Fleet will see that this is done. The determination of the future status of Formosa must await the restoration of security in the Pacific, a peace settlement with Japan, or consideration by the United Nations.

I have also directed that US forces in the Philippines be strengthened and that military assistance to the Philippine Government be accelerated.

I have also directed acceleration in the furnishing of military assistance to the forces of France and the associated States in Indo-China, and the dispatch of a military mission to provide close working relations with those forces.

Force V law

I know that all members of the United Nations will consider carefully the consequences of this latest aggression in Korea in defiance of the Charter of the United Nations.

A return to the rule of force in international affairs would have far-reaching effects. The US will continue to uphold the rule of law.

I have instructed Ambassador Warren R. Austin, as the representative of the US to the Security Council, to report these steps to the Council.

At present US land forces will not be committed to battle. But this possibility is not excluded if the situation worsens.

Invasion

On June 25, 1950, North Korean troops crossed the Parallel en masse in an attempt to unify the country. The North Korean People's Army (NKPA) invaded with tanks and full air support, surprising both the South Koreans and the US. It was immediately apparent that this would not be a local conflict; Stalin had approved the North Korean move, and Truman, then US President, sent troops within two days. He was acting in the name of the United Nations' Security Council, which had voted to resist North Korean aggression (the Russians were boycotting the Council at the time because it did not recognize Communist China). Truman authorized the use of air power against the North Korean tanks, and sent the US navy to patrol the channel between mainland China and Taiwan.

OPPOSITE ABOVE: **B-29 bombers fly in formation over Korea in September 1950. Over 24 million pounds of bombs were dropped from B-29s during the months of July and August.**

OPPOSITE BELOW: **An American radio operator of the 24th Infantry Regiment reads the latest news while eating a meal near Sangju, August 1950.**

TOP: **United Nations troops fighting in the streets of Seoul, September 1950.**

MIDDLE: **Two North Korean boys serving in the North Korean Army are interrogated by a US soldier after they were taken prisoner in the Sindang-dong area by the 389th Infantry Regiment in September 1950.**

RIGHT: **General Douglas MacArthur, commander of the UN force, gives orders to his two top aides, Major General E.M. Almond and Brigadier General John Church at Suwon Airfield.**

Arrival of the Americans

It was obvious that ground troops were needed, and the first US forces arrived on July 1. Their aim was to slow the NKPA advance so that more troops and equipment could be brought in before the North Koreans overran the whole peninsula, but they were outmanoeuvred and forced to retreat. Various defensive lines were drawn up running down the peninsula as the advance continued. The ROK virtually abandoned the western half of South Korea and were now moving further south and east towards the port of Pusan. There were further attempts to hold lines in order to allow an orderly retreat, but the most urgent need was for more soldiers. Troops from Britain and the Commonwealth were now arriving, and the UN forces were becoming more representative.

Pusan Perimeter

It was vitally important that the ROK hold on to Pusan, and US Marines began arriving there on August 2. Many of them were combat veterans of the Pacific War, and they were initially able to push part of the NKPA back. However, the NKPA had combat veterans too, from the Chinese Civil War, and a pattern of repeated advances and retreats set in. At the same time the NKPA were also advancing southwards down the eastern coast. Here the ROK forces had been able to hold them back at first, but the North Koreans were able to retake the city of Yongdok where they were fired on by US fighters, who also dropped napalm.

Despite their success, the NKPA forces had, however, fought themselves to a standstill by the end of August. They were fully extended and had failed to pierce the 'Pusan Perimeter'. Though still determined, they had little choice but to abandon their pattern of offensives, and stalemate set in. The entire Pusan Perimeter was now quiet, but the war was about to change.

Inchon

The commander of the UN forces, General Douglas MacArthur, was particularly experienced in amphibious warfare. He suggested landing forces behind North Korean lines on the coast at Inchon, only 25 miles from Seoul. The aim was to force a surrender by cutting the NKPA's supply lines. Inchon would not be an easy target; the approaches were difficult and defended, and Seoul was also well defended. A multinational invasion force assembled and the complicated attack began on September 15. A bridgehead was established, and troops were able to fan further out. The battle for Seoul began on September 22, marked by close-quarter fighting, and the city was retaken six days later.

Further south, the Eighth Army had broken out of the Pusan Perimeter and headed north, and by early October the situation had changed completely; the NKPA had been pushed behind the 38th Parallel, and any remnants had been effectively destroyed as a fighting force below it. It was a massive achievement for MacArthur.

On October 7, US troops were to the north of the Parallel. MacArthur urged the North Koreans to agree to a ceasefire, a call which was rejected – and the decision was then made to move further north. The North Korean capital, Pyongyang, fell on October 12, but Kim Il Sung and his government had already left. The swift northwards advance took the armies much closer to Korea's border with China, and altered the nature of the war once more.

OPPOSITE: B-29 'Superfortress' bombers drop bombs on North Korean targets.

OPPOSITE ABOVE RIGHT: United Nations troops shield their ears from the sounds of their own mortar and heavy machine-gun fire.

ABOVE: 'Little Joe', a South Korean war orphan dressed in a miniature GI uniform, proudly displays a captured North Korean weapon. He was adopted by a medical company of the American 25th Infantry Division.

ABOVE LEFT: British troops of the 1st Battalion, the King's Shropshire Light Infantry arrive at the port of Inchon after the sea voyage from Hong Kong.

LEFT: A young refugee carrying her brother on her back walks past a stalled M-26 tank at Haengju as she escapes the North Korean advance.

China's involvement

As the fighting came closer to the Manchurian border, where China met North Korea, the Chinese became more alarmed and mobilized troops. The Chinese offensive began in early November, and the war took a new and more dangerous turn. The Chinese were masters of a comparatively new style of fighting: their attacks were sudden and unpredictable, and their troops seemed to melt away afterwards. Chinese involvement also increased the potential strength of the North Korean side enormously; there were over five million troops in the People's Liberation Army, and they were familiar with fighting in similar territory and under comparable conditions.

Battle of the Chongchon River

The addition of Chinese forces was effective and the US Eighth Army was forced to retreat at the Battle of the Chongchon River, the worst US defeat of the war. This was followed by a series of Chinese offensives, one of which led to the abandonment of Seoul once more. It was recaptured in March 1951, as the UN forces retaliated and inflicted a major defeat on the Chinese. The spring of 1951 also saw the Battle of the Imjin, involving many British Commonwealth troops who just escaped destruction. There were severe losses, and this battle helped to halt the Chinese advance.

By late spring the Chinese offensive had stalled. Their armies were overextended, and though they reached the outskirts of Seoul on April 29, they lacked the resources to attack the city itself. Their general, Peng, regrouped his forces – and encountered resistance along the entire front for the first time.

BELOW: Trainee South Korean soldiers receive instructions on the use of the 3.5 inch rocket launcher.

RIGHT: Captured North Korean guerrilla fighters detained in a South Korean prisoner camp.

OPPOSITE TOP: Men of the King's Own Scottish Borderers stand guard on the Korean Western Front. Their battalion, together with a Battalion of the Royal Leicester Regiment, had recently repelled an entire Communist division.

OPPOSITE MIDDLE: General MacArthur inspects troops of the 24th Infantry at Kimpo Airfield in Korea during a tour of the battlefront.

OPPOSITE BOTTOM: The 16-inch guns of the USS *Iowa* fire on the North Korean city of Chongjin, a supply and transport centre for the enemy.

DAILY MAIL NOVEMBER 28, 1950

MacArthur fights stern defensive

Communist China is now fully committed to the war in Korea. The Chinese, operating a massive group of armies, have tonight deflated the United Nations' hope of any quick - or decisive - military victory.

Reports from all sectors of the north-western front show that General MacArthur's confidently launched offensive of four days ago has been transformed into a stern defensive. And this includes a right flank 'of no retreat' which has already been pierced by the Communists. Troops of the Republic of Korea Second Corps, who yesterday gave up Tokchon, were ordered today to 'hold at all costs' a line south of the town running east for 35 miles. But before the line could be organised an enemy combat team had infiltrated in the centre.

An official spokesman tonight described the situation in this sector as 'confused,' and admitted that the South Koreans have been forced to pull back between 12 and 20 miles in the past 24 hours.

All along the front commanders were reporting serious checks even where before the Red had offered comparatively little resistance. At the extreme west of the front the US 24th Division had to withdraw from the recently captured town of Chongju, 'in order to protect its flank.'

In other words, the whole impetus of the offensive has been lost and American veterans of the bleak days of the southern defensive box around Pusan are saying

'the situation now seems as grim as ever it did.'

It is now admitted here that 19 field formations of opposing Chinese have been identified. These were described as 'divisions, or elements of divisions.'

Prisoners say that an entire Chinese army, the 40th, is still in reserve, but is due to attack soon.

Expert Foot-sloggers

It seems certain that its existence was known before the boasted 'over by Christmas' offensive was launched, and therefore it is a fair inference that the effectiveness of the opposition may have been understood.

But the Chinese, who are also efficiently controlling the rebounding North Korean armies, have shown in four days that they are among the most formidable soldiers in the world. They have also achieved success without air support, and little or no artillery or armour has been used.

They have relied on infantry, expert mortarmen, night fighting and infiltration tactics. Today they have been stalling the US 2nd Corps position throughout the daylight hours.

Troops of the US 25th Division were forced to withdraw four miles. No reports have yet been received of British troops being committed to the battle, but it is obvious that General Walker, U.S. 8th Army commander, will need every man at his disposal - and quickly.

Stalemate

A general international agreement had developed that the situation in Korea must not be allowed to lead to a third world war. Truman now believed that the war in Korea could be contained – the prospect of it increasing in scope with the added possibility of the Atom Bomb being used was terrible, though it had been considered – but MacArthur's strategies were not consistent with the President's aim. He wanted to invade China if he thought it necessary, and was making important strategic decisions without reference to Truman. He was replaced.

By now the opposing sides were almost at a standstill, though serious fighting continued in what was becoming a war of attrition. Neither side could get much of an advantage over the other – they were both fighting from heavily fortified positions and preventing enemy incursions with the use of artillery and mines – though UN forces were superior in the air and at sea. It was becoming obvious that although the Chinese could keep North Korea fighting, they could not overturn South Korea in the face of US opposition. Nor could the US destroy North Korea by conventional means, and Truman was not prepared to launch a nuclear strike.

Peace talks

Negotiations of a sort began in the middle of 1951, opening with discreet discussions between the US and the Soviet Union; they were to take two years. Peace talks were set up and a month-long ceasefire was agreed for the end of the year. However, the war continued in 1952, with each side continuing to test the strength of the other without achieving a decisive outcome, a pattern which persisted into 1953. During that year a new administration under President Eisenhower came into power in the US. It was Republican and strongly anti-Communist, but it was felt that the real centre of the Cold War was Europe. There was also tacit agreement that the outgoing administration had demonstrated their ability to hold on to South Korea well enough.

An armistice was signed at Panmunjom at the end of July 1953, though there is still not a formal peace. Relations between North and South remain strained, as are North Korea's relations with many parts of the international community. The border between the two changed very little during the Korean War, but there had been many deaths – estimates range between three and four million, most of whom were Korean civilians. A demilitarized zone was established along the 38th Parallel, and it remains to this day.

DAILY MAIL JULY 27, 1953

Truce signed - no smiles

The Korean war - the war in which neither side could risk victory - ended today after three years and one month. The armistice was signed at 10.1 a.m. The guns will go silent at 10 o'clock tonight.

Under the terms mighty armies of both sides will be withdrawn one mile and a quarter from the battle line within 72 hours, and exchange of prisoners is expected to begin 'within a week - if the Communists co-operate.'

The chief Allied negotiator in the truce discussion, Lieut.-General William Harrison, landed at Panmunjom at 9.30 a.m. by helicopter and went straight into the prefabricated 'Peace Pagoda.' There were no smiles on either side.

He walked past a United Nations guard of honour representing all units and Services fighting in Korea on his way; the Communist delegation had arrived in jeeps five minutes earlier.

Bulky document

General Harrison entered the ceremony hall at exactly 10 a.m., sat down, and immediately signed the first copy of the bulky truce document. The Communist copies of the agreement were bound in dark brown leather, while the United Nation copies were covered simply by light blue paper.

The documents lay on two green-covered tables near the centre of the huge hall; between the United Nations and Communist tables was a third baize table for the actual signing. The Allied table was bare, with the exception of nine copies of the agreement -written in English, Chinese, and Korean - and nine copies of the supplementary agreement.

The Allied Command announced that front-line troops were prepared to make the withdrawal stipulated in the armistice agreement, but at the same time warned their troops to double their vigilance.

OPPOSITE BELOW: United Nations Command soldiers detained in North Korean prison camps.

OPPOSITE ABOVE: British troops of the King's Shropshire Light Infantry tear apart buildings in compound 66 of the UN's Koje Island Prisoner of War Camp. Communist agents had infiltrated the camp and the compound was suspected of housing their headquarters.

BELOW: South Korean soldiers move in single file towards the frontline near Lookout Mountain, east of the Pukhan River in June 1953. The South Koreans retook the mountain after being pushed off by a superior Chinese force.

RIGHT: Private Bill Speakman of the King's Own Scottish Borderers was awarded the Victoria Cross, Britain's highest honour for bravery, for his

actions in Korea. He led a team of six men in battle against thousands of Chinese soldiers in order to allow the rest of his company to evacuate.

ABOVE RIGHT: A large crowd gathers to welcome Private Speakman home from Korea.

Kenya Emergency
1952-1960

ABOVE: British soldiers and loyalist Kenyans capture a Mau Mau suspect in the Aberdare Hills.

RIGHT: Field Marshal Kanji, a leading member of the Mau Mau, is pictured in the Mount Kenya Forest. The origin of the name Mau Mau is uncertain. It was used by the British and the settlers and the rebels did not use it to refer to themselves.

BELOW: Suspected Kikuyu militants are rounded up on the day Governor Baring declared a State of Emergency in the colony. They were suspected of involvement in the assassination of Senior Chief Waruhiu, a prominent Kikuyu loyalist.

British colonial rule

During the Second World War the 30,000–strong European settler community took advantage of British distraction to increase their control over Kenya's government. When the British attempted to revive their colonial administration after the war, they realized they had to work with the settlers if London was to maintain its control. However, little was done to work with the native Kenyan population, a number of whom had fought and died on the British side in the war.

Mau Mau

The Kikuyu Central Association (KCA) was formed in the 1920s to politically organize the Kikuyu, Kenya's largest tribe. After the war, the KCA began demanding independence and called for a campaign of civil disobedience to meet their goal. However, by the end of 1951 it was clear that radical elements were intent on more violent methods of getting the British and white settlers out of Kenya. These radicals, dubbed the 'Mau Mau', started attacking Kenyans loyal to the British colonial administration. They were also blamed for a number of arson attacks on isolated white-owned farms and were widely rumoured to engage in barbaric oath-taking rituals. This shocked and appalled the European settler community who demanded that the colonial administration do something. The first post-war Governor, Sir Philip Mitchell, was not convinced of the threat, but the new Governor, Sir Evelyn Baring, who arrived in Nairobi in October 1952, had a rather different attitude. He declared a state of emergency in Kenya on October 20 following the murder of Senior Chief Waruhiu, a prominent Kikuyu loyalist. British troops were brought into the country and the supposed leaders of the Mau Mau rebellion were arrested.

The Ruck murders

The declaration of a State of Emergency only served to exacerbate the situation, and on January 24, 1953, white farmers were directly attacked for the first time. A group of Mau Mau, armed with machete-like implements called pangas, attacked and killed Roger and Esmee Ruck on their farm. Their six-year-old son and Kikuyu servant were also murdered. European settlers began to organize into vigilante groups, and white farmers became suspicious of their own Kikuyu labourers. More attacks on white farmers followed, but most Mau Mau attacks still focused on African 'collaborators'. Attacks generally came at night, and were concentrated in the countryside, but there were forays into Nairobi's suburbs.

British military victory

The British position was revitalized in the aftermath of the attacks. More troops were brought in, draconian measures were initiated and 'pseudo-gangs' were set up to infiltrate the Mau Mau. Nonetheless, it took some time before the British really recognized the scale of the movement. Nairobi was put under military control in April 1954, and lots of people were arrested or deported back to Kikuyu lands. As a result, Mau Mau sources of supply vanished. The effort then moved to other areas and by the end of the year many thousands of people were confined in overwhelmed internment camps. This did, however, mark the beginning of the end of the uprising, as very few Mau Mau were left at large. In 1955 an amnesty was declared, though peace talks collapsed and the Emergency remained in effect until January 1960. It was a clear military victory for the British, though the Mau Mau ultimately got what they wanted as Kenya was granted its independence in December 1963.

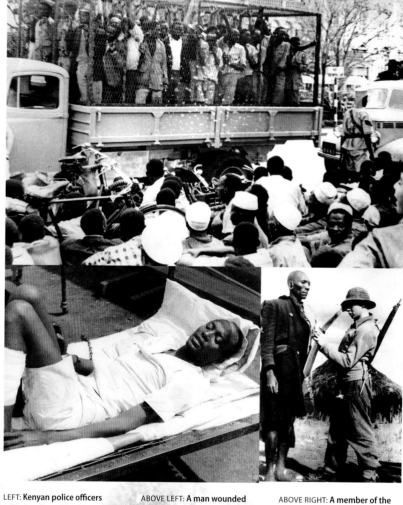

LEFT: **Kenyan police officers apprehend two Mau Mau suspects.**

TOP: **Hundreds of suspected Mau Mau rebels are rounded up by Nairobi police following a clampdown by the British Colonial Administration.**

ABOVE LEFT: **A man wounded during the uprising recovers in hospital. The majority of those targeted by the Mau Mau were Kenyans.**

ABOVE RIGHT: **A member of the Lancashire Fusiliers disarms a Mau Mau rebel of his panga during a sweep through the Aberdare Mountains north of Nairobi.**

BELOW: **Mau Mau are rounded up by local defense forces with the support of the British Army's Lancashire Fusiliers.**

DAILY MAIL DECEMBER 26 1952

Mau Mau Killers Run Amok

In the wildest night of killing and arson since the Mau Mau troubles began - Christmas Eve - terrorists murdered 10 Kikuyu, including a woman, and wounded five others - a man, a woman and three children. Two men escaped unhurt. At least four of the attackers are known to have been wounded. A joint store and two huts were burned down.

This record fulfils the fears that the terrorists were planning a violent outbreak over Christmas and it is significant that the attacks totalled seven -the ritual number used over and over again in Mau Mau ceremonies.

Nearly all the murders and all the cases of arson occurred in the notorious Mau Mau areas of Nyeri and Fort Hall. The only exception was a man killed in Nairobi. Two unknown assailants attacked a bus company employee in his house in one of Nairobi's African locations, shooting him in the head.

Three African homesteads were attacked in the Nyeri reserve by a gang of between 10 and 20. They killed four men with knives and seriously wounded a woman and two children. One man had his head hacked off.

Algerian War of Independence 1954-1962

French colonial rule

On All Saint's Day, November 1, 1954, Algerian independence fighters launched their long and brutal campaign for independence. It was becoming clear that the French Empire was slowly trending towards decolonization as earlier that year Indochina had won its independence and talks were underway for greater autonomy in Tunisia. However, Algeria was unlike other French colonies in that it had a massive French settler population and was widely regarded as an extension of mainland France. The French government committed itself to defending Algeria at all costs, putting itself on course for a violent showdown with the main Algerian rebel group, the National Liberation Front (FLN).

Terrorizing civilians

The FLN operated largely as a guerrilla army, which forced the French to use dubious methods to try to defeat them. The Algerian civilian population was held collectively responsible for FLN activity so as to get the natives to rein in the insurgents themselves, and the use of torture became a commonplace means of intelligence-gathering by the French military. For its part, the FLN also terrorized the civilian population: Algerians who worked for European-owned businesses were targeted in a bid to dissuade collaboration and undermine France's economic stake in the country, and the French population were subjected to brutal massacres in order to encourage the remainder to leave the country.

ABOVE: Security forces battle against a mob of French settlers opposed to President De Gaulle's attempts to negotiate with the Algerian nationalists.

MIDDLE: An armed French farmworker oversees the evacuation of women and children from his village to the relative safety of the city. FLN massacres on remote European-owned farms and villages terrified the settler population.

RIGHT: Young French settlers march through the streets of their town during the uprising of May 1958.

Return of De Gaulle

In April 1958, a new government came to power in Paris under Pierre Pflimlin, who had previously spoken out in favour of negotiating with the FLN. In response, a group of French generals in Algeria, backed by French settlers, rose up in rebellion and took control of Algeria and the island of Corsica. To prevent further unrest and avert a possible civil war, Charles De Gaulle, France's wartime leader, was called back to office in the hope that he could unify the country. De Gaulle sought to reduce the stranglehold Algeria was having over French politics and to shift the country's focus towards strengthening France's role in Europe. In 1959, De Gaulle came out in support of self-determination for Algerians. After a long negotiation process, a referendum was held on July 1, 1962. The electorate voted overwhelmingly in favour of independence, which was granted two days later.

The Secret Army Organization

When it became clear to French settlers in Algeria that they could no longer rely on the support of the French government, they organized into the Secret Army Organization (OAS), and began a campaign of bombings and assassinations against both the French authorities and the FLN. They were unable to stop Algeria from gaining its independence and merely prolonged the suffering on both sides. By the end of the war, hundreds of thousands of Algerians had been killed, 20,000 French soldiers had lost their lives, and almost one million European settlers had fled their homes in Algeria.

TOP RIGHT: **General Charles De Gaulle receives a rapturous welcome as he arrives in Algiers, June 1958. The French settler population initially believed he would oppose decolonization.**

TOP LEFT: **Algerians crowd around the President as he visits Tebessa in the Constantine Region of Algeria in August 1959.**

FAR LEFT: **A row of armoured cars defend Algiers' military General Headquarters during an army** insurrection in April 1961. A group of French generals rose up in opposition to De Gaulle's policy of self-determination for Algeria, but support for the French President remained strong and he was quickly able to defeat the mutiny.

LEFT: **A girl blows kisses to a group of paratroopers as they surrender following the failed army uprising in April 1961.**

ABOVE: **The scene in Algiers following an OAS attack near the Casbah. Women and children were among the thirty people killed when mortar shells were fired into a crowd of shoppers.**

BELOW: **The police of Algiers come under attack from a stone-throwing mob of French settlers opposed to De Gaulle's policies, November 1960.**

Suez Crisis 1956

British control of the Suez Canal

The Suez Canal had been built between Egypt and the Sinai Peninsula in 1869. Its creation meant that ships no longer needed to make the long and potentially dangerous journey around the coast of Africa, and it provided convenient European access to the oil fields of the Middle East, which were growing in importance. In a comparatively short period of time, it became a vital trade route and economic link for the West. Under a treaty of 1936, Britain had control of the Canal Zone.

The early 1950s were a time of strong anti-Western sentiment in many parts of the Arab world. The establishment of the state of Israel, supported by the US, had put many old alliances under strain, and Israeli success had, in its turn, encouraged the development of nationalist regimes in Iraq, Syria and Egypt. In 1952 a new government, led by army officers, was formed in Cairo.

ABOVE: **British troops backed by a tank search buildings for snipers who ignored the ceasefire order in Port Said, Egypt.**

RIGHT: **The British Peace Committee gathers to protest the war outside the Houses of Parliament in London where MPs had assembled for a special three-day session to discuss the crisis.**

Nationalization of the canal

One of these army officers was Gamal Abdel Nasser, and he became the head of the Egyptian government within two years. He also became, increasingly, the champion of Arab nationalism, and British control of the Suez Canal was impossible as far as he was concerned. He began agitating for the removal of British troops, and in October 1954 Britain signed an agreement to evacuate the Zone by 1956. The last British troops were evacuated in June of that year.

Nasser was a champion of the 'non-aligned movement', a group of countries who took neither side in the Cold War and sought to benefit by playing both sides. However, an arms deal with Czechoslovakia caused the United States to fear that the socialist Nasser was moving too far into the Communist camp. Consequently Washington announced it would halt plans to finance an ambitious dam construction project at Aswan on the Nile. The Aswan Dam was integral to Nasser's modernization programme, and he had to find new sources of funding. His answer was to seize control of the lucrative Suez Canal from the Anglo-French company who owned it. On July 26, 1956, Nasser announced the nationalization of the canal.

DAILY MAIL   JULY 27, 1956

Nasser grabs Suez Canal

Eden calls midnight meeting of Ministers and Service Chiefs after Egypt's rabble-rouser tears up the 1954 Zone Agreement

Colonel Nasser last night threw down his biggest challenge to the West. He seized the Suez Canal only five weeks after the last British troops had walked out. Within two hours Sir Anthony Eden called an emergency meeting of Cabinet Ministers and Service chiefs early today at 10, Downing-street. M. Picot, general manager of the Suez Canal Company, was called hurriedly from his West End hotel. Also present were Mr Selwyn Lloyd, Foreign Secretary; Admiral Earl Mountbatten, First Sea Lord; General Sir Gerald Templer, Chief of the Imperial General Staff;

Air Chief Marshal Sir Dermot Boyle; the American Charge d'Affaires, Mr. Andrew B. Foster, and the French Ambassador, M. Chauvel. King Feisal of Iraq, who had been Sir Anthony's guest at No. 10, was told the news.

In Alexandria Nasser told a wildly cheering crowd of 100,000 that Egypt had nationalised the Canal 'in the name of the nation.' And she would use the revenue to build the Aswan Dam - for which Britain and the US refused aid. Nasser thus tears up the 1954 Agreement under which Britain - biggest shareholder in the Canal and its biggest user - withdrew her troops. His action, in the opinion of some British experts, warrants the use of armed force to maintain our rights.

ABOVE RIGHT: **Britain and France amass the largest naval concentration in the Mediterranean since the Second World War as they prepare for the invasion of the Suez Canal region.**

RIGHT: **Prime Minister Anthony Eden tells the nation that 'this act of plunder must not succeed', following Egypt's nationalization of the canal.**

BELOW: **A ship passes through the Suez Canal just before Egypt's nationalization.**

The road to war

Attempts to reach a diplomatic solution to the crisis at the United Nations made slow progress and Britain and France began making contingency plans to retake the canal by force. Both countries were also motivated by a desire to strike a blow to Nasser's government for inciting national liberation movements in their colonies. They were joined by Israel, which had become angered after Nasser closed the strategic Straits of Tiran to Israeli shipping in September 1956.

In mid-October the Security Council, hampered by a Soviet veto, failed to agree a solution. On October 29, Israeli forces crossed into Sinai, and British ships left Malta for Egypt. The next day both Britain and France vetoed a UN motion demanding Israeli withdrawal. They also issued an ultimatum to Egypt (and, disingenuously, to Israel): to cease fighting and allow Anglo-French forces to occupy the Canal Zone. On October 31, there were British and French air attacks on Egyptian airfields and Israel finished occupying Sinai and Gaza. In response, the Egyptians sank some ships in the canal, blocking it to traffic. On November 5, the British and French launched a seaborne assault and landed ground troops in Egypt. They also denied any collusion with Israel, though it was evident that there had been some joint planning.

DAILY MAIL   NOVEMBER 1 1956

Britain at war

Britain is at war with Egypt. That is the grim, inescapable, over-riding fact of this November morning. It should serve to damp down the shrill partisan controversy which was raging in the Commons last night.

This morning British soldiers, sailors, and airmen face battle and sudden death for their country. It is for us all to uphold and support them by uniting behind the Government in the action they have taken.

Many people disagree violently with that action. Time may give them justification. It may prove the Government to have been mistaken in intervening in the Middle East with France, and at this juncture. But we can be sure that so grave a decision was reached only in the deep, sincere conviction that if we had remained quiescent Britain would have suffered irreparable damage.

Power

Questions and criticisms there will be, and must be. We may have some to proffer for ourselves. But let them wait.

Sir Anthony Eden reminded the House that Egypt had been stirring up trouble for a long time. There is no doubt that Colonel Nasser is a dictator of a most dangerous kind. Since he seized the Suez Canal he has repeatedly expressed determination to destroy Israel and drive the Western Powers from the Middle East.

So said the Prime Minister. He might have gone even farther back. The object of the Tripartite Pact of 1950, which has been quoted so much, was not intervention in a war but the prevention of a war by preserving the balance of armed power in that region.

Arms

The supply of arms to Israel and the Arab States was to have been carefully regulated. It was Nasser who deliberately upset that balance by importing large quantities of Russian arms - and thus made certain of the war which has now come to his country.

To ignore all this is, as Sir Anthony says, to shun reality. To ignore it is also to put our country in the wrong. It is true, also, that the Suez Canal is not vital to the US as it is to us, and that 'it is sometimes a Government's duty to take decisions for its own country.'

We must all agree with that, but many will agree, too, that it is a pity we could not have acted promptly on that principle when Nasser stole the Canal in July.

Regrets

There are other things in the present situation which are matters for regret.

It is a pity, for example, that Britain, had to impose her first veto after ten years of UNO on a motion tabled by the US.

It is a pity that Mr. Eisenhower's first intimation of the proposed Anglo-French movement was when he read it in the newspapers.

It is a pity that Australia felt it necessary to abstain from voting with Britain in the Security Council, and that Canada and New Zealand should not be wholeheartedly behind us.

It is a pity Britain got into a situation which the US and the U.S.S.R. together voted against her in the Security Council.

It is a pity, finally, that we have to open this grave chapter in an atmosphere of party faction and personal disagreement.

But we are in it now, and all our energies must be bent towards making it a short, sharp, successful operation. That is essential.

American intervention

However, Britain and France had made a serious error in judgement in assuming that they had the support of the United States. Eisenhower was not happy about being hoodwinked, especially as the Suez operation drew international attention away from the Soviet Union's invasion of Hungary, which had begun just days earlier. With the 1956 Presidential Election just days away, he was forced to criticize allies and put pressure upon them to halt the invasion. He even threatened to stop US support for pound sterling, which would have had far-reaching and disastrous consequences for the British economy. Eden had little choice, and gave way. Only two days after troops had landed, they stopped fighting.

End of the crisis

On November 12 Nasser accepted an international peacekeeping force, which arrived three days later. Both the French and British announced their withdrawal from Egypt, and completed it just before Christmas. Clearing the canal began soon afterwards. Israeli troops also gradually withdrew, leaving Gaza in March 1957; they had received a US commitment that they had shipping rights, including right of passage through the Gulf of Aqaba.

The Suez Canal reopened in April 1957, and remains in Egyptian control. Within weeks, the humiliated Anthony Eden had to resign, and Britain was forced into reassessing its entire foreign policy. The Suez adventure also confirmed Arab distrust of Israel, and enhanced Nasser's prestige. However, it did not have any lasting effect on the Cold War or on the overall balance of power in the region.

OPPOSITE ABOVE LEFT: **Royal Engineers construct a bailey bridge over the Suez Canal at Port Said.**

OPPOSITE MIDDLE LEFT: **British soldiers, backed by tanks, conduct ammunition searches after coming ashore at Port Said in the same landing craft as had been used for the Normandy landings on D-Day.**

OPPOSITE BELOW: **An Egyptian boy walks amongst the wreckage of buildings in Port Said, Egypt. British and French planes attacked military targets in the town from their bases in Cyprus in preparation for the landing of their troops.**

ABOVE RIGHT: **Locals in Rue Ababi, Port Said, assess the damage done during the Anglo-French bombardment.**

TOP: **British tanks roll down the Rue Mohamed Aly in Port Said.**

ABOVE: **Men of the Royal Scots Regiment break into a house in the Arab Quarter of Port Said, in their search for a kidnapped British soldier, Lieutenant Anthony Moorhouse, December 15, 1956.**

RIGHT: **Suspects arrested in the search for Lieutenant Moorhouse are marched in front of an Egyptian working for the British who has hidden his face to conceal his identity. Nasser later admitted Moorhouse had died in captivity.**

Soviet Invasion of Hungary 1956

Stalinist Hungary

After the Second World War, Stalin controlled Eastern Europe through closely allied Communist governments. In Hungary, as elsewhere, there were repressions during the Stalinist era: over 150,000 people had been imprisoned between 1948 and Stalin's death in 1953, and 480 public figures had been executed following show trials.

After Stalin's death, even the Soviets recognized that Hungary had suffered, and the leadership was replaced in 1953 with an administration led by Imre Nagy, a liberal Communist. He was backed by Moscow, and so was his reforming agenda – initially. Nagy held on to office until 1955, when conservative rivals in the Communist Party persuaded Moscow that he was unreliable. He was removed and the Stalinists returned to power. For about a year, Nagy and his supporters formed an unofficial opposition. Nagy's reforms when in office had attracted popular support, and there was little sympathy for another Stalinist regime.

ABOVE: War-torn Budapest during the Soviet invasion.

RIGHT: Hungarians gather around a fallen statue of Stalin in front of the National Theatre in Budapest.

The revolution begins

On October 6, the authorities allowed the reburial of some victims of the show trials. This spark ignited the Hungarian revolution by bringing people onto the streets. Ten days later, students in the provincial city of Szeged organized themselves into the League of Hungarian Students. Similar groups began to form everywhere, and none was allied with the official students' organization.

On October 22, the students at Budapest's Technical University launched a manifesto demanding free speech, economic reform and the return of Nagy. Demonstrations quickly spread on October 23, and escalated into rioting. After a statue of Stalin was overturned, the protesting crowds increased in size and enthusiasm. On October 25, Soviet tanks entered the city to restore order at the request of the Hungarian government and by evening Soviet troops were firing on the demonstrators. The country's Central Committee of the Communist Party announced the return of Nagy the following morning, after an all-night sitting.

ABOVE RIGHT: **Hungarians of London march on the Prime Minister's residence in Downing Street to appeal for British assistance in Hungary. However, the Prime Minister, Sir Anthony Eden was preoccupied with the imminent invasion of Egypt.**

MIDDLE RIGHT: **Hungarians walk past the body of a Soviet soldier lying in front of a wrecked truck in Budapest.**

BELOW: **Rebels ride through the streets of Budapest in a captured Russian tank.**

DAILY MAIL OCTOBER 25, 1956

The revolt spreads

The Hungarian rebellion is spreading through the country. Late tonight, while fierce fighting continued in Budapest, battles flared in three big provincial cities - Debrecen, 120 miles east of the capital, and Szolnok and Szeged in the south. Fighting there was admitted in broadcasts from Budapest and Moscow. Shooting was also heard at the little railway town of St. Gotthard, near the Austrian border.

Moscow radio called the rebels 'mutineers,' thus confirming reports that the anti-Russian rising was set off by Hungarian Army officers.

Budapest tonight is an occupied city and a city where many hundreds lie dead. The Red Army, called in because Hungary's new Government could not quell the revolt, has seized the radio station and other key buildings.

Tank ring

A state of emergency has been declared throughout the country. Martial law and a curfew remain in force in Budapest. Red Army tanks patrol the streets and have flung a ring of steel around the city.

Buildings are aflame, and Russian troops are attacking rebel troops who defied the Government's surrender ultimatum and are holding out against Soviet tanks, troops, machine guns, and artillery.

Hundreds of insurgents with machine-guns, pistols and grenades attacked the Robert Karolv military barracks and the Communist Party headquarters. More buildings went up in flames as the tanks wheeled back and forth, guns spattering.

The rebels resisted for several hours before the Red Army finally trapped them. For them capture meant death at the hands of new Premier Nagy's 'Titoist' Government. Red Army troops are said to have executed 'at least 28' Hungarian soldiers who refused to fight the rebels.

Hungary withdraws from the Warsaw Pact

On the streets barricades were being thrown up, and many of the revolutionaries had managed to acquire arms. Nor was protest confined to Budapest; activist groups had been forming everywhere. As the violence spiked, Nagy proposed a ceasefire and announced what was, in effect, a multi-party government. At his request, the Soviet leader, Nikita Khrushchev, withdrew Soviet tanks from Hungary, but sent more men to the border in case of future unrest.

However, Nagy went too far. He summoned the Soviet ambassador, Andropov, and stated that in response Hungary was now withdrawing unilaterally from the Warsaw Pact. At 7.50 p.m. on November 1 Nagy made a radio announcement that Hungary was now neutral, and asked for United Nations recognition. This was totally unacceptable to Moscow, who feared that other European nations would follow Hungary's example. The West had become distracted by the Suez Crisis and Khrushchev saw his opportunity to act. Negotiations were set up by the Soviet Government, but as soon as members of the Nagy government arrived at the talks, they were all arrested.

DAILY MAIL   NOVEMBER 5, 1956

The murder of Hungary

Hungary, the little country that dared to defy Russia, was murdered today. Russian troops struck at the freedom fighters all over the country. More than 1,000 tanks surrounded Budapest. Soviet soldiers stormed into the Parliament building after Premier Nagy had just broadcast to the world an agonised call for help.

They marched Mr. Nagy out at gun-point. He has been charged with supporting counter-revolutionary forces, East Berlin radio said tonight.

It was 2a.m. when the massacre of Hungary began.

AT 11a.m. telephone lines from Budapest to the free world went dead.

At noon Moscow announced: 'The Hungarian counter-revolution has been crushed.'

But tonight a Hungarian rebel station suddenly came on the air again. 'The Russian Air Force is bombing Budapest,' it announced. 'Smoke and flames can be seen for miles. Fighting is going on house by house and street by street.'

The Russians set up a puppet Government. The man they chose to lead it: Janos Kadar. He betrayed Nagy, because he was in Nagy's Government last week.

In a broadcast at 5 p.m., Kadar had to admit that the freedom men were still holding out. He said: 'There still exists the danger they may get the upper hand.'

Budapest radio came on the air again tonight under its new Communist masters. It reported that Erno Gero, former party boss whom Nagy purged, had been murdered 'in a barbarous fashion by the rebels.'

Last broadcast

One of the last broadcasts heard from the freedom fighters was a heart-rending call for help. 'Civilised people of the world. On the watch tower of 1,000-year-old Hungary the last flames begin to go out. The Soviet Army is attempting to crush our troubled hearts. Their tanks and guns

are roaring over Hungarian soil.

Our women - mothers and daughters - are sitting in dread. They still have terrible memories of the Army's entry in 1945. Save our souls. SOS – SOS. People of the world, listen to our call. Help us - not with advice, not with words, but with action, with soldiers and arms. In the name of liberty and solidarity we are asking you to help. Our ship is sinking. The light vanishes. The shadows grow darker from hour to hour.

Listen to our cry. Start moving. Extend to us brotherly hands. People of the world, save us. SOS. Help, help, help. God be with you and with us.'

Six thousand Soviet tanks, it is estimated, were used to crush Hungary. The rebels put up an heroic resistance against overwhelming odds. They matched rifles against armoured cars, stone barricades against tanks . . . courage against machine-guns. They flung on Stalin T.34 tanks and hurled petrol bombs into the midst of the crews.

Heroes seized At 'truce' talks

Much of the fighting in the provinces went on in snow-covered fields. And thousands of refugees from the Soviet terror trudged miles in bitter cold to find safety in Austria. Tonight they are still escaping over the frontier, crawling across the fields under cover of darkness. They cannot use the normal frontier roads - Soviet tanks have sealed them all.

For Russia wants nobody to know the ruthless butchery which went on today in the name of Communism.

The Russian attack began at the very moment when two Hungarian leaders were negotiating a settlement. Colonel Paul Maleter, hero of last week's rising, and Major-General Istvan Kovacs went to meet Russian commanders. They were going to discuss the withdrawal of Soviet troops. They came face to face with pistols and were arrested.

Soviet invasion

At 4.00 a.m. on November 4, Soviet tanks rolled into Budapest. An hour later, broadcasts were made from the east – which was occupied by the Soviets – announcing the replacement of Nagy by Janos Kadar. Nagy, still in Budapest, made a final dramatic broadcast, calling for resistance. He and his colleagues fled to the Yugoslav embassy, and were granted asylum.

There was intense resistance to the Soviet troops, but the resisters had little chance of success. The Russian army controlled Budapest within three days, and Kadar's government was sworn in on November 7. A few workers' councils survived to the end of the year, and there were sporadic strikes, but in January 1957 the death penalty was introduced for inciting strikes, and a new wave of repression began.

Execution of Nagy

Several thousand people were killed in the fighting, 341 were executed in the aftermath, and as many as 200,000 fled the country. Many thousands went to prison or internment camps, and others lost their jobs or were placed under surveillance. The international impact of the uprising and the unequivocal Soviet response was enormous.

Imre Nagy was tricked into leaving the Yugoslav embassy after three weeks. He was arrested and spirited away to Romania before being secretly returned for his trial on June 15, 1958. He was found guilty of inciting a counter-revolution and was executed at dawn the following day.

Times have changed. On the thirty-first anniversary of his execution, Nagy's remains were reburied with full honours, in the presence of about 100,000 people. A new national holiday was also introduced: October 23.

OPPOSITE LEFT: **A Soviet tank lies abandoned outside the Kilian Barracks in Budapest.**

OPPOSITE ABOVE INSET: **A young Hungarian rebel, holding a submachine gun, stands by a long line of slain Soviet soldiers.**

ABOVE LEFT: **Hungarians burn portraits of Stalin in the streets.**

LEFT: **Patrons and staff at a local store look on as members of the Hungarian revolutionary forces take aim at Communist secret police officers in Budapest.**

BELOW: **Hungarian rebels wave their national flag from a tank captured in Budapest's main square.**

Cuban Missile Crisis 1962

The Bay of Pigs invasion

In the early 1960s, the United States had a steadily growing arsenal of nuclear weapons. There had been 9 in 1946, there were 841 by 1952, and ten years later there were about 28,000. Some were based in Turkey, in striking distance of the Soviet Union. Though the US had clearly outpaced the Soviets, their nuclear arsenal was also growing. This added a very perilous element to the edgy situation between the two superpowers. Cuba was to become the most serious flashpoint.

The island of Cuba, physically close to the US mainland, had been allied to the States while under the leadership of Batista. However, Batsta's regime had been overthrown in 1959 and it became a Communist state with links to the Soviet Union under Fidel Castro. The US had been trying to depose Castro, and in 1961 an attempt to launch a counter-revolution was made at the Bay of Pigs by CIA-trained exiles. It failed, increasing Castro's wariness in the process, and making it likely that there would be another attempt.

DAILY MAIL APRIL 19, 1961

The truth about Cuba

Let us make no mistake about what is happening in Cuba. This is a trial of strength between the two Great Powers and ideologies which divide the world.

The situation in the island, which has become a Communist outpost, is a deadly threat not only to the US but to all the Americas and the free world. President Kennedy appears to be doing what he can to remove it. We say 'appears' because American 'intervention', if it can be so called, is obscure and confused. No US troops are to be employed, but the landings are certainly by American trained and equipped Cuban rebels.

Is this aggression? Is it Yankee Imperialism? Some people here are already saying it is. So is Mr. Kruschev, who, not for the first time, has organised anti-American demonstrations in Moscow and sent a Note full of menace to Washington.

No one doubts the gravity of what is happening. Everyone knows that military action on any scale anywhere can be a threat to world peace. But is Freedom always to be blackmailed into abandoning its rights? Must Democracy every time give way to Tyranny?

Castro has become a worse dictator than Batista, whom he displaced. He has betrayed his comrades, countrymen, and ideals, and has made Cuba a Red satellite. Such serious charges should be supported by facts and here are a few. In the past nine months more than 30,000 tons of arms, have poured into Cuba from the Iron Curtain countries. Castro's armed forces have been completely re-equipped by the Communists. Today Cuba has the largest ground forces in the American continent, apart from the US.

Such is the size of the military threat - begun, let us note, not by America but by Russia.

Soviet missiles in Cuba

During April 1962, the Soviet Union under Khrushchev supplied Castro with a range of cruise missiles. The following month the decision was taken to base nuclear missiles in Cuba, under Soviet control. Work began on preparing nine bases, and the first delivery was made during the night of September 8. This helped consolidate Castro's position and also – as far as the Soviets were concerned – went some way to redress the balance of power.

On October 8, the Cuban President Dorticos announced to the UN Assembly that his country would defend itself if attacked, and stated that it now had the means to do so. On October 14, reconnaissance photographs were taken by a US U-2 spy plane revealing that missile bases were under construction on the island. The photographs were shown to US President Kennedy two days later.

OPPOSITE ABOVE: **Anti-Castro Cubans train in the use of rifles, pistols and bayonets on No Name Key, about 15 miles from Marathon, Florida, in the Florida Keys.**

OPPOSITE BELOW: **The United States Naval base at Guantanamo Bay, Cuba, pictured just before the crisis. Reinforcements were sent to the base as the sensational events unfolded.**

ABOVE: **The revolutionary hero Ernesto 'Che' Guevara is sworn in as Cuban Industry Minister in 1961. He played an important role in facilitating the relationship between Cuba and the Soviet Union. He later left Cuba to export the revolution elsewhere, but was captured and executed in Bolivia in 1967.**

ABOVE LEFT: **President Kennedy and former President Eisenhower discuss the Bay of Pigs Invasion at Camp David in April 1961.**

ABOVE RIGHT: **Fidel Castro of Cuba and Soviet Nikita Kruschev embrace on the floor of the United Nations General Assembly in New York in 1960.**

RIGHT: **This image, taken by an American U-2 spy plane, revealed the presence of Soviet missile sites in Cuba and precipitated the crisis.**

DAILY MAIL OCTOBER 24, 1962

The evidence - US pictures show rocket sites

THIS is the spy-plane evidence taken from a high-flying U-2 which prompted the Cuban blockade. Here, according to United States experts, is unmistakable proof of Russian missiles being readied on Cuban soil.

Seven 1,100-mile medium-range ballistic missiles lie under canvas covers on their own trailers. In between are two maintenance shelters. To one side stands a giant erector-launcher.

This picture is a segment, enlarged 20 times, from a panoramic view of a square mile of Cuban woodland which is the scene of frenzied activity.

About 1,000 yards from the rockets are the first scars of concrete roads and launching pads under construction. Nearby is a tented missile town - in the open with no attempt at camouflage. Scattered through the woodlands are more erector-launchers and another rocket on its trailer.

The missiles are clearly identifiable as Russian medium-range rockets of a type seen before on sites close to the Iron Curtain. They are early liquid-fuelled type which can carry a warhead in the low megaton range - between 1m. and 5,000,000 tons T.N.T. equivalent. From this site they could reach Washington in minutes.

United States authorities last night released nine pictures as proof of their contention that a Russian build-up in Cuba had begun. The evidence includes photos taken obliquely by high-flying U-2s of rocket bases, airfields littered with Soviet jet fighters and bombers, and a harbour near Havana with Russian Navy patrol boats armed with anti-shipping guided missiles.

Russia on Alert

RUSSIA tonight cancelled leave for all armed forces and put them on 'battle alert.' Demobilisation of rocket troops, men from anti-aircraft detachments and submarine units was halted. The orders were given by Marshal Rodion Malinovsky, Defence Minister, after an emergency Kremlin meeting with Mr. Kruschev and the Council of Ministers of the U.S.S.R. Marshal Andrei Grechko, Commander-in-Chief of the satellite forces of the Warsaw Pact, also ordered an alert for all land and naval forces.

The official Russian news agency, Tass, said the measures were taken 'in connection with the provocative actions of the American Government and the aggressive intentions of the American armed forces.' The new American Ambassador, Mr. Foy Kohler, was called to the Foreign Ministry and handed the Soviet statement saying the blockade could 'unleash a nuclear war.' It was broadcast to the nation every half-hour this afternoon. The blockade was denounced as piratical and President Kennedy accused of cynicism and hypocrisy in declaring that Soviet rockets in Cuba were a menace to the United States.

American Response

There were several possible responses: to do nothing, to find a diplomatic solution, to attack the bases by air, to invade or opt for a naval blockade. The Joint Chiefs of Staff recommended invasion and a blockade, believing that the Soviets would not retaliate. Kennedy was less convinced; he pointed out that the US would retaliate in similar circumstances, and there was no reason to believe that the USSR might behave differently. Kennedy knew that he had to stand firm, but recognized this put him in a dangerous situation, especially if the Soviets retaliated in West Berlin.

On 22 October, Kennedy announced that the Soviet missiles should be withdrawn and ordered a naval blockade. He also said that any nuclear attack would be met by 'a full retaliatory response upon the Soviet Union'. US ships moved into position, and Khrushchev authorized Soviet commanders to launch nuclear missiles if there was a ground assault. Castro certainly believed this was likely, and Cuban forces were prepared.

DAILY MAIL OCTOBER 23, 1962

Cuba Blockade

President Kennedy tonight began a drastic military and naval blockade of Cuba. Any ship, Russian or otherwise, found carrying arms to Castro will be turned back.

After the President announced this massive military operation to 'quarantine' the island, the Defence Department said it was prepared to sink Soviet ships if necessary to prevent offensive weapons reaching Cuba.

In an atmosphere of crisis President Kennedy told the nation on television and radio that Russian medium- and long-range missiles capable of delivering nuclear weapons from Hudson Bay to Peru were being installed in Cuba.

President Kennedy announced these moves:

ONE - A strict quarantine on all offensive military equipment being sent to Cuba. 'All ships of any kind bound for Cuba from whatever nation or port will, if found to contain cargoes of offensive weapons, be turned back,' he warned. 'This quarantine will be extended if needed to other types of cargo and carriers. We are not at this time however, denying the necessities of life, as the Soviet attempted to do in their Berlin blockade in 1948.'

TWO - The President directed continued and increased United States air and naval watch on Cuba and its military build-up. He ordered American armed forces 'to prepare for any eventualities - I trust that in the interest of both the Cuban people and the Soviet technicians at these sites the hazards to all concerned of continuing this threat will be recognised.'

THREE - America's policy henceforth will be to regard any nuclear missile launched from Cuba against any nation in the Western hemisphere 'as an attack by the Soviet Union on the United States requiring a full retaliatory response on Russia.'

FOUR - He asked for an emergency meeting of the United Nations Security Council tomorrow to take action against 'this latest Soviet threat to world peace.' The American resolution will call for the prompt dismantling and withdrawal of all offensive weapons in Cuba under supervision of UN observers before the blockade can be lifted.

FIVE - 'I call upon Mr. Kruschev to halt and eliminate this clandestine, reckless and provocative threat to world peace and to stabilise relations between our two nations,' said Mr. Kennedy. 'I call upon him further to abandon this course of world domination and to join in an historic effort to end the perilous arms race and transform the history of man. He has an opportunity to move the world back from the abyss of destruction - by returning to his Government's own words, that it had no need to station missiles outside its own territory, and withdrawing these weapons from Cuba. By refraining from any action which will widen or deepen the present crisis and then by participating in a search for peaceful and permanent solutions.'

Back from the Brink

No one was in any doubt about the seriousness of the situation; it was taking the world to the brink of nuclear war and the two leaders seemed to be trapped in their relative positions. Finally Khrushchev, older and more experienced, made a move. At 6.00 p.m. on October 26, the State Department received a bargaining message apparently written by Khrushchev himself. It was considered overnight, and an exchange of telegrams and messages – and misunderstandings – between intermediaries began. The following day a spy plane was shot down, and at 3.41 p.m. shots were fired at others; these were later revealed as the result of purely local decisions. At 4.00 p.m. Kennedy sent a message to U Thant, the Secretary-General of the United Nations, asking him to ascertain whether the Soviets would suspend construction of the bases while negotiations took place.

At 9.00 a.m. on October 28 Khrushchev broadcast on Radio Moscow. He stated that there would be no further work undertaken on the bases, and that dismantling would begin. Kennedy praised this as 'an important and constructive contribution to peace'.

Behind the scenes there had been an agreement that the US would withdraw their own missiles from Turkey, but this was not made public and Khrushchev suffered as a result. The US had also agreed, this time publicly, that there would be no invasion of Cuba, ironically strengthening Castro's position. A hot-line was also set up, ensuring that the leaders of the superpowers could talk to each other directly should the need arise in the future. Disaster had been averted.

OPPOSITE LEFT: President Kennedy reports personally to the nation on the status of Cuban crisis, telling the American people that Soviet missile bases in Cuba are being destroyed.

OPPOSITE RIGHT: Fidel Castro denounces the American blockade as 'piracy' and puts Cuba on a war footing during a television broadcast to his nation on October 23.

OPPOSITE BELOW: Demonstrators stage a sit-in in Trafalgar Square, London, in opposition to the blockade against Cuba.

BELOW: At a meeting of the National Revolutionary Militia in Havana, Castro promises "No gratuitous attacks and no gratuitous hostile acts" against the United States.

BELOW INSET: Soviet tanks and troops parade through the streets of Havana, Cuba. Although the nuclear missiles were removed, Soviet influence remained, and the island remains Communist to this day.

DAILY MAIL OCTOBER 29, 1962

1962 Kruschev pulls out, President Kennedy applauds

The Cuban crisis is over. Mr. Kruschev has ordered all Soviet missile bases to be dismantled and shipped back to Russia. President Kennedy swiftly welcomed the surprise Kremlin move as 'a statesmanlike decision' and 'an important and constructive contribution to peace.'

Tonight, in a personal letter to Mr. Kruschev, the President said that perhaps now - 'as we step back from danger' - East and West could made real progress on disarmament. All signs point to an early Kennedy-Kruschev meeting, possibly burgeoning into a full Summit conference on every outstanding world issue.

Mr. Kruschev struck one sombre note in his 'no strings' offer to get out of Cuba. He charged that an American spy plane had this weekend flown over Russia - in the Chukotka Peninsula area near Alaska. And he warned: 'An intruding aircraft can easily be taken for a bomber with nuclear weapons, and that can push us towards a fatal step.'

Mr. Kruschev's complete surrender came in a new letter to the President early today in which: He conceded that his weapons in Cuba were 'in fact grim weapons,' and said he well understood the anxiety of the American people. He announced he had issued an order for the 'dismantling of the weapons, their crating and return to the Soviet Union' - with UN verification.

He took up as a firm guarantee a pledge by President Kennedy, during their rapid exchange of letters over the weekend, that there would be no invasion of Cuba by the United States or any other nation in the Western hemisphere. He called for a continued 'exchange of opinions aimed at a détente between NATO and the Warsaw Pact nations, a prohibition of atomic and thermo-nuclear weapons, general disarmament and other questions causing international tension.'

War of Liberation in Zimbabwe 1964-1980

Unilateral Declaration of Independence

By 1965 the decolonization of the British Empire was well under way and power had been transferred in all of Britain's major African colonies except Southern Rhodesia. This colony was home to a sizeable white settler community, which was largely hostile to decolonization on Britain's terms, namely the enfranchisement of Rhodesia's black population. To pre-empt British decolonization and maintain white minority rule, the Rhodesian government of Ian Smith unilaterally declared its independence from Britain on November 11, 1965. The British government's Prime Minister Harold Wilson opted against the use of military force to reverse the illegal declaration, but did impose economic sanctions.

ABOVE: Rhodesian government forces patrol the bush in search of ZANU guerrillas.

ABOVE LEFT INSET: Cecil Rhodes, the statesman who gave his name to Rhodesia, is pictured in the colony in 1896.

ABOVE RIGHT INSET: British Prime Minister Harold Wilson (left) welcomes the Rhodesian Prime MInister, Ian Smith (right), to Downing Street for talks just one month before UDI. Wilson refused to deploy the army to Rhodesia, believing such a move would be opposed by the British public.

National Liberation Movements

National liberation movements had begun opposing white minority rule in Rhodesia even before Ian Smith's unilateral declaration of independence. In 1964, the main movements, the Zimbabwe African National Union (ZANU) and the Zimbabwe African People's Union (ZAPU), were banned by Ian Smith's government and forced into exile in neighbouring Zambia. From there they began an insurgency that raged in the Rhodesian bush for the next fifteen years. ZANU, which came to be ruled by Robert Mugabe, drew its support from the majority Shona ethnic group and obtained its funding from China. ZAPU, under the command of Joshua Nkomo, was backed by the Ndebele ethnic group and was funded by the Soviet Union. In the early 1970s, the Zambian government began clamping down on ZANU and ZAPU, encouraging ZANU to relocate to Mozambique where a Chinese-backed resistance movement, FRELIMO, had liberated large areas from Portuguese colonial rule. From its new bases in Mozambique, ZANU was able to intensify the war in Rhodesia itself from 1972.

Rhodesian Isolation

In 1975 Portugal withdrew from Mozambique and FRELIMO took power. Not only did this greatly benefit ZANU, it also denied landlocked Rhodesia access to its nearest ports. Only the presence of a friendly government in South Africa to the south prevented Rhodesia from being completely encircled by hostile majority-rule governments. However, South Africa was seeking engagement with the continent's black leaders in the hopes of reaping economic rewards, leaving the Smith government increasingly isolated. Smith realized that some form of black participation in the government was necessary and wished to arrange this on his own terms rather than wait to have it imposed by ZANU and ZAPU, which had set aside their differences and joined together in a 'Patriotic Front'. Smith agreed to hold an election in April 1979 to bring moderate black politicians into the government, and Bishop Abel Muzorewa became Rhodesia's first black Prime Minister. However, violence persisted as ZANU and ZAPU did not participate in the election.

Majority Rule

In June 1979, Margaret Thatcher came to power in Britain and sought a lasting settlement to the crisis in Rhodesia. All sides were brought to Lancaster House in London to work out an agreement, which was finally reached in December 1979. Under its terms, majority-rule was introduced, but strict guarantees were issued for the rights of the white minority. Elections were held in March 1980, with ZANU winning a majority of the seats. Robert Mugabe became Prime Minister and Rhodesia was given the African name 'Zimbabwe'.

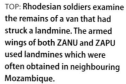

TOP: Rhodesian soldiers examine the remains of a van that had struck a landmine. The armed wings of both ZANU and ZAPU used landmines which were often obtained in neighbouring Mozambique.

ABOVE: Britain and America vote in favour of United Nations Security Council Resolution 415 in September 1977. The Resolution called for the expansion of economic sanctions against the regime, which the UN had first called for in December 1966. The United Nations Security Council met many times to discuss the situation in Rhodesia beginning in November 1965 when the Council condemned the unilateral Declaration of Independence.

LEFT: Major General John Acland, the commander of the Commonwealth Monitoring Force in Rhodesia, inspects a group of ZANU's guerrillas. The Commonwealth Monitoring Force was dispatched to the country to ensure that the country's first truly democratic elections were not marred by violence.

BELOW: Robert Mugabe of ZANU and Joshua Nkomo, the leader of ZAPU, announce agreement on the terms of the ceasefire at a press conference at Lancaster House in London. ZAPU merged with ZANU in the late 1980s to create the ZANU-PF party under Mugabe's leadership.

Vietnam
1965–1975

French Indochina

For over 1,000 years, between about 110 BC and AD 940, Vietnam was ruled by China. The collapse of the T'ang dynasty permitted a successful rebellion, which ushered in a period of independence that would endure until the end of the 14th Century. The Chinese would make repeated attempts to regain control, with varying degrees of success, until 1802, when they were expelled with the aid of the French. By 1883 however, France had claimed Vietnam as its own, and it would be subsumed into French Indochina along with Cambodia and Laos.

The First Indochina War

Resistance to French rule grew steadily into the 20th Century, and by 1941, a disaffected young man, originally named Nguyen That Thanh, had established the League for the Independence of Vietnam, or the Vietminh. By this time, he had also changed his name to Ho Chi Minh. During The Second World War, with US support, Vietminh forces defeated the Japanese in the north of the country and Ho went on to found the (largely unrecognized) Democratic Republic of Vietnam in 1945. In the south however, the British liberators returned control to the French, and within a year, skirmishes had broken out between French troops and Vietminh guerrillas that would ultimately escalate into the First Indochina War. France attempted to reunite Vietnam under former emperor Bao Da in 1949, but having previously cooperated with both the Japanese and French, he was mistrusted by Ho's government in Hanoi. The Vietminh continued to wage war and now had the backing of the new Communist government in China. Fearful of Communist expansion in the region, the US then began to supply French forces, but despite superior technology, most notably air support, the French would be overrun by General Vo Nguyen Giap's forces at the Battle of Dien Bien Phu in 1954, bringing the conflict to a close.

OPPOSITE ABOVE: **American GIs cautiously approach a South Vietnamese girl and woman during a search in Thuam Long for Vietcong weapons, December 1969.**

OPPOSITE BELOW: **French troops in an American-built amphibious vehicle manoeuvre through the swampy countryside of southern Vietnam**

BELOW: **French Legionnaires capture a Vietminh prisoner during their drive north on Thainguyen in North Indochina.**

LEFT TOP: **Indochinese peasants retreat towards Hanoi under the protection of French soldiers.**

LEFT MIDDLE ABOVE: **Female resistance fighters parade on the esplanade of the ancient Angor Wat temple in Cambodia.**

LEFT MIDDLE BELOW: **French troops scramble out of an amphibian tank and up a river bank during the hard fighting against Vietminh forces.**

LEFT BOTTOM: **French and colonial soldiers wade along a shallow stream in the search for Communist guerillas.**

A nation divided

At the Geneva Conference that followed, Vietnam was divided by a Demilitarised Zone (DMZ) along the 17th parallel, with Ho leading a Communist government in North Vietnam, and the French retaining control of South Vietnam, with a government headed by Bao Da's former Prime Minister, Ngo Dinh Diem. Reunification elections were scheduled for 1956, when the French planned to withdraw, but Diem, who had begun strengthening his position with US support, refused to participate. In response, Ho began planning to take back South Vietnam by military force.

US involvement under Kennedy

After World War Two, the US had adopted a strategy of containment, in order to prevent what Presidents Truman and Eisenhower referred to as the 'domino effect', whereby the fall of one nation to Communism would trigger the fall of neighbouring states. With Castro's seizure of Cuba in 1959, and the Cuban Missile Crisis of 1962, not only was the perceived threat of Communism brought right to America's door, but the very real possibility of nuclear war with the Soviet Union ensured that a conflict against a peasant army thousands of miles away would seem a far more attractive prospect.

However, despite gains by Vietnamese Communist (Vietcong) insurgents in South Vietnam, President Kennedy was reluctant to commit troops, and instead increased financial aid and sent hundreds of military advisors, who would train the Army of the Republic of Vietnam (ARVN) in counter-insurgency.

In early 1963 however, the ARVN were defeated at the Battle of Ap Bac, and the oppressive Diem regime was becoming increasingly unpopular. This led to a Buddhist revolt that culminated in the self-immolation of a number of Buddhist priests. By November, Diem had been overthrown and executed in a coup that was effectively endorsed by the US, and just three weeks later, Kennedy himself was assassinated, to be succeeded by Lyndon B. Johnson.

Operation Rolling Thunder

Throughout 1964, the political situation in South Vietnam became increasingly unstable as the North Vietnamese Army (NVA) began infiltrating the South along the 'Ho Chi Minh Trail' through neighbouring Cambodia and Laos. In response, the US began to plan attacks on the North, whilst sending more aid and personnel to the South.

By August, US-backed attacks had begun against coastal radar stations, during which the destroyer USS *Maddox* was reportedly fired upon in the Gulf of Tonkin. The incident would lead Congress to approve the Southeast Asia, or Tonkin Resolution, enabling the President to conduct military operations without a declaration of war.

Despite this, the Vietcong then stepped up their operations, attacking a number of military targets, as well as the Brinks Hotel in Saigon, finally prompting the US to launch attacks against North Vietnam. Operation Rolling Thunder, a sustained strategic bombing campaign began on March 2, 1965 and within a week, the first US ground troops had come ashore at Da Nang. By the summer, the US draft had doubled and the first major ground offensives had begun.

OPPOSITE LEFT: The body of a slain comrade is carried to an evacuation helicopter by soldiers of the US 1st Cavalry Division in the Ia Drang Valley early in November 1965.

OPPOSITE BELOW: US Marine helicopters drop troops near Da Nang amid reports of Vietcong activity in the area, April 1965.

OPPOSITE RIGHT: US Army helicopters fall into tight landing formation near Phouc Vinh in war zone 'D'.

RIGHT: A Chinook lifts the remains of another helicopter downed by Vietcong ground fire in the An Lao Valley near Bong Son.

BELOW: Men of the 3rd Marine Regiment's 3rd Battalion sit silently during Roman Catholic and Protestant memorial services at Da Nang Air Base for 18 Marines who died fighting near Van Tuong in August 1965.

DAILY MAIL JUNE 10 1965

All The Way With LBJ

The United States appears to be moving inexorably into a full-scale ground war in Vietnam.

Another 2,500 American soldiers landed today at Cam Ranh Bay, 175 miles north-east of Saigon. They are engineers who will build a new port and supply depot. Their arrival came only 24 hours after it was officially announced that henceforth US troops would be committed to 'combat support' of the South Vietnamese Army. These latest reinforcements bring US military strength to 53,500 men.

President Johnson's decision to engage US troops in the coming battles clearly springs from the assessment that on its own the South Vietnamese Army would be unable to withstand the Communist assaults. The President's move marks a critical shift in US policy. After the Korean war, Presidents Eisenhower and Kennedy decided that at all cost the US must avoid involvement in a new ground war on the Asian mainland.

Within six weeks US strength is expected to rise to 70,000. And already there is talk that the numbers will reach 100,000 by the end of the summer. American strategy will be to establish a series of powerful bases along the South Vietnam coast. From them American troops will be sent into battle against the Vietcong forces.

The ground war

Initially, US troops were sent on search and destroy missions, with the intention of engaging the enemy on the battlefield in large numbers, and defeating them with superior technology. However, the NVA and Vietcong were also prepared for a war of attrition, which they would conduct with small-scale guerilla actions; employing hit-and-run tactics to frustrate and demoralise the enemy. By the end of 1966, over 380,000 US servicemen had been committed to Vietnam, with over 5,000 combat deaths and over 30,000 wounded. Most had suffered as a result of snipers, ambushes, mines and home-made booby traps, in a war where the US and their allies (which now included troops from South Korea, Australia and New Zealand), seemed to be fighting a largely invisible foe.

As a result, in early 1967, US forces began clearing huge swathes of jungle north of Saigon with bulldozers, bombs, napalm, and chemical defoliants such as Agent Orange, which would not only expose miles of Vietcong tunnel systems, but result in the deaths and forced resettlement of thousands of civilians. It was hoped that the civilian population could be physically separated from Vietcong insurgents, but by 1967, when General Nguyen Van Thieu became president in the South, it was estimated that over half the rural villages below the 17th Parallel were under Vietcong control, and towards the end of the year, the NVA began launching attacks across the DMZ.

DAILY MAIL MAY 22 1966
Civil war threatens US base

South Vietnam's civil war erupted into new violence last night. Tanks and planes were thrown into a fierce battle in the northern rebel-held city of Da Nang. In Saigon police used truncheons and tear gas against Buddhist demonstrators. The rebels threatened to wreck an American air-base unless US Marines drive South Vietnam Government troops out of Da Nang.

Yesterday's day-long battles shocked the US and plunged the White House into deep gloom. Washington fears the revolt in South Vietnam's Army may grow and force America to disown Marshal Ky, the Premier.

And new Soviet threats of massive aid for North Vietnam could lead to a showdown between Russia and America.

Da Nang's worst day of terror ended last night in a 25-minute machine-gun and mortar battle. government troops, who now hold all the key points, went into action against a rebel relief column – believed to be South Vietnam's 2nd Division –marching on the city.

Government Skyraiders, making their first raid of Da Nang's civil war, strafed an advancing column and forced it back. The rebels said five of their soldiers were killed.

American Marines moved eight wounded to the pagodas where rebel troops and Buddhist monks are holding out.

OPPOSITE ABOVE: Two US soldiers stand with the wrapped body of a fallen comrade amid the smoke of a signal grenade in war zone D near Saigon.

OPPOSITE BELOW: Vietcong guerrilla suspects, blindfolded and linked arm to shoulder, are led by US infantrymen to a central interrogation point near Long Thanh.

ABOVE: A wounded veteran of the battle for Hill 881 is helped to a helicopter for evacuation, May 1967.

LEFT: A lone marine sits atop Hill 881, just days after the gruelling battle for the hill had been won.

TOP: A soldier fires at the Vietcong snipers who have just shot and wounded the man behind.

BELOW: In scenes reminiscent of D-Day, Marines from the 7th Fleet Amphibious Ready Group storm the beach at Vung Mu.

The Tet Offensive

By the end of 1967, the Border Battles at the DMZ had given the impression that an invasion of the South might be imminent, but US forces were completely unprepared when the Tet Offensive was launched on January 31, 1968. Breaking a ceasefire respecting the Vietnamese New Year, the NVA and Vietcong hoped to inspire a popular uprising by launching simultaneous attacks in towns and cities across the South. The US Embassy in Saigon was stormed, and battles raged for days in the streets of Saigon and Hué. When the fighting subsided, the US would claim a military victory, but the American public had seen the horrors of the offensive broadcast across the nation, and support for both the President and the war was rapidly eroding. As a result, by March, Johnson had announced that he would not be standing for another term, and by May, peace talks had begun in Paris. The negotiations quickly deadlocked, so Johnson tried to inject some momentum by announcing the cessation of Operation Rolling Thunder, during which almost a million tons of bombs had been dropped on North Vietnam with seemingly little effect. In fact, NVA infiltration into the South had continued to mount in 1968, as had US casualties, whilst social unrest had continued to grow across the US.

DAILY MAIL MARCH 1 1968

LBJ pours in troops

President Johnson has decided that the US war effort in Vietnam must be expanded. He has ruled out negotiations until the Allies regain the initiative in the fighting.

More troops will be sent to Vietnam as quickly as possible. The number still seems undecided but some reports say that General Westmoreland, military chief in Vietnam, has asked for 200,000. This would bring the total to 725,000. With the military manpower in the US almost exhausted, Mr Johnson has no alternative but to call up reserves.

Meanwhile American peace offers will remain officially open – but Mr Johnson has no intention of pressing them.

Saigon

US bombers struck heavily at North Vietnamese bases being enlarged to launch the first air raids on the south.

Main target was the heavily defended Vinh area, 150 miles north of the demilitarised zone. MiGs and bombers are expected to take off from Vinh to support an offensive along the border zone. Marines at Khe Sanh have been armed already with anti-aircraft weapons.

Hanoi was reported to have been bombed again today. So was the radio centre ten miles away, which controls anti-aircraft defences.

In battles last week 470 American Servicemen were killed – second only to the record 543 killed the week before. The Communists lost 5,769 dead and the South Vietnamese and other allies lost 453.

Hue

A hundred South Vietnamese soldiers and officials were found shot dead with their hands tied in caves outside Hue. This raised fears for another 200 kidnapped by the Vietcong when they held the city.

Anthony Carthew asks: But are they any good in a war like this?

There are 525,000 Americans tied up in Vietnam, but the generals say this is nowhere near enough. They say dangerous strategic gaps have appeared in the defences and the generals are right – at least in terms of the kind of war they are trying to fight here.

Since the offensive forcing the Americans and South Vietnamese to fall back on the towns and cities, there are great holes in the defensive net which was strung across the country to prevent enemy infiltration. The significant point about the way the Americans have organized their war is that, though half a million men may be serving in Vietnam, only 60,000 to 70,000 are fighting.

OPPOSITE ABOVE LEFT: **A Marine Armoured Vehicle, armed with six recoiless guns, patrols the streets of Hue at the end of the 26-day battle for control of the city during the Tet Offensive.**

OPPOSITE ABOVE RIGHT: **The 1st Brigade, 9th Infantry Division disembark from assault helicopters in rice paddies near Tan An after patrol helicopters report sighting Vietcong in the area.**

OPPOSITE BELOW: **Marines use empty shell casings to further strengthen the fortifications around the fort of Khe Sanh near the Vietnamese border. The North Vietnamese Army attacked the fort for ten days before the start of the Tet Offensive to draw US troops away from garrisoning towns and cities in the South.**

ABOVE: **A soldier runs for safety after dropping a grenade into the Vietcong bunker (seen on the left of the picture).**

RIGHT: **Marines help one another across a stream swollen by monsoon rains near Da Nang.**

BELOW: **Frightened refugees from the towns and villages around Khe Sanh shelter from North Vietnamese mortars at the American base.**

BELOW RIGHT: **Marines at Khe Sanh use sniperscopes attached to their M-16 rifles to get a better aim at the North Vietnamese encircling their base.**

Nixon and 'Vietnamization'

On January 20, 1969, Richard Nixon was inaugurated as the President of the United States. By March, secret bombing raids would be launched against the Ho Chi Minh Trail in Cambodia, despite the country's neutrality. Soon afterwards, the last major engagement between US and NVA troops would take place at Ap Bia, or 'Hamburger Hill', and the seemingly senseless loss of life entailed would herald not only a return to small-scale operations, but an escalation in anti-war sentiment both in the US, and amongst frontline troops.

Within five days of his inauguration, Nixon resumed peace talks in Paris. He proposed a simultaneous withdrawal of NVA and US troops from South Vietnam, but negotiations once again stalled, this time over Vietcong participation in a coalition government in the South. Nevertheless, by July the US began withdrawing troops as part of Nixon's plan for 'Vietnamization'; a gradual removal of US ground forces to allow the ARVN to take over more of the fighting. In parallel, Nixon's National Security Advisor, Henry Kissinger, began behind-the-scenes discussions with the North Vietnamese government. However, Ho Chi Minh died of a heart attack in September 1969 and was succeeded by Le Duan who pledged to continue to fight on until the US had pulled out of the war.

DAILY MAIL JUNE 9 1969

Nixon pulls out 25,000 troops

America is to withdraw 25,000 combat troops from South Vietnam, President Nixon announced in Midway Island today. The withdrawal will start within 30 days and will be completed by August 31.

President Nixon spoke during a lunchtime break in his talks with President Thieu of South Vietnam. He said the Americans would be replaced by South Vietnamese troops. Further withdrawals of United States forces will be considered as conditions in Vietnam permit.

President Nixon said President Thieu had recommended the initial troop withdrawal and the US Commander in South Vietnam, General Creighton Abrams, had given his approval.

President Thieu, speaking immediately after Mr Nixon, said the withdrawal was made possible by the improvement in the South Vietnamese Armed Forces and by progress in the pacification and rural development programmes. He expressed gratitude for 'the sacrifices generously accepted by the American people in joining us in the defence of Vietnam.'

He was now confident of a 'bright and beautiful tomorrow and long-lasting peace, prosperity and brotherhood in Asia.'

President Nixon's announcement reflects optimism that the Paris peace talks, which began in May 1968, may now make some progress after months of stalemate.

America has just over 500,000 troops in South Vietnam. More than 34,000 US Servicemen have been killed there since January 1961.

OPPOSITE LEFT: An American machine-gunner team fires as Vietcong close in on their position.

OPPOSITE RIGHT: Soldiers of the First Cavalry Division descend from a Chinook helicopter into thick brush near the Cambodian border.

ABOVE: Troops from the 1st Air Cavalry Division search for Vietcong in the underbrush with the assistance of the agile Cayuse helicopters.

FAR LEFT: Members of the 4th Battalion, 25th Infantry Division haul a sampan through a canal on the edge of the Mekong Delta. The 4th Battalion were the first into the Delta and were tasked with evaluating conditions before more troops were sent in.

LEFT ABOVE: General William C. Westmoreland, Commander of US Forces in South Vietnam from 1964 to 1968, stands beneath three combat-ready Hawk anti-aircraft missiles at Da Nang. In the aftermath of the Tet Offensive, Westmoreland was recalled to Washington, where he became Army Chief of Staff. General Creighton Abrams took over command in Vietnam.

LEFT: An infantryman suffering a gunshot wound to his hand receives treatment (left) before immediately resuming his duties (right).

DAILY MAIL OCTOBER 16 1969
Millions in Vietnam protest

Candlelit processions and vigils closed Moratorium Day across America tonight. It was a long day of non-violent protest marred only by a few disturbances and scuffles to involve the police.

In thousands of cities, towns and hamlets it was rallies, speeches, marches, prayers – with counter-protests by the people who opposed the massive call for the ending of the Vietnam war. The demonstrations centred on the college campuses – but elementary and high schools were half empty in many parts of the nation.

Tonight ten New York theatre shows closed down, and on the stages that stayed open curtain speeches were made in support of the Moratorium. When the curtains fell, many of the actors and actresses converged on garish Times Square for a demonstration – while on Fifth Avenue the candle-bearing marchers massed at St Patrick's Cathedral.

Streets were blocked as thousands of people thronged from the rallies to new assembly points – but all was still orderly.

Mayor Lindsay, Senator Eugene McCarthy and other prominent speakers at the series of rallies ran into opposition, with some counter-demonstrators flaunting placards like 'Moratorium Day is for Commies and pigs.'

But, by and large, as the sun fell and the candles were lit, the verdict was an impressive display of non-violent protest on a scale never before known.

DAILY MAIL NOVEMBER 21, 1969

The story that stunned America

The massacre of two Vietnamese villages is being felt here as a grave American defeat.

After 20 months of official secrecy all attempts to stifle revelations about the slaughter in My Lai and the neighbouring Son My villages broke down today. Cleveland, an American city the size of Liverpool, woke up to see the first, frightening evidence in pictures of the killings in My Lai. Their local newspaper, the Plain Dealer, was the first in the world to print pictures alleged to show the massacre.

Most of Cleveland's 800,000 people were dimly aware of reports of the massacre because the death toll was built up slowly over several days – first 30 civilians, then 109, then 300, now 567 according to the latest reports.

Terror

But not until the front page picture of scores of tangled bodies of men, women and children strewn across the ground reached them did the reports ring true. Vain attempts were made by the Army authorities last night to persuade the Plain Dealer's editor not to print pictures of the dead taken after the massacre.

The Plain Dealer printed the pictures as fact, not allegation pictures. It said nothing to suggest that their authenticity might be in doubt. One of the eight pictures showed three South Vietnamese women, one holding a little boy, cowering with terror on their faces and a small girl sheltering behind them.

The photographer, Ronald L. Haeberle, 28, an Army combat photographer, said in a page one article that moments after he took the picture the entire group was cut down. 'I noticed a woman appear from some cover and this one GI fired at her first then they all started shooting at her. I'd never seen Americans shoot civilians like that.'

Many Cleveland people refused to

believe that American soldiers could be responsible for the massacre. Others were upset and angry. Mr Haeberle added in his article that as troops moved in closer to the village 'they just kept shooting at people. I remember this man distinctly, holding a small child in one arm and another child in the other walking towards us. Then all of a sudden a burst of fire and they were cut down. They were about 20ft. away. One machine-gunner did it – he opened up. There was no reaction on the guy doing the shooting. That's the part that really got me. I turned my back because I couldn't look. They opened up with two M16s. On automatic fire they went through the whole clip – 35, 40 shots. I couldn't take a picture of it, it was too much.'

Haeberle said that the attack came at 5.30 a.m. on March 16, 1968. C Company, First Battalion, 20th Infantry Regiment, 11th Light Infantry Brigade went into the hamlet of My Lai Number 4. The Number 4 indicates that there are three other villages in the district with the same name.

'No one really explained the mission, but from what I heard it was suspected that these villages were Vietcong sympathisers and it was thought there were Vietcong there.' The newspaper said that it had checked with the Adjutant General's office at Fort Benning, Georgia, that Haeberle was present in the hamlet as an Army photographer on March 16.

The My Lai revelations come at a time when President Nixon is trying to muster world opinion against Hanoi's refusal to negotiate in Paris. They are a serious blow to his attempts to persuade 'the great silent majority' of his fellow-Americans not to join the camp of the peace marchers. The Pentagon is declining comment on the incident while it is decided whether to court-martial a lieutenant for 'multiple murder.'

OPPOSITE: The war clashed with the tenets of the 'Swinging Sixties' and a major peace movement spread. Millions of people took to the streets in cities across the world to protest against the war.

TOP: A US medic works on the shattered arm of a Viet Cong prisoner who had just been discovered hiding in a bamboo thicket near Duc Pho.

ABOVE: Placards at the ready, a group of mini-skirted girls assemble on the Victoria Embankment in London as they prepare to march on the Labour Party Headquarters to protest against the British government's support for the war in Vietnam.

TOP RIGHT: An aerial view of the destroyed Tu Cung and My Lai hamlets where on March 16, 1968, American troops massacred Vietnamese civilians and burned the villages.

Cambodia and Laos

The conflict took a dramatic turn in March 1970, when Prince Sihanouk of Cambodia was deposed in a coup by General Lon Nol. In order to regain power, Sihanouk aligned himself with the Cambodian Communist group known as the Khmer Rouge. By appearing to have royal assent, the Khmer Rouge saw its ranks swell, prompting further US incursions into the country. This apparent widening of the conflict prompted renewed protests in the US and four demonstrators were killed at Kent State University, Ohio, when National Guardsmen opened fire with live ammunition. From then on, anti-war sentiment in the US grew dramatically and by 1971, Congress had refused funding for any operations involving US ground troops in

DAIL MAIL MAY 1, 1970

2am: US troops in Cambodia attack

American combat troops poured over the Cambodian border in a massive attack early today.

In the most momentous statement of his career President Nixon told the American people in a nation-wide TV broadcast that he had just ordered the troops to make the night assault.

The soldiers were launched against what the President described as 'the headquarters for the entire Communist military operation in South Vietnam.' They moved in after US B-52 bombers made their first raids into Cambodia.

The area of the new attack is 50 miles north of the 'Parrot's Beak' which South Vietnamese troops were attacking with a hundred or so American military 'advisers.'

President Nixon dramatically dropped all pretence that the assault on the North Vietnamese bases behind the Cambodian frontier was a South Vietnamese affair with Americans giving only support and guidance. The President announced: 'This is not an invasion of Cambodia. The areas in which these attacks will be launched are completely occupied and controlled by North Vietnamese forces. Our purpose is not to occupy the areas. Once enemy forces are driven out of these sanctuaries and their military supplies destroyed we will withdraw.'

either Cambodia or Laos. This provided the opportunity to test Nixon's 'Vietnamization' policy in the form of Operation Lam Son 719, an incursion into Laos by 17,000 ARVN troops. Despite US air support, the operation was to prove a massive failure, with the incursion force being routed, having lost almost half of their number. Nevertheless, US troop withdrawals would continue, whilst Australia and New Zealand would announce their intention to pull out of the war.

DAILY MAIL MAY 5, 1970

Four students shot dead in riot

Four students – two of them girls –were shot dead and 15 people injured yesterday when a college demonstration against America's invasion of Cambodia erupted into a gun battle with National Guardsmen and police. The students who died were aged 19 and 20. Three were shot in the chest and one in the head. Four of the injured are in a serious condition.

The shooting broke out at Kent State University in Ohio after National Guardsmen broke up a 300-strong rally with tear gas. Students threw stones at the troops and hurled back tear gas canisters. Then snipers fired on the Guardsmen, who opened up with M1 semi-automatics.

'The crowd was harassing them, they turned and opened fire', said Jerry Stoklas, 20, a campus newspaper photographer. 'I saw five people go down.'

A state of emergency was ordered in Kent. Guardsmen sealed off the town and a curfew was imposed. The university, scene of three days of turmoil, was closed.

Mary Hagan, a student, said: 'The troops started pelting everyone with bullets. Some of the students fell. Then a Guardsman ordered a cease-fire.' Doug McLaran, another student, said: 'I looked towards the sound of guns and saw several people wounded. I ran like hell.'

Adjutant-General Del Corso said: 'The Guard expended its entire supply of tear gas and the mob started to encircle the Guardsmen. A sniper opened fire on the troops from a rooftop and they were also hit by stones and bricks. Guardsmen facing almost certain injury and death were forced to open fire on the attackers.'

President Nixon, who last week called dissenting students 'bums,' commented: 'When dissent turns to violence it invites tragedy. I hope this tragic and unfortunate incident will strengthen the determination of all ... to stand firmly for the right of peaceful dissent and just as strongly against the resort to violence.'

A Justice Department inquiry may be ordered into the shooting.

OPPOSITE BELOW: **An American mortar team fires 60mm shells against Viecong in support of US marines under attack at Cua Viet.**

OPPOSITE ABOVE LEFT: **A wounded paratrooper awaits evacuation during the battle for 'Hamburger Hill' (Dong Ap Bia). Forty-six Americans and more than 500 North Vietnamese died in the battle.**

ABOVE: **A helicopter picks up supplies to take to one of the 9th Infantry Division's forward base camps in the Mekong River Delta.**

ABOVE RIGHT: **Sandbagged bunkers topped with canvas play home to the 4th Infantry Division at a forward camp near the Cambodian border.**

MIDDLE RIGHT: **Army repairman Jerry Blackston passes time before being called to duty. His job is to fix the 'People Sniffers', electrical noses that are fitted to**

patrol helicopters to 'sniff' out enemy hiding places. They work by picking up traces of chemical compounds unique to humans.

BELOW RIGHT: **Battalion Commander Lt. Colonel Ardie E. McClure of the 1st Battalion 8th Cavalry Regiment calls for assistance as he evacuates Private First Class Lyle who was wounded in fighting near Bong Son.**

Peace at hand

Back in the US, the publication of the 'Pentagon Papers', secret documents that revealed a catalogue of military and governmental transgressions, were putting the Nixon administration under further pressure to find a peaceful solution. In early 1972, Nixon decided to open diplomatic relations with North Vietnam's allies, China and the Soviet Union. However, by the time of his visit to Moscow, the NVA had launched a concerted effort to invade the South, which would prompt the indefinite suspension of negotiations, and a massive resumption of bombing in North Vietnam. By the time talks resumed, the last US ground troops had left Vietnam, and in October both the US and Hanoi governments would agree to significant concessions. Kissinger would declare, 'peace is at hand', but before the year was out, negotiations had collapsed and the bombing had begun once more.

The end in sight

By January 1973, North Vietnam had returned to the negotiating table, and on the 23rd, the Paris Peace Accords were announced. A ceasefire would begin and the US would withdraw all remaining personnel, but NVA soldiers stationed in the South would be allowed to remain. Agreements were also made regarding the exchange of POWs, and an outline put in place for a political solution in the South. The Accords were signed on the 27th, and two months later the last US troops were withdrawn. By June, in a reflection of the public mood, Congress had forbidden US military involvement in Southeast Asia, leaving the Khmer Rouge free to seize power in Cambodia, and North Vietnam poised to reclaim the South.

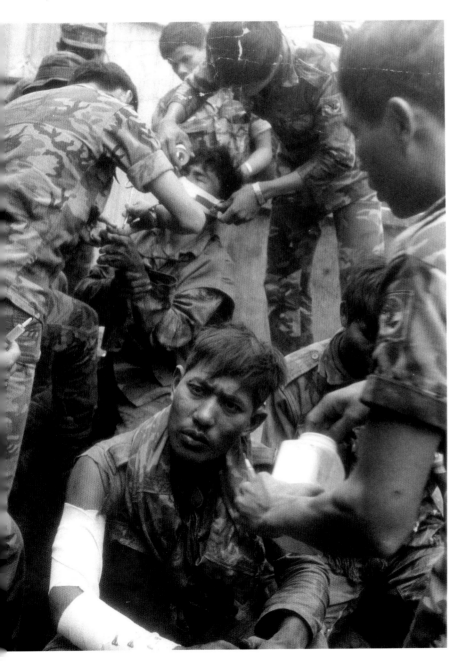

DAIL MAIL JANUARY 24, 1973

Nixon says it: Peace!

The Vietnam war is over. President Nixon went on nationwide television at 3 a.m. today to tell the world that America has achieved 'Peace with honour.'

The agreement initialled in Paris yesterday will effect a ceasefire throughout the war-torn country at midnight on Saturday. Within sixty days from then, said the President, all American troops will leave Vietnam and all US prisoners will be released by Hanoi.

The peace will achieve what America had fought for over so many bloody years, Mr Nixon said. 'South Vietnam has gained the right to determine its own future.'

Millions of Americans watched the Presidential broadcast, listening to the words they had waited so many years to hear. They saw Mr Nixon, calm, composed and matter of fact as he made his historic broadcast.

They saw him address himself to both North and South Vietnam in his vision of the peace to come. 'Ending the war,' he said, ' is only the first step to building the peace. All parties must now see to it that this is a peace that lasts and a peace that heals. This means that the terms of agreement must be scrupulously adhered to.

'Throughout the years of negotiations we have insisted on peace with honour,' the President said. 'In the settlement that has now been agreed to, all the stipulations I have set down have been met.'

Simultaneous announcements

As Mr Nixon spoke, simultaneous announcements were made in Hanoi and Saigon. In the South, President Thieu claimed that his refusal to accept the original peace accord last October and Mr Nixon's subsequent escalation of the bombing of the North had made a significant difference in the peace terms.

Hanoi, he said, had been forced to admit that North and South Vietnam were two separate countries and thus the sovereignty of the South was embodied into the peace agreement.

To the leaders of North Vietnam, the President pledged that the United States was prepared to make a major effort to help the country recover from the war. He said the United States would abide by the agreement but reciprocity would be needed to achieve peace.

President Nixon said: 'To the other major Powers that have been involved, even indirectly, now is the time for mutual restraint so that the peace we have achieved can last.

'Let us be proud that America did not settle for a peace that would have betrayed our ally, that would have ended the war for us but continued the war for the 50 million people of Indochina.'

DAILY MAIL FEBRUARY 13 1973

Goodbye Hanoi ... hello to freedom

The first group of repatriated American prisoners of war walked proudly back to freedom yesterday with smiles and waves to cheering crowds and thumbs up to television cameras to let America know they remained unbowed by their confinement in Communist camps. It was an emotion-packed homecoming for the 142 men. They walked down a long red carpet from the huge jets that had brought them from Vietnam and boarded ambulance buses for a swift ride to the military hospital where most of them will spend the next three days. There was a special cheer for Lieut.-Commander Everett Alvarez, 36, of California, who has spent almost nine years in captivity – the longest time spent by any prisoner in the North.

For 27 of the men there had been a nerve-tingling, last-minute hitch in Vietnam when a group of Vietcong prisoners refused to board their own freedom plane to Hanoi because they feared a trick. The Americans had to wait until the Communists were airborne before being whirled from Loc Ninh to Saigon by helicopter. By contrast, the release in Hanoi went like clockwork. Escort officer Lt. Col. Richard Abel said:

'When the men got off their buses, they were lined up by the ranking officer and marched to the North Vietnamese side. They didn't say anything. They stood at attention and looked straight ahead. But once aboard the planes, they embraced each other and began hugging the nurses and members of the crew. One PoW asked: "Tell me, who won the war?" He was told that South Vietnam didn't lose ... and North Vietnam didn't win.

The telephone rang in Marian Purcell's Kentucky home at 9.35 yesterday morning and the operator said 'Connecting you with the Philippines.' Then the voice she hadn't heard for nearly eight years came over crisp and clear: 'Hello Marian – how've you been?' asked her husband, Lt.-Col. Robert Purcell. Mrs Purcell, eyes swimming with tears, said: 'I saw you on TV – you were beautiful.' Another of the released men phoned the President – 'One of the most moving experiences I have had in the White House,' said Mr Nixon afterwards. Col. Robinson Risner made the call because he wanted to thank the President for his actions 'in getting us out of Vietnam.'

OPPOSITE LEFT: A South Vietnamese paratrooper wounded by a shelling attack on his unit southwest of Quang Tri waits for medics to give him an injection.

OPPOSITE RIGHT: Lt. Commander Mike Christian addresses a crowd during 'Mike Christian Day' April 7, 1973 in his hometown of Huntsville, Alabama. He spent six years as a North Vietnamese prisoner of war.

ABOVE: Released prisoner of war Lt. Col. Robert L. Stirm is greeted by his family at Travis Air Force Base in Foster City, California, March 17, 1973.

LEFT: Sentry geese help guard the strategic Y-Bridge in Saigon. The geese acted as an early warning system for the US troops guarding the bridge, which was Saigon's main highway link to the South.

The fall of Saigon

In August 1974, Richard Nixon resigned due to the Watergate Scandal, a 'dirty tricks campaign' stemming from the 1972 presidential election. His Vice President, Gerald Ford became Commander in Chief and had to deal with resumed North Vietnamese attacks in South Vietnam. Ford would call for increased aid to Saigon in early April 1975, but by this time the NVA were advancing on the city, and the evacuation of all remaining US personnel, as well as thousands of refugees had already begun. The final evacuation, 'Operation Frequent Wind', which centred around the US Embassy, was completed on the morning of April 30, just hours before the fall of Saigon. By midday, Communist forces had made their way to the Presidential Palace, where President Minh, who had been in power for less than two days following Thieu's resignation, would make his surrender, ending the Vietnam War.

For the United States of America, the conflict had been the longest, most expensive, and least successful that the country had ever engaged in. Of the almost three million US personnel rotated through Vietnam, some 60,000 had lost their lives, whilst many of those that returned home, found themselves deeply traumatized, unwelcome, and unable to readjust to a nation that was itself damaged and divided. For the Vietnamese meanwhile, the conclusion of the war marked an end to a struggle for unification, and a fight against foreign oppression, which had persisted for centuries. The country would be officially reunited as the Socialist Republic of Vietnam on July 2, 1976.

OPPOSITE BELOW: Mobs of Vietnamese people scale the wall of the US Embassy in Saigon trying to get to the helicopter pickup zone on April 29, 1975.

OPPOSITE ABOVE: Chaotic scenes on the roof of the American Embassy where evacuees try to board the last flight out of Saigon, April 30, 1975. A plainclothes American punches a Vietnamese man as he tries to board the helicopter.

BELOW: A US Marine helicopter lifts off from the landing pad during the frantic US evacuation of Saigon, April 30, 1975. The 11 Marines evacuated that day were the last remaining American troops to leave Vietnam.

ABOVE: Evacuees scramble up the ladder to get on board one of the Air America helicopters charged with transporting Americans and foreign nationals out of Saigon and on to navy ships waiting off the coast.

DAILY MAIL   MAY 1, 1975

I watched the tanks roll in

Well, they're here. And here is no longer Saigon, the capital of an independent South Vietnam. Today it is Ho Chi Minh City, named in honour of the man who began it all 32 years ago but who died before he could see the realisation of his dream – a united, Communist Indo-China.

Now, with Cambodia under their belt and Laos half digested, that reality has come near. For those who like historical records, it was exactly 10 a.m., Wednesday.

Handshakes

An errant tank ignored the gate hurriedly opened into the presidential palace by a hopefully smiling soldier and smashed its way through the fence. A soldier on the turret fell off. The Communists had arrived.

They arrived smiling and polite. They greeted newsmen with handshakes and Saigonese with kisses. They toured hotels to ask if it were at all possible for their soldiers to be accommodated.

They sat, somewhat self-consciously, in the open-air bar on the Continental Hotel where three days ago Americans drank dry Martinis and whisky sours and sipped orange juice.

They arrived in the middle of a panic-driven frenzy of looting by South Vietnamese soldiers and civilians who smashed into Government and American warehouses. On the streets, armed soldiers were holding up the few remaining Westerners, demanding our money and our cars. Within an hour, the looting stopped.

The guns were garlanded with flowers and one puzzled clerk said: 'We were told we would be killed. It looks as if that was another lie.'

The first Communist troops to drive in looked no older than 15. Their rifles were bigger than they were. Later I saw girl soldiers – all about 17 years old – in a tank column. They were in the Vietcong uniform of black pyjamas and watched unsmiling the Saigonese who came on to the streets to greet them with white flags, cheers and laughter.

Three hours after the occupation, the victors sat on the grass-lined boulevards of this beautiful, French-inspired city, talking and making tea. Children were given lifts on the tanks. People handed the troops cigarettes and fruit. They smiled and chanted 'Victory, victory!'

After thirty years of war, this city was so happy you could actually feel the relief.

At the Palace last night the Vietcong flag – red and blue, with a gold star in the middle – fluttered from a flagpole. It was run up by a soldier as the 'two-day President', Duong 'Big' Minh, was driven away an hour after broadcasting his surrender message. Last night he was in custody.

Pockets of resistance

There were, of course, isolated pockets of resistance. Some soldiers near the zoo saw the opposition and decided it wasn't worth it.

Another group, three miles outside the city on the Newport Bridge, were intent on a last minute redoubt. It collapsed in five minutes' fighting and some newsmen who had driven up to watch were forced from their cars by a South Vietnamese colonel who sped away in their vehicle. Apparently he hadn't worked it out that there was nowhere to go.

Salute

In the centre of Saigon, opposite the Assembly building, there is a huge monument of two soldiers, surging forward to fight the aggressor. To this, as the Communists entered, came a South Vietnamese police colonel. He saluted the statue, raised a gun to his head and pulled the trigger.

On the steps of the National Assembly Building, a Vietcong colonel said: 'This should be a great day for those who love peace. You will have more freedom. The curfew has been relaxed and will not begin until 6 p.m.'

At 5.55, the streets of Ho Chi Minh City were deserted. The Communists had arrived. Completely.

The victors

These are the conquerors of Saigon, the victorious troops of the North Vietnamese Army, some of them still only children. Boys of 15 in short-sleeved shirts and black strapped plastic sandals, dwarfed by the weapons they carried, marched with the units who took the city yesterday.

Girl soldiers of 15 and 17, stern and unsmiling, stood on the front of camouflaged tanks that rolled through the streets. They wore white and black silk suits, held their heads high and cradled rifles in their arms.

Yesterday the fighting was over and the Young Ones had their reward. They moved through the streets chanting 'Victory, victory' and giving clenched fist salutes. They loaded themselves with captured American-made equipment, grenades and rifles and drank picnic tea on the grass beside the roads. Their great day had come. To their nation they were the heroes of the revolution.

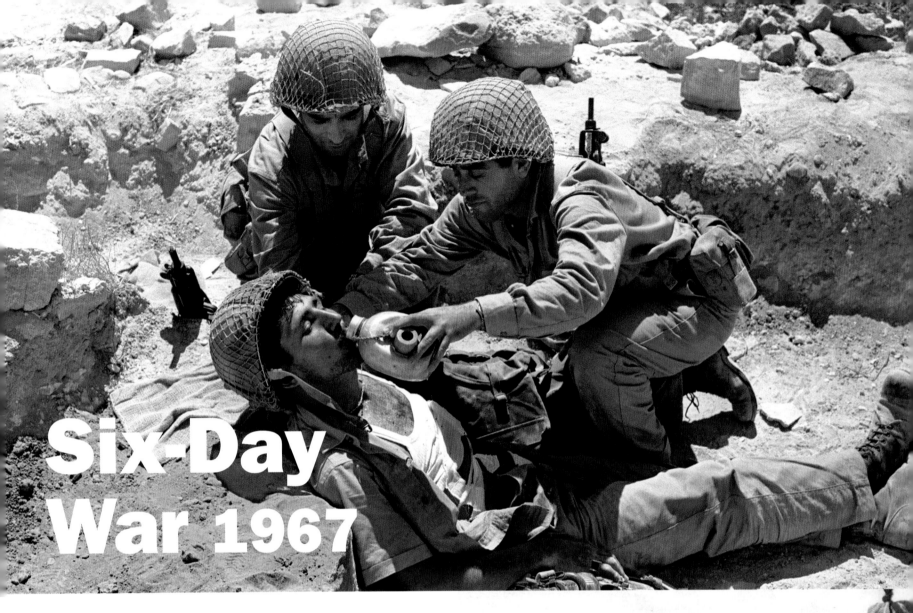

Six-Day War 1967

Pre-emptive strike

On June 5, 1967, Israel launched a pre-emptive strike on Egypt, sparking a six-day war against three of its Arab neighbours. The situation in the region had been deteriorating following the seizure of power by a militant anti-Israeli faction in Syria in February 1966. For more than a year, Israel and Syria had engaged in deadly skirmishes, and in November 1966, Egypt and Syria had joined together in a mutual defence agreement. In May 1967, President Nasser of Egypt demanded the withdrawal of the United Nations Emergency Force that had been stationed in the Sinai Peninsula following the Suez Crisis in 1956. He began moving his own troops in, closed the Straits of Tiran to Israeli shipping and brought Jordan into the defence pact. Israeli decision-makers became convinced that a war was imminent and launched a pre-emptive strike to destroy Egypt's air force.

ABOVE: An injured Israeli soldier is given water and medical attention during the Six-Day War.

RIGHT: Yitzakh Rabin was Chief of Staff of the Israel Defence Forces (IDF) at the time of the Six-Day War. He went on to become Israel's Prime Minister and was an instrumental player in the Peace Process. In November 1995, he was assassinated by a man who was opposed to negotiating with the Palestinians.

FAR RIGHT: An Israeli soldier looks down at the bodies of Palestinian guerrillas killed during the battle for Gaza. The Gaza Strip had been occupied by Egypt since the 1948 war.

Israeli Victory

The war was a disaster for Egypt, Jordan and Syria, who failed to coordinate their response. The Israeli army did not have to face a three-front war and was able to confront each adversary individually. After defeating Egypt and occupying the Sinai and Gaza, the Israelis turned their attention towards Jordan, capturing the West Bank and East Jerusalem, which includes some of the holiest sites in Judaism, Christianity and Islam. Israel then pressed on to engage Syria, which had been slow to mobilize, and took control of the Golan Heights after barely one day of fighting.

A ceasefire was signed on June 10. Within just six days Israel had grown to three times its original size. The United Nations Security Council passed resolution 242, which demanded that Israel withdraw from its newly won territories and also indirectly called upon the Arab States to acknowledge Israel's right to exist. None of the parties complied immediately and the Six-Day War has continued to shape regional politics to this day.

ABOVE LEFT: **Captured Egyptians carry their wounded comrades to a POW camp. The Israeli defence minister, Moshe Dayan, praised Egyptian soldiers for fighting much better than they had done during the Suez Crisis.**

ABOVE RIGHT: **An Israeli soldier is bandaged after being wounded on the Syrian front.**

BELOW: **Israeli soldiers defend a captured anti-aircraft gun along the banks of the Suez Canal. Israeli forces overwhelmed the Egyptian military and reached the canal within seventy-two hours of the start of the war.**

DAILY MAIL   JUNE 6, 1967

Tank Battle Rages In Sinai Desert

A fierce tank battle raged last night near the Egypt-Israel border. Armoured units said to be larger than those that fought at Alamein were locked in savage fighting in the Kuntilla area of the Sinai Desert.

Israel said she had advanced 43 miles. But Egypt claimed to have launched a successful counter-attack after Israel had thrown in an entire infantry brigade and large numbers of tanks. 'Our forces repulsed the attack and moved into Israel, destroying all enemy positions.' Cairo radio said. 'Israeli helicopter-borne troops were completely wiped out,' it added.

Earlier Israeli planes attacked airfields in the Cairo and Suez Canal area, Northern Sinai, and in Jordan and Syria.

Early today Israel's Premier, Mr. Levi Eshkol, and Army Chief of Staff, Major-General Yitzhak Rabin, claimed complete victory in the air.

Shot Down

General Rabin said 374 Egyptian, Jordanian, Syrian and Iraqi planes were destroyed in the day's fighting and 34 probably destroyed, for the loss of only 19 Israeli aircraft. General Moshe Dayan, the new Defence Minister, called it a 'devastating blow.'

Cairo Radio replied that 86 Israeli planes had been shot down. Claims by Jordan, Syria and Lebanon raised the number of Israeli planes brought down to 161.

In land battles Israel claimed her forces had slashed deep into the Sinai peninsula and captured Egypt's main base at El Arish - a key target in the 1956 Suez war. A large number of prisoners and big quantities of war material, including weapons, guns and tanks, were captured, said General Rabin.

Jordanian guns set up a bombardment of Tel Aviv, its airport area at Lydda, and other targets. Some of the shells landed a few hundred yards from where correspondents in Tel Aviv were waiting for a Press conference. One shell hit an electric power pole and switched on all the street lights in the blacked-out city. Engineers quickly had them off again.

Syrian planes were said to have bombed the oil refinery at Haifa and set it ablaze. Israel said her jet bombers hammered targets on the outskirts of Damascus in three-hour-long raids.

Other bombers were reported to have hit Amman, capital of Jordan, and set planes ablaze.

Jerusalem: Fighting raged until after dark between Jordanian and Israeli forces. Jordan claimed to have destroyed 38 Israeli tanks and 23 planes.

Gaza Strip: Israel said she had captured Khan Younis, cut off the Gaza Strip and trapped thousands of Palestine Liberation Army troops. Cairo denied the claim and said the Israelis lost 30 tanks and had been forced to withdraw.

Forces

This is the line-up of the forces of Israel and her Arab enemies:
Israel: Forces 250,000, tanks 800, modern jets 240, missiles 60.
Egypt: Forces 195,000, tanks 1,000, strike aircraft 70-plus, fighters 300-plus, missiles 100.
Jordan: Forces 65,000, tanks 132, modern jets 12.
Syria: Forces 81,000, tanks 350, modern jets 100.
Iraq: Forces 82,000, tanks 320, modern jets 87.
Saudi Arabia: Forces 55,000, modern jets 18.

Soviet Invasion of Czechoslovakia 1968

Prague Spring

Before the Second World War, Czechoslovakia was a democracy but after the war the Soviets took control and installed a Communist government in Prague. For many years Czechoslovakia was stable under Soviet influence, but in the 1960s the economy began slowing significantly. The Czechoslovakian military also wanted to develop its own defence strategy, feeling that the Soviets had overstated the threat from the West. In early 1968, during a period known as the 'Prague Spring', Antonin Novotny was ousted as the head of the Communist Party of Czechoslovakia and was replaced by Alexander Dubcek. The new government ended censorship and announced a planned series of reforms designed to improve the economy and allow more freedom to the army, although these were intended to fit within the existing Communist framework

TOP: A wounded Czechoslovakian civilian is rushed to hospital during the first day of fighting in Prague.

ABOVE: Prague residents build a barricade to halt the advance of Soviet tanks using the shells of two burnt-out streetcars.

LEFT: The streets of Prague burn as Soviet tanks enter the city on August 21.

Invasion

The developments in Czechoslovakia alarmed Soviet leaders – who were concerned that other parts of Eastern Europe might follow suit, leading to widespread rebellion against Moscow's leadership. On August 20, 1968, Soviet and Warsaw Pact troops entered the country. The invasion was intended to establish a more conservative and pro-Soviet government in Prague and it caught both Czechoslovakia and much of the Western world completely off guard. The Soviet Union had moved troops into place by announcing Warsaw Pact military exercises, but instead they swiftly took control of Prague and other major cities in Czechoslovakia. The United States was involved in Vietnam and had a policy of non-involvement in the Eastern Bloc, so although Washington condemned the invasion it did not take action. Resistance in Czechoslovakia continued into 1969, but in April 1969 Dubcek was forced from power. The new conservative leadership reinstated censorship and limited freedom of movement, but it also managed to improve economic conditions helping return stability to the country,

The invasion temporarily delayed the break-up of the Eastern Bloc but also briefly halted the progress of arms control agreements between the Soviet Union and the United States. After the invasion, Soviet leadership justified the use of force with the Brezhnev Doctrine, which established their right to intervene if a Communist government was under threat. This doctrine later led to the Chinese-Soviet split, as China feared it would be used to justify interference with Chinese Communism. The invasion not only led to a loss of support for the Communist Party in many Western countries but also raised doubts in many countries of Eastern Europe, who were alarmed at how quickly an ally could become an invading force.

DAILY MAIL AUGUST 21, 1968

The Russians invade

Russian troops and those of four of their satellites invaded Czechoslovakia today. The shock news came from Prague Radio at 3 a.m. The station said troops of the Soviet Union, Poland, East Germany, Hungary and Bulgaria started to cross the frontiers at 11 o'clock last night.

But the radio said the Praesidium of the Czech Communist Party appealed to the people not to resist the advancing troops.

The announcement said the invasion 'goes against the basic rights of States and relations between Socialist countries.' But it asked all Government and party officials to stay in their jobs and urged the people to keep calm.

A normal radio transmission had started to broadcast on the earlier crisis meeting of the Czech Communist Party Praesidium. Then it went dead.

TOP LEFT: **Soviet tanks and troops withdraw to the suburbs of Prague in September after successfully repressing the 'Prague Spring'.**

TOP RIGHT: **A Czechoslovakian boy climbs onto a Red Army tank as Soviet troops take a break.**

MIDDLE: **Supporters of Czechoslovakia's reformist government throw stones and paint at a Soviet tank to demonstrate their opposition to the invasion.**

ABOVE: **Soviet and Warsaw Pact troops, armed with heavy artillery, maintain their presence on the outskirts of Prague in late 1968 to dissuade any further dissent.**

LEFT: **Protesters in Wenceslas Square hold placards reading 'Go Home' and 'Why Are You Shooting At Us?'**

Northern Ireland Troubles 1969-2007

The background

The source of the conflict in Northern Ireland is centuries old – from the 12th century there have been constant revolts challenging British rule. The climax of these ongoing problems was the 1916 Easter Rising in Dublin, which sparked a chain of events leading to the partition of Ireland in 1921. In the south, 26 counties formed a separate independent state, while six counties in the north stayed within the United Kingdom. Over the years, the large Catholic minority in Northern Ireland suffered discrimination over housing and jobs, fuelling bitter resentment among a people who perceived themselves as culturally Irish. The Catholic community came to believe that the northern six counties should leave the United Kingdom and join the Republic of Ireland. However, the majority Protestant population, which sees itself as culturally British, has remained fiercely loyal to the union with the United Kingdom.

Start of 'The Troubles'

Although a few killings happened earlier, the modern conflict in Ireland resulted from a civil rights protest in 1969. On New Year's Day a small Catholic Civil Rights group named the People's Democracy set off from Belfast on a four-day protest march to Derry/Londonderry. On the last day the group was attacked by a group of loyalists, sparking riots in Bogside, the predominantly Catholic area of Derry/Londonderry. Bogside was declared a 'no-go area' for the authorities and dubbed 'Free Derry'. As the Catholic community began a growing campaign for equal rights, unionists began to feel that Protestant dominance of Northern Ireland was under threat.

Derry/Londonderry is the venue for the annual Protestant Apprentice Boys parade, which commemorates 13 young apprentices who closed the gates of the walled city in 1688 to stop the advancing forces of the Catholic King James' army. The 1969 August parade in Derry quickly led to clashes with local Catholic youths, and police trying to separate the two factions were stoned and petrol-bombed. This led to police entering Bogside with armoured vehicles and water cannons, resulting in two days of rioting known as the 'Battle of the Bogside'. It also led to serious violence erupting in Belfast, where Catholic homes were set alight.

On August 14, British troops were deployed on the streets of Northern Ireland to restore law and order, but they soon came into conflict with the Provisional IRA and the fighting escalated.

Bloody Sunday

On January 30, 1972, some 10,000 people gathered in Derry/Londonderry to take part in a banned Northern Ireland Civil Rights Association march against the British government's policy of internment without trial. Soon after it began, a British paratroop regiment shot dead 14 Catholic marchers. The soldiers later claimed that the IRA had fired on them as they moved forward to make arrests, but the Catholic community maintained that the crowd was peaceful and that the British Army murdered unarmed civilians. There was an immediate public outcry and the British government later made out-of-court settlements with the bereaved families. Bloody Sunday has come to be one of the most symbolic moments of The Troubles and – although even today it is not clear exactly what happened – to many sympathetic to the nationalist cause it represents the brutality of the British state against the Catholic community.

Bloody Friday

As the situation deteriorated, Northern Ireland's parliament was suspended and direct rule was imposed from London. However, a brief truce was declared in June 1972, when Republican leaders were secretly taken to London for talks with the British government. Unfortunately the talks failed and on July 21, a day that became known as Bloody Friday, the Provisional IRA detonated at least 22 bombs in Belfast city centre. The attack lasted for 65 minutes and included car bombs, mines and other devices; 11 people died and 130 were seriously injured. The horrific nature of the attack led some to believe that even if the Republican side had true cause for complaint, the Provisional IRA had passed far beyond justifiable action. At the end of July, British troops were ordered to dismantle IRA barricades in the no-go areas of Derry/ Londonderry and Belfast. Over the remainder of 1972 violence escalated and it became one of the bloodiest years of The Troubles, with most of those killed innocent civilians.

OPPOSITE ABOVE: **British troops are hit with petrol bombs on the streets of Belfast.**

OPPOSITE MIDDLE: **A British soldier of the Queen's Regiment mans a barricade in the Falls Road area of Belfast, October 1969.**

OPPOSITE BELOW: **Hunger strikers sit at 'Free Derry Corner' underneath a mural, painted in 1969, announcing the entrance to the Bogside area of the city.**

TOP RIGHT: **British paratroopers run through the streets of Derry/ Londonderry on Bloody Sunday, January 30, 1972.**

ABOVE RIGHT: **Violent rioting takes place on the streets of Derry/Londonderry in the aftermath of Bloody Sunday. Fourteen people lost their lives when British troops opened fire on the demonstrators.**

ABOVE LEFT: **Residents come upon an army roadblock as they carry white crosses through the** streets of Dungiven in memorial of the people killed on Bloody Sunday. The soldiers agreed to let the procession pass through.

BELOW: **Another day of civil disturbance in Derry/ Londonderry, more than two weeks after Bloody Sunday. British soldiers claimed they came under fire from the crowd before they commenced shooting. In 1998, the British government established the ongoing Bloody Sunday Inquiry to investigate.**

DAILY MAIL   JANUARY 31 1972
Derry's Hour Of Death

Thirteen men were shot dead in Londonderry yesterday in the bloodiest Northern Ireland battle yet between demonstrators and the Army. Another 16 people, including two women, were wounded. Two paratroopers were badly burned by acid bombs, two others were injured by lumps of rock and a fifth was wounded by a bullet. It all happened in an hour.

The Government will make a statement in the Commons today. And last night a huge row loomed as demonstrators accused the Army of firing first and of firing indiscriminately after paratroopers entered the Bogside to snatch suspects.

Mainland bombing campaign

In the early 1970s, the Provisional IRA began a bombing campaign against the British mainland. On October 5, 1974, they targeted two pubs in Guildford, known to have been popular with army personnel. The pub bombings claimed five lives and the police were immediately under pressure to locate the culprits. Three men and a woman, termed the 'Guildford Four' were apprehended and wrongfully charged for the crime. Their convictions were later overturned as their confessions had been obtained by torture. Just over a month later on November 21, a similar attack was made on two pubs in central Birmingham. 21 people were killed and six men, known as the 'Birmingham Six,' were found guilty and sentenced to life imprisonment. As with the Guildford Four, the Birmingham Six were later released when the evidence against them was discredited.

Margaret Thatcher targeted

On August 27, 1979, the Queen's cousin, Lord Mountbatten, was murdered when a bomb exploded aboard his boat, and hours later, eighteen British soldiers were killed in an ambush at Warrenpoint in Northern Ireland. These attacks were followed by a series of killings of Catholic civilians by Loyalist paramilitaries. The Provisional IRA continued their bomb campaign throughout the 1980s, striking two London parks on July 20, 1982, killing eleven people. In December 1983, Christmas shoppers were targeted by a bomb outside the Harrods store, six people were killed and scores were injured. The following year the IRA conducted their most significant attack on the mainland: a bomb exploded at a hotel hosting members of the British Cabinet during the Conservative Party conference in Brighton. The Prime Minister, Margaret Thatcher, narrowly escaped assassination, but five others, including a Member of Parliament were killed in the attack.

Warrington bombings

The 1990s saw a continuation of the bomb campaign and two boys were killed in an attack in Warrington. On April 10, 1992 the Provisional IRA launched a bomb attack on the Baltic Exchange in London that killed three and caused hundreds of millions of pounds worth of damage. As the peace process took hold, the bombings began to peter out, but in 1996, the IRA broke a ceasefire to launch a devastating attack on the London Docklands in February and the Arndale Shopping Centre in Manchester in June. As was their style, the IRA called in both bomb threats ahead of time allowing authorities to evacuate both areas, saving many lives.

BELOW RIGHT: The ruins of the Grand Hotel following the IRA bombing in October 1984. Provisional IRA member Patrick Magee had planted the bomb in the hotel weeks before the British Cabinet checked in.

RIGHT: British Prime Minister Margaret Thatcher dances with Brighton's Mayor just hours before the bombing.

BELOW LEFT: Warrington town centre is cordoned-off after two bombs explode on a major shopping street in the English town in March 1993. A three-year-old boy was killed instantly and a twelve-year-old boy died of his injuries in hospital. A gasworks in the town had been bombed by the IRA one month earlier.

Enniskillen bomb

On November 8, 1987, at a Remembrance Day parade to honour British soldiers killed in action, an IRA bomb ripped through the town of Enniskillen. The blast killed 10 people and wounded many innocent civilians who had come to watch the parade. Amateur video footage of the immediate aftermath was shown on television and it horrified people everywhere. The bombing was widely condemned and the IRA lost much of their support, both locally and across the world. At first Loyalist paramilitaries were intent on retaliation, but family members of the victims called for forgiveness, engendering a feeling of reconciliation and not long afterwards the first signs of a real change appeared.

LEFT: London City workers gaze up at the damage caused to the Commercial Union Building by the bomb on the Baltic Exchange in 1992.

BELOW: A worker assesses the damage done to the Baltic Exchange from the foyer of the building. The building was too badly damaged to be restored, and a new skyscraper, 'the Gherkin', was built on the site.

BELOW RIGHT: More than 100,000 people attend the funeral of Bobby Sands who died on hunger strike in the Maze prison in May 1981.

DAILY MAIL OCTOBER 27 1981

IRA target the children

IRA bombers brought death and chaos to the shopping heart of London yesterday -terror apparently aimed at children most of all.

As a bomb disposal man died when the device he was trying to defuse exploded, it was half-term in most London schools. The West End was crowded with children - young ones with their mothers, older ones with friends - up in town for early Christmas shopping.

The bomb that went off was planted in the basement seating area of a Wimpy bar in Oxford Street - just the place for mothers to take the kids for a break, just the place for teenagers to go and have a coffee. The suspicion that the terrorists had this specifically in mind was sickeningly

confirmed by these words in a statement claiming responsibility for the bombing issued by the Provisional IRA in Dublin: 'Let the British people take note that Irish children, the victims of plastic bullets fired by their soldiers, do not have the luxury of receiving warnings.'

There were about 20 children among the 120 or so people evacuated from the Wimpy bar after a telephoned warning from the terrorists. The warning also said there were bombs in two Oxford Street stores, Debenham's and Bourne's. One was found in Debenham's and quickly made safe. But six hours later, the police were still searching for the bomb supposed to be on the fifth floor of Bourne's.

Hunger strikes

In 1981 a number of IRA inmates at the Maze prison in Belfast went on hunger strike to demand to be treated as political prisoners rather than common criminals. The strikes turned into a test of will between the prisoners and the British Prime Minister Margaret Thatcher. Thatcher refused to relent even after one of the strikers, Bobby Sands, won a by-election and became a Member of the UK Parliament. The hunger strikers attracted media attention around the world and even the Vatican attempted to mediate. However, a solution was not reached and ten people, including Bobby Sands, died of starvation.

The Peace Process

Peace talks began in 1995, but the true breakthrough was not until three years later, when the 1998 Good Friday Agreement was signed. The process leading to that point had not been easy. Members of one of the main Loyalist parties, the Ulster Unionists, wanted assurances that no one with links to paramilitary groups still engaged in violence could take office in the proposed Northern Ireland Assembly. Instead, it was agreed that politicians linked to paramilitaries who refused to hand over weapons could not hold office – and that decommissioning would begin immediately after the Assembly came into being.

The final version of the Agreement was welcomed by three of the main parties in Northern Ireland, but Ian Paisley, the leader of the Democratic Unionist Party, the other major Loyalist party, called it 'treacherous'.

On May 22, 1998, a referendum on the Agreement was held in Northern Ireland and also in the Irish Republic, which gave up its constitutional claim to the north. The result was overwhelmingly in favour and a Northern Ireland Assembly was elected in September of that year. Nevertheless, almost every aspect of the Agreement has caused controversy – particularly the issue of decommissioning. Unionists demanded photographic proof that Republicans were decommissioning, and criticized Sinn Fein, the hardline Nationalist party, for failing to disarm the IRA. Sinn Fein argued that its influence on the IRA had limits, and also criticized the British government for failing to demilitarize.

The Omagh bomb

Just four months after the Good Friday Agreement, a car bomb in the town of Omagh killed 29 people, including seven children and 14 women. One of the worst atrocities in the history of The Troubles, the bombing was carried out by a radical offshoot of the Provisional IRA who had dubbed themselves the 'Real IRA'. The bombing was widely condemned by both sides, and the Real IRA quickly apologized, saying it had intended to hit only commercial targets, and pledged an end to all military operations. The tragedy raised fears that political groups could not control their military wings and increased pressure on Sinn Fein to ensure that IRA weapons were handed over. The Real IRA's apology and ceasefire proved to be short-lived, and they went on to carry out a string of small-scale bombings in Northern Ireland and London – including publicity-seeking attacks on MI6 and the BBC's headquarters.

ABOVE: **Irish Prime Minister Bertie Ahern (left), US Senator George Mitchell (centre) and British Prime Minister Tony Blair (right) at the signing of the Good Friday Agreement on April 10, 1998.**

RIGHT: **Prince Charles tours Omagh days after a Real IRA bomb ripped through the town killing 29 people.**

OPPOSITE ABOVE LEFT: **Ian Paisley (left) meets with Sinn Fein President Gerry Adams (right) for the first time as they announce that a powersharing deal had been reached at Stormont, the seat of the Northern Ireland Assembly, on March 26, 2007. Adams did not take a role in the Northern Ireland Assembly, making way for Martin McGuinness to become deputy First Minister.**

OPPOSITE ABOVE RIGHT: **Ian Paisley and Martin McGuinness share a joke after being sworn in as First Minister and deputy First Minister of the Northern Ireland Assembly on May 8, 2007.**

OPPOSITE BELOW: **Architects of the powersharing deal pictured at Stormont on May 8, 2007. From left to right, Martin McGuinness, Northern Ireland Secretary Peter Hain, Ian Paisley, Tony Blair and Bertie Ahern.**

The Mitchell Review

By the autumn of 1999, the peace process appeared to have stalled. The IRA showed no signs of giving up a single bullet, and Ulster Unionists were refusing to allow Sinn Fein to take their seats in the Assembly until decommissioning had taken place. To resolve the stalemate, US senator George Mitchell, who had chaired the talks leading to the Good Friday Agreement, returned to Northern Ireland to review the situation.

After weeks of patient diplomacy in strict secrecy, Senator Mitchell managed to get all parties to give ground in some areas in return for progress in others. Ulster Unionists accepted that Sinn Fein could sit on the executive before the IRA handed over any weapons and also recognized the Republicans' right to campaign peacefully for a united Ireland. Sinn Fein conceded that decommissioning was essential and made a commitment to peaceful progress. In May 2000, the IRA agreed to start taking its weapons 'completely and verifiably beyond use', providing that the Good Friday Agreement was implemented in full. Since then, several IRA arms dumps have been opened to international inspectors who have confirmed that the weaponry was beyond use.

Power-sharing

In 1998, elections to the Northern Ireland Assembly had been won by moderate parties on both sides and a power-sharing agreement was reached. However, the winners of the 2003 election, the Democratic Unionists and Sinn Fein, were more hard-line, and could not agree to work together. A series of negotiations took place, culminating in the St. Andrews Agreement in October 2006. Fresh elections were held in March 2007, which again saw the Democratic Unionists and Sinn Fein emerge on top. On March 27, 2007, it was announced that the two parties had agreed to a power-sharing deal, and, as the staunchest of foes began governing Ireland together, The Troubles finally seem at an end.

DAILY MAIL MAY 9, 2008

Time for peace in Northern Ireland

It is the scene many thought they would never see.

Reverend Ian Paisley and Sinn Fein's Martin McGuinness, bitter enemies for more than 30 years, sit together as the leaders of Northern Ireland's powersharing government.

Dr Paisley, famous for his mantra 'No Surrender' to the Republicans, appeared relaxed as he joked with former IRA commander Mr McGuinness, Mr Blair and Irish Premier Bertie Ahern over a pot of tea in his new office.

Later, the four men were met with rapturous applause as they descended Stormont's main stone staircase together, to the rather unlikely strains of Westlife's number one hit 'You Raise Me Up'.

Invoking the Bible, Dr Paisley declared there was "a time for love and a time for hate; a time for war and a time for peace." He added: "From the depth of my heart, I can say Northern Ireland has come to a time of peace. How good it will be to be part of a wonderful healing in this province".

Mr McGuinness paid tribute to Dr Paisley and said he was confident that both parties could put aside their longstanding differences to work together for the sake of the people of Northern Ireland. The Deputy First Minister said: "We know the road we are embarking on will have many twists and turns. It is, however, a road which we have chosen and which is supported by the vast majority of our supporters." He added that local politicians were embarking on "the greatest, yet most exciting challenge of our lives."

Nigerian Civil War 1967-1970

Republic of Biafra

After gaining independence from Britain in 1960, Nigeria became racked by ethnic tensions and economic problems. Nigeria had three distinct regions each containing different ethnic groups: the Hausa in the northern deserts, the Yoruba in the southwest, and the Ibo in the southeast. In 1966 a group of mostly Hausa army officers took power in a coup. The economic situation in the country started to deteriorate and ethnic tensions began to worsen. Thousands of Ibo were killed in fighting with Hausas and almost a million were forced to flee predominantly Hausa areas in the north. In response military leaders in the Ibo region seceded from Nigeria and proclaimed an independent Republic of Biafra in the southeast.

War and famine

The Nigerian government responded with force. They were unwilling to accept the territorial disintegration of the country, especially since the new Republic of Biafra was rich in oil and had taken much of Nigeria's access to the sea. After some military successes, Biafran forces were pushed back. Over the following two and a half years, one million civilians died, either in the fighting or from starvation. The results of the famine were made worse after the Nigerian government banned delivery of food aid to Biafra, although they allowed medical aid through. Finally, in January 1970, Biafra was reabsorbed into Nigeria and the Nigerian government pledged that Ibos would be treated equally with other citizens.

ABOVE: Troops of Nigeria's Federal Army man positions outside a school and church in the town of Ore after Biafran troops had been spotted in the area.

MIDDLE RIGHT: A Federal Army soldier demands that a dazed and hungry Ibo woman return to a refugee camp with her famished child.

RIGHT: Nigerian troops capture a former comrade who is suspected of defecting to the Biafran army.

LEFT: Images of starving children defined the conflict. The Nigerian government banned food aid to the shortlived Republic of Biafra.

Bangladesh War of Liberation 1971

East Pakistan

The Indian Subcontinent had been divided up arbitrarily as the British left in 1947, creating the two independent countries of India and Pakistan. Pakistan had two distinct parts that were not even connected geographically: West Pakistan and East Pakistan. East Pakistan was more populous and mainly comprised Bengali-speakers, but political power rested in the Punjabi-dominated West Pakistan. A charismatic leader from the East, Sheikh Mujibur Rehman, formed a party demanding more autonomy for East Pakistan and in the 1970 general elections they won a complete majority in the East. The West Pakistan ruling elite reacted by throwing the Sheikh into prison, causing widespread revolt on the streets of East Pakistan. Independence was declared and the country was renamed Bangladesh.

Indian Intervention

As the Pakistani Army attempted to quash the rebellion, hundreds of thousands of Bengalis died in a series of horrific massacres and more than 8 million refugees fled over the border into India. Left with the burden of supporting a massive influx of people, the Indian Prime Minister, Indira Gandhi, decided to help the Mukti Bahini (Bangladesh Liberation Army) liberate East Pakistan so that the refugees could return to their homelands. On December 3, 1971, the Pakistani Air Force (PAF) launched a pre-emptive strike on several Indian airfields. India responded by officially declaring war and attacking along the borders on both East and West. On the West front the aim was to avoid losing territory to Pakistan, while in the East the objective was to take as much of East Pakistan as possible, and install a Bangladeshi interim government. India was geographically closer to East Pakistan and defeated the Pakistani army within just two weeks. Hostilities ended when West Pakistan, now known simply as Pakistan, surrendered on December 16, 1971.

ABOVE: **Indian troops advance unopposed into Bangladesh following the unconditional surrender of Pakistan's army.**

MIDDLE LEFT: **Men suspected of collaborating with Pakistani forces are attacked by pro-independence militias in Dacca.**

MIDDLE RIGHT: **An injured member of the Mukti Bahini (Bangladesh Liberation Army) is**

helped to hospital following a battle with the Pakistani Army.

RIGHT: **Pakistani troops surrender themselves and their ammunition to Indian forces in Bangladesh.**

Yom Kippur War 1973

Legacy of the Six-Day War

Following the Six-Day War of 1967, the Arab world was thrown into disarray. The humiliating defeat and a dire economic situation had led to disillusionment with pan-Arab ideology. Instead each Arab state reverted to nationalism, and each adopted their own approach to their relations with Israel. Egypt, under Anwar Sadat, sought an approach based upon negotiation, while Syria, under Hafez al-Asad, wanted a military solution.

Egyptian-Syrian alliance

Egypt and Syria did still share the goal of regaining the territory they had lost to Israel in the Six-Day War. Although Sadat wanted to regain the Sinai through diplomatic channels, he believed Egypt might need to prosecute a limited war to bolster its negotiating position. In addtion, he thought that a brief war would diminish the defeatist attitude of his population and increase Egypt's regional standing.

Knowing that al-Asad wanted a retaliatory war against Israel, and knowing Egypt could not fight alone, Sadat entered into an alliance with Syria. A series of secret meetings took place between the two countries in late 1972, culminating in the establishment of a joint military command in January 1973. On October 6, 1973, a surprise attack was launched.

TOP: Israeli troops set Damascus in their sights during the Yom Kippur War.

MIDDLE RIGHT: A bandaged Major General Ariel Sharon and Major General Haim Bar-Lev confer over a map in the Israeli desert.

MIDDLE LEFT: Egyptian President Anwar Sadat. Sadat believed a war with Israel could reverse his country's fortunes and strengthen his position at the negotiating table.

ABOVE: An Arab family from Jabta al Chatab wave a white flag to the Israelis. Much of the town evacuated along with the Syrian army in the wake of the Israeli advance.

LEFT: Israeli troops pass a disabled Syrian tank as they move up in the Golan Heights.

DAILY MAIL OCTOBER 11, 1973

Big two send arms

The Middle East conflict took on a new dimension of danger last night as both Russia and America began airlifting fresh weapons to each side.

But Britain opted out. Foreign Secretary Sir Alec Douglas-Home told the Israeli Ambassador to Britain, Mr Michael Comay, that the Government had imposed an arms embargo on the Middle East. That, in effect, means Israel will no longer get vital spare parts for her British-built Centurion tanks.

This decision, bitterly attacked by Israelis, came at the close of a day of torment for Israeli commanders, who now know that they face a long, bone-crushing war before they re-establish ascendancy. They have recaptured the Golan Heights, but at great cost in men and material.

And Israeli military commanders admit that the major battle still to come against the Egyptians in the Sinai Desert will not be easy or quick.

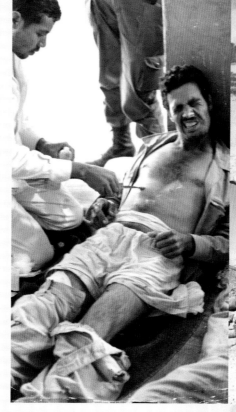

Great power intervention

In the first few days of the war, Israel appeared to be close to defeat. The Israeli army was under strength because many soldiers had been allowed leave to celebrate Yom Kippur and Egypt and Syria were experiencing the benefits of Soviet military aid.

Israel's defences held and the tide was turned two weeks later when American military supplies began arriving. Syria and Egypt were forced onto the defensive and the Israelis reached the outskirts of Damascus and completely routed the Egyptian Third Army. However, Israel ceased firing and adhered to a UN-sponsored ceasefire when the Soviet Union hinted it would send troops to help their allies if the war continued.

Peace treaty.

The 1973 war was pivotal in Arab-Israeli relations as it led to a groundbreaking peace treaty between Egypt and Israel in 1979. The treaty negotiated land for peace; Egypt was able to gain back the Sinai, the Suez Canal was opened to Israeli shipping, and each country bestowed diplomatic recognition on the other. As a result, Egypt was expelled from the Arab League and Sadat was assassinated by militant Islamists in 1981. Syria lost the most in the war; it was unable to meet its aim of regaining the Golan Heights, which Israel still controls to this day.

ABOVE LEFT: **An Egyptian prisoner of war is treated for his wounds by Israeli doctors.**

TOP RIGHT: **Israeli soldiers prepare to move into the Sinai peninsula.**

ABOVE RIGHT: **The Israeli army captures a Soviet-built Egyptian surface-to-air missile during their advance through Sinai.**

FAR RIGHT: **Following the ceasefire, Egyptian soldiers keep watch over Israeli positions from every available balcony of an apartment building on the desert road from Cairo to Suez.**

RIGHT: **Less than 30 metres away Israeli forces wait around for orders. United Nations mediators go back and forth between the two camps trying to arrange the passage of humanitarian supplies to the Egyptian Third Army, which had been routed in the Israeli advance.**

Turkish Invasion of Cyprus 1974

Colonial Cyprus

In 1570 Cyprus was conquered by the Ottoman Empire and Turks soon began arriving to settle among the Greek inhabitants of the island. The imperialists showed a relatively high degree of toleration for the Greeks and did not significantly suppress their language or religion. As a result, over the three centuries of Ottoman rule, two distinct communities developed; one Turkish and Muslim, the other Greek and Christian.

When the Ottoman Empire collapsed at the end of the First World War, the island came under the control of the British, who had been leasing it since 1878. In 1955, Greek Cypriots formed the National Organization of Cypriot Fighters (EOKA) with the goal of kicking the British out and unifying the island with Greece. The EOKA waged war against British interests on the island and also attacked Turkish Cypriots and any Greek Cypriots who were unsupportive of unification. In response, Turkish Cypriots established the Turkish Resistance Organisation (TMT) to repel EOKA attacks and to advocate a partition of the island between the two communities.

When the British granted Cyprus its independence in 1960, a political framework was established within which it was hoped that the Greek and Turkish populations could work together. However, the new government quickly became deadlocked by ethnic squabbles and Cyprus entered a decade of unrest. During this time EOKA was reorganized and placed under control of a new military junta in Athens. Members of the Greek Cypriot community had been slowly abandoning the idea of unification with Greece and the junta wanted to reverse the tide.

Turkey invades

In July 1974, the military dictatorship in Athens fermented a coup against the Cypriot government with the aim of replacing it with a regime loyal to the goal of unification. On July 15 President Makarios was overthrown and Nicos Sampson, a member of the reorganized EOKA, came to power.

Within five days of the coup, Turkey had responded by landing an invasion force on the island under an operation codenamed 'Atilla'. A bitter war broke out on the island as the Greek Cypriot forces tried in vain to halt the Turkish advance on the capital, Nicosia. In Athens, the military junta collapsed as a result of the crisis and a new civilian government came to power. Without the support of the military junta, Nicos Sampson's government fell and Makarios' government was restored.

Partition

On August 10 a conference began in Geneva to try and resolve the situation. Turkey demanded partition of Cyprus in a manner that would hand Turkish Cypriots a disproportionately large section of territory. The government of Cyprus refused partition and Turkey went on the offensive again to take what they could not get at the negotiating table. Turkish forces seized one third of the country within just two days and then called a ceasefire. This completed the division of Cyprus. A United Nations administered Green Line ran across the country from Morphou Bay in the northwest through the capital to Famagusta in the east. Both sides quickly set about ethnically cleansing their respective territories, forcing hundreds of thousands of people from their homes and across the new border.

OPPOSITE ABOVE: A Turkish army tank passes through the streets of Nicosia on July 24, 1974. The portrait of Kemal Ataturk, the founder of the modern Turkish republic, adorns one of the nearby buildings.

OPPOSITE BELOW LEFT: Greek Cypriot soldiers kneel with their hands behind their heads after being taken prisoner by Turkish troops.

OPPOSITE MIDDLE RIGHT: Turkish soldiers on the advance on the first day of the invasion, July 20, 1974.

OPPOSITE BELOW RIGHT: Turkish troops pull ashore a Greek Cypriot torpedo boat damaged during the fighting in Kyrenia.

LEFT: President Archbishop Makarios III was overthrown in a Greek-sponsored coup on July 15, 1974 and managed to escape to Malta. Makarios was reinstated after the new government collapsed. He died of a heart attack in August 1977.

BELOW: Greek Cypriot demonstrators march through the streets of London to protest the Turkish invasion. They set out from the Cyprus High Commission destined for the Turkish Embassy.

LEFT: The protest becomes especially heated as it passes by the American Embassy. Washington was unable to intervene decisively because it was allied to both Greece and Turkey through NATO.

Ethiopian Civil War 1974-1991

The overthrow of Selassie

The last years of Emperor Haile Selassie's long reign (1930-1974) had seen opposition to his regime growing due to rising government corruption, low living standards and the Emperor's failure to deal effectively with a recurrent famine. In 1974, Selassie was overthrown by a group of Marxist army officers and died in detention the following year. Initially the officers ruled together in a council called 'the Derg', but by 1977 it was clear that real power lay with one man, Mengistu Haile Mariam.

After consolidating power in a brutal 'red terror', Mengistu turned his attention towards ending the regional separatist conflicts in Eritrea and Tigray. Eritrea had been an Italian colony until the end of the Second World War, at which time it had been placed under Ethiopian control. Many Eritreans resented Ethiopian rule and an insurgency had been raging since 1961. Selassie had been unable to end the conflict, but Mengistu thought he could stamp it out once and for all.

Civil war

The Ethiopian government received financial and military aid from the Soviet Union and Cuba, which allowed Mengistu to score early victories, and Asmara, the Eritrean capital, was captured in February 1975. The government managed to retake territory around major towns and cities and along some principal roads in 1978 and 1979, but a decisive victory eluded Mengistu and the conflict proceeded to ebb and flow almost yearly. The main Eritrean rebel party, the Eritrean People's Liberation Front (EPLF), had a broad base of popular support and was a highly structured political and military organization, despite the fact that ideological disagreements had prevented it from forming a united front with other separatist movements. In addition, Eritrean and Tigrayan rebels soon began to cooperate, with the EPLF providing training and equipment that helped build the Tigrayan People's Liberation Front

End of the conflict

By the late 1980s, the tide had begun to turn; a devastating famine had distracted Mengistu's government and Soviet aid was beginning to dry up as the Cold War drew to a close. Rebels in Eritrea and Tigray managed to gain control of the majority of both regions by scoring decisive victories over the Ethiopian army in 1988. By May 1991, the EPLF controlled most of Eritrea and had declared independence for the province, setting up a Provisional Government under its leader, Isaias Afwerki. The Tigrayan People's Liberation Front joined forces with a number of other resistance movements to form the Ethiopian People's Revolutionary Democratic Front the EPRDF. In May 1991, they marched on the Ethiopian capital, Addis Ababa, and forced Mengistu to flee into exile, ending the civil war.

Ethiopian-Eritrean war

While Eritreans voted overwhelmingly in favour of independence from Ethiopia in a 1993 referendum, the EPRDF came to dominate the new democratic government of Ethiopia. Initially relations between the two countries were good, but they rapidly deteriorated over the two countries' poorly defined border. In June 1998 an incident in the disputed border town of Badme escalated into a war that was to claim tens of thousands of lives. The war ended in stalemate two years later, with the United Nations intervening to keep the peace. However, unless both sides can peacefully agree to officially demarcate the border, a recourse to war is likely.

OPPOSITE ABOVE: **Ethiopian troops occupy the National Palace days after the overthrow of Emperor Haile Selassie in September 1974.**

OPPOSITE MIDDLE: **Emperor Selassie addresses the Ethiopian parliament. Selassie is perhaps best known outside Ethiopia for being worshipped by Rastafarians. Rastafarianism holds that Selassie is a prophet in a similar manner to Jesus.**

OPPOSITE RIGHT BELOW: **Mengistu, the dictator of Ethiopia from 1977 to 1991, cheers during a peasants' militia parade in Addis Ababa in June 1977.**

LEFT: **Mengistu and Cuban President Fidel Castro ride in an open car through the streets of Addis Ababa. Castro was one of the Ethiopian regime's most important allies, and sent thousands of men to help Ethiopia defeat Somalia in a war over the ownership of the Ogaden province in 1977. Although the majority of Ogaden's population was Somali, the territory was governed by Ethiopia.**

BELOW LEFT: **Musician Bob Geldof visits Ethiopia's famine victims after staging 'Live Aid' concerts across the world on July 13, 1985 in order to raise money and draw attention to the Ethiopian famine.**

BELOW RIGHT: **Ethiopians bury famine victims. The famine distracted Mengistu's attention from the war with separatist groups.**

BOTTOM LEFT: **A young victim of the Ethiopian famine cries from hunger.**

BOTTOM RIGHT: **Famine victims are buried in a makeshift cemetery in Bati. The burial ground was surrounded by stones to prevent people and animals from walking over the gravesite.**

Famine

Many countries in Africa had been affected by famine in the early 1970s, and Ethiopia had never recovered. By the middle of 1984 another drought led to a further major famine in large parts of northern Ethiopia. Crops failed almost entirely in the north, and fighting hindered the delivery of emergency supplies by international aid organizations. The following year there was yet another drought, and by 1986 the famine had spread to the south of the country, made even worse by plagues of locusts and grasshoppers. The government had a policy of withholding aid shipments to rebel areas, which brought international condemnation even from the regime's supporters. By the end of this period the combined effect of famine and war had brought the economy of Ethiopia to a state of collapse.

Cambodian Genocide
1975-1979

Civil War

In March 1970, the ruler of Cambodia, Prince Norodom Sihanouk, was ousted by a group of right-wing generals led by Lon Nol. The monarchy was abolished and the country was renamed the 'Khmer Republic'. Khmer had been the name of a great empire centred round Cambodia during the Middle Ages. Prince Sihanouk formed a government in exile in China and enhanced his ties with Cambodia's Communist Party, which was later to become known as the Khmer Rouge. With royal support, the Communist Party grew in size and strength and began to present a formidable opposition to Lon Nol's government.

Civil war broke out as both sides became locked into a five-year struggle for control of the country. The Khmer Rouge scored remarkable victories in the countryside, and by 1974 Lon Nol's authority had been reduced the main urban centres. In early 1975, the Khmer Rouge launched a sustained push to take the capital, Phnom Penh. It fell in April and Lon Nol's government surrendered, officially ending the war.

ABOVE: The skulls of the Khmer Rouge's victims stand as a reminder of the murdrousness of the regime that ruled Cambodia from 1975 to 1979.

LEFT: Pol Pot emerged as leader of the Khmer Rouge in the early 1970s. He escaped from the Vietnamese invasion and continued to lead the movement into the 1980s. He was denounced by fellow members of the Khmer Rouge in 1997 and died under house arrest the following year.

ABOVE: The leaders of the Khmer Rouge, Pol Pot, Noun Chea, Leng Sary and Son Sen, pictured in Phnom Penh shortly after taking power.

LEFT: Khmer Rouge fighters celebrate the surrender of the Cambodian government at the Information Ministry in Phnom Penh in April 1975.

Genocide

After seizing power, the Khmer Rouge set about reorganizing Cambodia in line with their Communist ideology. The country was renamed 'Kampuchea', private ownership was abolished, and almost the entire urban population was forcibly relocated to the countryside to work on collective farms. Hundreds of thousands of people died from starvation, disease and overwork during the upheaval. Many more were killed in a Red Terror, which the Khmer Rouge instigated to get rid of anyone linked to the previous government or considered to be an enemy of the Revolution. Intellectuals, the bourgeoisie and foreigners were all targeted and often were tortured before they were killed so they would implicate others. It is estimated that more than two million people were killed as a result of the Khmer Rouge's brutal social reorganization.

TOP LEFT: **A camouflaged Khmer Rouge soldier trains with a rocket launcher in the Thai border region of northwestern Cambodia in 1980.**

TOP RIGHT: **Pol Pot parades through Tiananmen Square during an official visit to China in September 1977. The Khmer Rouge sided with China in its ideological and political split with the Soviet Union.**

ABOVE: **Guerrillas loyal to Pol Pot hold positions in the Cambodian jungle during the Vietnamese invasion.**

RIGHT: **Cambodian forces loyal to Vietnam move in to liberate Phnom Penh from the Khmer Rouge, January 7, 1979.**

BELOW: **Photographs of Cambodia's genocide victims hang at S21, a former prison camp turned into a memorial museum. The camp was established to 're-educate' enemies of the regime, but the majority did not make it out alive.**

Vietnamese Invasion

The violence and turmoil in Cambodia was only halted by the invasion of neighbouring Vietnam following a border dispute. The war was one of the first major conflicts between two Communist countries and highlighted the ideological and political division that had beset the Communist bloc.

The invasion began on December 25, 1978 and within weeks the Khmer Rouge had been forced from power. The Vietnamese installed a new government comprising Cambodian Communists who were politically and ideologically aligned to Hanoi. The Khmer Rouge established new bases in Thailand with the assistance of the United States and China and continued to skirmish the Vietnamese-backed government into the 1980s and early 1990s.

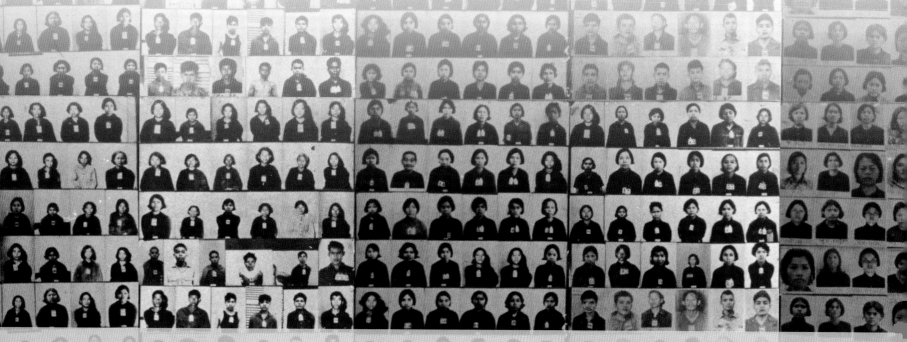

The Angolan Civil War 1975–2002

Portuguese withdrawal

The Angolan civil war, which started in 1975, lasted throughout the Cold War years and continued until 2002. It was one of the most prolonged of all the conflicts in Africa. By the time it ended, it left a country laid waste by war, a ravaged economy, and a generation that knew nothing but conflict. Millions of inhabitants had been displaced as thousands of refugees had left the country or fled to other areas of Angola. It is estimated that more than 500,000 people died and many tens of thousands more were left mutilated by anti-personnel mines.

The civil war erupted in 1975 shortly after Angola had gained independence from Portugal. Although there were a number of guerrilla movements involved, the two main factions were the MPLA (Popular Movement for the Liberation of Angola) and UNITA (National Union for the Total Independence of Angola) who had been fighting each other, as well as the Portuguese, throughout the War for Independence – which had lasted from 1961 until independence was granted on November 11, 1975.

The Cold War in Angola

The Communist MPLA, supported by Cuba and the USSR, and anti-Communist UNITA, backed by white South Africa and the USA, were bitter rivals even before the start of the civil war. As the Portuguese authorities and military forces withdrew from the territory UNITA and the MPLA stepped up their attacks on one another in a battle for supreme control of the country. Fearing Communist influence in southern Africa, South African troops invaded in October 1975 with the intention of putting UNITA in power. However, they were unable to capture the capital, Luanda, because Cuban troops arrived with Soviet equipment to shore up the MPLA. South Africa withdrew, allowing the MPLA to form a government under the leadership of Agostinho Neto, who became the country's first President.

The United States stayed out of the war during the 1970s because Congress had refused funding for operations in Angola. However, in the 1980s President Reagan stepped up American support for UNITA after taking a liking to its charismatic leader, Jonas Savimbi. Savimbi claimed his movement represented 'real Africans' – those living off the land as opposed to the wealthy urban elite. With UNITA strengthened by American support and with the MPLA weakening as the Soviet Union collapsed, the fighting escalated.

Towards agreement

As the Soviet Union disintegrated, Washington decreased its financial assistance to anti-Communist resistance movements worldwide. Cold War conflicts across the world were ending and initially the Angolan Civil War was no exception. Peace accords were signed and national elections were held in 1992. However, when he lost at the polls, Savimbi refused to accept the results and the fighting resumed with an even greater intensity. More peace talks followed and the UN sent in a peacekeeping force in 1995, but tension continued to mount and it withdrew in 1999 after one of its planes was shot down. The war finally came to a conclusion in 2002 when Savimbi was killed in battle. Devoid of its leader, UNITA quickly suspended its activities and entered into peace talks with the MPLA.

DAILY MAIL   FEBRUARY 23, 2002

UNITA leader 'killed by army'

The Angolan army has killed UNITA leader Jonas Savimbi, who led the rebel group's fight for power in Angola for more than 30 years, the government said in statements. The armed forces said Savimbi died during an army attack on UNITA forces in Moxico province in southeast Angola at around 3 p.m. (1400 GMT) on Friday. There was no independent confirmation of the claim. UNITA officials, who are hidden in the Angolan bush, were not available for comment.

Savimbi, who was 67, was a key player in the Cold War struggle for dominance in Africa but became internationally isolated after he resisted democracy. He has not been seen for several years. If confirmed, Savimbi's death could open the way for long-lasting peace in the Southwest African country where the devastating civil war has raged on-and-off for the past 27 years.

The civil war is believed to have killed about 500,000 people, though there are no confirmed figures. About 4 million people – roughly one-third of the population – have been driven from their homes by the fighting, creating a humanitarian crisis.

OPPOSITE LEFT: **Mine clearing in Angola, which is thought to have more landmines than anywhere else in the world. The MPLA government used mines to keep UNITA away from the main cities, while UNITA used landmines to deliberately incapacitate the civilian population in order to make them a drain on the government's resources.**

OPPOSITE LEFT INSERT: **Princess Diana walks through a cleared stretch of minefield during her Red Cross mission in January 1997. Her visit inspired her to call for an international ban on landmines.**

OPPOSITE ABOVE RIGHT: **Tanks on the streets of Luanda at the start of the civil war in 1975.**

OPPOSITE MIDDLE RIGHT: **These children are among the 50,000 Angolan refugees living in the Meheba refugee camp in Zambia, January 2001. The camp is also home to refugees from the war in the Democratic Republic of Congo.**

OPPOSITE BELOW RIGHT: **A refugee camp at Cambambe outside the city of Caxito, January 1999.**

ABOVE LEFT: **Jonas Savimbi at the UNITA base camp in Jamba. Savimbi refused to accept defeat in the Presidential Election in 1992 and the fighting continued until his death in 2002.**

ABOVE: **Angolan President Jose Eduardo dos Santos welcomes South African President Nelson Mandela on a state visit in April 1998. Dos Santos, the leader of the MPLA, became President of Angola in 1979 after the death of Agostinho Neto.**

The Lebanese Civil War 1975-1990

Sectarian violence

After independence from France, Lebanon's various religious and ethnic groups lived in relative harmony. However, by the 1970s, the Maronite Christians had grown prosperous and politically dominant, while the Shi'a Muslims had become the poorest and the most disenfranchised of Lebanon's sects. Resentment built and sectarian tensions grew, culminating in an attempt by Shi'a militias to assassinate a Christian leader in 1975. Christian militias responded by massacring scores of Palestinians on a bus in Beirut.

The tense political situation was further complicated by the Palestinian Liberation Organisation (PLO), which had created a state within a state in southern Lebanon. There had been a history of animosity between the PLO and the Christian militias, causing the Palestinians to support the Shi'a. Lebanon quickly became a war zone as reprisals met with counter-reprisals and the violence escalated.

In 1976, the fighting was halted by the intervention of neighbouring Syria. Although Damascus supported the PLO in its war with Israel, it held the Palestinians responsible for much of the instability in Lebanon and consequently backed the Christian militias in a bid to rein them in. Syria troops remained in the country and a relative calm returned until Israel invaded in 1978.

Israeli invasion

In March 1978, Palestinian militias hijacked a bus on the road from Haifa to Tel Aviv in Israel, killing thirty-eight passengers and wounding many more. The attack convinced the new Israeli government under Menachen Begin to stage a limited war against the PLO in southern Lebanon. The war was a success for Israel as they had managed to strike a blow at the PLO and to strengthen ties with Lebanese Christians. As the Israeli forces withdrew they handed over territory to the South Lebanon Army, a predominantly Christian militia group opposed to the PLO presence.

The PLO remained a serious threat to Israel and Begin and his defence minister, Ariel Sharon, began to plan another attack to remove the organization from Lebanon once and for all. The pretext for the invasion was an assassination attempt on Shlomo Argov, the Israeli Ambassador to the United Kingdom, on June 3 1982. Three days later Israel launched 'Operation Peace for Galilee'.

OPPOSITE ABOVE: **Syrian soldiers stand guard over West Beirut after Shi'a militias besieged the Shatila Palestinian Refugee Camp.**

OPPOSITE MIDDLE: **PLO leader Yasser Arafat pictured in southern Lebanon in 1978.**

OPPOSITE BELOW: **A Lebanese man thanks Syrian troops for bringing stability back to his country.**

ABOVE RIGHT: **Beirut residents and tourists take advantage of a lull in the fighting to go swimming in the Mediterranean Sea in the summer of 1979.**

BELOW: **Yasser Arafat inspects the bomb damage in the Arab University area of West Beirut following an Israeli bombardment in August 1982.**

BOTTOM: **Yasser Arafat attends a farewell gathering of PLO officers in West Beirut before leaving to establish new headquarters in Tunis.**

BELOW RIGHT: **Israeli soldiers pictured at the Litani River in Lebanon during the first Israeli invasion in 1978.**

The siege of Beirut

Israel laid siege to Beirut in July 1982 in a bid to force the PLO from its headquarters in the western part of the city. Israel was condemned for attacks on the city that resulted in many civilian casualties. The international community, including the United States, called for restraint and negotiation. However, Israel was able to fulfil its goal as the PLO leadership left Beirut for Tunis in Tunisia. In August, the US negotiated an Israeli withdrawal and announced the introduction of a multinational force comprising American and French soldiers who would help maintain political stability.

Despite the PLO withdrawal to Tunis, the cycle of violence continued. On September 14, the newly elected Christian President, Bashir Gemeyal, was assassinated in Beirut. Days later, with indirect Israeli assistance, Christian militias entered the Palestinian refugee camps of Sabra and Shatila and slaughtered more than one thousand people.

Hezbollah

The withdrawal of the PLO did not mark the end of the war in Lebanon; bitter sectarian violence continued and even reached new heights following the emergence of Hezbollah. In the early 1980s, the new Shi'a Islamist regime in Iran sought to export its style of government to Lebanon, where the Shi'a population was largely represented by a secular-leaning militia called Amal. Iranian revolutionary guards were sent to Lebanon with the assistance of Syria to unite the country's weak and divided Islamist groups under the banner of Hezbollah, the 'Party of God'. Resentment of the Israeli invasion certainly strengthened the movement's appeal as did a series of high-profile attacks: in April 1983 a group linked to Hezbollah bombed the US Embassy and in October of that year they bombed French and US military barracks, killing hundreds. During the war, Hezbollah became infamous for taking westerners hostage. Scores of people were kidnapped, and those who were not murdered were held in terrible conditions; Terry Waite, for example, was kept in solitary confinement for much of his four-and-a-half-year captivity.

Marine barracks bombing

After the tumultuous year in Lebanon in 1982, a multinational force led by the United States, France and Italy went to Lebanon to maintain peace and stability while Israel and the PLO withdrew. On the morning of October 23, 1983, an Islamist suicide bomber drove a truck into the lobby of the barracks housing US Marines and detonated the explosives packed inside. 241 American servicemen were killed in the terrorist attack, which made it the single most deadly attack on the American military since the Vietnam War, and on the United States Marine Corps since the Battle for Iwo Jima. A simultaneous suicide attack on the barracks of French paratroopers killed 58 people. As a result of the bombings the multinational force pulled out of Lebanon entirely by April 1984.

OPPPOSITE LEFT: **President Reagan** answers questions about two Americans held hostage in Lebanon. It later emerged that the Reagan administration had secretly sold arms to Iran in the hope of getting Tehran to use its influence to free the hostages. Funds from the sales of weapons to Iran were used to train the anti-Communist 'Contras' in Nicaragua in an episode known as the Iran-Contra Affair.

OPPPOSITE ABOVE RIGHT: **Terry Waite** is escorted by the Lebanese Army to his flight at Beirut Airport. Waite, an envoy of the Church of England and a veteran hostage negotiator, managed to secure the release of several hostages before being taken prisoner himself. He was held hostage for more than four and a half years, spending much of that time in solitary confinement.

OPPPOSITE BELOW: **Israeli artillery** pounds Hezbollah targets in southern Lebanon.

ABOVE LEFT: **A US marine stands** in front of the ruins of the marine barracks in Beirut, Lebanon, October 24, 1983.

ABOVE RIGHT: **Rescue workers** search the wreckage of the US marine barracks.

BELOW: **An explosion rips** through a Royal Jordanian ALIA airline Boeing 727 at Beirut Airport in June 1985. The hijackers, linked to Hezbollah, allowed their hostages to escape before detonating the explosives they had left behind.

The end of the Civil War

Between 1985 and 1986, the Shi'a Muslim militia group Amal fought a bitter battle against Sunni Muslim Palestinians in their refugee camps in Beirut and elsewhere. The 'War of the Camps', as it was known, resulted in thousands of deaths until Syria intervened.

In 1987, the fighting worsened when the Lebanon's Christian President engineered the succession of a Christian, General Aoun, as Prime Minister, despite an unwritten understanding among Lebanon's sects that the Prime Minister would always be a Sunni Muslim. Muslims refused to accept Aoun and followed Salim al-Hoss instead, meaning that Lebanon essentially had two parallel governments. The fighting was stopped once again with the intervention of Syria who pushed Aoun into exile in France, and it was this act that finally ended the civil war in October 1990.

Syria was the victor of the Lebanese Civil War, and the peace agreement, signed at Taif in Saudi Arabia reflected that. Backed by other Arab nations, the Taif Agreement gave Syria a mandate to keep the peace in Lebanon, and by extension it offered Damascus the opportunity to meddle in Lebanese affairs for the next fifteen years.

Soviet Invasion of Afghanistan 1979-1989

Revolution in Afghanistan

Afghanistan has long courted the interests of great powers on account of its strategic location in the heart of Asia, but its harsh terrain and severe climate has made it almost impossible to conquer. The country is crossed by largely impassable mountain ranges, which makes travel difficult and ensures that people's loyalties are usually regional rather than national.

In the 1950s the USSR began giving more aid to Afghanistan, which was then a monarchy. Roads and irrigation systems were built, as were some oil pipelines. The monarchy was overthrown in 1973, and the regime that replaced it was in turn overthrown in a revolution led by Communists five years later. The new regime tried to apply Soviet-style reforms to this conservative Muslim society, and met with resistance. A rebellion started in the remote area of Nuristan in 1978, and soon spread further.

Soviet troops enter Afghanistan

The Afghan government repeatedly requested Soviet assistance, and troops were deployed there in 1979. The USSR had several reasons for what was now, in effect, an invasion: not only could it support a friendly regime, it could also consolidate and extend its own position in Asia as well as protecting its existing interests. Kabul, the capital, was quickly secured by the 100,000 soldiers who were sent in.

However, controlling the countryside was a very different matter. Here resistance fighters, the Mujahideen, saw external rule as not only an infringement of independence but also as a defilement of Islam. They declared a jihad or holy war against the Soviets and received support from the Islamic world – and also from the United States, who were to send many millions of dollars' worth of arms and food aid over the years.

ABOVE: A Russian personnel carrier moves through the Salang Pass as the Soviet invasion of Afghanistan begins at Christmas 1979.

LEFT: Mujahideen on horseback in the rugged western region of Afghanistan in January 1980.

BELOW: British journalist Sandy Gall accompanies the Mujahideen in October 1985. He returned home to set up a charity to help landmine victims in Afghanistan.

The Mujahideen

The Mujahideen waged a guerrilla war against the invaders, one perfectly suited to the terrain, attacking quickly and then disappearing into the mountains. Their supply of weapons was somewhat improvised, with a mixture of inherited arms, more modern ones taken from Soviet troops and those supplied by the US, but this made no difference as fixed battles were not part of their plan. Nor did they have a single base; they were scattered throughout the country.

Soviet attempts to control the rural areas, where people supported the Mujahideen, were devastating. Villages were bombed, destroying homes, crops and ancient irrigation systems, as well as killing large numbers of civilians. Many more were left homeless and starving as a result. Land mines were scattered and caused appalling injuries and deaths, and many people fled across the Pakistani border where enormous refugee camps were set up.

Soviet withdrawal

There was a wave of international protests, with the United Nations condemning Soviet actions. Resistance grew and persisted instead of dying down, and the Soviet troops became bogged down in a vicious and unwinnable war for most of a decade. They achieved very little, except a level of brutality that affected both the Afghan people and their own lower ranks. Discontent spread at home. Not only did the USSR have a large Muslim population, but demoralized veterans were also returning and proving impossible to silence.

By the late 1980s it was becoming even more obvious that the war was unsustainable. In 1987, US shoulder-launched anti-aircraft missiles were introduced, and they had an immediate impact as the Mujahideen shot down helicopters and planes every day. In addition there were problems at home. The Soviet economy was essentially out of control and the country was in trouble; some commentators even thought there was a danger of a coup d'état from disaffected generals and veterans of the war. The Soviet leader, Gorbachev, decided that the time had come for the Soviet Union to withdraw. The first half of the Soviet contingent left in the summer of 1988; the rest were withdrawn by February 15,1989. This withdrawal was largely peaceful as ceasefires had been negotiated with the Mujahideen. Fighting between factions in Afghanistan continued, however, with ramifications to the present day.

During the occupation there were about 15,000 Soviet deaths, and almost half a million soldiers had been either wounded or were sick (with a variety of serious diseases, including typhoid and hepatitis). It is not certain how many Afghans died, but the figure is probably over a million. About five million fled to the refugee camps – an astonishing third of the pre-war population. The damage to the country's infrastructure was almost without parallel.

TOP LEFT: **Afghan resistance commander Abdul Haq urges Margaret Thatcher to exert pressure on the Soviets during a meeting in Downing Street in 1986.**

TOP RIGHT: **President Reagan meets Maulavi Yunis Khalis, the newly installed head of the Afghanistan resistance, at the White House.**

ABOVE LEFT: **Russian soldiers captured by the Mujahideen in 1984**

ABOVE LEFT INSERT: **Prime Minister Benazir Bhutto of neighbouring Pakistan tells a news conference that Moscow should scale down the conflict to encourage a political solution to the country's long-time civil war.**

LEFT: **A convoy of Soviet armoured personnel vehicles cross a bridge in Termez, at the Soviet-Afghan border, during the withdrawal of the Red Army from Afghanistan, May 1988.**

Iran-Iraq War 1980-1988

The Iraqi offensive

The eight-year war between Iran and its neighbour Iraq was the longest conventional war of the twentieth century. It was the result of a long-standing border dispute over the strategic Shatt al-Arab waterway combined with Saddam Hussein's fear that Iran was attempting to spread its Islamic Revolution to Iraq.

Iran's Revolution was barely a year old when Iraq invaded, and the Iranian military was severely weakened by internal strife. As a result, Iraq scored early victories in the oil-rich province of Khuzestan, capturing the city of Khorramshahr and closing in on Abadan, the centre of Iran's oil refining operation.

The Iranian counteroffensive

The Iraqi invasion helped Iran to overcome its military difficulties as hundreds of thousands of volunteers signed up to protect the Revolution and repel the invaders. By late 1981, the tide started to turn. Iranian warplanes began menacing the Iraqi army, whose supply lines were already overstretched, and the superior Iranian navy was able to impose a blockade against Iraq in the Persian Gulf. In May 1982, Khorramshahr was recaptured following a bloody battle in which thousands of Iraqis were taken prisoner.

TOP: Iranian troops man a position along the front lines. The trenches dug out in the Iraqi desert were reminiscent of France during the First World War.

LEFT: King Hussein of Jordan welcomes Saddam Hussein to a Pan-Arab Summit. Jordan tried to get the whole of the Arab world behind Iraq, but Syria and Libya refused and continued to back Iran.

ABOVE INSET: Saddam Hussein weclomes Yasser Arafat to Baghdad soon after the outbreak of the conflict. The Palestinian Liberation Organization tried to mediate a ceasefire between the two countries and re-focus their attention on the Arab-Israeli conflict.

ABOVE: Victorious Iranian soldiers crowd in for a photograph following the liberation of Ahvaz, the provincial capital of Khuzestan, in May 1982.

The fight for Basra

In July 1982, Saddam pulled his armies out of Iran and called for a ceasefire. The Iranians rejected it and pushed into Iraqi territory, focusing their attacks on the southern port city of Basra. However, they met with determined Iraqi resistance and resorted to futile 'human wave' tactics to make use of their numerical superiority and to compensate for their relative lack of military hardware. These waves proved easy targets for the Iraqis, but the Iranians continued to threaten Basra. In response Saddam allowed the use of chemical weapons against Iranian soldiers and began pummelling Iran's cities from the air. The Iranians began bombing Iraq's cities in return, giving rise to the so-called 'war of the cities', in which thousands of civilians lost their lives.

The Tanker War

Iran and Iraq attacked tankers carrying one another's oil in the Persian Gulf, and Iran later widened this offensive to include tankers carrying oil supplies from Iraq's allies, Kuwait, Saudi Arabia and other Arab nations. This seriously affected the global supply of oil and drew the superpowers into the conflict. The United States and the Soviet Union had already been supplying weapons to Iraq, but the Tanker War drew them directly into the conflict. Tankers belonging to Arab nations were 'reflagged' so they could be given legal protection by the superpower whose flag they were flying so as to maintain the flow of oil.

Ceasefire

The land war had reached a stalemate: the Iranians were unable to take Basra, but the Iraqis were unable to repel them. In July 1987, the UN Security Council passed a resolution calling for a ceasefire and return to the pre-war border. Iran had more to lose from this and so refused to accept the terms until a major Iraqi offensive in 1988 drove its forces back across the border. In August 1988, both sides agreed to a ceasefire with both claiming victory. The exact death-toll is not known, but it is estimated to be upwards of one million, making the Iran-Iraq War one of the deadliest of the twentieth century.

TOP RIGHT: **Iranian troops celebrate as they press on Basra. They were never able to capture the strategic port city, despite making it the focus of their resources.**

MIDDLE RIGHT: **Iranian troops open up with a US-made 103mm howitzer. Much of the Iranian arsenal comprised old American hardware that was bought during the Shah's rule. However, an American arms embargo on the new regime made it difficult for Iran to get spare parts. In** 1986, it emerged that members of the Reagan Administration had been selling arms to Iran in order to get Tehran to convince Hezbollah to release American hostages being held in Lebanon. The funds from arms sales to Iran were being used to train right-wing rebels in Nicaragua.

RIGHT: **Saddam Hussein visits a kindergarten to try to convince the Iraqi public that it is business as usual, despite the war with Iran.**

BELOW: **A group of Iranians pictured in northern Iraq in January 1988. The Iranians allied with the Kurdish people of the region who resented being ruled from Baghdad. They waged a guerrilla insurgency which distracted Iraq from the war with Iran. Saddam responded with great ruthlessness, culminating in a deadly chemical attack on the Kurdish settlement of Halabja. Thousands of people were killed instantly.**

Falklands War 1982

Disputed Ownership

The Falklands War lasted for just 74 days and arose from the disputed ownership of a collection of islands, situated in the South Atlantic some 350 miles off the southeast coast of South America. Both Britain and Argentina claimed the Falklands, which also administer the tiny uninhabited islands making up South Georgia and the South Sandwich Islands to the east and southeast. A small band of Argentinians had settled on the Falkland Islands in 1826, but after a dispute over seal hunting a US warship arrived in 1831 and declared the islands free of government. In 1832 a British expedition landed and in 1833 Britain expelled the Argentine governor and declared sovereignty over the territory, although this was never recognized by Argentina. Over the intervening years the population on the islands had grown to 1800 inhabitants, who were happy to live under British government and had British traditions – even though most people in Great Britain would not have been able to point to the islands on a map.

Argentina invades

In March 1982 the military junta ruling Argentina decided to invade the Falklands, known to them as Las Malvinas, and restore them to Argentina. The junta believed that a short and successful war would engender a bout of national pride, divert attention from the shattered economy, and restore their waning popularity. They were also under the mistaken belief that Britain would not be able to defend the islands after it was announced that HMS

Endurance was being withdrawn from the South Atlantic, and would consider the barren land of a region so far away from home not worth fighting for. The Argentinian invasion, codenamed Operation Rosario, was to begin in either May or July to coincide with one of the important national celebrations. However, mounting domestic pressures led to the date being moved forward, and on March 28 reports reached Britain via amateur radio that five Argentinian warships had been sighted off South Georgia. On April 2, the Argentine navy and thousands of troops landed on the Falklands and soon also seized South Georgia and the Sandwich group, despite resistance from the British Royal Marines based locally. Although the UN Security Council immediately called for troops on both sides to withdraw and renew negotiations for a peaceful solution, Argentina refused to comply and Britain began to assemble a large naval taskforce.

Over the first few weeks of April, British ships, aircraft and troops all headed for the South Atlantic, along with the P&O cruise liner *Canberra* and the *QE2*, which were acting as troopships. Meanwhile, the United States began trying to negotiate a peace treaty with the military junta, but they had little success and talks very soon broke down. By April 22 the British task force had arrived in Falklands waters and a few days later a small British commando force re-took the island of South Georgia. The British Government then proceeded to impose a 200-mile exclusion zone around the islands, which at one point was extended to within just 12 miles of the Argentinian coastline.

OPPOSITE TOP: **A Lynx helicopter comes into land on a County-class guided missile destroyer. In the background, a Wasp helicopter hovers forward of a frigate.**

OPPOSITE LEFT: **Britain's Prime Minister, Mrs Margaret Thatcher leaves 10 Downing Street in London after the latest development in the Falklands crisis.**

OPPOSITE RIGHT: **The Argentine Army stands to attention as their national flag is hoisted up the flagpole outside Government House in Port Stanley, the capital of the Falkland Islands.**

ABOVE RIGHT: **The Union flag and white ensign are raised on South Georgia, after the island's recapture by the British.**

BELOW: **Sea Harrier jump jets on the flight deck of HMS *Hermes*, a British aircraft carrier built at the end of the Second World War.**

ABOVE: **British paratroopers come under fire while carrying out emergency medical treatment on Mount Longdon.**

DAILY MAIL MARCH 29, 1982

Britain Sends In Marines

Forty-Two Royal Marine Commandos were on their way to the disputed Falkland Islands last night amid growing friction between Britain and Argentina. Their arrival will double our military strength in an area where tensions have increased because of an Argentine 'invasion' of South Georgia, an island dependency.

They will be stationed in the Falklands capital of Port Stanley – base for the past year for 40 other Marines, 12 of whom are now aboard HMS Endurance off the South Georgia coast 800 miles away. There they await orders to 'evacuate the intruders if necessary'. The latest detachment to be sent out to the South Atlantic made the

first leg of the journey, to Uruguay, by chartered jet. Then in Montevideo they trooped aboard the Antarctic survey ship, the John Biscoe.

As they headed for Port Stanley two of Argentina's missile-carrying corvettes were steaming towards South Georgia with a heavy patrol boat capable of putting ashore 400 marines, and a supply vessel. According to a spokesman in Buenos Aires, the warships would 'protect' the remaining ten members of a party of scrap metal dealers who last week made an illegal landing on South Georgia and flew the Argentine flag.

DAILY MAIL MAY 31, 1982

Surrender at Goose Green

David Norris reports from Goose Green, where he saw 1,400 Argentine troops throw down their arms in front of 600 Paras. I was the only British newspaperman to see the climax of the Paras' outstanding victory at Goose Green – the official surrender of the Argentines who outnumbered us by more than two to one. I was asked by the acting commander of the Second Battalion the Parachute Regiment, Major Chris Keeble, to be an official witness of the surrender, with BBC correspondent Robert Fox. It was a great moment for us.

The tragedy was that the architect of the victory was not there to see the ultimate triumph of his men. It had been Lieutenant-Colonel 'H' Jones's leadership and courage which had brought about this moment. But he had died in the achieving of it. The actual ceremony at mid-afternoon on Saturday in the grey Falklands light had all the necessary traditional military sense of theatre about it to satisfy both sides. The Argentine troops and air force men were lined up hundreds deep around the Goose Green airfield. Around them a guard from the 600 battle-scarred British paratroopers who took Goose Green and its twin settlement of Darwin.

No choice

The senior Argentine officer, Vice-Commodore Wilson Doser Pedroza, turned and addressed his airmen. His voice hoarse, he harangued them for several minutes. The speech obviously dealt with the rightness of the Argentine cause. He told them they had fought well, but they had no choice but to surrender. He led his men in the singing of the Argentine National Anthem. Then he

officially surrendered the settlement and its airfield to Major Keeble, and Argentine officers gave the orders to their men to lay down their weapons. This they did... not with surliness but with relief. They threw their automatic rifles and pistols into piles at the end of each rank. Many took off their steel helmets and threw them on to the heaps of weapons. One group gave loud whoops of joy. Their meaning was clear... they were not going to die.

After some 250 airmen had thrown down their weapons came the Argentine Army troops. More than 800 of them filed past the Paras throwing their weapons and ammunition into piles. On the airfield itself were two Pucara planes. There were dumps of bombs, rockets, ammunition. There was aviation fuel. Four modern 30mm anti-aircraft guns around the field can now be manned by British troops. So can other field guns and heavy machine guns. Amazingly, when all the ancillary Argentine troops were rounded up we found we had 1,400 prisoners.

Union Jack Raised

I then saw the Union Jack raised over the settlement from the flag pole outside the Goose Green settlement school, where it had flown for years until eight weeks ago. At the other end of the village flies the proud flag of the airborne forces, the blue Pegasus on a maroon background. The other witnesses to this historic scene had reason to feel grim satisfaction. They were the inhabitants of this little settlement who have suffered severely at the hands of the Argentines. They welcomed us with shouts of joy and arms thrown round the soldiers.

Sinking of the *Belgrano* and the *Sheffield*

On May 2 the British nuclear submarine HMS *Conqueror* torpedoed the Argentine cruiser ARA *General Belgrano* some 30 miles outside the exclusion zone. The *Belgrano* sank quickly and 323 crewmembers died in the attack, although over 700 more men were rescued from the ocean despite the stormy weather. The incident hardened the attitude of the Argentinian junta and they refused to consider a comprehensive peace plan that had just been proposed by the President of Peru, Belaúnde Terry. However, the sinking did have a major effect on the course of the war, since the entire Argentine fleet returned to port afterwards and did not leave again during the hostilities.

A few days later, on May 4, the British destroyer HMS *Sheffield* was struck by an Exocet missile, launched by an Argentinian aircraft. The missile hit amidships, and although it is not clear whether it actually exploded it did cause massive fires to break out, which led to the loss of 20 men, and severe injuries to another 24 crew members. The *Sheffield* was abandoned to burn and later sank as it was being towed out of the exclusion zone. The destruction of *Sheffield* had a profound impact in Britain, making people realize that the 'Falklands Crisis' was a real war with real people dying. Britain accepted the peace plan proposed by Peru, but without Argentinian approval it could not proceed.

OPPOSITE BELOW: **Argentine soldiers take position in Port Howard in May.**

OPPOSITE ABOVE: **The destroyer HMS *Sheffield* burns on May 25, after being hit by an Exocet missile fired by an Argentine Navy aircraft. The ship sank with the loss of twenty lives.**

OPPOSITE MIDDLE: **Paratroopers of the British Falkland Islands Task Force clean out a mortar on East Falkland before the final push on** the capital Port Stanley.

BELOW: **The Union flag flies over Port Howard, West Falkland in June 1982. It is the first time in more than two months and is hoisted by 40 Commando, Royal Marines.**

RIGHT: **The launch of HMS *Coventry* which sank with the loss of 20 lives.**

DAILY MAIL   JUNE 10, 1982

Disaster At Bluff Cove

Argentine jets have mounted a devastating attack on exposed British supply ships unloading men and ammunition near Port Stanley. The number of killed was not known, but was believed to be 'substantial' and between 78 and 80 men were badly burned from explosions.

The attack came when the most daring tactical gamble of the Falklands war was within an hour of total success. Even in its bloody aftermath, the British operation had established a crucial beachhead for the assault on the Falklands capital Port Stanley, under 15 miles away.

Brigadier Tony Wilson, commanding Five Infantry Brigade, had discovered that the Argentines had abandoned the settlements of Fitzroy and Bluff Cove. There was low cloud and fog. He gambled on getting thousands of men in by sea, undetected by the Argentines and by-passing their patrols on land. The risk was that he had no anti-aircraft cover. Setting up Rapier ground-to-air missiles on the hills around the landing site took time. For two days, men and materials poured ashore. Still the Argentines did not discover the operation.

Heroism And Selflessness

Michael Nicholson, of ITN, watched from the shore what he described as 'a day of extraordinary heroism and selflessness.' He reported:

The attack happened so fast there wasn't even time to think of finding cover and as the ships were hit many men aboard hadn't even time to put on their anti-burn asbestos masks and gloves to save them from the heat flash as the bombs exploded. Many were brought ashore with second degree burns.

'Our air defences which had come off the ships that morning were still being set up on the hillside overlooking the estuary and had the Argentine planes come just that one hour later we would have been ready for them.

'As it was the Skyhawks came in to attack and were out again with our gunfire chasing them too late. The bombs hit Sir Galahad aft through the engine room and accommodation sections.

'As I watched from the shore less than 400 yards away the impact of boxes of ammunition aboard exploding shook the ground beneath us. We crouched with other soldiers around us as bullets from the ship whistled and whirled past us. We could see them coming by the red tracers.

'I saw hundreds of men rush forward along the deck, across the hold, putting on their lifejackets, putting on their survival suits, some, the ship's crewmen just off watch, putting on shirts and trousers. Many, trapped on the wrong side of the fire, jumped overboard.

Horror

But one hour away from unloading the last men and equipment – and from the Rapiers being set up ready to fire – the weather suddenly cleared. An Argentine patrol spotted the landing and radioed its position. The Argentines sent a wave of Skyhawk jets, heavily loaded with bombs and missiles, to attack the British ships. Their main target was the supply ship Sir Galahad, which together with its sister ship Sir Tristram was unloading hundreds of men 200 yards off-shore. On Sir Galahad were up to 400 men, many of them sleeping and resting before transferring to landing craft.

The ship had no warning and little to fight back with. The troops on shore could only look on in horror as bomb after bomb crashed into Sir Galahad setting it and the surrounding sea ablaze. Last night it was feared it might have sunk.

TOP LEFT: An Argentine POW waits for a prisoner transport ship in San Carlos Water.

ABOVE: A British Royal Marine guards some of the 1,400 Argentine prisoners captured during the battle at Goose Green.

TOP: Survivors are helped onshore at Bluff Cove, East Falklands, after two British landing ships the Sir Galahad and the Sir Tristram suffered air attacks. One week later the Argentine forces surrendered Port Stanley, ending the Falklands War in which 255 Britons and 652 Argentines died.

OPPOSITE: HMS Hermes returns to a hero's welcome in Portsmouth, England, on July 21.

OPPOSITE RIGHT: The luxury liners, the QE2 and the Canberra, bring Falklands veterans back to Southampton.

Battle at Goose Green

Throughout May the conflict escalated, although Britain continued to offer ceasefire terms to the Argentinians and the UN was still trying to negotiate a peaceful solution. British troops landed on the Falklands near Port San Carlos on May 21, and on May 28 they took Darwin and Goose Green, which were blocking further progress and were being defended by a large section of the Argentine army. The British lost 17 men, including Lieutenant-Colonel Herbert 'H' Jones, who was later awarded a Victoria Cross. The Argentine death toll was ten times greater and 1,400 prisoners were taken. Many military sources believe that the death toll would have been much lower if the impending attack had not been announced on the BBC World Service just before it took place. Goose Green was a significant victory for the British, however, as it put a sizeable part of the Argentinian army out of action and opened the way for troops to move forward towards the capital, Port Stanley.

Bluff Cove

As a preliminary to making an attack on Port Stanley itself, British troops advanced on Fitzroy and Bluff Cove. To back them up, early on June 7 RFA *Sir Galahad* and RFA *Sir Tristram* arrived with more troops who were due to be shipped ashore at Fitzroy. However, due to mistakes and mix-ups the troops were ferried the far longer journey to Bluff Cove instead, leaving the *Sir Galahad* and the *Sir Tristram* vulnerable to attack for some considerable time. On June 8, Argentine Skyhawk aircraft took advantage of the opportunity: the *Sir Galahad* caught fire and sank, while the *Sir Tristram* was badly damaged but salvageable. Their escort ship, the HMS *Plymouth*, was also hit. A total of 48 British servicemen were killed in the attack, and many more were seriously wounded – some of them suffering terrible burns. The disaster led to harrowing and sobering images of war being sent around the world, as television news footage showed helicopters hovering in thick smoke to winch survivors from burning ships.

The Fall of Stanley

On the night of June 11, the British launched the first major assault on the heavily defended high ground around Port Stanley, taking the areas of Mount Harriet, Two Sisters and Mount Longdon. Two days later the areas of Wireless Ridge and Mount Tumbledown were captured, which were Port Stanley's last lines of defence. On June 14, the Argentine garrison at Port Stanley was finally defeated and Brigade General Mario Menéndez surrendered to Major General Jeremy Moore, marking an end to hostilities. By June 20 Britain had also retaken the South Sandwich Islands. A Falklands Protection Zone of 150 miles later replaced the 200-mile exclusion zone.

Grenada 1983

Soviet threat in America's backyard

In 1983 Grenada was ruled by a leftwing government that had seized power in a coup in 1979. The government was aligned to the Soviet Union and Cuba, and both countries had been helping to build an airstrip on the island, ostensibly for commercial use. However, President Reagan feared that Moscow's real intention was to turn the small Caribbean island into a Soviet military airbase. His fears were shared by members of the Organization of East Caribbean States, who appealed to Washington for assistance in the matter.

Coup d'état in Grenada

In October 1983, the political situation in Grenada rapidly deteriorated. The Prime Minister, Maurice Bishop, was overthrown and later murdered by members of his own party. Bishop, a relative moderate, was considered too close to Washington by the coup plotters. The worsening political situation, combined with the strategic threat to the United States and its regional allies convinced Reagan of the need to intervene. The final trigger came when the new regime imposed a strict 'shoot-on-sight' curfew, which compromised the safety of some 1,000 US nationals in the country, mostly medical students at St George's University.

Operation Urgent Fury

Operation Urgent Fury, as the invasion was codenamed, began early in the morning of October 25, 1983. In what was the US military's first major foreign operation since Vietnam, 1,900 marines were airlifted on to the island with the support of over 2,000 members of the army. They faced limited resistance from Grenada's 6,500 troops and a contingent of 700 Cuban construction workers. The US secured control of the island within just two days, but at a cost of 19 American and up to 100 Cuban and Grenadan deaths. Democratic elections in 1984 brought to power a pro-American government and Soviet influence on the island was removed.

OPPOSITE ABOVE: **An American soldier stands next to an anti-Communist sign on the Caribbean Island of Grenada on November 11, 1983. There are few pictures of the actual invasion because Washington ordered a media blackout.**

OPPOSITE BELOW LEFT: **President Ronald Reagan defends the use of US troops in Grenada during a press briefing at the White House on November 3, 1983. Standing by is Donald Rumsfeld who has just been named Middle East Envoy in the wake of the Marine Barracks bombing in Beirut.**

OPPOSITE BELOW RIGHT: **Margaret Thatcher takes part in a live phone-in on BBC World Service where she is criticized for letting down President Reagan by refusing to support the invasion of Grenada. She declared: 'You can't go walking into other people's countries just because they are Communists.'**

BELOW: **American soldiers arrest a man suspected of belonging to a Marxist militia group.**

ABOVE LEFT: **Demonstrators chant 'Reagan-Thatcher hands off Grenada' as they protest the invasion outside the American Embassy in London.**

LEFT: **President Reagan outside 10 Downing Street during his state visit to the United Kingdom in June 1982. Reagan rode with Queen Elizabeth on horseback and became the first American President to address the Houses of Parliament. Reagan had supported Thatcher in the Falklands War and there was some anger in America that she did not respond in kind.**

Sri Lankan Civil War 1983 -

Ethnic divisions

The origins of the conflict lie mainly in disagreements between Sri Lanka's two main ethnic groups, the Sinhalese and the Tamils, over language and access to education and citizenship. After independence from Britain in 1948, a democratic government was established in Sri Lanka. This favoured the majority Sinhalese population which comprised more than two-thirds of the eligible Sri Lankan voters. The Tamil population was totally politically marginalized and had to stand by as successive Sinhalese-dominated governments introduced legislation to benefit the Sinhalese people. In 1956 Sinhala was made the official language of Sri Lanka, which led to employment problems for many among the minority Tamil-speaking population, and during the 1970s it was agreed to standardize university admissions, which benefited Sinhalese students at the expense of Tamils.

During these years, there had been some grassroots violence between the two communities, but it was not until the late 1970s, when the Tamils began organizing themselves, that Sri Lanka stood on the precipice of civil war.

TOP: Sri Lankan government soldiers move into the Jaffna Peninsula, a Tamil Tiger stronghold in the north of the island, during an offensive in April 1996.

LEFT: Tamil Tigers patrol the streets of Jaffna in 1987.

ABOVE: Flanked by bodyguards, a Tamil Tiger makes a show of strength during a photoshoot at a safehouse in Jaffna.

ABOVE INSET: Leaders of the Tamil Tigers are said to carry a capsule of cyanide with them at all times; it is to be taken in the event of their capture.

Tamil Tigers

In 1976, the Liberation Tigers of Tamil Eelam (LTTE) was formed. Commonly known as the Tamil Tigers, they staged their first major attack on Sri Lankan government forces in July 1983, when they ambushed and killed 13 government soldiers. Outraged Sinhalese took to the streets of Colombo, the capital, to protest and hundreds of Tamils were killed by the mob. Thousands more were forced to flee their homes and move to the Tamil-dominated areas of the north, further polarizing Sri Lankan society.

On the first anniversary of the riots, Tamil guerrillas began a series of attacks, each leading to retaliation by armed forces. Attempts were made to negotiate between the two sides in 1985, but fighting intensified through early 1987 with Sri Lankan government forces pushing deep into Tamil territory in the north, laying siege to the main Tamil city of Jaffna in May.

Indian intervention

In 1987, the Indian government intervened to stop the bloodshed and managed to impose a short-lived peace agreement. The Indo-Sri Lanka Peace Accord of July 29, 1987 demanded official status for the Tamil language and for the Tamil Tigers to surrender arms to a peacekeeping force from India. However, violence soon broke out between the Tamil Tigers and the Indian Peace Keeping Force, leading to full-scale conflict. The IPKF was called back to India in 1989 and after the Tamil Tigers assassinated the former Indian prime minister, Rajiv Gandhi, in 1991, Indian support evaporated.

Ceasefire

After brief ceasefires in 1990 and 1995, both sides turned on each other again. A more lasting ceasefire agreement was signed in February 2002 with the assistance of Norway, and Tamils achieved autonomy in the north and east of the country. However, there have been numerous violations of the ceasefire by both sides, and on January 2, 2008 it came to an end. The conflict continues.

ABOVE RIGHT: **Defence minister Anuruddha Ratwatte addresses government troops after hoisting the Sri Lankan flag over Jaffna in December 1995. Several thousand died during the offensive to capture the Tamil stronghold.**

BELOW: **Two policemen monitor a curfew in the deserted capital, Colombo following a bomb blast in October 1994.**

RIGHT: **A Tamil Tiger guerrilla drapes himself with bullets before going out on patrol in a truck modified with a mounted machine gun.**

First Intifada
1987-1993

Grassroots uprising

By 1987 the West Bank and Gaza had been under Israeli occupation for two decades. The Palestinian population had grown weary, and the widespread belief that the Arab world had lost interest in their cause only added to their sense of frustration. This frustration translated into a full-scale uprising following an incident at the Jebaliya refugee camp in Gaza in December 1987. The Israel Defence Forces (IDF) used heavy-handed 'Iron Fist' tactics to disperse rioters in the camp, causing an outpouring of anger across Gaza and the West Bank, and giving rise to the First Intifada.

The Intifada, which means 'shaking-off', was very much a grassroots protest involving various acts of civil disobedience ranging from non-payment of taxes and general strikes to stone-throwing. The Palestinian Liberation Organization (PLO), in exile in Tunisia, was keen to coordinate and lead this spontaneous protest, but they were by now rivalled by Palestinian Islamic Jihad and Hamas, two Islamist movements vying for influence. The differing agendas of these three groups served to prolong and radicalize the uprising. The advent of militant Islamist groups saw a rise in the use of terror tactics, which would come to define the Second Intifada a decade later.

TOP: Palestinian youths set fire to tyres and debris to block the entrance to the Bureij refugee camp in the Gaza Strip.

ABOVE: A Palestinian woman protests against the Israeli occupation outside the Palestinian Affairs Department in Amman, Jordan. When the Intifada broke out in 1987, many Palestinians felt the Arab world had lost interest in their cause.

LEFT: PLO guerrillas train at a camp in Damascus, Syria, in 1986. The Intifada began as a grassroots uprising and initially the PLO had to respond to events rather than lead them.

Peace Process

The image of Palestinians throwing stones at Israeli tanks and well-armed soldiers caught the attention of the world and galvanized the Peace Process. This process began with a conference sponsored by the United States and the Soviet Union in Madrid in October 1991, and culminated in the signing of the Oslo Accords in September 1993. This Norwegian-brokered agreement secured the withdrawal of Israeli troops from parts of the West Bank and Gaza, and placed these areas under the administration of a newly created Palestinian National Authority. The PLO and Israel also bestowed formal recognition upon one another, and their leaders, Yasser Arafat and Yitzakh Rabin, famously shook hands on the White House lawn on September 13, 1993. Despite international jubilation, violence continued as Hamas and other militant Islamist groups remained outside the agreement and pressed on with their campaign against Israel. The Peace Process subsequently stalled as agreement could not be reached on controversial areas not covered by the Oslo Accords, namely control of East Jerusalem, the future of Israeli settlements in the West Bank and the right of Palestinian refugees to return to their homes.

ABOVE RIGHT: **Palestinian youths jeer at an Israeli soldier in the Nuseirat refugee camp in the Gaza Strip. Many Palestinians who took part in the Intifada were youths who had spent their whole lives under the Israeli occupation.**

ABOVE LEFT: **Armed with catapults, Palestinians fire marbles at Israeli troops following Friday prayers in the casbah of Nablus.**

BELOW: **Yasser Arafat, Shimon Peres and Yitzakh Rabin share the 1994 Nobel Peace Prize for their role in the Peace Process. The following year, Rabin was assassinated by a Jewish extremist who was opposed to the Peace Process.**

TOP: **Israeli troops are on high alert as they patrol along Baghdad Street in Gaza City.**

ABOVE: **Israeli troops respond to a group of stone-throwers in the Jebaliya refugee camp in the Gaza Strip.**

Panama 1989

American invasion

On December 20, 1989 the US launched Operation Just Cause, a surprise invasion of Panama. President Bush sought to protect American citizens in the country after an American serviceman had been killed by the security forces of the Panamanian ruler, General Manuel Noriega. Bush also had a legal obligation to protect the Panama Canal Zone and sought to restore democracy and the rule of law in the country following rigged elections. Noriega had fixed a May 1989 Presidential election when it became clear that his opponents would win.

The US already had almost 15,000 men in Panama policing the Canal Zone in 1989, and another 15,000 were brought in for the invasion. Within days the Panamanian Defense Force was defeated and a new government was formed under Guillermo Endara, the legitimate winner of the rigged May 1989 elections. On January 3, 1990, Noriega was captured and later sent to the United States to face trial on charges of drug-trafficking and money-laundering.

ABOVE: **US Marines advance through a hostile neighbourhood in Panama City during Operation Just Cause.**

MIDDLE: **Manuel Noriega talks to the press to deny claims that he rigged the election in May 1989.**

RIGHT: **President Bush welcomes General Maxwell Thurman, the commander of the US Forces in** Panama, to the White House to commend him and his troops for their 'outstanding' work. Twenty-three American servicemen lost their lives during the operation.

Kashmir Insurgency 1989 -

The Kargil War

In May 1999, India discovered that Pakistani troops had crossed the Line of Control near Kargil during the winter while Indian troops had retreated to lower altitudes. The Indian army was mobilized and the Pakistani positions were attacked from the air in what became known as the Kargil War. The Pakistani government denied the incursion, claiming that the troops were insurgents, and criticized India for using airstrikes in Kashmir. The international community quickly intervened to prevent a wider war between the two nuclear powers, and the conflict ended in July 1999, by which time India had already pushed most of the insurgents out of the country.

The Line of Control

Ever since Partition in 1947, both India and Pakistan have claimed ownership of Kashmir, the mountainous territory lying between them in the north. The two countries went to war over the territory in 1948, following which a UN resolution stated that a plebiscite should be held, allowing the Kashmiris to choose. This never happened, and the situation still remains unresolved. War broke out between India and Pakistan again in 1971, after which the old ceasefire line became a formal Line of Control, dividing Indian-controlled Kashmir from the part administered by Pakistan.

Insurgency

In 1989, Islamic militants began an insurgency in Indian-controlled Kashmir. Some of the insurgents were Kashmiris demanding independence from India, while others were veterans of the Soviet-Afghanistan war, looking for a new location to fight their Holy War. In addition to attacking and killing Indian soldiers and Hindu civilians, the insurgents targeted moderate Muslims in an attempt to radicalize and divide the population. Clashes have continued ever since; thousands have been killed, and more than 250,000 people are believed to have fled from their homes.

Despite establishing the Line of Control, the issue of Kashmir has continued to sour relations between India and Pakistan. The Indian government argues that Pakistan has been stirring up the insurgency by helping outside militants enter Indian-controlled Kashmir. Pakistan consistently denies this, charging that the militants fighting against Indian rule are natives.

Continued hostilities

India and Pakistan continued to trade gunfire across the Line of Control and the insurgency in Indian-controlled Kashmir persisted. In October 2001 scores of people were killed when militants attacked the Kashmir Assembly in Srinagar. Two months later they attacked the Indian Parliament building in New Delhi killing seven people and outraging public opinion in India. The Indian government blamed Pakistan for sponsoring the audacious attack and deployed thousands of extra troops to Kashmir. A full-scale war was again averted, but only after General Musharraf, the ruler of Pakistan, made a speech pledging to do more to stop Pakistan-based militants from entering Indian-controlled Kashmir.

Talks between India and Pakistan led to a ceasefire in November 2003. Since then fewer militants have crossed the border and there has been a reduction in violence in Kashmir, although terrorist attacks have occurred in cities across India. The situation remains fragile; with political instability in Pakistan and the presence of large armies on both sides of the Line of Control, a return of hostilities is likely.

TOP: **Indian forces patrol their side of the Line of Control in Kashmir, the world's highest battleground.**

LEFT: **Kashmiri separatist leader Shabir Shah leads a march in Srinagar in Indian-controlled** Kashmir. Pakistan claims the insurgency is being fuelled by separatists from within Indian-controlled Kashmir. India argues that the insurgents are coming in from outside with the help of the Pakistani government.

ABOVE: **A camouflaged Pakistani soldier takes position in a bunker near Chakoti on the Line of Control.**

Romania 1989

The Communist monarchy

By 1989 Nicolae Ceausescu and his wife, Elena, had ruled Communist Romania like King and Queen for more than two decades. In relation to other East European Communist leaders, they were mavericks who broke with Soviet domination and asserted an independent foreign policy. However, the cost of maintaining an independent military, as well as paying for a series of grandiose construction projects, took its toll on the Romanian economy. In the 1980s, Ceausescu instituted a severe austerity programme designed to clear the debt in only a few years. The programme was a failure and resulted in shortages of food, electricity and consumer goods across the country. This led to widespread dissatisfaction with the regime, but the Ceausescus had a well-oiled security apparatus and dissenting voices were normally silenced before they could spread.

Spillover

By December 1989 Eastern Europe had witnessed great upheaval; the Communist regimes in Poland, Hungary, Czechoslovakia and East Germany were all in the process of collapse. The Ceausescus believed their independence from the Soviet bloc and their muscular security services would insulate them from the contagion. However, Romania had an Achilles' heel in the form of a sizeable Hungarian population in the east. These Hungarians watched as Communism unravelled in Hungary, and dissent soon spread across the border.

BELOW: Bucharest, December 22, 1989. With the Ceausescus in flight, thousands fill the centre of Bucharest. However, security officers still loyal to the regime continued to engage in a violent counter-revolution.

LEFT: Romania's dictator delivers his last speech from the balcony of the Communist Party Headquarters in Bucharest, December 21, 1989. A stunned Ceausescu listened as the crowd began jeering during his speech.

OPPOSITE ABOVE: The end of an era: a statue of Lenin is removed from a square in Bucharest. Although the National Salvation Front was made up of members of the Communist party, they set Romania on a path to democracy and later EU membership.

OPPOSITE BELOW: A soldier guards Ceausescu's bedroom at his private residence.

The Romanian revolution began on December 16, 1989 when a protest broke out in the eastern city of Timisoara. The regime had tried to evict a Hungarian pastor named László Tökés for publishing an article critical of the regime's policies. Emboldened by changes occurring in Hungary, the town's Hungarian population gathered outside his home and refused to allow the eviction to take place. The insurrection quickly spread as the repressed, impoverished Romanian population of the town took up the cause. The protestors chanted anti-Communist slogans and attempted to burn down the regional Communist party headquarters. Secret police arrested protesters or beat them up, but were unable to stop the protests.

On December 17 martial law was declared and the army was sent in to disperse the crowds. They opened fire and a number of protestors were massacred. The fighting escalated on both sides and Timisoara became a warzone.

DAILY MAIL DECEMBER 26 1989

The Tyrant Is Dead

Deposed Rumanian tyrant Nicolae Ceausescu and his wife Elena were executed last night after a secret court martial. The couple who misruled Rumania with megalomaniac zeal for almost 25 years were found guilty of the genocide of 60,000 people, stealing one billion dollars from the state and undermining the national economy.

The announcement by Rumania's interim government, the National Salvation Front, was carried on state radio and television. The TV said: 'Nicolae and Elena Ceausescu have been sentenced to death, and their property has been confiscated. The sentence is definitive and has been carried out.'

It took viewers completely by surprise and was followed moments later by a cheerful bearded Santa Claus driving through snow and singing Jingle Bells. 'Oh, what wonderful news,' a Bucharest radio announcer said. 'The anti-Christ died on Christmas Day.'

The broadcasts did not specify how or where the executions were carried out or where the two were tried. Executions in Rumania have usually been carried out by firing squad.

There was no word of the fate of the couple's son and daughter Nicu and Zoia-Elena, who were paraded before television viewers after their arrests on Friday and Sunday.

The news was of the executions also given by the French ambassador in Bucharest, M Le Breton. He told French TV viewers: 'I have just been informed that the Bucharest Military Tribunal brought the Ceausescus to trial on a charge of genocide. They were both found guilty and the death sentence was carried out immediately.'

Ceausescu, 71, and his wife, who would have been 71 next month, fled the capital on Friday in a helicopter and were reportedly captured in an underground bunker on Saturday.

The Ceausescus fall

On December 21, after returning from a trip to Iran, Ceausescu addressed an assembly of 110,000 people from the balcony of Communist headquarters in Bucharest. He tried to stoke ethnic tensions by blaming the unrest on Hungarians, but many Romanians in the crowd were unconvinced and began chanting insubordinately. Loud bangs were heard and a rumour quickly spread that the secret police were firing on the crowd. The scene quickly descended into a battle between ordinary civilians and the Ceausescus' security forces. The riots spread as workers downed their tools and joined the revolution. The army switched sides, but the secret police remained loyal and continued to fight, prolonging the bloodshed. The Ceausescus fled the city by helicopter, but they were captured by the army and taken to a barracks for trial. They were found guilty of crimes against the state and were executed on Christmas Day 1989. The violent revolution petered out and a new government called the National Salvation Front came to power promising an end to the one-party system.

ABOVE: **The collapse of the Ceausescu regime revealed the terrible plight of Romania's orphans. The Ceausescus outlawed abortion and contraception in a bid to raise** the birth rate. However, the country was unable to care for the number of abandoned children and they were forced to live in terrible conditions. A shocked world poured aid into the country during the 1990s and conditions improved.

The Gulf War 1990–1991

Operation Desert Storm

The Gulf War, codenamed Operation Desert Storm, lasted for just 42 days in 1991, but the build-up to the conflict played out over a much longer period. The origins of the conflict lie in the bloody Iran-Iraq war, during which more than 200,000 Iraqis were killed in Saddam Hussein's attempt to win military glory and defeat the Islamic Revolutionary government in Iran. Most Arab nations, including Kuwait, supported Iraq, fearing that Iran wanted to dominate the region and spread its revolution.

By the time the war ended in an inglorious stalemate in 1988, Iraq had amassed huge debts in countries across the world. Iraqi oil production had been affected by the war, meaning that Saddam was in no position to repay his foreign creditors. Matters were made much worse when Kuwait increased its oil production by 40 per cent over its OPEC quota, causing a slump in world oil prices. Eager for a clear military victory, unable to finance his foreign debts and desperate to keep his military occupied, Saddam saw an easy answer to all his problems in the oil-rich kingdom to his south.

Iraq invades Kuwait

In 1988 and 1989, the Iraqi government attempted to extract territorial concessions from Kuwait in compensation for fighting the war against Iran on its behalf. Kuwait did not accept the proposal leaving Saddam outraged and on a fast track to war. Emboldened by the belief that Iraq had a historic claim to Kuwait and convinced by a conversation with the US ambassador that Washington would not intervene, Iraq invaded. The pretext for the war would be that Kuwaiti oilrigs were slant drilling and illegally tapping into Iraqi oil fields.

ABOVE: Abandoned vehicles line the 'Highway of Death', the road between Kuwait City and Basra. Following the Allied invasion, Iraqi soldiers tried to flee Kuwait in any available means of transport, but most were intercepted and destroyed.

MIDDLE: An Iraqi tank rolls into Kuwait City during the invasion in August 1990.

FAR RIGHT: The Commander in Chief of British military during the Gulf War, General Sir Peter de la Billiere, was a member of the SAS and had led the Special Forces during the Iranian Embassy Siege in 1980.

RIGHT: As commander of United States Central Command (CENTCOM), the operations in the Gulf fell under the jurisdiction of General Norman Schwarzkopf. Schwarzkopf had distinguished himself during two tours in Vietnam, the 1983 campaign in Grenada and as a teacher at West Point.

OPPOSITE ABOVE: RAF Tornado jets at Bruggen in Germany prepare to fly to the Gulf, August 17, 1990.

OPPOSITE MIDDLE RIGHT: Iraqi President Saddam Hussein appearing defiant on Iraqi Television.

OPPOSITE MIDDLE LEFT: Allied troops try out new equipment designed to protect against chemical warfare. Saddam had used chemical weapons during the war with Iran as well as against his own people in the Kurdish village of Halabja in 1988.

OPPOSITE BELOW RIGHT: Wreckage of British Airways Flight 149 at Kuwait International Airport.

British Airways flight 149

British airways flight 149 from London to Kuala Lumpur stopped as scheduled in Kuwait to refuel in the early hours of the morning on August 2, 1990. Just hours earlier, the Iraqi invasion of Kuwait had started leaving the passengers of flight 149 stranded in a war zone.

The Iraqi army quickly overran the airport and the passengers were rounded up and taken to Baghdad. From there they were relocated to strategic sites across the country to act as human shields to deter the West from airstrikes.

After months in captivity Saddam released the hostages. None was killed by the Iraqis, but all were shaken by their ordeal and one man died from a heart attack.

From the moment the crisis began, questions arose as to why British Airways had landed a passenger airliner in a country teetering on the brink of a war. It has been alleged that the British government used the plane to transport agents into the country ahead of the invasion. British Airways maintains that it had no knowledge that the invasion had started when the plane landed.

DAILY MAIL AUGUST 3, 1990
I'll make Kuwait a graveyard

America, Britain and Russia yesterday gave Iraq's President Saddam Hussein 48 hours to end his invasion of Kuwait. They warned of international 'collective measures' against Iraq as the rape of the tiny Gulf state was condemned worldwide. But Hussein, the Butcher of Baghdad, had already issued a chilling warning against any outside interference. 'We will turn Kuwait into a graveyard to anyone who tries to commit aggression or is moved by the lust of invasion,' said a statement from his mouthpiece, the Revolution Command Council.

The international ultimatum was issued after the United Nations Security Council passed a unanimous emergency resolution condemning the Iraqi attack as 'a breach of international peace and security'. Today, in an unprecedented Superpower move, US Secretary of State James Baker flies to Moscow to issue a statement with Soviet Foreign Minister Eduard Shevardnadze calling on Iraq to withdraw.

The lightning invasion, launched at midnight London time, stunned the world.

Hussein, furious at Kuwait's refusal to capitulate to his demands in a quarrel over land, oil and loans, hurled his battle-hardened forces against the neighbour which backed him with millions of dollars in his war with Iran. Iraqi troops reached the centre of Kuwait City.

Operation Desert Shield

On August 2, 1990, Iraqi forces crossed the border and quickly seized control of the smaller nation. However, across the world this move was seen as a threat to Middle East stability and to worldwide oil supplies, so within days the United States, along with the United Nations, demanded Iraq's immediate withdrawal. Within a week King Fahd of Saudi Arabia had requested help to protect his country from possible attack, since Iraqi troops were now within striking distance of major Saudi oil fields. Iraqi control of these, along with the Kuwait and Iraqi reserves, would have given them ownership of the majority of the world's reserves, so the United States and other UN member nations began deploying troops in Saudi Arabia under the codename Operation Desert Shield. Iraq's access to the sea was quickly blockaded, and a trade embargo was put in place.

By November, with no sign of Iraq complying with requests to leave Kuwait, the UN Security Council authorized the use of 'all means possible' to eject Iraq from Kuwait, and UN member countries began putting together a force to achieve this. By the end of 1990 it was clear that diplomatic measures had failed to achieve an Iraqi withdrawal from Kuwait and meanwhile over half a million Allied troops had been deployed in Saudi Arabia and throughout the Gulf region.

ABOVE: **The 1st Battalion of the Staffordshire Regiment keeps watch for an Iraqi invasion along the Saudi side of the border with Kuwait.**

FAR LEFT: **Military police stand guard in their dugout. They are on hand to police more than half a million men who arrived in Saudi Arabia in a short space of time.**

FAR LEFT BELOW: **From Saudi with love. Soldiers send messages home.**

FAR LEFT BOTTOM: **Food rations being carried by stretcher across the desert.**

LEFT: **General Schwarzkopf arrives on a tour of the area to see Operation Desert Shield firsthand.**

OPPOSITE ABOVE: **The Challenger tank is put through its paces in the Saudi desert.**

OPPOSITE MIDDLE LEFT: **The Desert Rats, the British Army's 7th Armoured Brigade, are interviewed in the Saudi desert.**

OPPOSITE BELOW LEFT: **Allied soldiers train in desert camouflage in Saudi Arabia.**

OPPOSITE RIGHT: **Allied troops man positions along the Kuwaiti border.**

DAILY MAIL SEPTEMBER 15, 1990

Return of the Desert Rats

The Desert Rats are returning to the Middle East to confront Iraqi dictator Saddam Hussein with a stunning array of firepower.

The 7th Armoured Brigade, a powerful unit of 114 battle tanks and 6,000 troops, received its orders for Gulf duty yesterday. It will sail for Saudi Arabia in the biggest movement of British tanks, artillery and armoured infantry since its military forebears blazed across North Africa in World War II. Another 18 Tornado aircraft are also being sent to Saudi, raising the number of RAF warplanes in the region to 54.

Mrs Thatcher turned up the heat on Saddam as tension in the Gulf was increased by the Iraqis. Their invasion troops yesterday burst into French, Canadian and Belgian diplomatic residences in Kuwait. They seized four people and were still holding three last night.

The brigade's transfer from its base at Soltau, north of Hanover in West Germany, is expected to begin within the next fortnight and will take almost until mid-November to complete. The force will sail on ten roll-on, roll-off ferries. The first to be hired is the Stena Searider, owned by a friend of Mrs Thatcher, Swedish shipping magnate Dan Stan Olsen.

The brigade, a self-contained unit packing tremendous firepower, is heir to a proud tradition. The Desert Rat nickname, retained in its modern emblem, eventually became synonymous with the entire Eighth Army, which, under Field Marshal Montgomery's leadership, recaptured North Africa from Germany's Desert Fox, Erwin Rommel.

The air offensive

The most powerful and successful air assault in the history of modern warfare began on January 17, 1991. After disabling the Iraqi early-warning systems by introducing a virus into the computer systems, Allied forces began a devastating campaign from both land and sea, targeting Iraq and the Iraqi forces still in Kuwait. The bombs and missiles were aimed to destroy Iraq's command and control centres in order to hinder their ability to make war effectively, while at the same time damaging civilian infrastructure to destroy the population's morale. Saddam Hussein immediately ordered the launch of his SCUD missiles in retaliation, targeting both Saudi Arabia and Israel. Although Israel was not directly involved in the attack on Iraq, Saddam hoped that they would be provoked into striking back, igniting the ongoing hostility between Israel and the Arab world and causing the Arab nations to split away from the Allied coalition. Although Israel did indeed want to retaliate, President George Bush pledged to protect Israel from the SCUDs if they held back. As a result, US missile batteries were deployed in Israel to shoot down SCUDs. The SCUD launches successfully diverted Allied air power, since planes were tied up hunting for the mobile SCUD missile launchers rather than continuing to attack. Despite this, the air strikes and cruise missile attacks against Iraq were truly devastating and successfully cleared the way for the ground attack that was to follow.

Baghdad on the morning of January 18, 1991. The skies erupt with anti-aircraft fire as US warplanes strike targets in the Iraqi capital.

DAILY MAIL JANUARY 17, 1991

Blitz on Baghdad

American and British warplanes blasted the centre of Baghdad early today. Other raids were launched on military targets throughout Iraq in 'Operation Desert Storm'. US Defence Secretary Dick Cheney confirmed that chemical and nuclear plants had been attacked. Iraqi ground fire was largely ineffective, and all the allied planes were said to have returned safely to their bases.

At least five waves of bombers swept in to blitz Baghdad. Saudi Arabian and French planes also took part. The attack, 16 hours after the expiry of the UN deadline for Saddam Hussein to withdraw from Kuwait, took the Iraqi capital by surprise, and the city was still brightly lit as bombs exploded. In Israel a radio ham intercepted messages from the British military network saying the raids had gone 'exceptionally well'.

President George Bush said in a broadcast to America: 'Tonight battle has been joined ... the world could wait no longer.'

Attack on Saudi Arabia

On January 29, Iraq attacked and occupied the Saudi city of Khafji, which had only been lightly defended. However, within a couple of days the Iraqi troops were driven out of the city again by Saudi and Qatari forces, supported by US Marine Corps and with back-up air strikes. Khafji had become an important strategic position immediately after the Iraqi invasion of Kuwait, since it was ideal as a base for the Iraqis to move into the eastern part of Saudi Arabia and take control of the major oil fields there. It would also have provided an excellent defensive position from which to fight Allied troops, so Iraq's failure to commit armoured divisions to hold onto the city is seen as a grave strategic error.

OPPOSITE LEFT: Colin Powell, chairman of the Joint Chiefs of Staff, gives a detailed score card of Allied progress one week into the operation. He announced that after 12,000 sorties, coalition forces had gained air superiority.

OPPOSITE BELOW LEFT: A Stealth F117A bomber closes in on a Baghdad communications building.

DAILY MAIL   JANUARY 22, 1991
What has he done to them?

A shocked world yesterday saw the brutal treatment of captured British and US fliers by Saddam Hussein's regime. Two RAF men paraded on TV by Iraq bore the signs of vicious abuse - by drugs, torture or brainwashing. And the latest threat to Tornado pilot John Peters and his navigator Adrian Nichol is that they will be among more than 20 prisoners used as human shields against air raids.

The Iraqi dictator's cruelty made a mockery of his country's signing of the Geneva Convention on treating PoWs - but he could face fierce retribution. Prime Minister John Major told the Commons yesterday that those responsible for outrages would be brought to account. This could mean Saddam facing a war crimes trial.

President Bush, questioned about the parading of US prisoners, said: 'America is angry, the rest of the world is angry.' Asked whether Saddam would be held accountable, he replied: 'You can count on it.'

ABOVE: **Flight Lieutenant John Peters and his navigator, Flight Lieutenant Adrian John Nichol (below).**

DAILY MAIL   JANUARY 18, 1991
Israel hit by missiles

The world's worst nightmare began to unfold early today when Saddam Hussein fulfilled his terrifying promise and sent missiles thundering into Israel. They hit the suburbs of Haifa and Tel Aviv and within minutes Israeli jets were being scrambled for a retaliatory strike across Jordan and into Iraq. Allied jets were also in the air seeking out the Scud launchers.

The Pentagon said that Iraq launched 10 missiles at Israel. Of the eight which landed, two hit Tel Aviv, one near a major hospital. Another fell in the Haifa area, three in unpopulated areas and one was unaccounted for. The Pentagon said it believed they were not carrying chemical warheads.

The Allies believed earlier that their devastating air strikes had taken out all of Saddam Hussein's Scuds in their silos.

OPPOSITE BELOW RIGHT: **Iraqis search among the rubble of homes in the Suq Ag Ghaddim District of Central Baghdad on March 12, 1991. These are among the 14 private homes destroyed during the air offensive.**

ABOVE: **The aftermath of an Iraqi missile SCUD attack on Tel Aviv.**

RIGHT: **Tornado pilot Flight Lieutenant John Peters and his navigator, Flight Lieutenant Adrian John Nichol are paraded on Iraqi television after being shot down during a bombing raid over Iraq. Both showed signs of having been tortured.**

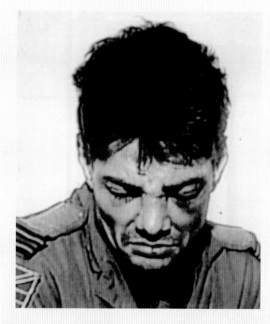

The ground offensive

When the Allied armies launched the ground war on February 23, the Iraqi occupation forces in Kuwait were in disarray and thousands of soldiers simply gave themselves up. The Allied coalition had managed to convince the Iraqi command that they would attack along the Saudi-Kuwait border and by amphibious assault. However, two entire corps of US forces, supported by British and French divisions, had been swiftly moved to the west under cover, in one of the largest battlefield troop movements in history. More than 250,000 soldiers, spread across a hundred miles, moved deep into Iraqi territory from the Saudi border to deliver a fatal blow behind the Iraqi lines and cut off all avenues of retreat north and west of Kuwait. The Allies pushed through most of Iraq's defences with ease, and even where elite Iraqi forces stood and fought they were no match for superior Allied equipment and training.

DAILY MAIL FEBRUARY 27, 1991

Freedom

Kuwait city was back in the hands of its people last night, 209 days after being seized by Iraq. Elated residents poured onto the streets, weeping and shouting, after the invaders fled in their thousands leaving resistance leaders to take control. On the outskirts of the capital, a massive Arab army was poised to drive into the centre at dawn to raise the flag of liberation.

But despite a widespread Iraqi retreat across Kuwait, the war was still raging. Just ten miles south of the city, a fierce tank battle was being fought for control of its airport. The Allies said they expected to gain control by dawn.

And on the Iraq border, the Desert Rats were involved in a massive Allied troop movement to surround the Republican Guard after President Bush and Prime Minister John Major both demanded total Iraqi surrender as the price of a ceasefire.

A Republican Guard division of up to 12,000 troops was said to have been defeated in darkness and pouring rain by the US VII Corps late last night. A second division was being engaged but the elite units were offering 'stiff resistance', a senior military officer said. Fifty of the Guard's best T-72 tanks were captured as they fled northward.

DAILY MAIL   FEBRUARY 6, 1991

My nightmare, by Stormin' Norman

The tough, uncompromising commander of 550,000 Allied troops in the Gulf yesterday revealed the private emotional toll of war. 'Every waking and sleeping moment my nightmare is the fact that I will give an order that will cause countless numbers of human beings to lose their lives,' said General Norman Schwarzkopf. 'I don't want my troops to die. I don't want my troops to be maimed. It's an intensely emotional thing for me.'

The 56-year-old, four-star general said he didn't think he was getting enough rest. 'I wake up 15, 20, 25 times in a night and my brain is just in a turmoil over some of the agonizingly difficult decisions that I have to make...it's awful lonely at the top.'

Stormin' Norman said he had no specific timetable for the war and the final decision for a ground attack would be based on a compendium of results and 'gut feel.'

Liberation of Kuwait

On February 26 Iraqi troops began retreating from Kuwait, setting fire to Kuwaiti oil fields as they left. Retreating Iraqi troops streamed along the main Iraq-Kuwait highway, which was bombed extensively by the Allies and came to be known as the 'Highway of Death'. Allied forces pursued retreating Iraqis over the border into Iraq, and to within 150 miles of Baghdad before withdrawing. The Allied coalition, along with Kuwaiti resistance forces, now controlled Kuwait City. After the ceasefire on February 27, surviving Iraqi troops were allowed to escape back into southern Iraq and the Emir of Kuwait was quickly restored to power. On March 3, 1991, Iraq accepted the terms of the cease-fire and the fighting ended. However, Saddam Hussein still remained in power in Iraq – although many hoped that he would soon be brought down by an internal rebellion.

OPPOSITE: As the Iraqi troops withdrew they implemented a scorched earth policy, setting alight to Kuwait's oil wells. The blazes took months to put out and adversely affected both the economy and environment. Eleven years later, on December 7, 2002, Saddam Hussein apologized to the Kuwaiti people for his invasion, saying he was not speaking from weakness but a desire to set the record straight.

OPPOSITE ABOVE LEFT: A devastated convoy of vehicles on the road to Basra, March 1, 1991.

OPPOSITE ABOVE RIGHT: British Prime Minister John Major poses with the Desert Rats of the 7th Armoured Brigade in Kuwait.

FAR LEFT: General Norman Schwarzkopf is met at Heathrow airport by British army commander General Sir Peter de la Billiere in July 1991. Throughout the conflict the two generals met daily to make sure the Allies worked in harmony.

LEFT: Saddam Hussein fires his gun into the air in celebration of George Bush's election defeat, during a visit to the city of Ramadi. A defiant Hussein warned other enemies to learn from Bush's mistake.

BELOW: A column of Iraqi prisoners of war, captured by Task Force Ripper of the U.S. First Marine Division marches to a processing area in Kuwait on February 26, 1991.

Algerian Civil War 1991-1999

Economic crisis

By the late 1980s, Algeria's economy was almost totally reliant upon its oil exports. A collapse in the price of oil in 1986 sparked a serious economic crisis and led to major rioting by urban youths who were feeling the pinch as unemployment rose sharply. The riots, combined with a global trend towards democratization at the end of the Cold War, convinced the ruling National Liberation Front (FLN) to relinquish its thirty-year-old grip on power and allow democratic elections in Algeria.

With Algeria's leftwing weakened by decades of incumbency, the poor turned towards Islamists to help navigate a way out of the crisis. As a result, the main Islamist party the Islamic Salvation Front (FIS) won a decisive victory in the first round of legislative elections in 1991. However, fearing that the FIS would install Sharia Law and make Algeria an Islamic state, the army staged a coup before the second round of voting could occur. The FIS was banned and its members fled into exile or were sent to internment camps deep in the Sahara desert.

Civil War

The suppression of the elections led many supporters of the FIS to seek non-democratic paths to power. Militant Islamist groups had already been operating in Algeria on a small scale during the 1980s, but their support base swelled in the aftermath of the coup and Algeria plunged deep into a bloody civil war.

The young urban poor supported an Islamist movement called the Armed Islamic Group (GIA), which was a splinter of an Islamist faction founded in the early 1980s. They were assisted by veterans of the war in Afghanistan, who moved to Algeria to continue their jihad following the Soviet Union's withdrawal. GIA's campaign against the government was marked by exceptional violence as Algerian civilians were attacked indiscriminately in order to demonstrate that the military regime could not protect their citizens. GIA also conducted a series of terrorist attacks in France, including the hijacking of an Air France plane in December 1994 and a series of attacks on the Paris Metro in the autumn of 1995.

Infighting

Some of the worst bloodshed occurred as a result of infighting within the Islamist movement. The Algerian army had a great deal of success at decapitating GIA, which caused a rapid turnover in its leadership. This resulted in bloody power disputes as the various factions of radical Islam fought over the future direction of the movement. In addition, violent clashes often broke out between GIA and the more moderate Islamic Salvation Army (AIS). The AIS was created by members of the FIS who abhorred the violence of GIA, but believed armed resistance was necessary to ensure the party maintained a role in Algerian political life.

End of the Civil War

The leadership of GIA became ever more extreme and some of the worst atrocities of the war occurred in 1997 and 1998. As a result, militants began abandoning the movement in droves, especially after the new president, Abdelaziz Bouteflika, introduced a new law giving amnesty to the majority of guerrilla fighters. Those who did not surrender their campaign broke away from GIA to distance themselves from the atrocities. They formed the Salafist Group for Preaching and Combat (GSPC), which soon began targeting civilians once again. The GSPC, which has strong links with Al Qaeda, has been unable to find much support among the war-weary Algerian population and its operation has largely been confined to the desert.

OPPOSITE TOP: **The scene in the Ben Aknoun area of Algiers in the aftermath of a bus bombing on January 20, 1998. One person was killed and scores injured in the attack, which was designed to coincide with a visit by an EU delegation investigating the upsurge in the massacres.**

OPPOSITE MIDDLE: **A soldier stands in a tank in Oued Allel, 12 miles south of Algiers, as the army begins a major offensive on a stronghold of the Armed Islamic Group (GIA), October 4, 1997.**

OPPOSITE BOTTOM: **A soldier takes shelter behind a tank in Oued Allel. The army's offensive came in the wake of some of the worst massacres of the entire war. In August 1997 GIA slaughtered the population of the small village of Rais, and one month later the villagers of Bentalha met a similar fate.**

BELOW: **Algerians search through debris in the village of Sehanine, located in the Ouarsenis mountains near Relizane. The village was devastated and its inhabitants decimated during an attack by presumed Islamic militants on the first day of the Muslim holy month of Ramadan, December 1997.**

LEFT: **Citizens of Daira de Ramika on the outskirts of Relizane organize themselves for self-defence. Daira de Ramika and three neighbouring villages were attacked in January 1998, just days after the massacre in nearby Sehanine.**

TOP: **Berbers protesting in the Kabyle region of Algeria, May 2001. As the Civil War petered out, the Algerian government had to turn its attention toward its Berber population which was aggrieved about its economic and cultural marginalization. The violent street protests broke out after a teenage boy was shot to death while in police custody.**

ABOVE: **A fresh round of protests in Kabyle in December 2001.**

Sierra Leone Civil War 1991-2002

Child soldiers

A civil war broke out in Sierra Leone in 1991 when a rebel group named the Revolutionary United Front (RUF) began attacking settlements in the east of the country. The rebels were opposed to the government's corruption and an unequal distribution of the nation's wealth, especially the funds derived from diamond sales. The war became infamous for the use of child soldiers by the rebels. After being kidnapped from their families or being orphaned in the fighting, these children were turned into killing machines by the rebels, often with the aid of drugs. The pro-government militias, the Kamayors, are also thought to have employed child soldiers.

TOP: **An armed man patrols the streets of Freetown, Sierra Leone, during the country's decade-long civil war.**

ABOVE RIGHT: **Civilian workers pan for diamonds under the watchful eye of the Kamayor.**

MIDDLE RIGHT: **People mutilated by rebels wait for hospital treatment in Freetown. The rebels were infamous for mutilating civilians during the war. By injuring and not killing the civilian population, the rebels were able to increase the burden on the government's resources.**

BELOW RIGHT: **Pro-government Kamayor militias patrol near a diamond mine in the village of Hanga. Some of the most severe fighting occurred when government and the rebel forces fought for control of the country's lucrative diamond mines.**

LEFT: **Child soldiers man a checkpoint sixty miles outside the capital, Freetown.**

Nigerian intervention

Amid the civil war, Sierra Leone held elections in 1996, which were won by Ahmad Kabbah. However, Kabbah was ousted in a coup in 1997 by a group of army officers who called themselves the Armed Forces Revolutionary Council and allied themselves with the RUF. Kabbah was reinstated following the intervention of a Nigerian-led force from the armed monitoring group of the Economic Community of West African States (ECOMOG). The two sides were brought to the negotiating table at Lome in Togo in 1999 and a UN force was sent in to oversee the implementation of the peace. However, the rebels, supported by Liberia, continued to fight and were poised to take the capital, Freetown, in 2000.

TOP RIGHT: **American Marines arrive in Sierra Leone to evacuate Americans from the country in the aftermath of the coup.**

TOP LEFT: **Soldiers aligned with the Armed Forces Revolutionary Council show off the weapons they discovered in Freetown during the coup.**

LEFT: **Nigerian soldiers inspect weapons confiscated from the rebels during the ECOMOG mission to reinstate President Kabbah.**

ABOVE: **A member of the RUF is attacked by a mob of government-loyalists in Freetown.**

BELOW FAR LEFT: **British troops from 42 Commando Royal Marines patrol through the jungle of Sierra Leone, May 2000.**

BELOW LEFT: **British experts train new recruits for Sierra Leone's army at a training camp in Benguema.**

British Intervention

The UN mission was too small to stop the rebel advance, so the British government under Tony Blair sent more than 1,000 men to stop the fighting and protect foreign nationals. The presence of British troops provided much-needed stability and security in the country and the civil war ended quickly. Elections were held in 2002, which President Kabbah won comfortably, and British forces withdrew later in the year. The United Nations has remained in the country, but peace and democracy remain fragile, especially while Sierra Leone remains one of the world's poorest countries, despite its diamond wealth.

Yugoslavia 1991-1995

Tito's Yugoslavia

At the end of the Second World War, the Socialist Federal Republic of Yugoslavia was formed, with Josip Broz Tito as the head of state. This diverse country was made up of eight republics and major provinces, including Croatia, Slovenia and Boznia-Herzegovina – and Serbia, the largest and the seat of the Federal Republic's capital of Belgrade. The republics had varied ethnic backgrounds, but held together under Communist rule. Following Tito's death in 1980, and during a longstanding economic crisis, ethnic tensions – which had always simmered in the background – began to grow.

Breakup of the Federation

In the Serbian province of Kosovo, which was ethnically Albanian, resentment at Serb domination was expressed in a series of strikes and demonstrations which were suppressed by force. Some other republics supported the Kosovans, and called for more independent representation as well, and the January 1990 Communist Party Congress broke up when Slovenian and Croatian delegations walked out in protest following a speech by the Serbian leader Slobodan Milosevic which only served to emphasise Serbian dominance. There was consternation in Belgrade and a call for martial law to be imposed on the 'rebel' provinces by the People's Army. This action would need to be approved by a majority of the republics, and a vote was accordingly taken. The result was inconclusive; Slovenia, Croatia, Bosnia and Macedonia voted against; Serbia and its dependents – Kosovo, Vojvodina and Montenegro – voted for action. There were few options for Slovenia and Croatia under the existing system.

ABOVE: **Croatian forces pass through a village on the way to the front line.**

RIGHT: **Josip Broz Tito led Yugoslavia's resistance against Nazi occupation and went on to rule the country after the war. After his death in 1980 the Yugoslav federation began to unravel.**

FAR RIGHT ABOVE: **A Slovenian soldier fires on a Federal Army tank from his hiding place in the woods near the Slovenian town of Dravograd.**

FAR RIGHT: **Residents of Slovenia's capital Ljubljana fly their national flag in defiance of the invading Federal Army. Much of the city's population remained indoors for safety.**

Slovenia

Elections were held, and pro-independence leaders were elected in a landslide victory; Slovenia declared formal independence on June 25, 1991. Yugoslavia – the Serbs, essentially – then declared war. However, and in contrast to what was to follow, this was something of an anti-climax: after ten days the Serbs withdrew to focus their attentions on Croatia, which had a sizeable Serb population and was geographically closer to Serbia.

Croatia

Croatia declared its independence at the same time as Slovenia, but it was not in the same position. It was ethnically more diverse, with some ethnically Serbian inhabitants – about 12 per cent – whom Milosevic felt should not be forced to live outside the Serbian state. The attack began with the Serbians shelling Croatian cities but this only strengthened the Croatian spirit of resistance, especially after the fall of the city of Vukovar which had resisted a three-month siege. Vukovar was almost totally destroyed and many people died; survivors were sent to camps by the Serbs. The mixed ethnic composition of Croatia led to what has been called 'ethnic cleansing', which took place on both sides, as each attempted to move – and sometimes kill – those whom it perceived as inappropriate residents of a particular area.

UN Peacekeepers

The worsening situation was of increasing international concern, and the United Nations intervened, sending in a multinational, 14,000-strong, protection force of peacekeepers. Their aims were to bring about a ceasefire and ensure the Serbs retreated, and maintain peace thereafter. The two strongly Serbian provinces of Croatia then declared their own independence, which helped delay the signing of a peace treaty until Croatia snatched them back in 1995. An international arms embargo was imposed, but had little effect on the Serbs. Yugoslavia had previously had a thriving arms industry which they were able to exploit; the same was not true of their opponents, particularly the Bosnian Muslims who were soon to suffer from Serbian attention.

TOP: An ethnic-Serb guerrilla from the Croatian town of Vukovar prepares to launch an anti-armour rocket at Croatian Army postions following the country's declaration of independence from Yugoslavia.

ABOVE: Vocin's fourteenth-century Roman Catholic church lies in ruins in the aftermath of a massacre in the village in December 1991. Serb militias rounded up and murdered almost forty Croat inhabitants as part of their campaign of ethnic cleansing in the Slavonian region of Western Croatia.

LEFT: A member of the United Nations Peace Keeping force assesses an abandoned Croatian village. The 14,000-strong force began arriving in early 1992 to broker a ceasefire, oversee the Serbian retreat and uphold the peace.

BELOW: Two inhabitants of Vukovar are evacuated from their ruined homes as the siege of the city comes to an end. Croat residents and soldiers held out for three months before the city fell to the Federal Army.

Bosnia

Bosnia's path to independence – originally declared in April 1992 – was similarly stormy, and its ethnic background was even less straightforward. There were three main groups, Serbs, Croats and Bosnian Muslims (Bosniaks). The Serbs, who comprised about a third of the people, violently objected to independence and were able to occupy most of the country. Then the Croats, about 17 per cent of the population, occupied almost all of what remained, and the Muslim population – who were in the majority, at 44 per cent – were left with very little. The Bosnian Serbs began to 'ethnically cleanse' their territory of Muslims, with open support from Serbia itself, in an attempt to create an ethnically homogenous area which could be incorporated into Serbia. As a result, there was a widespread movement of people, and many deaths and reports of atrocities on both the large and small scale.

Siege of Sarajevo

The cities of Sarajevo and Mostar were besieged and bombarded by the Serbs, with heavy loss of life; Sarajevo, the Bosnian capital, was under siege for almost four years during which time it came under heavy shell and sniper fire. At first there was anti-Serbian unity between the Croats and the Bosnian Muslims, but they eventually fought each other over territory; peace between them was brokered after about a year, but worse was to come. The UN forces in Croatia were asked to cover Bosnia as well and established safe zones which, it was hoped, would provide some protection. One of these was the town of Srebrenica and the area immediately around it, which has since become notorious.

FAR RIGHT: UN peacekeepers come to the aid of a Bosnian man injured during a heavy artillery bombardment on a village near Vitez. The man later died of his injuries.

ABOVE: A UN helicopter patrol monitors the frontline near Sarajevo Airport after reports that UN planes were coming under sniper fire.

BELOW: Bosnian Serb soldiers cover their ears as they fire a missile at Bosnian Muslim positions on the outskirts of Bihac.

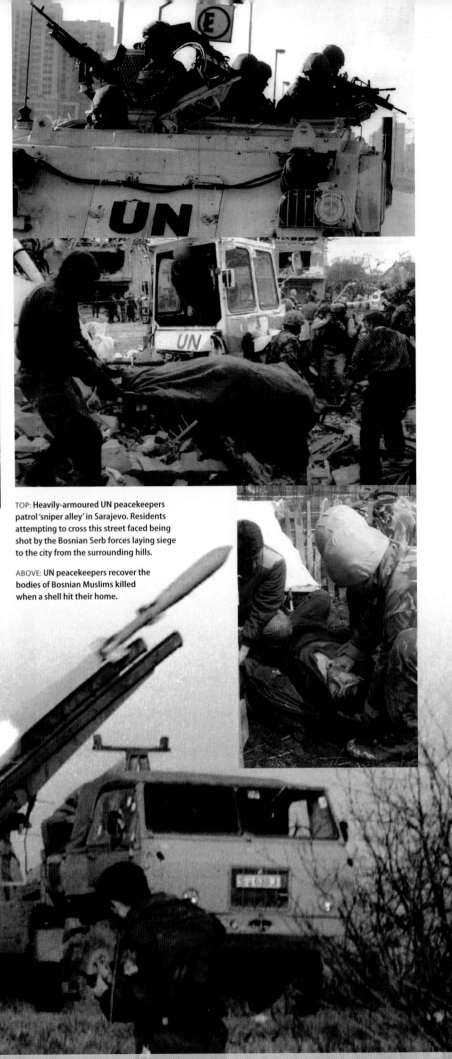

TOP: Heavily-armoured UN peacekeepers patrol 'sniper alley' in Sarajevo. Residents attempting to cross this street faced being shot by the Bosnian Serb forces laying siege to the city from the surrounding hills.

ABOVE: UN peacekeepers recover the bodies of Bosnian Muslims killed when a shell hit their home.

DAILY MAIL AUGUST 29 1995

Slaughter At The Market

They were not soldiers. They were women, children, old people, trying to buy some pitiful provisions to survive in the hell of Sarajevo. Yesterday they were the targets again for the Serb gunners who have the besieged city at their mercy.

Nearly 40 died when two mortar bombs blasted the Markale market place, 50 yards from the scene of a similar outrage last year. Even though gatherings had been banned since then, because of the danger, the area was teeming with people yesterday. They had to buy food or starve.

That was when the Serbs in the hills around Sarajevo decided the time was right to loose another round of carnage on the helpless civilians below.

The scenes that followed were unspeakable. Screaming women and children wandered dazed among bodies. 'Killers, bastards!' screamed a woman covered in blood. 'They all deserve to be slaughtered.'

Scores of wounded were taken to hospitals already overwhelmed with victims of the war. At Kosevo, the main hospital, many people with shrapnel wounds were forced to wait outside. Inside, the more seriously wounded were crowded in the halls and patients' rooms.

The Moslem-led government and the separatist Serbs, who have been laying siege to the Bosnian capital since April 1992, were quick to condemn each other.

Bosnian Serbs accused the government of staging the massacre to put pressure on them as the peace mission by Assistant Secretary of State Richard Holbrooke got under way. The attack, said Bosnian Serb army commander General Ratko Mladic, was 'constructed to stop the peace process and trigger Nato strikes'.

But UN spokesman Alexander Ivanko noted that the mortar was fired from the south of the city where 'most of the positions are Bosnian Serb'.

Srebrenica massacre

In July 1995 Ratko Mladic, one of the main Serbian commanders, led his troops into the zone. It was overflowing with Muslim refugees, and though there were also some 400 UN peacekeepers from the Netherlands, they were able to do little to resist Mladic's forces or prevent what happened. The men and boys were separated and in the following few days – the precise dates are difficult to establish – more than 8,000 Bosnian Muslims were massacred. This was the worst mass-murder in Europe since the Second World War and it was perpetrated under the eyes of the United Nations.

NATO Airstrikes

There was an eventual outcry when the full facts became known, and international opinion – which had already been shifting steadily in that direction – swung round even more firmly against the Serbs, bolstered by the increasingly appalling situation in Sarajevo. When Bosnian Serb forces shelled a busy Sarajevo market on August 28, 1995, NATO decided to use military force for the first time in the organization's history. Operation Deliberate Force began on August 30 with attacks on Serbian munitions dumps. It was quickly obvious that the Serbs actually had few options left despite their much-vaunted military might. A ceasefire was negotiated, becoming the basis for the Dayton Peace Agreement which was reached in November 1995 and signed the following month in Paris. This established a semi-divided Bosnia, one which had a Serb Republic and a separate Croat–Bosnian Muslim Federation.

LEFT: **President Bill Clinton had long called upon the international community to do more to assist the Bosnian Muslims, but other countries were worried that sending in more weapons and conducting airstrikes would jeopardize the safety of UN peacekeepers. In the event, several hundred peacekeepers were used as human shields by the Bosnian Serbs during Operation Deliberate Force.**

BELOW: **The aftermath of a NATO strike on an arms dump in the Bosnian Serb stronghold of Pale, August 31, 1995.**

BELOW LEFT: **Bosnian Serb paramilitaries come under fire from Croat forces amid NATO airstrikes in September 1995.**

Rwandan Genocide 1994

Belgian colonial rule

On April 6, 1994, a plane carrying the Presidents of Rwanda and Burundi was shot down as it arrived in Kigali. Although Hutu extremists were probably responsible, they blamed the attack on the Tutsi minority and launched a brutal retaliation.

The origins of the Rwandan genocide lie in the nature of Belgian colonial rule. Belgium used the minority Tutsi to help them govern the colony and used identity cards to establish a clear distinction between who was a Hutu and who was a Tutsi. This system allowed little room for social mobility, which caused Hutus to grow jealous of the economically and politically dominant Tutsi.

When Belgium hastily decolonized in the late 1950s, the majority Hutu took power and set about stripping the Tutsi of the positions they had been given in the colonial government. Over the following decades, the Hutu subjected the Tutsi to a number of attacks, forcing many of them to flee into exile in neighbouring Uganda.

The Civil War

During their time in Uganda, the displaced Tutsi matured into a fighting force called the Rwandan Patriotic Front (RPF). In 1990, with the assistance of the Ugandan government, the RPF invaded Rwanda in a bid to regain a stake in their homeland. War dragged on until 1993 when the Rwandan President, a Hutu named Juvenal Habyarimana, agreed to sign the Arusha Accords, which granted the RPF representation in the Rwandan government.

Fearing that any form of power-sharing agreement with the RPF would undermine their power and patronage, Hutu extremists in Habyarimana's government began planning to expunge the Tutsi from Rwanda once and for all.

The genocide

In preparation for the genocide, these extremists stepped up their propaganda campaign against the Tutsi and began arming their militia groups, the Interahamwe and the Impuzamugambi. After President Habyarimana's plane was shot down, the attacks began in earnest. Roadblocks were set up in the capital, Kigali, and the militias went hunting for Tutsi with machetes, clubs and guns. The genocide was spread quickly across the north and east of the country, in the provinces of Gisenyi and Ruhengeri, which were the heartlands of Hutu extremism. South-Western Rwanda initially resisted the genocide until militias were shipped in from the north.

Massacres

Many Tutsis sought refuge in churches or schools, but this often increased their vulnerability and some of the worst atrocities of the genocide occurred in these supposed havens. One such massacre took place in a church in Nyarubuye in eastern Rwanda in April 1994. The thousands of Tutsis who had taken refuge in the church proved easy prey for the Hutu militias and their accomplices. The attacks were thorough and those who survived did so only by hiding under the dead bodies of others. Similar brutal stories unfolded across Rwanda during the genocide. The victims were often lured to communal buildings by people in positions of trust, such as mayors and clergymen, so as to make the killing-machine quicker and more efficient.

Liberating other Tutsi from the genocide gave extra impetus to the invading RPF. As the RPF moved in, thousands of Hutus fled into neighbouring Zaire, being told by the extremists' propaganda machine to expect a retaliatory genocide at the hands of the Tutsi invasion force. In reality, the RPF did not engage in genocide and demonstrated relative restraint as it took over the country. By the time the RPF took control and stopped the genocide, up to one million Tutsis and moderate Hutus had been murdered. In addition, millions of Hutus had fled to neighbouring countries where they were run down by diseases, which added more names to the long list of victims of Hutu extremism.

LEFT: **British soldiers arrive in Zaire to help facilitate the return of the first Hutu refugees to Rwanda in November 1996.**

MIDDLE LEFT: **French-trained recruits of the Rwandan National Army pause in a banana forest close to the front lines in June 1994.**

BELOW LEFT: **Bodies of cholera victims are left piled in the street. A cholera epidemic ravaged through refugee camps killing thousands of refugees who fled to Zaire in the aftermath of the genocide.**

OPPOSITE TOP: **The bodies of Tutsi genocide victims lie outside a church in Rukura where more than 4,000 people were killed while taking refuge. Mass murders in churches and schools became a recurring feature of the genocide.**

OPPOSITE ABOVE RIGHT: **Members of the RPF pose with a French-built armoured car, which had been captured from the Rwandan Army at Kagitumba, in northeastern Rwanda in April 1994.**

OPPOSITE MIDDLE LEFT: **RPF soldiers push into the Rwandan bush on April 9, just days after the plane crash killing President Habyarimana.**

OPPOSITE MIDDLE RIGHT: **A Rwandan Government soldier holds his position against the RPF advance at Rwankuba, southwest of Kigali.**

OPPOSITE BOTTOM LEFT: **RPF soldiers fire on Rwandan Government positions near Mukaranye, north of Kigali.**

ABOVE LEFT: **A young Rwandan genocide survivor with a bandaged wound on his face. Many Rwandans have been left with not only the physical scars of genocide, but also the emotional ones.**

ABOVE: **Rwandans bury their dead in the aftermath of the genocide.**

BELOW: **Hundreds of thousands of Hutu refugees pour over the Tanzanian border to escape the RPF invasion in May 1994.**

International response

At the outbreak of the genocide, the United Nations already had a mission in Rwanda to help implement the Arusha Accords. However, it did not have the appropriate authority to intervene in the genocide and the UN peacekeepers had to stand idly by while the mass killing went on around them. There was little appetite for strengthening the UN's mission in Rwanda, especially in the United States, where the recent loss of US servicemen in Somalia played heavily on President Clinton's decision-making. Following the murder of ten UN peacekeepers from Belgium, the UN opted to scaled down its operation and pull most of its peacekeepers out of the country.

The only country to intervene decisively in Rwanda was France. Backed by a UN mandate, French troops began arriving in late June as part of Operation Turquoise. French troops established a safe zone, which helped to save many lives, but which also gave haven to Hutu extremists from the invading RPF. The RPF believed that France showed deliberate bias towards the French-speaking Hutu because members of the RPF had become Anglophonic while in exile in Uganda. In August the French withdrew and the RPF moved in and occupied the remainder of the country.

Chechnya 1994-2000

The first war in Chechnya

In November 1991, amid the chaotic demise of the Soviet Union, Chechnya declared its independence. However, Moscow only tolerated the break-up of the Union into its fifteen constituent Republics, and was unwilling to accept the independence of Chechnya, which was an autonomous province within Russia. Troops were sent in, but they were repulsed by Dzhokhar Dudayev, an ex-Soviet general turned Chechen leader.

When Russia had somewhat recovered from the tumultuous years of the Soviet collapse, President Yeltsin turned his attentions towards the breakaway Republic. He feared that unless Chechnya was brought back under Moscow's control, it would set a precedent for other autonomous regions to break away, and would result in the collapse of the Russian state. Moreover, he feared that the predominantly Muslim Chechens would establish an Islamic state within Russia's borders and was concerned that the province had become a haven for organized crime.

After helping to ferment political unrest in Chechnya, Moscow launched an attack in December 1994 under the pretext of restoring order. The Russian military planned a lightning attack on the breakaway region, but they became mired in a quagmire that was to cost many lives. The Russian army was still reeling from the collapse of the Soviet Union and was not able to defeat the Chechen rebels who used effective forms of guerrilla warfare. To try to regain the initiative the Russian military carpet-bombed the capital, Grozny, killing thousands of civilians.

The war dragged on, but Russia was unable to score a decisive victory against the Chechen guerrillas. Support for the war among the Russian public was lacklustre and Yeltsin, facing a Presidential Election in 1996, began to seek exit strategies. A ceasefire was finally signed in August 1996 after Grozny had once again become a bloodbath. The war was over, but the underlying causes had not been addressed, and a return to hostilities was inevitable.

The second Chechen war

Tension in the region flared up again in 1999 against the backdrop of a power transfer from Yeltsin to Vladimir Putin. Russian troops were sent back to Chechnya following a spate of bombings in Moscow and elsewhere in Russia that killed hundreds and outraged Russian public opinion. Chechen militants had also begun operating in the neighbouring province of Dagestan, threatening to widen the conflict and further break-up the Soviet Union.

Again the Russians faced stiff resistance from Chechen rebels using guerrilla tactics. They reached the outskirts of Grozny within weeks of beginning the ground offensive in October 1999, but soon became bogged down in months of bitter urban warfare. Thousands of civilians were caught in the crossfire and Grozny was utterly destroyed before the Russians claimed victory in the city in February 2000. Some rebels escaped Grozny and moved further south where they continued to resist Russian forces for another month. The climax of the fighting in the south came in the village of Komsomolskoye, where hundreds of rebels were killed following a fierce battle in March 2000. Two months later, Moscow reimposed direct rule and the war was essentially over. However, Chechen rebels were not entirely beaten and they have still been able to mount a number of attacks on Russian civilian and military targets.

OPPOSITE ABOVE: **Chechen women carry their belongings through the ruins of Grozny in February 2000.**

OPPOSITE ABOVE RIGHT: **Russian President Boris Yeltsin meets with his American counterpart, Bill Clinton, at an OSCE Summit in Istanbul in November 1999. Russia's war in Chechnya topped the agenda of the summit.**

OPPOSITE MIDDLE RIGHT: **Rescue workers search through the rubble of an apartment building in Volgodonsk after it had been destroyed in a terrorist attack in September 1999. The attack was one of a series of atrocities blamed on Chechen separatists, serving as a reason to send Russian troops back into Chechnya.**

OPPOSITE BELOW RIGHT: **The Khankala military base near Grozny is pictured awash with Russian troop activity amid the second Chechen war in February 2000.**

ABOVE LEFT: **Russian soldiers wait at the Slepcovck crossing on the Ingushetian border to check for militants amid the Chechen refugees arriving from Grozny.**

ABOVE RIGHT: **A Russian multiple missile launcher fires on Grozny during an intense offensive in the closing days of 1999.**

TOP: **Russian President-elect Vladimir Putin meets with Defence Minister Igor Sergeyev at the Kremlin to get the latest military intelligence reports on the war in Chechnya.**

MIDDLE: **A column of Russian tanks moves into the foothills of mountains in southern Chechnya where many Chechen rebels fled in the wake of the Russian onslaught.**

ABOVE LEFT: **Workmen remove debris that was once a hospital in Mozdok on Chechnya's border with North Ossetia, August 2003. Scores of people were killed when a Chechen suicide bomber rammed a truck packed with explosives into the building.**

BELOW: **Russian soldiers walk through Komsomolskoye, which was destroyed in heavy fighting in March 2000.**

ABOVE RIGHT: **Russian special forces end a school siege in Beslan in September 2004. Chechen separatists entered the school on the first day of the new academic year and took hundreds of children and a number of parents hostage. Special forces stormed the building after two days, but more than 300 people, mostly children, were killed.**

Democratic Republic of the Congo 1996–2008

The First Congo War

In the 1990s, while democratization was spreading across Africa, the powerful ruler of the vast country in the continent's midsection was reluctant to follow the tide. Mobutu Sese Seko had ruled Zaire as a personal fiefdom for three decades, exploiting his country for as much as it could give.

During his three decades of misrule, Mobutu developed many enemies, but they were too weak to mount a serious challenge. However, the opportunity for change finally presented itself when genocide spilled over the border from neighbouring Rwanda in 1994. Mobutu had supported the genocide and provided a safe haven for the Hutu extremists who had perpetrated it. The post-genocide, Tutsi-dominated government in Rwanda was looking for revenge and allied with one of the main Zairian opposition groups, the Alliance of Democratic Forces for the Liberation of Congo-Zaire (AFDL), under the command of Laurent Kabila. The AFDL also found support among neighbouring countries such as Uganda and Angola which had interests in Zaire's great mineral wealth.

With outside support, Kabila's AFDL was able to march rapidly and seize the capital, Kinshasa. Mobutu was dying of cancer and did not put up much of a fight. Kabila proclaimed himself President and began limited reforms of the country – starting with a reversion to the country's original post-colonial name: the Democratic Republic of the Congo.

ABOVE: Bands of militias rove across the country engaging in extreme acts of violence. Rape was often used as a weapon during the war; tens of thousands of women and children suffered horrific abuse.

ABOVE RIGHT: Hundreds of displaced Congolese line-up to receive food aid donated by USAID in Bunia, Democratic Republic of Congo, July 2003.

Each family of five receives 15 kilograms of cornmeal, 5 kilograms of beans and 1.5 litres of cooking oil, for a week.

OPPOSITE ABOVE RIGHT: Congolese children stand behind razor wire next to a United Nations compound in Bunia after fleeing their villages in the Democratic Republic of Congo.

OPPOSITE BELOW: British troops, hovercraft and helicopter in the Congo River as they begin the evacuation of their nationals from Kinshasa as Kabila's men march on the city during the First Congo War. While regional powers played a central role in the conflict, the wider international community has been criticized for turning its back on the country.

The Second Congo War

In 1998 a new civil war broke out after Rwanda turned against Kabila because he had failed to tackle the Hutu extremists and had instead grown hostile to the Tutsi minority. The Rwandan government backed a new rebel coalition in the eastern part of the country, which almost ousted Kabila, but Zimbabwe and Angola came to his aid at the last minute.

A brutal war dragged on till 2001, when Laurent Kabila was assassinated. The Congolese Parliament unanimously agreed to replace him with his son, Joseph. Laurent had been resistant to democratization, but his western-educated son proved more open. He soon made peace with Rwanda, Uganda and the rebel coalition. In 2006 the nation held its first elections and much of the country has managed to avoid further conflict.

While Congo began its reconstruction, a violent rebellion continued in the east of the country. Tutsi rebels led by Laurent Nkunda rejected the peace process in order to continue the fight against Hutu extremists in the region. Nkunda was finally forced to the negotiating table in Goma in January 2008. Although an agreement was reached, East Congo is rich in resources and may yet experience further bloodshed as a result.

DAILY MAIL DECEMBER 9, 2004

Congo mired in 'deadliest crisis'

Over 1,000 Congolese civilians a day are dying, nearly all from disease and malnutrition, due to a festering conflict that has killed 3.8 million people, an aid agency has said today. Although the Democratic Republic of Congo's five-year war was declared over last year, the International Rescue Committee (IRC) said it was still the 'deadliest crisis' in the world, but the international community was doing too little to stop it. 'In a matter of six years, the world lost a population equivalent to the entire country of Ireland or the city of Los Angeles,' said Dr Richard Brennan, one of the authors of a study by the private New York-based refugee relief agency. 'How many innocent Congolese have to perish before the world starts paying attention?'

The mortality study updates a previous widely agreed death toll of three million people from the war which sucked in six neighbouring countries. Based on a survey of 19,500 households, it found almost half of those who died were children under five and 98 per cent of people were killed by disease and malnutrition resulting from a healthcare system destroyed by the years of war.

Peace deals were signed in 2002 and a transitional government set up last year, charged with leading the vast central African nation to elections in 2005, but huge tracts of the east remain unstable. Highlighting the discrepancy between the $3.5 billion aid budget for Iraq in 2003 and the $188 million earmarked for Congo in 2004, the IRC labelled the international community's response to Congo's crisis 'grossly inadequate in proportion to need'.

Kosovo 1996–99

Balkan tensions

After the Second World War, the Kingdom of Yugoslavia became a socialist federation consisting of six republics: Bosnia-Hercegovina, Croatia, Macedonia, Montenegro, Serbia and Slovenia. Kosovo was not a federal republic, but an autonomous province within Serbia. Located within southern Serbia, the majority of the population of Kosovo was ethnic Albanian, but there was a sizable Serb minority in the north. Initially the province had a high degree of autonomy, but in 1989, amidst growing ethnic tension, Serbian leader Slobodan Milosevic brought Kosovo under the direct control of Belgrade. Yugoslav troops and police were sent in to replace ethnic Albanian security forces and the official language was changed from Albanian to Serbian.

The outbreak of war

In 1996, after six years of Serbian oppression, many among Kosovo's Albanian population had come to feel that armed aggression to achieve independence for the province was the only answer. Four of the six republics had already broken away from the Serb-dominated Yugoslavia and Kosovo's Albanians wanted to follow suit. They established a resistance militia called the Kosovo Liberation Army (KLA), which carried out its first attacks against Serbian security forces in April 1996. The international community supported greater autonomy for Kosovo, but opposed the KLA's demand for independence. However, concern was soon being expressed over the Serbian military's disproportionate response to KLA attacks and Slobodan Milosevic found himself under increasing pressure to bring an end to the escalating violence in the province.

Massacre at Racak

One of the worst atrocities of the war occurred in the village of Racak on January 15, 1999. KLA attacks in the vicinity of the village had resulted in the deaths of four Serb policemen. The Serbs responded by shelling the village early in the morning of the 15th. Later in the day, Serbian soldiers entered the town, rounded up villagers, and marched them to the outskirts. Once there, the Serbs opened fire, killing 45 people in the manner of an execution. This massacre proved to be a turning point in the war as it was an important factor in convincing NATO of the need to intervene.

OPPOSITE ABOVE: **The divided town of Mitrovica. The river Ibar separates the ethnic Serbs in the north of the town from the ethnic Albanians in the south.**

OPPOSITE MIDDLE: **A Serb soldier lies dead after a KLA attack.**

OPPOSITE BELOW: **Serbian riot-police forces face down the ethnic Albanian protest over university access. They later used teargas to disperse the crowds.**

ABOVE: **Thousands of ethnic Albanians march through the streets of the Kosovan captial, Pristina, demanding free university access, October 1, 1997.**

BELOW LEFT: **Serbian youths wave Serbia's national flag chanting 'All English and Albanians are stupid'.**

ABOVE LEFT: **Kalashnikov in hand, a sixteen-year-old member of the KLA stands in front of a car riddled with his bullets that killed the Serb policemen inside. They were ambushed close to a field where more than 120 Kosovan civillians were killed.**

NATO intervention

As far back as June 1998, amid worldwide concern at what was happening in Kosovo, NATO had begun to consider possible military options to resolve the conflict. Air strikes were planned to support diplomatic efforts to make the Milosevic regime withdraw forces from Kosovo, cooperate in bringing an end to the violence and facilitate the return of refugees to their homes. However, at the last moment, President Milosevic agreed to comply and the air strikes were called off. The UN Security Council called for a cease-fire by both parties and limits were set on the number of Serbian forces allowed in Kosovo. Despite these steps the situation in Kosovo flared up again at the beginning of 1999, following a number of acts of provocation on both sides.

Renewed international efforts to find a peaceful solution to the conflict began, with peace talks in Paris. At the end of the second round of talks, the Kosovan Albanian delegation signed the proposed peace agreement, but the talks broke up without a signature from the Serbian delegation. Immediately afterwards, Serbian military and police forces stepped up operations against ethnic Albanians in Kosovo, moving extra troops and modern tanks into the region. Tens of thousands of people began to flee their homes and US Ambassador Richard Holbrooke flew to Belgrade in a final attempt to persuade President Milosevic to stop attacks on the Kosovan Albanians, or face imminent NATO air strikes. However, Milosevic refused to comply and on March 24 the air strikes began. The strikes focused primarily on military targets in Kosovo and Serbia, but extended to a wide range of other facilities, including bridges, oil refineries, power supplies and communications. Over the next 77 days, NATO flew more than 38,000 sorties involving 1,200 aircraft from bases in Italy and aircraft carriers in the Adriatic Sea. The mission was a success for NATO since none of its pilots was killed, and Serb forces only managed to shoot down two of its planes. However, the operation was not without its controversy; several hundred civilians perished in the air strikes, and on May 7, NATO accidentally struck the Chinese Embassy in Belgrade causing outrage across China. Nevertheless, after a relentless bombing campaign, on June 10, 1999, Milosevic finally gave in and ordered a full withdrawal of his forces from Kosovo.

BELOW LEFT: Kosovan refugees in Albania take to the river Drina to cool off in summer 1999. Hundreds of thousands of ethnic Albanians fled the country during the fighting.

LEFT: The British 5th Airborne Brigade moving out of Petrovac Camp in Macedonia as they head into Kosovo, June 1999.

BELOW LEFT: Two Puma helicopters landing at Pristina airport, Christmas 1999.

BOTTOM: British troops in an AS90 self-propelled gun of the 26th regiment of the Royal Artillery guard a church outside the town of Podujevo on Christmas Day, 1999.

OPPOSITE ABOVE: The US Airforce's B2 stealth bomber had its combat debut during 'Operation Allied Force'.

OPPOSITE MIDDLE: The remains of the neurology department at Dragisa Misovic Hospital in Belgrade. Three patients were killed in the attack.

OPPOSITE BELOW RIGHT: In June 1999, after Milosovic agreed to withdraw Serb forces from Kosovo, NATO's Kosovo Force, KFOR, was sent in to maintain peace and security. Here, British paratroopers cross the border from Macedonia into Kosovo.

OPPOSITE BELOW LEFT: Paratroopers secure the only road between Macedonia and Kosovo's capital, Pristina. These men discovered two mass graves in this village with almost 100 people in them.

OPPOSITE BELOW MIDDLE: Nepalese soldiers of the British Army's Gurkha brigade are airlifted from a bridge in Kosovo.

The aftermath

After the conflict ended, Kosovo was placed under United Nations administration and NATO peacekeepers, called the Kosovo Force (KFOR), were sent in to maintain security in the province. Negotiations over the future status of Kosovo began in 2006, but were doomed to failure because the interests of the West and Russia could not be reconciled. The West wanted 'supervised independence' for Kosovo, but Russia, which has historical ties to Serbia, refused to support independence of any kind. With UN negotiations stalled, Kosovo decided to unilaterally declare independence on February 18, 2008. It was immediately recognized by the West, but Russia has refused to follow suit.

Slobodan Milosevic lost a presidential election in 2000, and although he refused to accept the result he was forced out of office by strikes and massive street protests. He was later handed over to a UN war crimes tribunal in The Hague, and put on trial for crimes against humanity and genocide. He died of a heart attack in his cell in March 2006. The relationship between Serbia and the remaining Yugoslav republic, Montenegro, deteriorated as Montenegrin leaders distanced themselves from the conflict in Kosovo. Montenegro declared its independence from Serbia following a referendum in May 2006.

East Timor 1999

Indonesian invasion

Between the sixteenth and twentieth centuries, the South East Asian island of Timor was split between Portugal, who ruled the east, and the Netherlands, who controlled the west. The Dutch withdrew in the late 1940s and West Timor became a part of Indonesia, but the Portuguese remained for three more decades. The new government that came to power in Portugal following a 1974 revolution quickly instigated the process of decolonization and East Timor unilaterally declared its independence in November 1975. However, within days of the declaration, Indonesian forces invaded and turned East Timor into an Indonesian province.

Independence referendum

In 1998, the Indonesian President, Suharto, was ousted after three decades in power and Indonesia underwent a democratic transition. Following talks with Portugal, the new government announced plans to hold a referendum on independence in East Timor in August 1999, but this alarmed members of the Indonesian military who responded by assisting pro-Indonesian militias on the island. When the vote came overwhelmingly in favour of independence, the militias stepped up their campaign of killing and destruction, which had been going on for some time prior to the referendum. Thousands were killed or made homeless and the country's infrastructure was almost completely destroyed. The violence was only halted when an Australian-led United Nations peacekeeping force arrived on the island in late September 1999.

TOP: An Australian peacekeeper passes a burning building in Dili, the East Timorese capital.

ABOVE FAR LEFT: The head of the Indonesian army, General Wiranto, defends his role in East Timor at a tribunal held in Indonesia. He denies the allegation that his forces and the allied pro-Indonesian militias were responsible for human rights abuses in East Timor.

BELOW FAR LEFT: Indonesian troops take aim during the 1975 invasion.

ABOVE LEFT: Xanana Gusmao, a hero of the East Timorese resistance, addresses a crowd during a political rally. Gusmao became the first President of East Timor in 2002.

ABOVE RIGHT: Australian troops applaud as the 2nd Battalion Royal Gurkhas end their tour of duty in East Timor and prepare to return to barracks in Brunei. The Gurkhas were among the first UN troops to arrive following the outbreak of violence.

Second Intifada 2000 -

Outbreak of the uprising

By 2000 the Arab-Israeli peace process had stalled and economic conditions in the Palestinian territories were worsening. In September, a second Palestinian Intifada broke out after Ariel Sharon, the leader of Israel's main opposition party, visited a disputed religious site. Palestinians began rioting and attacking Israeli worshippers leading to gun battles between Israeli police and Palestinian fighters. The conflict rapidly escalated two days later when a twelve-year-old Palestinian boy was killed in the crossfire.

Suicide bombings

The uprising was far deadlier than the First Intifada, in part because the conflict saw the widespread use of suicide bombing against Israeli civilian targets. In one particularly deadly attack, almost thirty people were killed when a suicide bomber struck a hotel during Passover in March 2002. In response Israel launched a major military operation in the West Bank, dealing a blow to Palestinian militants, but killing a large number of civilians in the process.

Hamas-Fatah split

In November 2004, Yasser Arafat, the leader of the Palestinian Liberation Organization (PLO), died. Since his death, Hamas, the militant Islamist group responsible for much of the suicide bombings, has grown in popularity at the expense of Fatah, the main faction of the PLO. Hamas won a majority in the elections to the Palestinian Authority in January 2006 and ousted Fatah from the Gaza Strip in June 2007. Fatah has shown a commitment to a renewed peace process, but Hamas has been excluded and the conflict continues.

ABOVE: **Masked Hamas militants march through the streets of Khan Yunis in the Gaza Strip to celebrate the organization's nineteenth anniversary in December 2006. Hamas has orchestrated many suicide attacks against Israel and** is deemed to be a terrorist organization by the United States and the European Union.

ABOVE RIGHT: **Palestinian** demonstrators taunt the Israeli tanks defending Netzarim, a Jewish settlement in the Gaza Strip, on October 29, 2000.

BELOW RIGHT: **Palestinian boys** throw stones at an Israeli tank in Nablus on September 29, 2003, the third anniversary of the Intifada.

Afghanistan 2001-

Taliban rule

When the Soviet troops withdrew from Afghanistan in 1989, they left a largely unstable country, ravaged by years of war and with its infrastructure either destroyed or badly damaged. They also left a country with a ready supply of weaponry, some Soviet, some supplied by those nations which had aided the Mujahideen. Within a few years, it had degenerated even further, becoming a fragmented and anarchic place, with regular outbreaks of fighting and areas ruled by local warlords. In 1994 alone, thousands of people died in the capital, Kabul. This situation was perfect for the rise of the Taliban, a fundamentalist Sunni Islamist movement, and they were able to seize control of Kabul in 1996. Afghanistan under Taliban rule was marked by severe human rights abuses and heavily restricted freedom for everyone, especially women and girls.

ABOVE: Afghan women and children crouch by a wall as a soldier passes by while searching for Taliban at a compound near their home in Southern Afghanistan.

FAR RIGHT: Smoke billows out of the twin towers of the World Trade Center in New York City following the terrorist attacks of September 11, 2001. Another two planes were hijacked; one struck the Pentagon in Virginia and the other crashed in a field in Pennsylvania after passengers confronted the terrorists.

RIGHT: New Yorkers run from the debris as the South Tower crashes to the ground. Almost 3,000 people, mostly civilians, were killed in the attacks.

Daily Mail
SPECIAL EDITION
Newspaper of the Year 40p
WEDNESDAY, SEPTEMBER 11, 2001

APOCALYPSE
New York. September 11, 2001

9/11 Attacks

The terrorist attacks of September 11, 2001 had an immediate impact on the international situation with regard to Afghanistan. Al-Qaeda, the Sunni Islamist group which claimed responsibility for the attacks, had been based in the country since soon after the Taliban came to power in 1996. Immediately after the attack, the stunned United States sought to bring those involved to justice and the Taliban were asked to hand over Bin Laden. When the Taliban refused, the US began mounting a diplomatic offensive with the aim of achieving consensus and moral support for a retaliatory strike, in an attempt to destroy al-Qaeda and ensure there would be no further such attacks. Most countries responded positively, including some of the Arab states as well as Russia and China. There was also some general support from the United Nations Security Council, and specific support from NATO.

TOP RIGHT: **A wall is filled with the details of missing people at the Bellevue Hospital in midtown Manhattan, in the hope that they might be found alive after the attacks.**

RIGHT: **A Pakistani man holds a poster of Osama Bin Laden while a young boy totes a toy gun during a pro-Taliban demonstration in Karachi, Pakistan.**

ABOVE: **Union Square in New York awash with floral tributes to those who lost their lives in the 9/11 attacks.**

BOTTOM: **A Taliban supporter waves a picture of al-Qaeda leader, Osama Bin Laden, from a lamppost in Karachi during a demonstration called by the pro-Taliban Afghanistan Defence Council.**

Operation Enduring Freedom

The assault on Afghanistan, codenamed Operation Enduring Freedom, began on October 7, 2001. It involved mostly US forces, with some from Britain and other NATO countries, and with the emphasis on attacks from the air; initially, few ground troops were deployed. There were several objectives, but they all centred around the removal of al-Qaeda and the destruction of their camps – and, hopefully, the capture of Bin Laden himself. A tape of Bin Laden was released to the Arab news channel al-Jazeera just before the assault; in it he called for a jihad, a holy war against the US.

Airstrikes were made against targets in and near Kabul and two other cities, Jalalabad and Kandahar. They met little resistance; though the Taliban had been able to make use of some of the munitions left over from the struggle against the Soviet Union, it appeared that anti-aircraft weapons were not among them.

ABOVE RIGHT: **The remains of a Taliban jeep lie at the bottom of a huge crater after it sustained a direct hit during an American airstrike.**

ABOVE: **Marines conduct a nighttime patrol in search of Taliban positions in Southern Afghanistan.**

BELOW: **United Nations vehicles cross a river, bypassing a bridge destroyed during a US airstrike, as the organization attempts to provide food relief before the winter sets in.**

US airstrikes

In the longer-term the Coalition attack had two phases: first came the destruction of the training camps, of both the Taliban and al-Qaeda, and then an attack on the Taliban's communications infrastructure. Civilian casualties began to mount up, and it became evident that the Taliban were receiving unofficial aid and support from the tribal areas of Pakistan. By early November, however, the Taliban forward positions had been extensively bombed and their regime began to collapse; as it did so, al-Qaeda assumed control in some areas. Resistance to the Coalition centred on the Tora Bora mountains east of Kabul. This difficult terrain, with a useful cave system, was where both the Taliban and al-Qaeda appeared to be dug in, and the mountains were heavily attacked as a result.

The Northern Alliance

The United States relied upon a native anti-Taliban coalition named the Northern Alliance to do much of the fighting on the ground and relatively few American troops were sent in during the initial invasion. The Northern Alliance largely drew its support from the three main minority ethnic groups, the Tajiks, the Uzbekhs and the Hazara, but they also had some backing among the majority Pashtun ethnic group. The Alliance still controlled territory in the north of the country, which they were able to use as a springboard for their attack.

The Alliance enjoyed considerable success, thanks largely to the US airstrikes and the support of American and British Special Forces. On November 9 the city of Mazar-i Sharif was taken, and during the night of November 12, almost all of the Taliban fled from Kabul itself. The Northern Alliance arrived the following day and found only a small group of Taliban fighters. The fall of Kabul sparked the almost total collapse of the Taliban; local warlords assumed control in many areas, notably the north and east.

Tora Bora mountains

Fighting continued in the Tora Bora mountains and though many Taliban fighters did surrender, a lot also escaped, most likely to the relatively close tribal areas of Pakistan. The Coalition established their first ground base on November 25 near the Taliban centre of Kandahar and the city fell on December 9, essentially concluding the invasion. However, some al-Qaeda members were still holding out in the Tora Bora, though tribal forces were pushing them out. The cave complex was eventually taken, but there was no sign of Bin Laden and it was suspected that he had already been moved to the tribal areas across the Pakistani border. The US forces based themselves at Bagram, close to Kabul. An interim Afghan government was formed under the auspices of the United Nations and aid began arriving.

TOP: Suspected members of the Taliban are held by the Northern Alliance in a makeshift prison camp near the city of Taloqan. Some in the west expressed misgivings over the human rights record of the Northern Alliance and criticized their summary judgement of Taliban suspects.

ABOVE: Northern Alliance soldiers shell Taliban positions along the frontline in Afghanistan.

BELOW: A Northern Alliance fighter garrisons the village of Kashmond Kala in the mountains north of Jalalabad, which was liberated after the withdrawal of al-Qaeda and Taliban forces in mid-November 2001.

Insurgency

A period of consolidation began, but it was not long before it was interrupted. It soon became clear that neither the Taliban nor al-Qaeda had been destroyed and that they were, in fact, regrouping with the intention of launching a guerrilla insurgency. Many were now based in Pakistan, but some remained hiding in the caves of the Shahi-Kot mountains of eastern Afghanistan. In March 2002, the United States launched Operation Anaconda to drive the insurgents out, many were killed, but many also escaped across the border into Pakistan, from where they continued to launch cross-border raids.

This set the pattern for the next few years – attacks, followed by a Coalition assault, at which point the insurgents would disappear into the mountains and caves or the tribal region of Pakistan. Mobile training camps had been established there, and there had also been something of a recruiting campaign, with a renewed call for jihad. Throughout 2003–2005 there were Taliban rocket attacks, raids and ambushes, often involving the use of IEDs – improvised explosive devices, frequently in the form of roadside bombs. There was also evidence that the Taliban were back inside Afghanistan in increasing strength, using the remoter parts of the south as a base. Joint offensives began with the aim of rooting them out, utilizing troops from both the Coalition and the Afghan Government.

LEFT: British Royal Marine Commandos search Malmand in southern Afghanistan in November 2007 after reports that the town was being used as a Taliban logistics base. More than 8,000 British troops are stationed in the country, mainly in the restive Helmand Province, where much of the world's opium poppy crop is grown.

TOP: France's President, Nicholas Sarkozy makes his first visit to Afghanistan to pledge French support for the NATO-led ISAF mission in December 2007. Sarkozy later announced that he would bolster the number of French soldiers in Afghanistan to more than 2,500. His troop increases were approved by the French parliament despite the loss of ten soldiers in a deadly Taliban attack in August 2008.

ABOVE: Afghanistan's President Hamid Karzai inspects a guard of honour in Kabul with British Prime Minister Gordon Brown. In October 2004, Karzai, an ethnic Pashtun, became the first democratically elected leader of Afghanistan, winning more than 50% of the vote despite facing 17 other candidates.

ISAF

In January 2006, the NATO-led International Security Assistance Force or ISAF began taking the place of many of the US troops, for whom the war in Iraq was assuming greater importance. They were largely British, Canadian and Dutch, though there were also some Australians, Danes and Estonians. Initially their aim was reconstruction, but the Taliban announced that they were opposed to their presence and would resist it. This led to one of the deadliest periods of fighting in southern Afghanistan for the whole of the war. There were various attacks, many operations and even some more formal battles, such as the Battle of Panjwaii which involved the Canadians and resulted in the removal of the Taliban from the area. The fighting was intense, especially in Helmand Province where the British were based, and though there were some victories for the ISAF forces, there was no really complete defeat for the Taliban.

This situation continued much the same in 2007, and more major anti-Taliban offensives were launched. The numbers of ISAF troops were increased, and it seems likely that there was a similar increase in the number of insurgents, though this is difficult to determine.

Instability in Pakistan

For the Americans, the situation in Afghanistan has continued to be largely eclipsed by the insurgency in Iraq, though there are signs that this may now be changing slightly. A sense of frustration has been growing, especially with Pakistan and the apparent unwillingness or inability of the government there to do anything to control either the militants on their territory or the exceptionally porous border between Pakistan and Afghanistan. The latter would be difficult, given the extremely mountainous nature of the terrain, but the situation with the Taliban and al-Qaeda fighters has been a source of real irritation if not open anger. In September 2008, the fighting in Afghanistan finally spilled over into Pakistani territory, with a commando raid on a village near a known Taliban settlement. Just weeks later, Pakistani troops fired on two US helicopters hovering near the border; the incidents were followed by recriminations and denials on both sides. The suspicion had been growing for some time that Pakistan, itself somewhat unstable, was unable to deal with the situation in its tribal territories.

Future

International military attention is now beginning to return to Afghanistan, and it is likely that many more troops will have to be deployed there to deal with the Taliban. One of the main problems is that though an area may be 'cleared', it cannot be continually policed with anything like the same degree of intensity, allowing the Taliban and their supporters to slip back in. The situation remains unresolved, though the war did achieve its aims to some extent: the Taliban were removed from power and al-Qaeda no longer appears to be operating in the country.

ABOVE: A resident protests as ISAF troops search his home for evidence of the resurgent Taliban.

LEFT: Pakistani President Pervez Musharraf was largely an ally of the United States in the War on Terror. However, he has been criticized for not doing enough to tackle militants operating in his country. During his last year in power, Pakistan was beset by political uncertainty which has continued to destabilize the country, despite Musharraf's resignation in August 2008 .

FAR LEFT: Britain's Prince Harry on duty in southern Afghanistan in January 2008. News organizations agreed not to report that Harry had been serving on the frontline so as not to make him and other servicemen vulnerable. However, an Australian magazine reported the story and the Prince was pulled out of the country having served ten weeks.

Darfur
2003 -

'Genocide'

Since gaining independence from Britain and Egypt in 1956, Sudan has fought two bloody civil wars as the non-Muslim, non-Arab south has resisted the authority of the predominantly Muslim, Arab government based in the capital, Khartoum, in the north of the country.

In February 2003 as the Second Civil War was drawing to a close, a rebellion broke out in the Darfur region in the west of the country. The rebels accused the government of neglecting the region, especially its non-Arab population. The government responded to the rebellion with air strikes and by mobilizing their Arab militias, the 'Janjaweed'. Since then, the Janjaweed have engaged in killing, raping and looting on a large scale in Darfur. An estimated 300,000 people have been killed and millions have fled their homes in what the United States government has labelled genocide. The Sudanese government has said it is attempting to rein in the Janjaweed and African Union troops have been dispatched to the region, but the killing continues.

DAIY MAIL JULY 23, 2004
Arab militias blamed for further Sudan raids

Rebels in western Sudan have said that Arab militias had attacked twice in Darfur this week, despite the government's insistence that it is cracking down on them.

The rebel Justice and Equality Movement (JEM) said the government had integrated more than 6,000 of the militiamen into the regular police, giving them uniforms and new weapons.

JEM general coordinator Abu Bakr Hamid al-Nur said by telephone that police including some of the militiamen, known as Janjaweed, had attacked a rebel camp on Wednesday in the Orshi area north of el-Fasher, capital of North Darfur state.

He said that two days earlier, Janjaweed had killed more than 30 people and kidnapped many women and children at Kfour, between el-Fasher and Kutum, about 120 km (75 miles) to the northwest.

The Janjaweed are at the centre of a conflict that has displaced more than a million people in remote Darfur and created what the United Nations says is one of the world's most serious humanitarian crises.

The rebels and human rights groups say the government has armed and supported the Janjaweed.

The government says they are outlaws and it has started a campaign to disarm them.

The JEM and another rebel group in Darfur, the Sudan Liberation Movement, pulled out of political talks with the government last Saturday because Khartoum rejected their preconditions, including disarmament of the Janjaweed.

The rebel groups took up arms in early 2003 to protect the settled non-Arab people of Darfur from attacks by Arab nomads who have traditionally competed with them for land and grazing.

The US Congress passed a resolution saying that genocide was under way in Darfur - a description many international observers on the ground say is an exaggeration.

The African Union has plans to send a peace force to Darfur to protect monitors and humanitarian workers.

Chadian influence

The conflict in Darfur has been complicated by the intervention of neighbouring Chad. Many of the victims of violence in Darfur belong to the Zaghawa tribe, which is the tribe of Idriss Deby, the President of Chad. Deby has given funding, arms and medical supplies to the rebels in Darfur, and his government most likely played a role in an ambitious rebel attack on the Sudanese capital, Khartoum, in May 2008. This has allowed the Sudanese government to claim the war in Darfur is in part an act of self-defence against Chad. The Sudanese government has reciprocated by supporting rebel groups in Chad and most likely assisted with an unexpected rebel attack on the Chadian capital, N'Djamena, in February 2008.

ABOVE: Irish troops, part of a European Union force, patrol through the desert in eastern Chad. The French-led European operation is designed to offer protection for refugees and humanitarian aid workers. Hundreds of thousands of people have fled across the Chadian border since the war in Darfur began.

OPPOSITE ABOVE: A member of one of Darfur's main rebel groups, the Sudan Liberation Army, races through the desert near the city of El Fasher in Darfur in November 2004.

OPPOSITE LEFT: Refugees from Darfur lobby the British government to intervene in Sudan during a rally outside the Prime Minister's residence at Downing Street in London, September 2007.

TOP: Nigerian troops of the African Union patrol the town of Habila Konare in Darfur in March 2006. The AU force was merged into a larger United Nations force at the start of 2008. The UN plans to send 26,000 peacekeepers to the region, but so far have fallen short of this total.

ABOVE: Protest rallies and marches have been held across the world to draw attention to the humanitarian crisis in Darfur.

LEFT: Refugees cram into the sprawling Riyad camp near the town of Al-Geneina in Darfur. The Janjaweed militias often patrol the desert surrounding the camps making it difficult for the refugees to search for food or water.

Iraq 2003-

Resolution 687

During the Iran-Iraq War, Iraq's President Saddam Hussein had shown a willingness to use 'weapons of mass destruction' (WMDs) against both his enemy and his own people. After the Gulf War in 1991, the United Nations Security Council passed Resolution 687 calling upon Iraq to destroy its WMDs and UN weapons inspectors were sent in to monitor and verify Iraq's disarmament. In addition, no-fly zones were established over Kurdish and Shi'a areas to stop the Iraqi army attacking these communities from the air, and economic sanctions were introduced.

Operation Desert Fox

During the 1990s, Saddam became increasingly non-compliant. He began blocking access to sites suspected of housing WMDs and later began demanding that American members of the weapons inspection team be expelled from the country. Throughout 1998, the UN mission became mired in confusion, until it was withdrawn altogether in December. The following day, the United States and the United Kingdom launched 'Operation Desert Fox', a four-day-long air blitz on Iraq. The aim was to target and destroy sites suspected of housing WMDs and demonstrate that non-compliance had penalties.

ABOVE: **A US Marine drapes the American flag over a statue of Saddam Hussein in Firdos Square. The statue was toppled shortly after, symbolizing the fall of Baghdad and Saddam's regime.**

RIGHT: **A soldier working for UNIKOM, looks across the border from Kuwait into Iraq in February 2003. UNIKOM, the United Nations Iraq-Kuwait Observation Mission, was set up to monitor the border between the two countries following the first Gulf War.**

The path to war

In the aftermath of the 9/11 terrorist attacks, the US government stepped up its demand that Iraq readmit the weapons inspectors and comply fully with the United Nations. Throughout 2002 UN and Iraqi negotiators met to discuss the readmission of inspectors. Saddam was inconsistent in his position, sometimes agreeing to give them full access, and at other times listing sites that were off-limits. On November 8, 2002, the UN Security Council voted unanimously in favour of Resolution 1441, which gave Iraq one last chance to comply with the weapons inspectors, but did not sanction the use of military force if he did not. Saddam accepted the resolution and the weapons inspectors were readmitted immediately. As per the terms of the resolution, Iraq submitted a lengthy written declaration of its weapons programme, but the US and Britain believed it to contain glaring omissions and war seemed ever more likely. In early 2003, international opposition to a US and British invasion mounted; a long list of countries including France, Russia and Germany refused to support it, millions of people took to the streets in cities around the world to protest, and government ministers in Britain resigned. Knowing that a new Security Council Resolution calling for the use of force would be vetoed, Britain and America decided to press ahead without a UN mandate. On March 17, 2003, the US President, George W. Bush, gave Saddam 48 hours to leave Iraq or face war.

TOP RIGHT: **Hans Blix, the head of the UN weapons inspector team in Iraq, was a key figure in the run-up to the Iraq War as his reports on Iraq's compliance with the UN shaped the international response.**

TOP LEFT: **US and British troops, massing in Kuwait, watch as US Secretary of State Colin Powell gives a speech to the UN just days before the invasion.**

RIGHT: **Millions of people gathered in cities across the world to protest against the war in Iraq in early 2003. On February 15 an estimated one million people converged on London for the largest demonstration in British history.**

ABOVE: **Troops of the 16 Air Assault Brigade train by night in Kuwait.**

BELOW: **US General James Conway of the 1st Marine Expeditionary Force addresses allied British troops in Kuwait on March 14, 2003. By this time it had become clear that other major powers - France, Russia and Germany - would not support an invasion of Iraq. Australia and Poland also sent troops for the initial invasion.**

Invasion

The invasion of Iraq began in the early hours of the morning on March 20, 2003. Airstrikes were launched against Baghdad and troops began pouring across the border from Kuwait. Unlike in Afghanistan, the decision was taken to stage the ground and air offensives in parallel so as to prevent Saddam's forces from destroying the oilfields of Southern Iraq. American and British troops were joined by soldiers from Australia and Poland for the invasion and a number of other countries agreed to play supplementary roles.

The Coalition planned a two-pronged attack with the aim of reaching Baghdad as quickly as possible. One thrust was made to the west of the Euphrates River while the other was made further east closer to the Tigris River. The southern port of Basra was to be captured and occupied by the British but, by and large, major population centres were avoided at first. The US had hoped to make another thrust on Baghdad from northern Iraq, but the Turkish government refused permission for an invasion to be staged from its territory. In the event, a smaller number of troops were parachuted into the region to team up with Kurdish guerrillas who had been fighting Saddam's regime for years.

BELOW: **Iraq's Planning Ministry on the Tigris River in Baghdad is hit by a US missile, on the opening day of the invasion.** Thousands of bombs were targeted on sites linked to Saddam's regime in a campaign of 'shock and awe' designed to soften up resistance to the ground troops crossing the Kuwaiti border in the south.

ABOVE RIGHT: **As coalition troops head north they pass thousands of refugees fleeing the bombing of Basra. The city had been left without water and most refugees pleaded with coalition troops for a drink.**

BELOW RIGHT: **A Royal Air Force Harrier jump jet takes off from an airfield in Kuwait on its way to bomb Iraq.**

Daily Mail **WAR ON SADDAM**

Newspaper of the Year   40p

FRIDAY, MARCH 21, 2003

INVASION

- First British deaths as the Royal Marines lead charge into Iraq
- Bombs and missiles blitz Baghdad

Onslaught: Thick smoke plumes hundreds of feet into the air as U.S. cruise missiles slam into a key target in Baghdad last night

17 PAGES OF BRILLIANT REPORTS, PICTURES AND IN-DEPTH ANALYSIS

Iraqi resistance

The US army was expecting to encounter a similar situation to the first Gulf War, but that was not what happened in practice. There was considerably more resistance, and it was better organized. It was also different; American troops faced opposition from guerrilla fighters in built-up areas, who held them back for some time despite the invaders' much superior firepower. This led to a general suspicion of any Iraqi civilian – the guerrillas wore no uniforms – which often had appalling consequences. The local people also remembered the terrible penalties many had paid for welcoming the invading forces in 1991, and often did not greet the incomers as liberators.

The Coalition forces were able to advance swiftly across the desert and open countryside, but they came into problems when they reached Nassiriyah. Here US forces were bogged down by a heavy sandstorm as well as guerrillas and sustained considerable casualties before taking control of the city. Meanwhile, air and missile attacks on Baghdad continued. Although these used precision-guided weapons, and were only aimed at specific targets, mistakes were sometimes made: on the seventh day of the invasion a US plane dropped two bombs on a busy market in northern Baghdad killing and injuring a number of civilians.

Baghdad falls

Saddam Hussein had planned a last-ditch defence of his capital, and expected that his Special Republican Guard would prevent US troops from approaching. In the event, the result looked like a foregone conclusion and the trusted and feared Guard disappeared. Public opinion seemed to be swinging around as the Iraqi people began to believe that, this time, the regime might fall. For his army officers, this meant that there was little point in obeying orders, and the Americans were able to capture Saddam International Airport on April 4. Five days later, Baghdad itself fell, symbolized by the toppling of a large statue of Saddam in Firdos Square in the centre of the city.

Though the mood had changed to some degree, it had not taken the direction the Americans had anticipated. Many people wanted them as little as they had wanted Saddam Hussein, and saw them more as conquerors than liberators. Looting and civil disorder broke out in Baghdad and spread to cities across the country. The looting began with government and Ba'ath Party buildings, but it spread much more widely and the Coalition troops were unable to contain it. Hospitals, schools, museums: nothing which had even the vaguest connection to the regime was immune.

TOP: **Paratroopers in the desert during Operation Iraqi Freedom. Coalition forces spent considerable time in the desert as they pushed on Baghdad;** conditions could be very inhospitable and sandstorms blighted communications and supply lines.

ABOVE: **A British soldier with the 'Desert Rats', Seventh Armoured Division, walks past ruined buildings in Mushirij, a village amid the oil fields west of Basra.**

LEFT: **Coalition troops camp under the bright light of burning oil wells in Southern Iraq. Iraqi troops managed to set several wells alight, but not as many as had been feared.**

Occupation and Insurgency

When the city of Tikrit – Saddam's hometown – fell on April 15, the invasion as such was over. On May 1, President Bush stood aboard the USS *Abraham Lincoln* and declared that major combat operations were at an end. The occupation had now begun. A temporary provisional government was installed and the time that followed was marked by attempts to establish an elected and more representative democratic government. It was also marked by the outbreak of violence against the Coalition forces and among various sectarian groups. Initial opposition to the Coalition came from Saddam's remaining loyal supporters, many of who were tracked down. Saddam Hussein himself was found hiding on a farm near Tikrit on December 13, 2003, and following a year-long trial, he was hanged on December 30, 2006.

RIGHT: Saddam Hussein sits in his cell awaiting trial for the torture and murder of the Shi'a population of Dujail in 1982. Saddam was alleged to have ordered the massacre after narrowly escaping an assassination attempt in the town. He was found guilty and sentenced to death by hanging.

BELOW: American soldiers search Iraqi youths who were thought to be selling guns on the streets of Baghdad.

ABOVE: A US Marine of the Light Armored Reconnaissance Company checks a residential district in Fallujah for insurgent activity during Operation Phantom Fury, the Second Battle for Fallujah, in November 2004.

Fallujah

On March 31, 2004, Sunni insurgents ambushed a convoy driving through the predominantly Sunni city of Fallujah. Four private American security contractors were killed then their mutilated bodies were hung from a bridge in the city. US troops retaliated in what became the First Battle of Fallujah, but a ceasefire was declared after it emerged that various key members of Iraq's Provisional Government were opposed. Fighting resumed in November when it was clear that Sunni insurgents had tightened their control over the city. Civilians were given a chance to evacuate before the city was pummelled from the air and US troops were sent in. By the end of the operation, half of Fallujah's buildings lay in ruins and many of the insurgents had been killed or captured.

Islamic extremism

Saddam loyalists were later followed by others who stood against the occupation, especially religious extremists of various kinds. Sunni fundamentalists, drawing inspiration from Osama Bin Laden's terrorist network, called themselves al-Qaeda in Iraq (AQI), and began attracting many foreign fighters to help them wage jihad against the occupying 'infidels'. AQI has employed terror tactics, notably suicide bombings and hostage-takings, to terrible effect; thousands of people have been killed and Iraq has been severely destabilized. Since its founder and leader, Abu Musab al Zarqwi, was killed in a targeted US airstrike in June 2006, AQI appears to be in decline, but it remains capable of conducting serious atrocities against civilians and soliders alike.

The main Shi'a insurgent group, the Mahdi Army, has been less inclined to adopt terror tactics, preferring instead to engage Coalition and Iraqi forces in gruelling street battles in Shi'a strongholds in southern Iraq and Baghdad. The Mahdi Army is led by the radical cleric Mutada al-Sadr and gets some support from neighbouring Iran. In August 2007, Sadr agreed to a ceasefire, which has largely held, and he now appears to be pursuing less violent routes to power. However, Shi'a extremists claiming to be linked to the Mahdi Army continue to operate in Southern Iraq, despite the Iraqi government's attempts to disarm them.

Sectarian violence

The insurgency against the foreign occupiers soon gave way to a civil war between Iraq's various extremist factions. The country has been plagued by sectarian violence for years, but it was the bombing of the al-Askari Mosque in Samarra – an intensely holy place for Shi'a Muslims – that unleashed a new level of sectarian bloodshed. Across Iraq Shi'a groups responded by massacring Sunni Muslims and destroying Sunni mosques. This led to a cycle of sectarian violence only somewhat mitigated by a 'surge' in US troop numbers during 2007. August of 2007 saw the single most deadly suicide-bomber attack, when more than 800 members of the non-Muslim Yazidi community died in an attack on the town of Qahtaniya. Al Qaeda in Iraq probably conducted the attack in revenge for their execution of a convert to Islam. Towards the end of 2008 the situation seemed to be a little calmer, and there has been a general trend towards handing over control to the new Iraqi security forces so as to free up Coalition troops for redeployment to Afghanistan where they face a resurgent Taliban.

ABOVE RIGHT: **US President George W. Bush meets Marines during his visit to Al-Asad Air Base in Anbar Province, Iraq, in September 2007.**

RIGHT: **British Prime Minister Tony Blair meets students from an elementary school in Basra during a visit to postwar Iraq. Blair was a solid supporter of the Iraq War, despite facing widespread opposition from within his own party.**

BELOW: **A US soldier carries an Iraqi girl away from the scene of three explosions in Baghdad. Insurgents attacked a US military convoy as it passed by the opening ceremony for a sewage station, killing 35 people and wounding scores of others.**

Israel-Lebanon War 2006

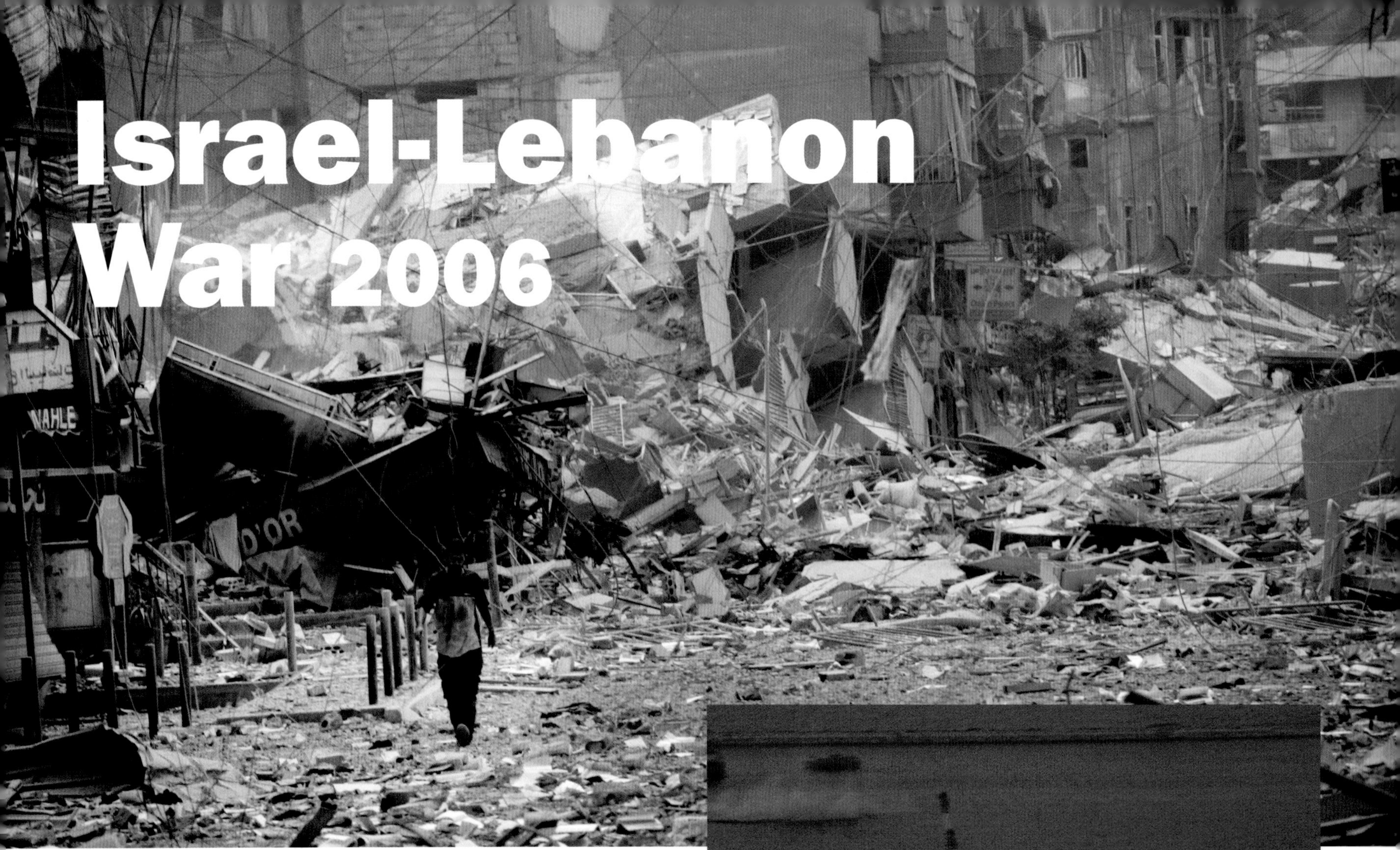

Operation Grapes of Wrath

After the end of Lebanon's civil war in 1990, Hezbollah remained armed in order to fight the Israeli occupation of Southern Lebanon. Intermittent attacks occurred over the years, but the closest the two sides came to war was in 1996, when Israel launched 'Operation Grapes of Wrath', a two-week blitz on Lebanon to take out the missile sites Hezbollah had been using to fire rockets into northern Israel. During the operation, Israeli planes struck a UN compound in Qana, killing more than one hundred civilians who had taken refuge there.The strikes were halted after the United States intervened.

Israel withdrew from Southern Lebanon in May 2000, but Hezbollah has argued that a narrow stretch of territory is still being occupied so as to justify its continued attacks on Israeli military targets. The territory, named the Sheeba Farms, was taken from Syria during the 1967 war and was therefore not included in Israel's pullout from Lebanon.

Cross-border raid

On July 12, 2006, Hezbollah captured two Israeli soldiers during a cross-border raid. The Israeli Prime Minister Ehud Olmert perceived this as an act of war and initiated a full-scale offensive aimed at securing the release of the soldiers and more broadly at dealing a decisive blow to Hezbollah. Israel began by bombing cities across Lebanon, concentrating on Hezbollah's strongholds in the south and in Beirut. For its part, Hezbollah stepped up its rocket attacks on northern Israel, killing a number of people during strikes on the country's third-largest city, Haifa. While the air war was ongoing, the Israeli army staged a ground invasion of Southern Lebanon in an attempt to take out the rocket sites.

ABOVE: **A man walks through the devastated Musharachea district of Dahiye, a Hezbollah stronghold in the southern suburbs of Beirut.**

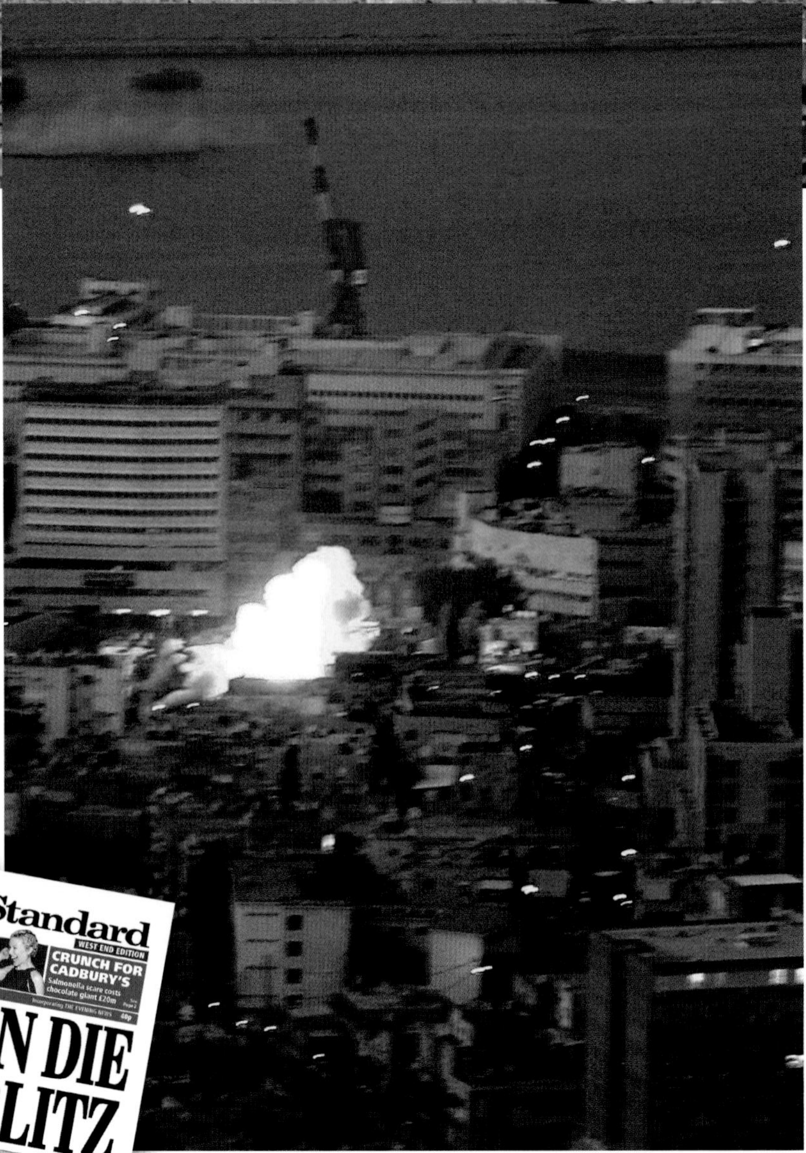

RIGHT: **Flames rise above the skyline of Haifa as a Hezbollah rocket strikes the city, killing at least three people. At the height of the conflict more than one hundred rockets were hitting northern Israel each day.**

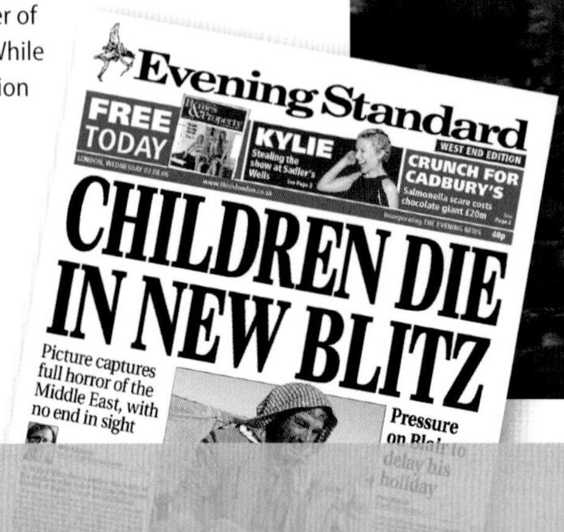

Evening Standard

FREE TODAY

KYLIE Stealing the show at Sadler's Wells

WEST END EDITION

CRUNCH FOR CADBURY'S Salmonella scare costs chocolate giant £20m

CHILDREN DIE IN NEW BLITZ

Picture captures full horror of the Middle East, with no end in sight

Pressure on Blair to delay his holiday

Ceasefire

The cost to both sides was high, and more than 1,000 civilians are estimated to have been killed during the raids on Lebanon. The civilian suffering galvanized the international community to act and the United Nations passed a resolution demanding a ceasefire and an Israeli withdrawal. Both sides accepted the resolution and the ceasefire came into effect on August 14 after more than one month of fighting. A strengthened United Nations force was sent into the south to maintain peace and security following the withdrawal of Israeli troops. The war failed to deal a decisive blow to Hezbollah or secure the return of the two captured soldiers, leading many Israelis to question the wisdom of the war. In July 2008, it emerged that the two soldiers had been killed and their remains were returned to Israel as part of a prisoner exchange.

DAILY MAIL   JULY 17, 2006

Lebanon plunged back into the devastation of the 1980s

Bombs, bloodshed and burials marked the fifth day of Israel's merciless bombardment of Lebanon yesterday. Jets blitzed Beirut and the south of the country, killing at least 36 and turning the clock back a quarter of a century.

In the south of the capital, heartland of the Hezbollah militants, entire buildings were reduced to rubble. One apartment block toppled on to its side while the upper floors of others collapsed on to homes below.

Furniture, blankets, mattresses, clothes and soft toys were scattered on the streets. The wrecked home and office of Hezbollah leader Sayyed Hassan Nasrallah were still smouldering after repeated raids.

The airstrikes, in revenge for Hezbollah's kidnapping of two Israeli soldiers, have so far killed 140 people, almost all of them civilians. Eight Canadians from a single family died when warplanes flattened a house in the border town of Aitaroun. They had come for a summer holiday with relatives.

Only a week ago, Beirut was the self-proclaimed cultural and party capital of the Middle East. It was a magnet for tourists and investors again after years of rebuilding an economy shattered by a long and bloody civil war and the Israeli invasion of 1982. Now Israel has killed

not only scores of its people but Lebanon's future too. It has been plunged back into the devastation of the 1980s when Beirut was a byword for misery, destruction and death.

As well as disbelief, there is despair. 'We feel the entire world has left us alone to be slaughtered,' said Ali Al-Amin, a 40-year-old civil engineer who has stayed at his Beirut home with his sister and mother because they have nowhere else to go. At a nearby school, 11-year-old Aya Al-Siblam wrote on the blackboard: 'Today is the worst day of my life.'

A visibly emotional Prime Minister Fouad Siniora denounced Israel for turning his country into a 'disaster zone' and appealed for foreign aid. Blankets, sheets and medical equipment are all in short supply.

The most horrific attack of the campaign came on Saturday, when at least nine children were among 21 people incinerated when a bomb was dropped on their convoy. They had been following Israeli instructions to leave their border town.

Anger and terror grip Lebanon. No one expects Hezbollah to surrender its arms, and no one expects Israel to end its attacks. Trapped in the middle are the ordinary people.

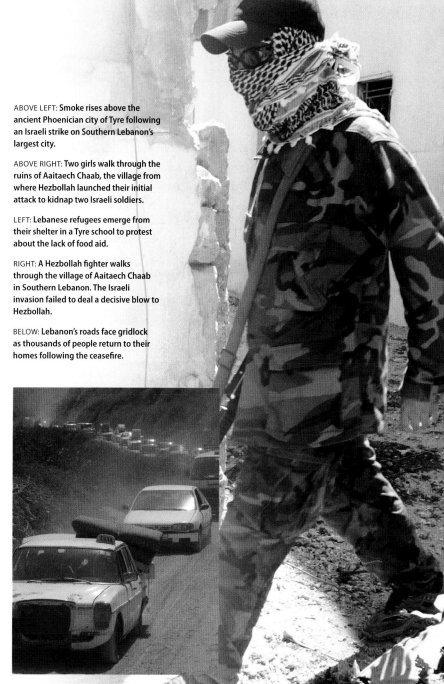

ABOVE LEFT: **Smoke rises above the ancient Phoenician city of Tyre following an Israeli strike on Southern Lebanon's largest city.**

ABOVE RIGHT: **Two girls walk through the ruins of Aaitaech Chaab, the village from where Hezbollah launched their initial attack to kidnap two Israeli soldiers.**

LEFT: **Lebanese refugees emerge from their shelter in a Tyre school to protest about the lack of food aid.**

RIGHT: **A Hezbollah fighter walks through the village of Aaitaech Chaab in Southern Lebanon. The Israeli invasion failed to deal a decisive blow to Hezbollah.**

BELOW: **Lebanon's roads face gridlock as thousands of people return to their homes following the ceasefire.**

Ethiopia-Somalia War 2006

The Ogaden war

Frequent clashes have occurred between neighbouring Somalia and Ethiopia ever since Somalia was granted independence from Britain and Italy in 1960. Large-scale war broke out in 1977 when Somalia tried to reclaim the Ogaden region which had come under Ethiopian control. The efforts of Somalia's dictator Siad Barre failed and his troops were forced to retreat in 1978.

In 1991 Siad Barre's regime collapsed when an uprising of the Issk clan in the north-west of the country precipitated a nationwide rebellion. Since then, despite global efforts to help the situation in Somalia, the country has been plagued by violence and has been without a recognized government. The latest phase in the Somalia crisis came in 2006 when Ethiopia intervened to aid the weak Transitional Federal Government in their fight to release the Islamic Courts Union's hold over Mogadishu.

American intervention

On December 3, 1992, the UN passed Resolution 794 authorizing the use of all necessary means to create a secure environment for aid operations in Somalia. The United States led the taskforce, known as UNITAF, under a mission codenamed 'Operation Restore Hope'. In May 1993, following another UN vote, UNITAF was transformed into UNOSOM II and the American mission was renamed 'Operation Continue Hope'.

The US involvement came to a quick end when 19 American servicemen were killed during fighting in Mogadishu on October 3, 1993. Somali militias managed to shoot down two Blackhawk helicopters and then engaged American troops in bitter street fighting.

Shocking pictures filtered through the Western press of the soldiers' bodies being dragged through the streets and the American public began to question the necessity of their presence in a country of seemingly limited strategic importance. In March 1994, President Clinton withdrew US troops from Somalia and the UN followed suit a year later. The debacle reduced America's appetite for further intervention on the African continent over the following decade.

Islamic Courts Union

Barre's demise and the rebellion in 1991 gave way to violent clan warfare in Somalia. The only real force of law that existed in the country at this time was regulated by the Sharia-based courts. The courts began to develop into an institution that provided education and health services as well as regulating the police force. As the role of the courts expanded, they gained a wider support base, and in 1999, advocates of the courts formed the Islamic Courts Union. The ICU was assisted partly by Eritrea, who supplied arms to the militia group, which allowed them to gain control of Mogadishu. Following their seizure of Mogadishu, the Islamic Courts brought a degree of stability to Somalia that had not been experienced for years.

As the Islamic Courts strengthened their grip over the country, they threatened to spread their Islamist militancy across the border to Ethiopia's substantial Muslim minority. Ethiopia's Prime Minister, Meles Zenawi felt compelled to act to prevent the destabilization of his country. In July 2006 reports that Ethiopian troops had crossed into Somalia began to emerge, but Zenawi claimed that they were military trainers in the country helping the Transitional Federal Government. Three months later he declared Ethiopia in a state of war with the Islamic Courts Union.

Islamists in Retreat

Battle ensued in Baidoa and in the towns of Bandiradley in Mudug and Beledweyne in the Hiran region. The fighting came to a head at the Battle of Jowhar on December 27, the last major town on the road to Mogadishu. Ethiopia gained control of the town and took the fighting to the capital. The leaders of the Islamic Courts Union could not withstand Ethiopia and its hold over Mogadishu collapsed. Ethiopia sought the assistance of African Union troops to bolster the Transitional Federal Government and allow the unpopular Ethiopian troops to withdraw.

As yet, the African Union has not sent in sufficient numbers of troops and Ethiopian troops remain in the country to avoid another power vacuum, which might allow the Islamic Courts Union to return to power. The collapse of the Islamic Courts Union has led to a re-emergence of clan fighting with almost 2 million Somalis displaced from their homes in Mogadishu alone.

OPPOSITE ABOVE: **Somali youths are trained by the Islamists for the impending war with Ethiopia at the Arbiska training camp near Mogadishu in September 2006.**

OPPOSITE MIDDLE: **Siad Barre, the dictator of Somalia from 1965 to 1991. His overthrow has left Somalia without an effective government.**

OPPOSITE BELOW: **UN food aid arrives at a camp for internally displaced Somalis at Wajid. Millions of people have been displaced by relentless fighting in the country.**

TOP: **Members of the Islamic Courts Union hold an anti-American protest in Mogadishu stadium in December 2006.**

ABOVE LEFT: **An aerial view of Mogadishu on December 31, 2006, days after Ethiopian troops had taken control of the city.**

LEFT: **Troops of the weak Transitional Federal Government ride through the town of Bur Haqaba on December 28, 2006. Before the war, the Ethiopian government helped train these forces in the hope that they could contain the Islamists and reduce the need for direct Ethiopian intervention.**

Russian invasion of Georgia 2008

Russia's 'near abroad'

The Russian government has had a history of opposing the emergence of Western-leaning governments in former Soviet States, which Moscow claims to fall within its sphere of influence and names the 'near abroad'. In defiance of this, the Georgian government of President Mikhail Saakashvili, which was swept to power in the popular 'Rose Revolution' in 2003, has sought closer ties with the West and has even bid to join NATO. In response, Moscow has supported separatist movements in the Abkhazian and South Ossetian regions of Georgia, which have helped to undermine Tbilisi's chances of getting into NATO.

Until 2008, the Russian government opted for a subtle approach towards reining in its 'near abroad' so as not to appear too adversarial on the international stage. However, the West's recognition of Kosovo's independence in February 2008, in spite of strong Russian objections, encouraged the Kremlin to play a more overt role in Georgia. Tensions mounted throughout the spring of 2008 and relations reached an especially low point when Russia was implicated in the shooting-down of an unmanned Georgian reconnaissance plane over Abkhazia in April.

War in South Ossetia

Less than four months later, on August 7, border skirmishes between Georgian and South Ossetian forces turned into a full-scale offensive. The Georgian government, which had been calling for peace negotiations, moved troops into South Ossetia and began bombing the capital, Tskhinvali. The following day, Russia came to the assistance of South Ossetia under the pretext that it was protecting its citizens as many South Ossetians had been issued with Russian passports. On August 9, Russian planes began bombing the town of Gori in Georgia and moved tanks and troops into Georgian territory. Over the next few days, the bombing offensive against Gori continued and was widened to include military targets across the country.

Soon after the war broke out, the international community began calling for a cessation and French President Nicholas Sarkozy proposed a peace plan whereby all sides would withdraw to their pre-war positions. On August 12 President Medvedev agreed to Sarkozy's terms and announced a ceasefire. Russia had met its aim of forcing Georgian troops out of South Ossetia and demonstrating that it still had authority over its 'near abroad'. However, the invasion came at a cost to the country's international reputation and has encouraged many countries to re-evaluate their relations with Moscow.

DAILY MAIL   AUGUST 12, 2008

INVASION:
Russia launches blitz on Georgia as Putin brushes aside calls for ceasefire

Russian troops invaded Georgia yesterday as Vladimir Putin brushed aside the West's appeals for a ceasefire. Soldiers and armoured vehicles advanced 25 miles inside the former Soviet satellite to capture two towns in the west. There were unconfirmed reports that the strategic central city of Gori had fallen after a Georgian retreat.

Georgia was urgently moving troops back to defend its capital Tbilisi from further Russian onslaught. 'The Georgian army is retreating to defend the capital,' a statement said. 'The government is urgently seeking international intervention to prevent the fall of Georgia.'

In Gori, where artillery fire could be heard, Georgian soldiers warned the public that Russian tanks were approaching and advised them to leave. Hundreds of terrified families fled toward Tbilisi, using any means of transport they could find. Many stood along the roadside trying to flag down passing cars. Russia opened up the new fronts as the Kremlin continued to defy international calls for a halt to the four-day conflict.

Moscow said it had moved into Georgia to end military resistance in the area around the disputed enclave of South Ossetia. Georgia's president Mikhail Saakashvili described Russia's actions as the 'cold-blooded, premeditated murder of a small country.'

OPPOSITE ABOVE: **A Russian tank rolls past a house in Kvemo-Achebeti set on fire by South Ossetian militia.**

OPPOSITE BELOW LEFT: **Firefighters tackle a blaze in an apartment block in Gori after it had been hit by Russian bombers.**

OPPOSITE MIDDLE RIGHT: **Russian troops move into the Khurcha settlement in the breakaway region of Abkhazia. Abkhazian separatists, backed by Russia, used the war in South Ossetia to push Georgian troops out of Abkhazia entirely.**

OPPOSITE BELOW RIGHT: **Georgian police face down Russian tanks and soldiers on the outskirts of Gori.**

BELOW: **A Georgian military convoy heads north on the road between Gori and Tbilisi to halt the Russian advance.**

TOP LEFT: **Georgia's President Mikhail Saakashvili condemns the Russian military action during a nationwide address.**

TOP RIGHT: **A Russian soldier takes aim as a Georgian tank convoy enters Tskhinvali in South Ossetia.**

ABOVE MIDDLE: **Georgian troops assemble the military convoy on the outskirts of Tbilisi.**

ABOVE: **A burnt-out Georgian tank lies abandoned at the roadside two kilometres outside Gori.**

LEFT: **Russian soldiers in military vehicles wait for orders on the outskirts of Gori.**

Index

Picture Acknowledgements

The photographs in this book are from the archives of the Daily Mail.
Thanks to many of the photographers who have contributed.

Getty Images: 226t; 254t; 255b; 260t; 280t; 291t; 300; 302; 304; 305; 306
Corbis: 154b; Front cover central band: David Leeson.

David Eldan 173b; Arpad Hazafi 190b; Sanjor Bojar 191m; Bela Jarmai 192b;
Paul Vathis 195bl; Peter Arnett 202l; Henri Huet 204b; Slava Veder 215t; Hoang Van Cuong 216t;
Neal Ulevich 216b; Paul Faith 227l, 227r; Niall Carson 227b; Alex Lentati 225m;
Jeremy Selwyn 225l, 288tr, 289bl, 289bm; Monty Fresco 230bl, 230br; Bill Cross 231tl, 231bl, 231br;
Mark Ellidge 231tl; Karel Prinsloo 238rm; Manuel de Almeida 238br; Luis d'Orey 239l;
Peter Andrews 239r; Mourad Raouf 241al; Menhem Kahan 242b; Jim Hollander 243tl 259c;
Vitaly Armand 245b; Ghislain Zoccolat 252bl; Barry Thumma 254bl, 260b; Mick Forster 257r;
Keith Pannell 258t; Rabih Moghrabi 258r; Martin Cleaver 259ml; Jerome Delay 259mr;
Pascal Guyot 264t; Dominique Mollard 268t; Jean-Philippe Ksiazek 274ml; Corin Dufka 275l, 275ar;
Alexander Joe 275br; James Miller 276t; Christopher Birbeumer 276m; Steve Bent 277l;
Lynn Hilton 277r; Oliver Chukletovic 277b; Giles Penfound 278r; Nick Sharp 278b;
Wally Santana 279l; Sayyid Azim 280bl, 280m, 284b; Jaques Collet 280ml;
Jean Marc Bouju 280br, 281ml; Murray Sanders 283l; Nikolai Gaiayev 283m; George Mulala 284t;
Antony Njuguna 285tr, 308b; David Crump 286t; Nick Skinner 287tl, 288bl;
Alex MacNaughton 288br; Ed Wray 290t; Muchtar Zakaria 290l; Charles Dharapak 290r;
Fayez Nureldine 291m; Alaa Badarneh 291b; Jamie Wiseman 292t, 294tr, 295t, 296l, 297t; 302m,
303t, 306t, 307; Cavan Pawson 292br, 292bl; 293tr 293l, 302t; Stephen Shaver 293r;
Zahid Hussein 293b; Ian McIlgorm 295b; Eric Febeberg 296tr; Peter Macdiarmid 296br;
John Stillwell 297bl; Finnbarr O'Reilly 299; Bruce Adams 301tl, 303b; Glenn Copus 301tr;
Steve Waters 301r; Mark Richards 301b, 303m, 311b; Michael Thomas 304b; Jason Reed 305t;
Guy Calaf 309b; Denis Sinyakov 310tl; Vladimir Popov 310m; Irakli Gedenidze 311tl;
Mikhail Metzel 311tr; Gleb Garanich 311ml; Scott Hornby 311br.

Every effort has been made to trace any photographers and
copyright-holders not mentioned here.
The publishers apologise for any unintentional omissions and would be pleased,
in such cases, to add an acknowledgement in future editions.

Acknowledgements

The photographs in this book are from the archives of the Daily Mail.
Particular thanks to Steve Torrington, Alan Pinnock, Katie Lee and all the staff.

Thanks also to Alison Gauntlett, Lauren Oing, Michael Quiello, Bradford Swann,
Laurence Socha, Christopher Sullivan, Patricia Annunziata,
Caitlin Gildea, Cliff Salter, Jill Dorman and Richard Betts

Dedication
For Eric McDonald Good